Bazhanov and the Damnation of Stalin

Boris Georgievich Bazhanov circa 1928.
From the French edition *Bajanov Revele Staline*, Boris Bajanov
(Gallimard, Paris, 1979). Photography by Jeffrey S. Caldwell.

Boris Bazhanov

BAZHANOV AND THE DAMNATION OF STALIN

Translation and Commentary by David W. Doyle

 Ohio University Press, Athens

Library of Congress Cataloging-in-Publication Data
Bazhanov, Boris.
 [Bajanov révèle Staline. English]
 Bazhanov and the damnation of Stalin / Boris Bazhanov ;
translation and commentary by David W. Doyle.
   p. cm.
 Includes bibliographical references.
 ISBN 0-8214-0948-4
 1. Stalin, Joseph, 1879–1953. 2. Bazhanov, Boris. 3. Heads of
state—Soviet Union—Biography. 4. Secretaries—Soviet Union—
Biography. 5. Defectors—Soviet Union—Biography. 6. Soviet
Union—Politics and government—1917–1936. I. Doyle, David W.
II. Title.
DK268.S8B3213 1990
947.084'2'092—dc20
[B]   89-35310
                                                         CIP

Contents

Translator's Introduction

Boris Georgievich Bazhanov escaped from the USSR on 1 January 1928. He was the first and for many years the most important of a new breed—the Soviet defector. His risky escape through eastern Persia into India, just ahead of the Obiedinyonnoye Gosudarstvennoye Politicheskoye Upravleniye (Unified State Political Administration) (OGPU) assassins sent after him by Stalin, and his period of waiting at Simla while the British Raj and an unimpressed bureaucracy in London tackled the question of what to do with him, took eight months. Finally, this human treasure trove of new, intimate knowledge on the Soviet leadership and its Party and governmental mechanisms settled in Paris in September 1928. The French, unlike the British, immediately understood and exploited Bazhanov's unique information and his rare ability to decipher what was going on in Russia.

Bazhanov had been Stalin's assistant, and concurrently secretary to the Politburo, from 1923 until 1925. Prior to that he had spent 1922 and half of 1923 in the Orgburo, where he quickly rose to be its secretary. His relative youth (he was born in 1900) was evidently offset by his keenly organized and competent mind, retentive memory, breadth of perception, and capacity for work. He was invaluable to Stalin and the Politburo and, had Bazhanov stayed in Stalin's service, he might well have enjoyed the same meteoric career as the man who replaced him when he left, Georgy Malenkov.

But Bazhanov came to despise the unethical and brutal regime he was serving. It was apparently in the nature of this uncompromising man, once he became anticommunist, to seek to bring down the regime and so to prepare his departure carefully. He brought with him sample documentation which not only revealed some of the innermost secrets of the Kremlin but which he could "trade" for onward passage to Europe.[1] Once in France, he set about describing the nature and ambitions of Stalin's regime to a skeptical West which, preoccupied with problems of the Great Depression and burgeoning fascism, had difficulty accepting the priority and the content (then seemingly outrageous) of Bazhanov's blunt message: the Soviet plan to destroy Western civilization, and they will succeed if you let them. They will use *any* means to achieve their goal.

The French military interrogation of Bazhanov produced hundreds of pages of detail on Soviet plans and efforts to undermine the West and on the power struggle in the Kremlin. It must have been a pleasure for Lieutenant Colonel Josse to interrogate this well-informed and least-complicated of the early defectors.[2] The British realized what a prize they had had in their hands only after they knew of this interrogation. Bazhanov's information included the first description received in the West of the awesomely callous and effective security, disinformation, political action, and espionage machine that we now know as the Komitet Gosudarstvennoy Besopasnosti: (Committee for State Security) (KGB), then the OGPU.

As soon as he got to Paris, Bazhanov set to work writing his message to the West. He wrote extensively for the newspapers and for the émigré press. In 1930 Les Editions de France, in Paris, published Bazhanov's book: *Avec Staline dans le Kremlin*. Editions P. Aretz of Berlin published a German translation of the book in 1931 as *Stalin: Der rote Diktator, von seinen ehemaligen Privatsekretär*. He also wrote a book describing the Soviet kidnapping of General Aleksandr Pavlovich Kutepov, which Editions Spes published in French in Paris in 1930 as *L'Enlèvement du Général Koutepov*, and in Russian, *Pokhishenie generala A. P. Kutepova Bol'shevikami*.[3] None of his books were translated into English for publication, although some of his articles were summarized by U.S. and British embassy officers for Washington and London. Bazhanov was not again published in book form until 1977, as we see later.

Stalin watched Bazhanov and his activities very carefully, and several attempts were made to assassinate him.[4] But the intended victim knew Stalin and his OGPU all too well. He carried a pistol, which he had deliberately learned to handle expertly before he defected and was fully prepared to use. He watched for, and evaded, the attempts on his life that he knew he had to expect. He never married, fearing that his wife would become either a victim—or a widow—of Stalin's vengeance. He lived a life of constant caution until Stalin's death in 1953 removed the source of his danger. Bazhanov may have feared for his life much of the time, but he was a man of courage and conviction and he damned Stalin as often and as publicly as he could.

Bazhanov was vindicated and his dire message confirmed as the rest of the pre–World War II defectors followed him into exile: Georgy Agabekov, Aleksandr Barmin, Grigory Z. Bessedovsky, Walter Krivitsky, Aleksandr Orlov, Boris Souvarine, and so on. They confirmed his dour prediction that Western civilization had much to fear from Stalin and might not be up to the task of countering him. Stalin tried to silence them, but despite his spectacular murder of Trotsky and other successes of the OGPU (and its successor, the NKGB and the Narodnyi Kommissariat Gosudarstvennoy Besopasnosti (People's Commissariat for State Security) and Narodnyi Kommissariat Vnutrennikh Del (People's Commissariat of Internal Affairs) the NKVD), Stalin couldn't kill them all.[5]

The West listened, but even the Terror and the Purges did not convince them that Stalin had long surpassed even Hitler in the fields of state-induced fear and mass murder at home and surgical murder abroad.

Almost laconically, Bazhanov describes his time in Finland in 1940 raising a small force of Russian prisoners to help the Finnish army fight off the Red Army; his dismay at the West's failure to appreciate the danger from the Kremlin; and his 1941 convocation to Berlin, where Hitler's staff asked him to help colonize and oppress the Russian population that Operation Barbarossa (the Nazi code words for their invasion of Russia) was going to overrun. His refusal must have taken some courage, whatever his reasons.

There followed a period of suspicion that he had been a Nazi sympathizer, based in part on the fact that Hitler let him go back to Paris a free man, despite his refusal to be the German-controlled gauleiter of German-colonized Russia. This and the wartime alliance of the Western democracies with Stalin against Germany helped induce Bazhanov to be silent for thirty years.

It was only after Aleksandr Solzhenitsyn had urged him, in 1976, to write his memoirs, that Bazhanov (now aged seventy-six) again wrote a book. This time he revised, updated, and substantially changed his 1930 book about Stalin. By now Bazhanov's friends inside the USSR had died or no longer needed him to be discreet on their account. The 1976 manuscript, therefore, goes far beyond his 1930 work in such details as what Lenin's secretaries told Bazhanov about Lenin's "testament" and "codicil."[6]

Bazhanov's 1976 manuscript was accepted for publication in Germany, France, and Italy. A German translation, *Ich war Stalins Sekretär*, was published by Verlag Ullstein, Berlin, in 1977. The French version, *Bajanov révèle Staline,* translated from the Russian by Catherine Maillat and reviewed by Bazhanov (who spoke French), was published by Gallimard, Paris, in 1979. An Italian version was also published in 1979, and in 1980 the original Russian version, *Vospominaniia byvshevo pomoshnika Stalina,* was published in Paris by Tret'ia Volno (Third Wave). Again, there were no takers for the English rights, which Ullstein returned to the author in 1980. Bazhanov died in Paris in 1983.

The 1979 French version, presented here in translation, (in the hope that it will illuminate from a unique perspective, a corner of Kremlin history that has not been generally available in English) is about four times longer than his 40,000 word book of 1930. It contains all the essentials of the 1930 book and adds materially to that earlier manuscript. The 1979 version includes his interesting experiences in Finland in 1940 and in Germany in June 1941. The update of the 1930 book differs mostly in that it offers much more detail than he was then prepared to give on Stalin and the dictator's entourage and methods, naming more names and giving explanations that, in 1930, might have caused his friends inside the USSR to be harmed. Some of the differences are both interesting and logical.

In 1930, for example, he stated quite categorically that, as an anticommunist, he had joined the Communist Party and then applied for work in the Central Committee staff, in a deliberate and (he made the point frequently) courageous effort to penetrate the Kremlin and be there "like a good soldier" when some unnamed force was ready to overthrow the regime. Bazhanov reversed this claim in his 1976 text, describing at some length how he became a communist *by conviction* and then was so disgusted by what he saw in the Kremlin that he came to hate the regime and its system. His later version is far more convincing, and from what I know of Bazhanov and his writing style, my guess is that some other person, perhaps a now-unidentified editor or translator, "helped" him in 1930 by adding some racy text designed better to sell the book and simultaneously to improve Bazhanov's image. In those days defectors were an almost unknown breed and were rather suspected of being turncoats. Added to that, he was the first senior communist to defect and, as such, the émigré population of Paris, almost all either White Army or Provisional Government escapees, distrusted him profoundly. It must have been a priority at that time in Bazhanov's mind to convince his readers that secretly he had never been a communist.

In 1930 Bazhanov claimed that his sister had poisoned herself in horror at the Civil War's excesses and that his parents "perished" when the communists took over his town. The clear implication was that they had been killed by the Bolsheviks. By 1976 there was no mention of his sister, and his parents had died of typhus in 1920, after he had joined the Communist Party (in the summer of 1919). Obviously, the 1930 version was written to support his Trojan-horse-inside-the-Kremlin claim of that time.

In 1930 Bazhanov recounted the story of chekist Yakob Bliumkin's role in the assassination of German Ambassador Count Wilhelm von Mirbach in Petrograd in 1918 and Bliumkin's subsequent execution by the OGPU as a traitor working for Trotsky. The 1930 Bazhanov book, however, did not mention Bliumkin's vain attempt to kill him (Bazhanov) after Bazhanov got to France. Since Bliumkin was put to death in December 1929, his attempt to kill Bazhanov must have been prior to the publication date, 1930. Perhaps in 1930 Bazhanov, even if he already knew of that first OGPU assassination attempt, felt it wiser to avoid any publicity about Stalin's efforts to murder him. Perhaps he somehow learned from inside the USSR that Stalin thought the attempt successful and hoped to avoid further attempts. That was not to be, however, because as he describes in the 1979 version, while Stalin did indeed think Bliumkin had killed Bazhanov, the OGPU and its successors knew that Bazhanov was still alive, and they continued efforts to murder him until Stalin died in 1953.

The 1930 book was written with more humor, and in more vivid language, than its 1976 successor, perhaps the combination of a much younger author with a more imaginative, less restrained translator or publisher. Whatever the cause, and while there is reason to doubt some of what Bazhanov says about his own motivation (he's never modest), there is no reason to doubt most of his descriptions of events, many of which have been confirmed by other sources (and some used by plagiarists). His accounts of the mechanics of Politburo sessions and of Troika preparations for those sessions, are unique. His assessment of people is generally in line with other sources. He is a prime source on Stalin from 1923 to 1928.

Some questions have arisen in my mind while working on this that I cannot answer but now set forth for the reader to ponder. Did Bazhanov wittingly help Stalin's rise to power by organizing key elements of the inner Party bureaucracy and giving Stalin the levers to control them? For example, did Bazhanov obtain Troika approval to organize a system to follow up on Politburo decisions in order to help Stalin rise to power or for his own career purposes? Bazhanov stoutly denies wishing to help Stalin after he got to know the dictator, yet a careful reading of the text makes one wonder. Did Bazhanov really defect for ideological reasons, or did he stub his toe and feel it wiser to get out, then once out, take up the anticommunist cause? Was he less repelled by Nazism than he tells us, or did the Nazis really have such a poor reading of him that they wasted hours of Rosenberg's and Leibbrandt's time at a critical planning moment? Although I would rate Bazhanov "a usually reliable source," he should be read with caution where he displays bias or discusses his own motives.

The principal value of Bazhanov's work is in the "feel" that he gives the reader of what the power struggle in the Kremlin was like as Stalin carefully prepared the "spicy dish" (Lenin's words when he tried to warn the Central Committee about Stalin) that would carry him to the top over the bodies of his semihypnotized competition. As Bazhanov sheds more light on that struggle than has been available to date in English, it is again clear how many times along Stalin's road to power he could have been stopped—by men and women who knew the threat he represented but mysteriously failed to act to protect themselves or their colleagues. Trotsky was perhaps the man who most visibly failed to act, since in 1924 he was still the most likely successor to Lenin. Trotsky, writing notes for his book *Stalin* shortly before his assassination in Mexico, quoted Bazhanov's description of the Central Committee session at which Kamenev first made Lenin's Testament known. After this quote Trotsky stated (p. 376): "Lenin's return to activity would mean the political death of the General Secretary. And conversely: only Lenin's death could clear the way for Stalin."

Then Trotsky went on to describe the strange manner in which Stalin kept insisting that Lenin was asking for poison and kept hinting that it might be for the best to give him some. Did Trotsky acquire suspicions only in retrospect? Bazhanov thought not, and his reasons appear to be sound. Lenin had tried to remove Stalin from power a short time before, and had broken off personal relations with Stalin a few days before he supposedly asked Stalin for poison. Also, Trotsky thought this of Stalin's demeanor when discussing Lenin's so-called poison request (p. 377): "This episode is one of those that leave an indelible imprint on one's consciousness for all time. . . . Stalin's behaviour, his whole manner, was baffling and sinister." Trotsky wasn't as naive as Bazhanov relates in regard to Stalin's willingness to murder his colleagues. Trotsky, discussing Frunze's death, said (*Stalin*, p. 418): "The very nature of the suspicion is significant. It shows that by the end of 1925 Stalin's power was already so great that he could rely on a submissive concilium of physicians armed with chloroform and a surgeon's knife."

And yet, if Trotsky saw this, if he really thought that Lenin's death would "clear the way for Stalin," then why did he virtually stand aside and let it happen? Why didn't he assert the role that Lenin's Testament and

Codicil and Trotsky's own background and Party support would have allowed and step in to claim the throne? Bazhanov's story helps to clarify what Trotsky did not do but doesn't help us understand why he didn't do it. Trotsky certainly doesn't seem to have had a death wish, but there's no doubt that in many instances when Trotsky sniffed danger he reacted slowly and did strangely little to protect himself. It was to cost him his life in August 1940.

His late awakening to his own risk from Stalin appears in Trotsky's notes for *Stalin*, page 418–19:

In 1930 when Bazhanov's book appeared this [Bazhanov's fear that Stalin's exile of Trotsky to Turkey was only a half measure and that Stalin normally would have poisoned Trotsky to get rid of him] seemed to me merely a literary exercise. After the Moscow trials I took it more seriously. . . . Bazhanov had received his training in Stalin's ante-room—there the question of Koch bacilli and Borgia methods of poisoning were evidently under discussion as early as prior to 1926, the year Bazhanov left Stalin's secretariat. Two years later he fled abroad and subsequently became a reactionary émigré.

Stalin's nature is well documented, but Bazhanov adds texture from his unique viewpoint at Stalin's right hand. He gives Stalin no free credit, although it is clear from his account that he understood and respected the skills (if not the methods) of his employer. One gets the impression that Bazhanov's contempt for Stalin may have blinded him to the possibility that Stalin—brutal and amoral as he was—had a higher cause than the simple urge to be supreme for its own sake. Bazhanov relates, for example, the disagreement between Stalin and Trotsky on whether the Soviets should seek "communism in one country" first or world revolution first (chapter 5) but doesn't credit Stalin for taking the more practical view for reasons other than the vendetta.

Bazhanov's account of the Czech telephone technician's gruesome "reward" for installing a secret Kremlin telephone tap system for Stalin has not, as far as I can tell, been related by another original source. The tale certainly supports Bazhanov's view of Stalin.

Whatever the truth about Stalin's motivation, the fact is that the Soviet communists of the 1920–53 period and their system made it possible for a man like Stalin to act barbarically with impunity and to stay in power until he died. Bazhanov adds to our appreciation of just how hard it must be for the "reformers" in the USSR to overcome Stalin's legacy. Even today the dictator's stamp is still heavily on the Party and the government, and the old guard has many followers in the immense bureaucracy that is apprehensive of *glasnost*. To understand how Stalin and his acolytes made it so and how, for example, Khrushchev could be brought down is to glimpse how powerful and pervasive that machine became, as Bazhanov predicted.

Bazhanov's story about the cynical Politburo exploitation of foreign ventures (such as the Lena-Goldfields heist) gives warning of what could happen should today's Politburo decide to repeat the procedure. The mechanics to do so are still in place, no matter how well meaning the reformers are.

Bazhanov's predictions regarding what Stalin would do inside the USSR were accurate: the Terror and the Purges were cataclysmic. They were planned and conducted in traditional tsarist style, embellished by Lenin and Stalin and their chekists, over the strangely inert bodies of Trotsky and his dwindling allies.

Bazhanov's message to the West regarding the menace from the Kremlin was accurate in that, for that period of history, it reflected the nature of Stalin's regime and its ambitions to spread communism outward from the USSR by subversion or force or both. His suggested cure, tasking the Western democracies with reconversion of Russia from communism, had a flaw: it assumed that the Soviet regime could be brought down from the outside and that the Western democracies would be able and willing to try it. But they weren't. Only Hitler was willing to attempt to unseat the regime. But Hitler didn't want the help of the Russian people; he wanted a colony, and he paid the cost of his fatal mistake. Just as Bazhanov predicted in Germany in 1941, the Russian people didn't want to trade a known despot for an unknown, foreign colonizer of equal ferocity.

Bazhanov's book follows, in free but complete translation. The text is his. The notes, bibliography, and index are mine and are intended to clarify or to help the general reader evaluate or understand what Bazhanov said. The index covers both Bazhanov's text and my notes and comments.

My translation from the French was checked against Bazhanov's Russian text by Professor Donald J. Raleigh of the University of Hawaii, Department of History, before he joined the faculty of the University of North Carolina, Chapel Hill. Dr. Raleigh also provided unstinting editorial and substantive comment on my footnotes and commentary and helped me select the bibliography. Without his encouragement and assistance this would not be as serious an offering as it is.

My wife, Hope, who saved my life and made this book possible, has provided daily support and encouragement since the project began, ranging from profound insights drawn from her personal acquaintance with many Soviet defectors, to the nit-picking work of finding typographical errors in the first drafts. Without her, there would have been no book at all.

I am also deeply grateful to a large number of friends, acquaintances, and strangers who have provided assistance in this project. First among them are Patricia A. Polansky, University of Hawaii Hamilton Library bibliographer, and her assistant Kevin Moore. They helped greatly in the tedious search for biographic and background data. University of Hawaii Professor Emeritus Ella Wiswell gave needed encouragement and helped in the search for Bazhanov's will.

Special mention goes to Dr. Gabriel Declercq, a Belgian friend of long standing, who introduced me to Bazhanov's book in the first place. And to my sister, Professor Suzanne Doyle Miers, a fine historian, whose advice and support were very important.

Photographic credits go to Mr. Jeffrey S. Caldwell of Wahiawa, Hawaii.

Preface

These memoirs go back principally to the period when I was the assistant to the general secretary of the Central Committee of the Communist Party of the Soviet Union [CPSU], Stalin, and secretary of the Central Committee's Politburo. I was appointed to these functions on 9 August 1923. Having become anticommunist, I fled the USSR on 1 January 1928, via the Persian frontier. In France, in 1929 and 1930, some of my observations were published in the form of newspaper articles and a book. Their basic value lay in my description of the real mechanics of the communist regime—very little known then in the West—of certain of the regime's leaders, and of certain historical events of the period.[1]

I have always forced myself to be scrupulously precise, and I have only described that which I saw or which I knew to be incontestably true. The Kremlin authorities have never tried to contest what I've written (they wouldn't have been able to) and have preferred to choose the tactic of total silence: My name was not to be cited anywhere. Stalin was the most assiduous reader of my articles and defectors from the Soviet diplomatic mission in Paris have told how Stalin insisted that each new article I wrote be sent to him at once by airmail.[2]

While describing facts and events with complete accuracy, I arranged, for the security of my friends who stayed in Russia, to modify one detail concerning me—the date on which I actually became anticommunist. In fact the date makes no difference to my story; I will explain later in this book when I describe preparations for defection, why my friends asked me to obscure the date.

In addition, I was not able to speak of a large number of facts and people who were still living. For example, I could not reveal what Lenin's personal secretary told me about a very important matter. It could have cost her dearly.[3] Now that almost a half century has gone by and most of the people of that era are dead, I can speak of almost everything, without anyone risking a Stalinist bullet in the back of the neck.

In describing today past events of which I was an eyewitness, I can share with the reader ideas and conclusions I drew from having seen these things myself. I hope this will help the reader understand the events of which I speak and this period of the communist revolution.

1. Entering the Party

School. University. Shooting of the demonstrators. Entry into the Party. Yampol and Mogilev. Moscow. The Higher Technical School. Discussion of trade unions. The Kronstadt Insurrection. The NEP. My studies.

I was born in 1900 in the village of Mogilev-Podolsky, in the Ukraine.[1] At the time of the February 1917 Revolution, I was a senior in high school. During the spring and summer of 1917, our town knew all the vicissitudes of the revolution and, especially, progressive disintegration of the old way of life. This process was even more accented by the October Revolution. The front broke up, the Ukraine seceded, and the Ukrainian nationalists contested Bolshevik power in the Ukraine. Anarchy was widespread in my area. But in early 1918 German troops occupied the Ukraine, and with their support a certain amount of order was reestablished. A strange regime was formed under Pavel Petrovich Skoropadsky,[2] "hetman" of the Ukraine—theoretically a Ukrainian nationalist but in fact vaguely conservative.

Life returned more or less to normal, my high school classes resumed, and I graduated in the summer of 1918 and left for the University of Kiev, for the department of physics and mathematics. Alas, the university's classes didn't last long. In November Germany was defeated and their troops began leaving the Ukraine. Revolutionary activities—meetings, discussions—boiled at the university, which the authorities closed. At that time I was not involved in politics. At eighteen I believed I didn't know enough yet about the fundamental problems of the life of society. But like most of the students I was very angry at the cessation of classes. I had come from a faraway province to Kiev to study. That was why, when a student demonstration in front of the university to denounce its closure was announced, I went along.

I learned a very important lesson there. A detachment of state police came by truck, formed up in front of the demonstrators, and with no warning opened fire. The crowd had quickly dispersed at the sight of the police, but three or four dozen people stayed rather than flee like rabbits. Of their number about twenty were killed and the rest wounded. I was among the wounded, a bullet in the jaw. But it was a glancing blow, and I got away with two or three weeks in the hospital. Courses having ceased and fighting between the Bolsheviks and the Ukrainian nationalists having resumed, I returned to my hometown to recuperate and reflect on the events in which I had participated against my will.

The Civil War flared up in 1919, and the White armies made their way toward Moscow. But the Podolsky region was outside this campaign, and the fight for local power was only between Simon Vasilievich Petliura's Ukrainian nationalists[3] and the Bolsheviks. During the summer of 1919 I decided to join the Communist Party.

For us, the student youth, the Party at that time looked like an exciting effort to create a new, socialist society. If I wanted to participate in politics in my small provincial town, the only choice was between Ukrainian nationalism and communism. The first choice didn't attract me at all, for in my view it was a renunciation of the Russian culture in which I was raised. I wasn't enthusiastic, either, about the practice of communism as it appeared around me, but I told myself (and I wasn't alone) that one mustn't ask too much of these uncultivated, primitive Bolsheviks, recruited from among uneducated workers and peasants who understood and applied communist dicta like savages. It was up to better-educated and more competent people to correct their errors and to build the new society so that it would better match the ideas of the leaders who—seen from afar—were obviously working for the welfare of the people.

The bullet that struck me in Kiev had little effect on my political outlook, but the problems posed by war played a large role. The last years of my adolescence witnessed the long, insensate killing that was World War I. Despite my youth I understood that war could never bring any benefit to the belligerents that could justify the millions of victims and the colossal damage inflicted. I understood that the techniques of extermination had reached such a level that the ancient process of settling disagreements between large powers by war had become insane. If the leaders of these powers were still motivated by outmoded concepts of nationalism, acceptable a century earlier when it took two months to travel from Paris to Moscow and countries could exist independently of each other, then today when all nations were linked and that voyage took only two days, these leaders were following a false trail. They had a large share of the responsibility for the revolutions which followed war and shattered the old ways of life. I took on faith the antiwar arguments of the internationalists at Zimmerwald and Kienthal.[4] It was only much later that I understood how war had served and enchanted the partisans of Lenin. Only war could have won them the Revolution.

Once I joined the local Party organization, I was soon elected secretary of the district organization. It is significant that from the first I quarreled with the chekists, sent from the provincial capital to organize a local Cheka.[5] This district Cheka requisitioned the house of the notary Afeniev, an old and inoffensive rich man, and they shot him. I urged the Party to close the Cheka office immediately and send its men back to the provincial capital, Vinnitsa. The Party organization was reluctant, but I quickly convinced them. The town was mainly Jewish, and the Party members were mostly Jews. I asked them if they understood that the Jewish population, under threat of a pogrom following each of the frequent shifts in government, would be the first victims of the mindless executions of these sadistic chekists. They understood and supported me. The chekists were sent back to Vinnitsa.[6]

The Soviet authorities didn't last long, and Petliura's men arrived and took over. I stayed some time in Zhmerinka[7] and Vinnitsa where, in January 1920, I was suddenly appointed head of the provincial department of education. My activities were interrupted by a recurrent fever, then by news of the death of my parents from typhus. I hastened back to my native town. Petliura's men were still there, but they did me no harm. The local population certified to them that I was an "idealistic communist" who had done only good and had saved the town from the chekist terror.

Soon power changed hands again. The Bolsheviks came, then left again. It was the time of the Soviet-Polish war. In the summer of 1920 the town of Yampol[8] was again in Soviet hands and I was appointed member and secretary of the town revolutionary committee. Since the October Revolution, Yampol hadn't known such a peaceful and benign authority. The president of the revolutionary committee, Andreev, and its two members—Trofimov[9] and I—were well-intentioned and peaceful men. At least that was what the widow of a government servant in whose house we lodged must have thought. We all three took our more than frugal meals there, which in view of all our power, astonished her.

Mogilev was occupied a month later. I was transferred there and again elected secretary of the Party district committee. The Soviet-Polish war ended in October, and the Crimea was occupied in November. The Bolsheviks had won the Civil War. I decided to go to Moscow to continue my studies.

I arrived in Moscow in November 1920 and was admitted to the

Higher Technical School. The school had, of course, a Party cell, but it was basically inactive. The Party considered that the country lacked competent technicians and that our duty, as Party students, was above all to study—which we did. Nevertheless, in the capital I got to know a lot more about the Party.

The Civil War over, the country had to be peacefully rebuilt. During the three years since the Bolshevik Revolution, communist methods of running the country seemed to have taken shape. However, those methods were the object of furious debate in the Party hierarchy during the well-known discussions on the trade unions, at the end of 1920. For all of us, simple Party members, the object of the debate seemed to be to decide methods to run the economy, or more exactly industry. There was the position of the Trotsky faction, which held that the Red Army should be transformed into a work army, to restore the economy on the basis of severe military discipline. Another faction (Aleksandr Gavrilovich Shliapnikov[10] and his Workers' Opposition), held that the economy should be run by the trade unions. Lenin and his group were against both solutions and held that the economy should be run by Soviet economic organs, abandoning military methods. Lenin's thesis won, not without some damage.

I only understood, several years later when I was secretary of the Politburo and had access to its archives, that the debate had been fabricated out of whole cloth. In fact what was involved was Lenin's struggle to have a majority in the Central Committee of the Party. At that time he feared that Trotsky had acquired excessive influence and he was trying to weaken Trotsky and diminish his power. The matter of the trade unions, a secondary question, had been inflated artificially. Trotsky sensed the hypocrisy of Lenin's ploy, and for almost two years their relations were much colder. This episode and its consequences played a significant role in the struggle for power that was to follow.

In March 1921, during the Tenth Party Congress, all members of our cell at the Higher Technical School were urgently convoked by the regional Party committee. They declared us mobilized, issued us rifles and cartridges, and sent us to the factories—most of which were closed. Our job was to mount an armed guard against the possibility of workers' uprisings against the authorities. This was the period of the Kronstadt Insurrection.

For almost two weeks three of us mounted guard in a closed factory. I was with my friend "Yurka" Akimov,[11] a communist student like me, and a blue-eyed Russian of German origin, Hans Lemberg.[12] Several years later I had Lemberg appointed secretary of Sportintern, where he intrigued on the lowest level. I lost track of Akimov a couple of years later but recently read in the Soviet Encyclopedia that he was a professor emeritus of metallurgy.

At the March Party congress, Lenin presented a report proposing to replace the grain requisitions by a (much lower) tax in kind. All official Soviet documents claim this to be the moment of birth of the NEP [New Economic Policy] but that's not quite accurate. Lenin didn't come that quickly to the idea of the NEP. During the Civil War and the summer of 1920, wheat was taken by force from the peasants. The authorities calculated about how much wheat the peasants had in each district. The amount of wheat that was required was set for districts and households, and then the wheat and other products were simply taken by force, in the most arbitrary manner, to feed (albeit meagerly) the army and the cities. In exchange the peasants received virtually no industrial products, since there practically weren't any. Peasant revolts broke out in the summer of 1920. The best known of these, that of the peasant guerilla Antonov (in Tambov province) lasted until the summer of 1921. In addition, planting was greatly reduced as the peasants didn't want to produce any excess wheat just to have it confiscated. Lenin saw that a catastrophe was approaching and that they would have to abandon dogmatic communism to return to the real world, to give the peasants a sensible reason for working.

The Kronstadt Insurrection incited Lenin to push his ideas further. In the country there was hunger, general discontent, and an absence of industrial products. To put not only agriculture but the whole economy back on its feet would be possible only by giving the population an economic stimulant. It would be necessary to abandon unrealistic communism and return to a normal system of economic exchange. That was what Lenin proposed at the end of May to the Tenth Party Conference, but he didn't take his NEP formulation to its logical conclusion until the end of October at the Regional Moscow Party Conference. (I will relate later on what his secretaries told me after Lenin's death about his most secret thoughts during this period.)

I continued to study and was elected secretary of the Party cell. This was no bother because of the much reduced Party activity at the Higher Technical School. Famine raged throughout the country all of 1921. Commerce was nonexistent, and we had to survive on our meager rations. That consisted of four hundred grams of bread daily (a sort of mess made of God knows what debris), and four pounds of dried herring per month. In addition the school canteen served a small daily portion of millet boiled into a soup, without a trace of fat or salt. One couldn't subsist for long on this diet. Luckily summer came, and we could go to summer work in a factory. With three friends (we were studying chemistry), I chose summer work in a sugar refinery in my home district of Mogilev. There we were able to recover a little; the ration was delivered in sugar, which could be bartered for any other foodstuffs.

In the autumn I returned to Moscow to resume my studies. But by January I was again very thin and depleted by hunger. At the end of January I decided to go back to the Ukraine. Once there, in the quantitative analysis laboratory [of the sugar refinery] I worked next to a very nice young student named Sasha Volodarsky. Sasha was the brother of Moisei Markovich Volodarsky, commissar for press affairs in Leningrad, assassinated by the worker Sergeev.[13] Sasha was a charming and modest adolescent, and when one asked him, "Aren't you related to the well-known Volodarsky?" he would respond, "No, no. I just have the same name."

I asked him whom I might propose to take my place as Party cell secretary. He asked why. I explained that I wanted to go [back to Moscow] but I could no longer endure the hunger. "Then why not do as I do?" he asked. "What's that?" "Well, I study half a day and the other half I work at the Party Central Committee. They've got work one can take home and do. Right now the Central Committee apparatus is expanding considerably, and they need educated help. Try it!"

I gave it a try. The fact that I had once been Party district committee secretary and was now secretary of the Higher Technical School cell were serious arguments in my favor. The man responsible for the Central Committee's administration, Ivan Ksenofontovich Ksenofontov[14] (former member of the Cheka central collegium), who undertook the initial selection of candidates, sent me to the organization section of the Central Committee, where I was accepted.

2. The Central Committee

The Organization Bureau of the Central Committee. Kagano-vich's article. Party Congress. Lenin's report. New Party statutes. Kaganovich, Molotov, and Stalin. My statutes approved. Los-kutka, the Volodarskys, Malenkov, Tikhomirnov, Lazar Kagano-vich. "We fifty-year-olds . . ." Mikhailov. Molotov. Instructional Commission. Handbook for Party militants. The Central Com-mittee's Izvestya.

The Party apparatus was, at this time, considerably expanding and strengthening itself. I was attached to the section responsible for organization and circular instructions, which was then perhaps the most important of the Central Committee's sections [bureaus]. Shortly after-ward, it was reorganized and became the section for organization and distribution [Orgburo]. Along with its principal subsections (organization and information) an unimportant subsection was formed, responsible for studying local experience. It had the vaguest of functions. I was appointed a simple employee of this subsection, which consisted of five employees and the chief, an old Party member called Rastopchin.[1] Rastopchin and three of his five employees considered their work as a temporary sinecure. Rastopchin himself only showed up once a week for a few minutes. When asked, "What should we do?" he smiled and said, "Demonstrate some initiative." Three of his five people demonstrated their initiative by finding better jobs, and they did so rapidly. After some complex intrigues, Raiter became the chief instructor of the Central Committee and later secretary of some provincial Party committee. Kitsis waited patiently until Raiter got his job, then left to join him. Zorge (not the famous one in Japan) wanted to work overseas in Comintern affairs. The only one who wanted to achieve something was Nikolai Bogomolov, a very intelligent and pleasant worker. Later he became deputy to the head of the organization and distribution section, responsible for selecting Party cadres, and then he replaced the chief. Finally, for reasons unknown to me he became Soviet commercial representative in London. He disappeared in the 1937 purges, doubtless liquidated.

At first I did almost nothing. I observed what went on around me and continued my studies. My food and lodgings were greatly improved over the difficult year 1921. All that year I had not only suffered from hunger but also lived in dreadful conditions. By order of the borough soviet, Yurka Akimov and I lived in one tiny room requisitioned from "the bourgeois." There was neither heat nor furniture (except for a washbowl and a water jug, on the window sill). In winter the inside temperature often went down to −5 degrees Celsius [about 27 degrees Fahrenheit] and the water in our pitcher froze. Luckily the floor was wood, so Akimov and I slept on a corner of the floor, wrapped in our fur coats and tightly (squeezed) together to gain warmth, with books under our heads in place of the nonexistent pillows.

Now, however, the situation was different for the employees of the Central Committee. A room was assigned to me in the Fifth House of the Soviets—formerly the Hotel Loskutnaya, at 5 Tverskaya Road—commonly called House No. 5 of the Central Committee. It was exclusively inhabited by simple Central Committee employees. The senior people lived either in the Kremlin, or in House No. 1 of the Soviets, at the corner of Tverskaya and Mokhovaya roads.

I didn't have much work, but soon I had to do with Lazar Moiseevich Kaganovich,[2] chief of the organization section. A conference on problems of Soviet construction [of socialism] took place under his leadership, and I was named secretary of the conference (by chance, because I happened to be there). Kaganovich gave a very intelligent speech. I seldom wrote up the minutes of the sessions, so I took no notes on his speech. Several days afterward the magazine *Soviet Construction* asked him for a substantive article on the subject. The problem was that although he was very talented and active, Kaganovich was very ill-educated. A shoemaker with no formal education, he made gross grammatical writing errors and had no concept of literary style. Because I had been the conference secretary, the magazine editors asked me to do it. I agreed to try.

Remembering Kaganovich's words, I formed them into an article. Because they were his ideas, not mine, I went to him and said, "Comrade Kaganovich, here is your article on Soviet construction. I wrote what you said at the conference." He read it and was enchanted: "True, I said all that. But how well it's expressed!" I responded that the writing was purely secondary; the ideas were his, and he should sign the article and send it to the magazine. Inexperienced in these things, Kaganovich was embarrassed: "But you wrote it, not I." With some difficulty I persuaded him that I had simply written it for him, to save him time. The article was printed, and Kaganovich was extremely proud of it. It was "his" first article, and he showed it to everyone.

This incident had a sequel. The [Eleventh] Party Congress occurred at the end of March and the beginning of April. Along with a large number of other young employees of the organization section, I was assigned to help in the secretariat of the congress. Various commissions were formed at the congress: the voting mandate commission, the editorial commission, etc. They were composed of longtime Party adherents, members of the Central Committee, significant local militants, but the actual work was done by the young employees of the Central Committee apparatus. Specifically in the publishing commission, where I was sent, the work was done in this manner: an orator spoke, a stenographer took down his words and then dictated them to a typist. This first text was full of mistakes, for the stenographers didn't understand or hear much of what went on, or in some cases couldn't keep up the pace. So an employee of the publishing commission was attached to each speaker and had to listen carefully to the presentation. He then undertook to correct the text. After that, the orator had only to add his corrections, thus saving him much time.

The political report of the Central Committee was presented to the [Eleventh] Congress (for the last time) by Lenin. A question arose; who should undertake the task of listening to and correcting the text of his report? Kaganovich said, "Have comrade Bazhanov do it. He'll do it perfectly well." It was decided thus.

The platform of the congress was raised about 1.5 meters [about 4 feet] above the floor of the hall. The Presidium of the congress was on the platform. On the right side of the platform (if you faced the hall) was the lectern behind which the speaker stood, papers on the lectern to prompt him. In these early days of the Soviet regime such reports were never written out beforehand. They were improvised, and the speaker would, at most, have noted down a brief outline of his speech and maybe some figures and citations. In front of the lectern a small staircase led down to the floor of the hall, for the use of the orators. Given that nobody should mount the platform during Lenin's report, I sat on the top step, a meter from Lenin, to hear everything clearly.

During Lenin's report the official photographer (I believe it was Otsup)[3] took pictures. Lenin detested being filmed during his presentations, it bothered him, distracting him and interrupting his train of thought. He allowed only the two inevitable official photographs. One, taken from Lenin's left, showed the Presidium as background. The other, from the right, showed only Lenin and behind him a corner of the hall. In both pictures I was visible in front of Lenin.

These photos have often been published in the newspapers: "Vladimir

Ilich speaking for the last time to the Party congress," or "One of the last public appearances of Comrade Lenin." Until 1928 I could always be seen in these photographs. Once I arrived in Paris, I read Soviet newspapers. There was the familiar photo in *Pravda* or *Izvestia* but without me in it. Stalin had undoubtedly ordered that I be obliterated from the picture.

During this spring of 1922, I became progressively more involved in my work and in my studies. My point of observation was excellent, and I quickly grasped the main developments in the life of the country and the Party. Sometimes a few details told more than long studies. For example I don't recall much of the Eleventh Party Congress (1922), which I attended [as a helper], but I remember clearly that labor leader and Politburo member Mikhail Tomsky[4] said, "They chastise us abroad for having a single-party system. But it's not accurate. The difference between us and the foreign countries is that we have one party in power, and the others in prison." The hall reacted with loud applause.

(I wonder if Tomsky remembered this fourteen years later when Stalin's prison gates opened before him? In any event he committed suicide, not wishing to go to prison.)

Honesty requires me to note that at that time I still had confidence in our leaders; if the other parties were in jail, it was because it had to be so.

In April and May 1921 I came to understand how Soviet authority was evolving. Obviously, power was being concentrated more and more in the hands of the Party, and more and more in its apparatus. I was struck by an important fact. The organization of the work of the Party—and of its apparatus which determined the efficiency of that work—were laid out in the form of statutes. But the Party's statutes were almost exactly as they had been adopted in 1903. The Sixth Congress in 1917 changed them slightly. The Eighth Party Conference in 1919 had added some timid modifications, but the statutes, adopted during the prerevolutionary period of clandestinity, were inappropriate to a government in power. They hindered its activity, being unsuitable, unclear, and imprecise.

I got to work and wrote a proposed set of new statutes. Having checked everything, I typed two parallel texts: the old statutes on the left and the new ones on the right, underlining all the modified original text, and my additions. I visited Kaganovich's office, the document in hand. His secretary Balashov[5] told me that Comrade Kaganovich was very busy and could see no one. I insisted, "Tell him anyway. I have a matter of great importance." "What affair of great importance?" "Announce me anyway. I'll not go until you do." He announced me, and Kaganovich received me. "Comrade Bazhanov, I'm very busy. I can give you three minutes. What is it about?"

"Comrade Kaganovich, I have brought you a proposal for new Party statutes." He was sincerely stunned by my audacity: "How old are you, Comrade Bazhanov?"

"Twenty-two."

"How long have you been in the Party?"

"Three years."

"And do you know that in 1903 our Party split into Bolsheviks and Mensheviks solely because of a dispute on the first article of the statutes?"

"Yes, I know that."

"And yet you dare to propose new Party statutes?"

"Yes, I dare."

"Why?"

"Very simple. The statutes have become outmoded. They worked well for a party operating in clandestinity, but they're not at all right for a party in power. They don't provide the required formulas for its work and evolution."

"All right, show me." He read the first and second sections of the old text and those of the new text and reflected for a moment.

"You wrote this yourself?"

"Yes."

He asked me to explain some points, which I did. A few minutes later, Balashov's head appeared in the doorway to remind him that there were people waiting who'd been promised an audience and that it was time for a very important meeting. Kaganovich told him to go: "I'm very busy and can see no one. Put back the meeting to tomorrow."

For two hours Kaganovich read my statutes, reflecting on and weighing them, asking me for an explanation or justification of this or that point. When done, he smiled and declared: "Well, Comrade Bazhanov, you're putting us on a laborious track." After that he phoned Vyacheslav M. Molotov[6] (who was at that time second secretary of the Central Committee) and asked to see him on an important matter. Molotov replied that if it wouldn't take long, it was all right.

"Look," said Kaganovich when we entered Molotov's office, "this young man proposes to us nothing less than new statutes for the Party." Molotov, in his turn, was stunned: "And does he know that in 1903 . . ."

"Yes, he knows it."

"And even so . . . ?"

"Even so."

"You've read the proposal, Comrade Kaganovich?"

"Yes, I have."

"And how do you find it?"

"Perfect."

"In that case, show it to me."

There reoccurred the same scene. For two hours Molotov read my statutes, pulling the text to pieces point by point as I explained each item. Then: "You wrote this alone?"

"Yes."

"There's no doubt," Molotov said when he finished it. "We must go and see Stalin."

As with Molotov, I was presented to Stalin as a crazy young man who dared to question something sacred and untouchable. We went through the same ritual: ". . . how old are you? Do you know that in 1903 . . .?" After I had explained my reasons for proposing the changes, he read and questioned me, also asking: "Did you do this yourself?" But this time the question was followed by another: "Where do you think your text will take the Party in terms of the evolution of its work and its well-being?" I responded that I had addressed this question very well, and saw the Party's evolution in such-and-such a manner. Stalin looked at me long and hard. He understood, as I did, that my statutes represented an important instrument for using the Party apparatus to gain power.[7]

The epilogue was unique. Stalin picked up the phone: "Vladimir Ilich [Lenin]? Stalin here. Vladimir Ilich, *we* think *here in the Central Committee* that the Party's statutes have aged and no longer respond to the new work conditions of the Party. Now that the Party is in power . . ." and so on. It seemed that Vladimir Ilich was agreeable. "Well, then," said Stalin. "*We* thought about it and *we* have prepared new statutes which we'd like to propose to you." Lenin approved and said that the question should be on the agenda of the next Politburo session.

The Politburo agreed in principle and sent the matter for examination to the Orgburo. On 19 May 1922 the Orgburo named a commission charged with revision of the statutes, presided over by Molotov and including Kaganovich, his deputies Lisitsyn and Okhlopkov, and me as secretary.

From that moment I entered the orbit of Molotov for a year.

We worked on the statutes for about two months. The project was sent to the local Party organizations for comment, and in early August the All-Russian Party Conference was convoked to discuss adoption of the new statutes. The conference lasted three or four days. Molotov presented the project, and the delegates gave their opinions. Finally a commission was formed to prepare a definitive version, always presided over by Molotov, which included Kaganovich and certain local dignitaries. One such was Anastas Ivanovich Mikoyan who was then secretary of the Southeast

Bureau of the Central Committee.[8] I was member and secretary of the commission. After that, the conference definitively adopted the new statutes (but later the Central Committee interred them in its turn).

I spent all of 1922 at the same House No. 5 of the Central Committee, at the Loskutka. The employees of the Central Committee who lived there formed little circles based on friendship or because of similar work. Brought into this milieu by the good offices of the student Sasha Volodarsky, I joined a circle grouped more about three close girlfriends—Valeria ("Lera") Golubtsova, Marusia Ignatieva, and Lida Volodarskaya—than about the Volodarsky couple. Lera and Marusia were, like Sasha Volodarsky, "informers" of the organization section's information subsection. The "informers" were in fact writers, each of whom was involved with one or two provincial Party organizations. An "informer" received all documents pertaining to the daily activities of these organizations and reduced them to periodic reports on all that went on in these organizations, sending them to the head office of the organization section.

Volodarsky and his wife were most sociable. They were very proud of entertaining the writer Boris Andreevich Pilniak at their place.[9] I learned, to my great astonishment, that the gentle and modest Sasha had, during the Civil War, been the secretary of the bloodthirsty Rozalia Samoilovna Zemliachka, who was in the Party commissariat of the Eighth Army and who became famous for committing executions and all sorts of cruelties.[10]

In addition to me, our circle included Georgy Maximilianovich Malenkov[11] and German Tikhomirnov.[12]

Georgy Malenkov was married to Lera Golubtsova. He was a couple of years younger than I but put on an air of being an old Party hand. In reality he was only twenty years old and had been in the Party a bit more than one year. During the Civil War he was a junior political militant at the front. Then, like me, he studied at the Higher Technical School, but since he had not gone to high school, he had to begin by taking "worker's" preparatory courses sponsored by the school. He spent about three years at the school. Then his wife, to whom he was in fact indebted for his career, got him into the Central Committee staff and pushed him along the same track as I had taken. First he was secretary of the Orgburo, and then after I left he became secretary of the Politburo. His wife was much more intelligent than he. Georgy Malenkov gave the impression of being a very ordinary man with no special talent. He always had an important and haughty air about him, but it's true that at that time he was very young.

German Tikhomirnov was a year older than I. He was the second assistant of Molotov. This is why: When Molotov was only fifteen he studied at the Kazan high school, during the first quasi-revolution of

1905. With his classmate Viktor Tikhomirnov[13] (son of a very rich family, incidentally), Molotov organized the revolutionary committee of the students of the high schools of Kazan. Viktor Tikhomirnov played an active role in the 1917 revolution, at Molotov's side. During World War I Viktor gave a very large sum of money to the Party, which enabled it to publish *Pravda*. Molotov was appointed secretary to the *Pravda* editorial board, because the money had come thanks to him.

Molotov didn't stay in that position long. In the spring of 1917, during the first weeks of the Revolution, he had a very important role in the Party. He ran the central press organization, but the Party didn't at all consider him to be a political leader. Soon, members of the Central Committee began to arrive in Petrograd: Kamenev, Sverdlov, and Stalin, followed by Lenin, Trotsky, and Zinoviev; and Molotov was sent to the provinces. In 1919 he was the Central Committee's delegate to the Volga region; in 1920, in the Party committee and member of the executive regional committee of Nizhny-Novgorod; then in 1920–21, secretary of the Donets regional committee. But beginning in March 1921 he became a member of, and secretary to, the Central Committee. For a year he was the responsible secretary of the Central Committee—not secretary general, it's true, but neither was he a technical secretary as his predecessors had been (for example, Elena Dmitrievna Stasova).[14] On 3 April 1922 Stalin took office as first secretary of the Central Committee, and then it took very little for Molotov to remain head of the Party bureaucracy, which was advancing relentlessly toward power. Zinoviev and Kamenev preferred Stalin, for one reason only: They needed a sworn enemy of Trotsky in this post, and Stalin was just that.

In 1917 Viktor Tikhomirnov became a member of the collegium [in Russian, *kollegia*, "board"] of the NKVD[15] and essentially devoted himself to administrative and repressive activities. In 1919 he was sent to Kazan to reestablish order, and he died there (of typhus, I believe).

His younger brother, German, had joined the Party in 1917. Until 1921 he stayed in the army, and during some of that time did chekist work in special sections. It left him a bit mad—it seems that chekist "work" was not at all that easy. Upon his arrival in the Central Committee staff, Molotov took him on in his secretariat, where he worked for several years as Molotov's second assistant. They were on a "thou" [familiar] basis, but Molotov drove him hard and incessantly reprimanded him and spoke to him harshly. His intellectual capacity to be private secretary to Molotov wasn't outstanding. Molotov's first assistant, the very competent and intelligent Vasilievsky, had a great deal more responsibility than German. German considered himself a professional chekist. At first I was greatly surprised that German didn't live at House No. 1 of the Soviets, in accordance with his job. Then I understood: Molotov and Vasilievsky "fished" in the Loskutka, where the simple workers of the Central Committee lived, looking for the more intelligent personnel, whom they needed. German spotted such people, watched how they lived, and studied them in the Cheka way of assessment, then gave his analyses of them and whether they could be trusted or not. It was thanks to her relationship with German that the intelligent Lera Golubtsova was able to push her Georgy and get him into the Orgburo's secretariat—Molotov's fief.

As a result of the statutes affair, I was viewed with interest, but until the end of the year I continued to work with Kaganovich and Molotov.

Lazar Kaganovich was remarkable for one thing; he was one of only two or three Jews who stayed in power throughout the Stalin period. In view of Stalin's anti-semitism, this was possible only because Kaganovich completely disavowed all his own relatives and friends. For example, when the Cheka brought to Stalin's attention the affair of Mikhail Moiseevich Kaganovich, minister of aeronautic industries and brother of Lazar, Stalin asked Lazar for his opinion. Lazar, knowing full well that a pure and simple assassination was being prepared, without the slightest grounds for it, replied that this was a matter for the "competent authorities" and it didn't concern him. Before being arrested, Mikhail Kaganovich shot himself in the head.[16]

Beginning in 1917 Lazar Kaganovich, who had consecrated himself to the Revolution, traveled quite a bit on revolutionary business. At Nizhny-Novgorod he met Molotov who promoted him to the position of president of the executive committee of the province of Nizhny-Novgorod, and it was this that determined his career. Lazar continued his travels, going to central Asia via Voronezh, then working on trade union matters at the Central Trade Union Council. In 1922 Molotov made him head of the Organization section of the Central Committee, and it was from that point that his career improved rapidly.

There was an incident that played an important role in his ascension. At a 1922 Politburo session Lenin told its members: "We (meaning Trotsky and himself) are fifty-year-olds; you other comrades are in your forties. We must prepare for our eventual replacement—we must choose thirty- and twenty-year-olds and gradually prepare them to be leaders."

At that point they selected only two, both in their thirties: Vasily Mikhailovich Mikhailov[17] and Lazar Kaganovich.

Mikhailov was then twenty-eight, secretary of the Moscow Party Committee, and a candidate member of the Central Committee. In 1923 he was elected full member of the Central Committee and was named its secretary. It didn't last long, unhappily for him. It was soon apparent that important matters of state were beyond him, and little by little he was demoted back to less important work. Eventually he was manager of the work site at the Dnepr dam and electric generating station. In 1937, having been imprudent enough to side with Bukharin in 1929, he was shot with all the rest of them. Looking back, his selection as a "replacement" was not a happy one.

Kaganovich was much more talented. At first junior to Molotov, he progressively joined Molotov as one of the principal Stalinists. Stalin moved him about from one important Party post to another, and so he was secretary of the Central Committee for the Ukrainian Communist Party, secretary of the Central Committee, member of the Politburo, first secretary of the Moscow committee, again secretary of the Party Central Committee, and peoples' commissar for transport. He undertook whatever mission Stalin gave him. If at first he had a conscience and other human qualities, they disappeared later on as he adapted himself to the requirements of his master and became, like Molotov, 100 percent Stalinist. Little by little he became accustomed to everything, and the millions of victims left him untouched. It is significant that after Stalin's death, when Khrushchev was denouncing Stalinism—although Khrushchev too had adapted himself to the excesses of his master—Kaganovich, Molotov, and Malenkov were not in favor of a less repressive regime. They thought, quite rightly, that they would sleep more soundly with the vice turned to maximum pressure in a regime of Stalin's type—such a regime would run no risks, whereas the possible consequences of Khrushchev's liberalization for the regime itself and their leadership in it could not be judged.

During the second half of 1922 I continued to work in Kaganovich's department. He and Molotov made me secretary of several commissions of the Central Committee. Having a gift for fast and precise writing, I was useful to these commissions. Kaganovich was quick and intelligent, and rapidly understood things, but literary skills were not his strong suit. I was of great value to him. But in the commissions I was of even more value to Molotov.

Molotov was not a brilliant man. An untiring bureaucrat, he worked without stopping from morning to night. He had to spend a good deal of time in commission sessions. In these meetings there was rapid agreement, but then the process of reducing the agreements to writing was endless. They would try to write up a point, but then objections and amendments rained down in profusion. The discussions became heated, they lost track of the starting point, and eventually they forgot what they were arguing about. Molotov, who understood very well the heart of each matter, had great difficulty formulating appropriate wording.

By good fortune I was able to find the right wording very quickly and easily. The moment I saw that a solution had been agreed upon, I would raise my hand. Molotov would immediately stop the debate: "We're listening to you." I would state the formulation. Molotov would jump on it: "There, there. Exactly what we need; note it immediately, if not we'll forget it." I would reassure him, "I won't forget."

"Repeat again." I would repeat it. And thereupon he would end the session, with much time spared.

"You save me a great deal of time, Comrade Bazhanov," said Molotov. As a result he appointed me secretary of all the innumerable commissions over which he presided (the Central Committee worked through a system of commissions). After prior discussion of each important question they would create a commission to study the question and specify the definitive text of whatever resolution it might be, which would then be presented for ratification in either the Orgburo or the Politburo.

One of the most important commissions of the Central Committee was the Instructional Commission. On all important matters the Central Committee adopted directives, which were then sent to the local Party organizations. These were the Central Committee's instructions, the text of which was composed by the Instructional Commission. Sometimes Molotov presided over this commission, sometimes Kaganovich, and I was solidly implanted as the permanent secretary of it. If the local Party organizations had to initiate an agricultural sowing campaign, or run a census of Party membership and issue new Party cards, or manage a campaign of subscriptions for a new publication, the directives arrived in the form of circular instructions.

I soon became interested in this work. New circulars went out daily, and nobody knew which ones were still in force, which were no longer valid, or which had been modified by the course of events or by new Central Committee resolutions. And how were the local organizations to handle the accumulated mass of circulars? How to find what one needed among these thousands of documents? I had no illusions about the organizational talents of the local Party bureaucrats. So I went through the entire mass and threw out those which were no longer valid. I reorganized those which were still valid by subject, by association, by time periods, and alphabetically, with an index so that one could instantly find what one wanted. I went to see Kaganovich, who by this time expected only serious things from me. Not without mischief, I told him in words that would

intrigue him, "Comrade Kaganovich, I propose to codify the Party's legis-
lation." It had a solemn ring to it. Comrade Kaganovich was enchanted by
the expression, and the entire machine was set in motion. Molotov, in
turn, was very pleased. The work made up a volume of five-hundred pages
which was entitled *Handbook for Party Activists*. The Central Committee
press published it, and it was to be reedited each year.

Molotov also appointed me secretary of the editorial staff of the Central Committee's *Izvestya*. This was a periodical that was entirely different
from the daily newspaper *Izvestya*. It was the internal Party organ. Molotov was editor-in-chief, which is why it was a bureaucratic product,
extremely dry and boring. It reflected nothing of the daily life of the Party,
only Central Committee directives and guidances. My role as secretary
was also entirely bureaucratic, and I had begun to ask myself how to get
out of it when, suddenly (suddenly for me, whereas Molotov and the
others had been preparing this for a long time) I was appointed to an
important position: At the end of 1922 I was promoted to secretary of the
Orgburo.

3. Secretary of the Orgburo

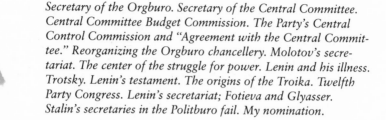

I was beginning to be a somewhat more important cog in the Party's government machinery. I lost myself in my work in the bosom of the apparatus, totally detached from the reality of life. I learned what was happening in the country solely through the prism of the Party apparatus. I only began to work my way out of the sea of paper after about six months. By then I had learned all the information necessary to face all the facts; I could then judge, draw conclusions, make deductions, and see what was really happening and where the Party was actually leading us.

Meanwhile I participated more and more in the work of the central apparatus of the Party, and there were fewer and fewer secrets held from me.

What were the duties of the secretary of the Orgburo? I attended the sessions of the Orgburo and those of the Central Committee's secretariat. I also attended meetings of the Conference of the Central Committee chiefs of sections, where proposed resolutions were prepared for the meetings of the Central Committee's secretariat. Finally, I attended sessions of the various Central Committee commissions and directed the secretariat (in other words, the chancellery) of the Orgburo.

According to the statutes, the hierarchy of the central organs elected by the Party was as follows: First, the three secretaries of the Central Committee, known as the Secretariat. Above the Secretariat was the Orgburo, and above that the Politburo. The Secretariat of the Central Committee was at that time evolving rapidly, taking giant steps toward absolute power in the country—not so much in and of itself but in the form of the person who was its general secretary. In the years 1917–19, Stasova was the secretary, purely technical, of the Central Committee, while its then-

rudimentary apparatus was directed by Yakob Mikhailovich Sverdlov.[1]
After his death in March 1919, and until March 1921, Mikhail Vasilevich
Serebriakov[2] and Nikolai Nikolaevich Krestinsky[3] were the secretaries of
the Central Committee (partly technical, partly responsible). From March
1921, Molotov was the "responsible" secretary of the Central Committee.

But in April 1922, at the time of the plenum of the Central Committee,
three secretaries were elected: Stalin was the general secretary, Molotov
the second secretary, and Mikhailov the third secretary (soon replaced by
Valerian Vladimirovich Kuibyshev).[4] It was from this time on that the
Secretariat began to function regularly.

The statutes defined the Secretariat's functions poorly. Although they
specified that the Politburo was created to resolve the most important
political matters, and the Orgburo to resolve problems of organization, it
was in fact understood that the Secretariat must resolve problems of lesser
importance and prepare the more important ones for the Politburo or the
Orgburo. But on the one hand this was nowhere in writing, and on the
other hand the statutes stipulated the qualification that "all decisions of
the Secretariat, if not challenged by any one member of the Orgburo,
become automatically the latter's decision, while all decisions of the Orgburo, if not challenged by any one member of the Politburo, become the
Politburo's decision—hence a decision of the Central Committee. Any
member of the Central Committee can contest a Politburo resolution
before the plenum of the Central Committee, but that does not annul its
execution."

Put another way, imagine that the Secretariat takes upon itself to
resolve political problems of the greatest importance. From the viewpoint
of the Party's internal procedures and its statutes, there can be no objections. The Secretariat isn't usurping the legal right of a superior level,
because that level can annul or modify the Secretariat's decisions at any
time. But if all power is already in the hands of the general secretary, as
was the case after 1926, he can do all he wants through the Secretariat,
without any interference.

In actual fact it was not like that, for until 1927–28, the Politburo and
its members still had enough weight so that the general secretary didn't
fight uphill battles. But from 1928 the Politburo was so dependent upon
Stalin that he didn't need to act other than through the Politburo. A few
years after that, the Politburo and the Secretariat became simple executors
of his instructions, and power was in the hands of not only the one who
was highest in the hierarchy but the one who was closest to Stalin. His
secretary carried more real weight than the president of the Council of
Ministers or any member of the Politburo.

But for now we are only at the beginning of 1923. The meetings of the Secretariat were presided over by Jan Ernestovich Rudzutak,[5] third secretary of the Central Committee, who had already replaced Kuibyshev (who became president of the Central Control Commission). Stalin and Molotov attended, because only the secretaries of the Central Committee could make decisions. The heads of the sections of the Central Committee, with only the right to make recommendations, also attended: Kaganovich, Sergei Syrtsov,[6] Sofia Nikolaevich Smidovich,[7] Knesofontov, Raskin (head of the finance section), Smitten (head of the statistics section), as well as the newly appointed section heads for information, press, etc., and the principal assistants of the three secretaries of the Central Committee. Rudzutak was a very good president. He was very kind to me. He had just stopped smoking and sucked on candies all the time; he stuffed me with candies.

Molotov presided over the meetings of the Orgburo, which consisted of the three secretaries of the Central Committee; the heads of the principal sections of the Central Committee, Kaganovich and Syrtsov; the political director of the Revolutionary Military Council, which was the equivalent of a Central Committee section; plus one or two members of the Central Committee at the Orgburo in their individual capacities. Most often these were the secretary of the Central Trade Union Council, and the first secretary of the Moscow Party Committee.

Stalin and Molotov had an interest in keeping the Orgburo as small as possible, consisting of only their own trusted men drawn from the Party machinery. That was because the Orgburo was responsible for work that was of vital importance to Stalin. It selected and appointed senior Party members, first in general—for all administrations, which was of relatively less importance—but also for jobs in the Party apparatus: secretaries and leaders of Party provincial, regional, and territorial organizations, which was of the greatest importance for it would ensure Stalin a majority in the next Party congress—a precondition to achieve absolute power. This work went ahead at an energetic pace. But Trotsky, Grigory Yevseevich Zinoviev,[8] and Lev Borisovich Kamenev,[9] who floated in more elevated political clouds, paid no particular attention to it and understood the importance of it only when it was too late.

The first Orgburo was created in March 1919 after the Eighth Party Congress. It consisted of Stalin, Aleksandr Georgievich Bieloborodov,[10] Serebriakov, Stasova, and Krestinsky. As one can see from its composition, it was to handle the organization of the technical apparatus of the Party and the assignments of its personnel. From then on, everything changed. Once Stalin was secretary general, the Orgburo became his main choice for the selection of his cronies and his capture of all the local Party organizations.

Molotov and I had already known each other for a long time. He was very content with my work and continued to appoint me secretary of the Central Committee's various commissions. This enabled me quickly to get to know all the wheels of the apparatus.

There existed, for example, a budget commission. It was a permanent commission, presided over by Molotov, with me as its secretary. It consisted of two secretaries of the Central Committee, Stalin (who never attended a single session) and Molotov, and Raskin, chief of the Central Committee's finance section. I soon learned that Raskin and I were present at the commission's sessions only to record Molotov's decisions. Fortunately Raskin had very little speaking to do. He was a Russian Jew who had emigrated overseas as a child and had lived in a large number of countries. He spoke a Russian that was very difficult to understand, and it seems that the same was true in his other languages. His section workers said, "Comrade Raskin speaks all languages except his native tongue."

The Budget Commission discussed and approved the budgets of the various sections of the Central Committee. Their chiefs tried to defend their interests, and Molotov would talk it over with them, but of course he alone made the decisions. In addition, large sums of money were involved as the Budget Commission ratified the budgets of all the communist parties of other countries. But not one representative from the brother parties was ever admitted to a session. Only the Comintern secretary general, Osip Aronovich Piatnitsky,[11] presented a report. Molotov spread the money around according to his own wishes, and there was no appeal. The circumstances which guided him in this were not always clear to me. It was Raskin who explained to me in a friendly fashion the technique of aid to brother parties: The transfer of secret funds was made possible by the state's monopoly of foreign commerce.

I also learned very quickly how the "conscience of the Party" worked. This was the collegium of the Party Central Control Commission.

It was the rule in the country that the mass of the population had no rights and was entirely under the GPU's supervision. A citizen who was not a Party member could, at any moment, be arrested and exiled, jailed for many years, or shot, simply on the verdict of an anonymous GPU "tribune." In 1923 the GPU could still not arrest a Party member—that came later, in eight or ten years. If a Party member committed a theft, an assassination, or a violation of Party rules, he was first judged by the local control commission. If it concerned a more senior Party member, he was judged by the collegium of the Central Control Commission—that is to say, several members of the commission, designated for that purpose. Only those Party members expelled by the collegium fell into the hands of the GPU's justice. Party members trembled before the collegium of the Party. One of the worst possible threats was to say, "Your case will be transmitted to the Central Control Commission."

At the sessions of this commission some of the older hypocrites, like Aaron Aleksandrovich Solts,[12] gave their judgments accompanied by grandiose phrases about the high moral level of Party members; they presented themselves as the "conscience of the Party." In reality there were two procedures: In cases of lesser importance or matters of criminal law (such as a theft by a party member), members like Solts had no business playacting. But in cases of more important Party members, the unknown GPU information apparatus came into play. It operated with prudence, with the assistance of the GPU leadership, Yakob Khristoforovich Peters,[13] Martin Ivanovich Latsis,[14] and Vasily Nikolaevich Mantsev,[15] who, for the purposes of a particular case, would be brought into the Central Control Commission proceedings. If the case involved a Party member opposed to the Stalin group, GPU information—true or especially invented to compromise the individual in the case—would arrive secretly into the hands of Stalin's Secretariat—to his assistants Grigory ["Grisha"] Kanner[16] and Ivan Pavlovich Tovstukha.[17] It was sent to them by the intermediary of the head of the administrative section of the Central Committee, Knesofontov, or his deputy Brizanovsky (also a chekist). After that, the collegium of the Party would receive an equally secret directive as to what must be done: "expulsion from the Party," or "demotion from supervisory post," or "severe censure with warning." It was up to the collegium to find an appropriate indictment, which was quite easy. For example, a Party member wrote an article for publication and was paid thirty rubles over the maximum set by the Party. That was enough for Solts to put on a scene worthy of the Art Theatre. In a word, after being told what to do by Kanner, Solts or Emelian Mikhailovich Yaroslavsky,[18] acting out their parts, would pose as indignant that a communist had dared to undermine the purity of the Party. Then the verdict dictated to them by Kanner would be pronounced. (I'll have more to say later about Kanner and Stalin's Secretariat.)

But the statutes specified that the decisions of the Control Commission must be in accord with the appropriate Party committees, and those of the Central Control Commission with the Central Committee's approval. They got around that with the following technique.

When the sessions of the Orgburo were over and the members had left, Molotov and I would stay behind. Molotov scanned the minutes of the

Central Control Commission, which contained numerous resolutions regarding different matters. For example: "In the case of Comrade Ivanov, accused of such and such. Decision taken: Expel Comrade Ivanov from the Party." Or perhaps: "Deny Comrade Ivanov any supervisory responsibility for three years." Molotov, who was up to date on all directives of the Party collegium, would mark up the resolution, and I would note in the minutes of the Orgburo: "Agree with the resolutions of the Central Control Commission on the cases of comrades Ivanov, Sidorov, etc." But if Molotov didn't agree, if, for example, the Central Control Commission had decided to "Pronounce severe censure," Molotov would cross it out and write, "Expel from Party," and then I would write in the minutes of the Orgburo, "In the matter of Comrade Ivanov, propose to the Central Control Commission to review its decision of X date, in the case of X person." Once he had received his [unmarked] copy of the minutes, Solts would telephone me and ask, "What is the decision?" I would tell him by phone what Molotov had written on his copy of their minutes. Then the next set of minutes of the Central Control Commission would read, "After having reviewed its decision of X date, in view of the gravity of the accusations brought against Comrade Ivanov, the collegium of the Central Control Commission has decided to expel him from the Party." Obviously the Orgburo (that is to say, Molotov) would be in agreement with this decision.

My secretariat in the Orgburo was composed of a dozen or so employees, devoted and handpicked. All the work of the Orgburo was considered to be secret (and that of the Politburo top secret). Also, in order to keep the secrets in the hands of the smallest number, our personnel was kept at a minimum. Because of that, we were overworked and had virtually no private lives. Work began at 8:00 AM. We ate at our places, as quickly as possible, and we worked until 1:00 in the morning. And despite that we couldn't keep up with the work. In the sea of paper that drowned the Orgburo, the mess was such that we couldn't find anything. The documents were registered according to an outdated method of tracking them in and out. When the secretary of the Central Committee wanted some information or a document from the archives, we would search for hours in the ocean of paper.

I could see that this organization was worthless. I cleaned things up and established several card files where each document was recorded in three different alphabetical indexes. Bit by bit things fell into place. After two or three months, information or documents requested by the secretary of the Central Committee were sent to him minutes later. The sections of the Central Committee which previously had thought it useless to address the

Orgburo secretariat, were now amazed by the speed with which everything was accomplished. Molotov was very pleased and sang my praises constantly. But he was getting ready to move me. In the Politburo secretariat, the mess was even greater, and Stalin had begun to ask himself if it wouldn't be useful for me to put things over there in order. But as we shall see, it wasn't a simple matter.

For the personnel of my secretariat, the consequences were unexpected. At first they protested my reforms energetically, complaining to the secretaries of the Central Committee that it was impossible to work with me. Once I had nevertheless realized my reforms with a firm hand and the results could be seen, the protests ceased. Before, their time was mostly lost in lengthy and fruitless research. Now, the work was well and quickly done, and there was less of it. They came at 9:00 AM, and by 5:00 to 6:00 PM the day's work was all finished. They had free time and could lead their own lives. Were they happy? Not at all. Before, they saw themselves as martyrs making a sacrifice for the Party. Now, they were merely bureaucrats in an apparatus that was functioning well. I could sense their disappointment.

I was by now working in daily contact with the secretaries of Molotov and already to some extent with those of Stalin.

Vasilievsky, Molotov's first secretary, was head of his secretariat. A fast and energetic worker, he was intelligent and efficient. He was thin, with an intelligent, emaciated face. He organized all Molotov's work, understood all the problems quickly. He called his boss [familiarly] "thou" and enjoyed his full confidence. I was unable to decipher his past. I believe he was a tsarist army lieutenant who, right after the October Revolution, became chief of staff of the Bolshevik military district of Moscow. After I left the Central Committee in 1926, I lost track of him and have never heard anyone speak of him again.

The second assistant of Molotov was German Tikhomirnov, of whom I've spoken before. He certainly "never set the world on fire" and more than once I was astonished that Molotov put up with such a secretary. But the third and fourth secretaries of Molotov, Borodayevsky and Belov, were no better. German and Molotov called each other [familiarly] "thou." Molotov wasn't pleased with German's work, but he put up with it. Two or three years later he made him head of the Central Archives of the Party's Central Committee, but only for insignificant documents. All important papers were held by Stalin's secretary, Tovstukha.

Through my work with Molotov's secretariat, I became more and more familiar with the Party's secrets. I began to understand the hidden core of the power struggle.

After the Revolution and during the Civil War, collaboration between Lenin and Trotsky was perfect. At the end of the Civil War (end of 1920) the country and the Party considered these two men as the chiefs of the Revolution, way above all other Party leaders. In fact it was Lenin who always played the major role of the two, during the Civil War. The nation didn't understand this too well, and there was a tendency to attribute the victory principally to Trotsky, organizer and head of the Red Army. This "halo" surrounding Trotsky didn't please Lenin, who foresaw a significant and dangerous crossroads as the country turned to peacetime rebuilding. To maintain himself as head of the country when it would be needed, Lenin had to keep his majority among the Party leadership in the Central Committee. During this period, both before the Revolution and in late 1917, Lenin was often in a minority position in the Party he had created, and he retrieved his majority with great difficulty. The same thing happened after the Revolution, for example, when Lenin was defeated in the Central Committee and was in a minority position over such a vital matter as the Brest–Litovsk peace treaty with Germany.

Lenin wanted to be certain of having a majority. He saw Trotsky as the only possible threat to his preponderance. At the end of 1920, during the debate on the trade unions, he endeavored to enfeeble Trotsky and reduce his influence. He went so far as to place Trotsky in a ridiculous position on the transportation problem. It was urgently necessary to put the ruined railroads back into working order. Lenin knew perfectly well that Trotsky had no aptitude for this task and had no appropriate talent to accomplish it. Nevertheless Trotsky was appointed peoples' commissar for transport. He brought to the task his enthusiasm, his zeal, his eloquence, and his leadership methods, but the only result was confusion. Trotsky, conscious of his failure, resigned from the job.

Lenin organized a group of his close collaborators in the Central Committee from among Trotsky's adversaries. Zinoviev and Stalin were his fiercest enemies. Zinoviev had become Trotsky's enemy after the autumn of 1919, when General Nikolai Nikolaevich Yudenich[19] was successfully advancing on Petrograd. Zinoviev was in a complete panic and had totally lost the ability to command. Trotsky arrived, saved the situation, and treated Zinoviev with contempt. That is how they became enemies. Stalin detested Trotsky just as much as Zinoviev did. Throughout the Civil War Stalin took part in revolutionary war committees with several armies on several fronts and was subordinated to Trotsky. The latter required discipline, attention to orders, and the use of military experts. Stalin, for his part, depending on local bands of undisciplined partisans, didn't obey the orders of the general staff, and he couldn't stand

Trotsky because he was a jew. Trotsky violently attacked Stalin, and Lenin constantly had to play referee.[20]

Kamenev had no personal reasons to be hostile to Trotsky. He was less vain and less inclined to intrigue, but he attached himself to Zinoviev and followed his lead. Lenin promoted the group to high posts. Zinoviev was made head of the Comintern (to which Trotsky had no objection, being himself in the important job of commander of the Red Army during the Civil War). Lenin made Kamenev his premier and principal assistant in the Council of Peoples' Commissars (Sovnarkhom) as well as charging him with supreme direction of the country's economy (on the Council of Labor and Defense). When, at the April 1922 Plenum of the Central Committee, Kamenev proposed acceptance of Zinoviev's idea of making Stalin general secretary of the Central Committee, Lenin—although he knew Stalin all too well—had no objection. That was how in March and April 1922 the group ensured Lenin his majority while remaining subordinate to him, and Trotsky ceased to be a danger.

But in May 1922 an unexpected incident changed everything: Lenin's first stroke. During the past few years he had been ill a number of times. In August 1918 he was wounded when Fanny Kaplan tried to kill him.[21] In March 1920 he was very ill, while at the end of 1921 and in late March 1922 illness kept him from working. He recovered and on 27 March 1922 he presented the political report of the Central Committee to the Party congress and took everything back in hand. His stroke of May 1922 brought confusion. Until October he was away from his work, and the doctors' diagnoses (secret, for the Politburo only, not the country) announced that it was the "beginning of the end." It was after this attack that Zinoviev, Kamenev, and Stalin organized the "Troika." They saw Trotsky as their principal rival but did not start fighting him because, against all expectations, Lenin began to do better in June. His condition improved and he went back to work at the start of October. On 20 October he was on the dais at the plenum of the Moscow Soviet, and on 3 November he presented a report to the Fourth Congress of the Comintern. During this period he was again master. He took Stalin to task sharply on the matter of his nationalities policy: Stalin had proposed formation of a Soviet Socialist Republic of Russia, whereas Lenin wanted a *Union* of Soviet Socialist Republics in expectation of later adherence of other countries as the revolution spread east and west. Lenin also was preparing to attack Stalin because of his conflict (and that of Stalin's acolytes Grigory Konstantinovich Ordzhonikidze[22] and Feliks Edmundovich Dzerzhinsky)[23] with the Georgian Central Committee, but there was no time for it. In October 1922 the plenum of the Central Committee, sitting without

Lenin, made decisions that weakened the state's monopoly over foreign trade. In December Lenin came back and annulled these decisions at a new plenum. He held, it seems, the reins of power once again, and the Troika resumed its role of being the group of his closest collaborators and executors.

But the doctors had seen clearly. His recovery was of short duration. Syphilis, poorly treated earlier in life, had reached the terminal stage.[24] The end was near. On 16 December Lenin's condition worsened severely, and turned even worse on 23 December.

Lenin already knew by the beginning of December that he had not much longer to live, hence the evaporation of his concern about his majority in the Central Committee and his rivalry with Trotsky. More, he was surprised by how much the Party apparatus—hence that of Stalin—had reinforced its power during his months of illness. He was sketching out a rapprochement with Trotsky and seriously considering how to limit Stalin's growing power. In the course of reflecting on the matter, he thought of a series of steps basically involving problems of organization. He could no longer write and had to dictate to his secretaries. He began with a double measure: on the one hand to enlarge substantially the composition of the Central Committee, thus diluting, as they say, the power of the Party apparatus; on the other hand to reorganize and expand considerably the Central Control Commission so that it would be a counterweight to the Party bureaucratic machinery.

On 23 and 26 December, Lenin dictated his first "letter to the Congress," which was to be the Twelfth Party Congress in March/April 1923, where the question of increasing the size of the Central Committee would be brought up. This letter was sent to the Central Committee, to Stalin. Stalin hid it and, at the April congress, taking advantage of Lenin being completely out of circulation, he proposed the increase as if it were his own idea (but in line with Lenin's thinking). It was approved, and the Central Committee expanded from twenty-seven to forty members. But Stalin had maneuvered this with the opposite intention than Lenin, to bring in *his* men and so obtain *his* majority.

On 24 and 25 December, Lenin dictated his second "letter to the Congress," the one usually referred to as his "testament." In it he gave his assessment of the principal Party leaders, raising the question of leadership of the Party in the event of his death. In general he leaned toward a collegial leadership, with Trotsky in the first position. This letter was also addressed to the next congress (the Twelfth), but Lenin had ordered that it be sealed and only opened after his death. This stipulation was not written on the envelope by the secretary on duty, but she did explain his wishes to Lenin's wife, Nadezhda Konstantinova Krupskaya[25] and to the other secretaries. Bound by this order, Krupskaya did not have the letter opened at the Twelfth Congress because Lenin was still alive.

Meanwhile Lenin continued pondering the problem and concluded, several days later, that Stalin must be relieved of his position as secretary general. On 4 or 5 January Lenin composed the well-known Codicil to his Testament, in which he emphasized Stalin's crudeness and other faults and recommended to the Party that they demote him from the post of general secretary. This codicil was appended to the "letter to the Congress" and sealed and of course not opened by Krupskaya before the Twelfth Congress. But Lenin's secretaries knew the contents of the Testament and explained them to Krupskaya.

Lenin then exposed the second part of his plan in an article entitled "How to Reorganize the Rabkrin," which he dictated until the beginning of March. This article was transmitted to the Central Committee by normal channels and the Rabkrin was reorganized in June but in reality also to serve Stalin's interests.

In February and March Lenin's condition was stable. At that time he had definitely decided to fight as much against Stalin as against the bureaucratic machinery that Stalin directed. On Lenin's urging, a Central Committee commission against bureaucracy was created at the end of February. Lenin, who expected to direct the struggle against Stalin at the next congress—even from his sickbed—was especially targeting the bureaucratism of the Orgburo, the Central Committee's Bureau of Organization.

Meanwhile, after a new mid-December turn for the worse in Lenin's health (the doctors considered it a second stroke), Stalin decided he had no more reason to hold back. He became rude with Krupskaya, who spoke to him in Lenin's name. In January 1923, Lidia Aleksandrovna Fotieva,[26] Lenin's secretary, asked him for documents on the Georgian problem, which interested Lenin. Stalin replied with a refusal, "I cannot give them without the advice of the Politburo." In early March he insulted Krupskaya to the point where she ran to Lenin in tears, and he—outraged—dictated a letter to Stalin telling him that he was breaking all personal relations with him. But the incident greatly upset Lenin, and on 6 March he had a third stroke which robbed him of the power of speech, leaving him paralyzed and semiconscious. He never again appeared on the political scene, and the ten months which followed were nothing but a progressive agony.

(I learned all that I have related here in early 1923 at secondhand, from the secretaries of Molotov. Several months later it was confirmed to me at firsthand, by the secretaries of Stalin and Lenin.)

The Troika took power as of January 1923. During the first two months they still feared collusion between Trotsky and the moribund Lenin, but after the March attack Lenin was no longer a factor and the Troika could put into action its preparatory steps in the struggle to eliminate Trotsky. The Troika consolidated and fortified its position as summer approached.

The Twelfth Party Congress was from 17 to 23 April 1923. A major problem arose: Who would present the congress with the Central Committee's political report, the most important political document of the year? This task had always been Lenin's. Whoever did it would be considered by the Party to be Lenin's successor.

At a Politburo meeting Stalin proposed that Trotsky present the report. This was Stalin's style. He was conducting an energetic campaign to put his supporters in place, but that would only give him his majority in the congress two years hence. In the meantime he had to gain time and lull Trotsky's vigilance to sleep.

With astonishing naïveté, Trotsky refused. He didn't want the Party to think he was usurping the place of a sick Lenin. In his turn, he proposed that Stalin give the report as general secretary of the Central Committee. I can just imagine Zinoviev's emotions at that moment. But Stalin also refused. He understood perfectly well that the Party would not understand and wouldn't accept him, for nobody then considered him as one of the top Party bosses. In the end, with Kamenev's help, Zinoviev was tasked with presenting the report. He was president of the Comintern, and if anyone should temporarily replace the ill Lenin, it was he. Zinoviev gave the political report to the congress in April.

In May and June the Troika continued to consolidate its position. The Party considered Zinoviev not so much as its chief but as its "number one member." Kamenev was "number two" and effectively Lenin's replacement as president of the Council of Peoples' Commissars and as president of the Council of Labor and Defense. He also presided over Politburo sessions. Stalin was "number three," but his principal activity was clandestine: The process of preparing his future majority. Kamenev and Zinoviev weren't thinking of that. Their main concern was to discredit Trotsky politically and remove him from power.[27]

Lenin had quit the ranks, but his secretariat continued to function by force of its inertia. He had two secretaries: Maria Ignatievna Glyasser,[28] and Fotieva. Toward the end of his illness, two others—Voloditcheva,[29] and Sarah Flakserman—helped as "duty secretaries," taking turns to be completely at Lenin's disposal should he wish to dictate a letter, an instruction, or an article. Later, Sarah Flakserman went to the "Little Sovnarkom" (a sort of commission that gave legal form as needed to Sovnarkom decrees) and became its secretary. Fotieva, who was officially secretary of the USSR Sovnarkom, continued to work with Kamenev. She told him enough of the little secrets of Lenin's secretariat to enable her to keep her job. But Kamenev, unlike Stalin, had little interest in the details of Lenin's daily life.

Of Lenin's two secretaries, the first and principal one was Glyasser. She took care of Lenin's secretariat for Politburo matters, and Fotieva for Sovnarkom matters. All of Russia knew Fotieva's name. For years she had signed her name with Lenin's to all government decrees. But nobody knew of Glyasser, because the Politburo's work was top secret. It was there that all fundamental questions were handled, and Glyasser drew up the minutes noting all the decisions and all pertinent decrees at Politburo sessions. The Sovnarkom merely executed them afterward, and it was up to Fotieva to be sure that the Sovnarkom decrees exactly mirrored the Politburo's decisions. But she didn't participate, as Glyasser did, in their preparation and their formulation.

Glyasser functioned as secretary at all Politburo sessions, Central Committee plenums, and for the principal commissions of the Politburo. She was a small, humpbacked woman with an intelligent and inscrutable face. A good secretary, very intelligent, she herself never originated concepts, but she understood very well all that took place in the Politburo debates, and the matters which Lenin dictated to her, and she recorded it rapidly and exactly. Guardian of Lenin's spirit, she understood his hostility during his last months to Stalin's bureaucratic machinery, and she made no effort to transfer into it.

Stalin decided it was time to get rid of her and replace her with one of his own men. The post of secretary to the Politburo was too important to him: all the secrets of the Party and the government converged there.

At the end of June 1923 Stalin obtained agreement from Zinoviev and Kamenev to replace Glyasser. But it was not so easy to find a suitable replacement. The Politburo secretary's work required a number of skills. At the sessions he must not only understand everything that was going on but also: (1) follow the debate carefully; (2) ensure that each Politburo member had before him all necessary documents; (3) direct the entry and exit of all persons convoked to testify on each agenda item; (4) interrupt each time an error was committed, such as forgetting that a different decision had been made already on the same point; (5) take the time, all the while, to record all decisions; and (6) function as the Politburo's "memory," furnishing instantly all necessary information.

Glyasser was up to all that. Stalin tried to replace her with two of his secretaries, Amayak Markarovich Nazaretian[30] and Tovstukha, hoping that the two, sharing the work, could do it.

But it was a complete failure. Nazaretian and Tovstukha were unable to concentrate on all the tasks; they got confused, didn't follow things, didn't understand, and weren't prompt. The work of the Politburo was disorganized. The members saw it was a failure, but for the moment they kept quiet.

Finally, it was Trotsky who exploded. His pretext was discussion of a note from the Peoples' Commissar for Foreign Affairs to the British government. Trotsky had drafted the note, and several corrections were made to it during the Politburo discussion. The secretaries, failing to understand their essence, didn't make the desired changes. After the meeting, it was necessary to go to each Politburo member and correct his copy. At the next Politburo session Trotsky scribbled a note which I kept (it was given me by Nazaretian): "*For Politburo members only.* Comrade [Maxim Maximovich] Litvinov[31] says that the secretaries of the session made no record of my note. That won't do. One must ensure better procedures in the future. The secretaries should have had the text of the note (which I sent) in front of them and recorded everything. Otherwise we risk misunderstandings. Trotsky."

Zinoviev wrote on the same note, "We must get a stenographer. G.Z."

And Bukharin: "I agree. N. Bukh."

Stalin, very unhappy at this failure, wrote with his customary crudeness and unscrupulousness: "*A trifle.* The secretaries would have made note if Trotsky and Georgy Vasilievich Chicherin[32] hadn't done so themselves. On the contrary, the secretaries should record nothing *regarding such questions,* to maintain secrecy. J. St."

Tomsky: "A stenographer is useless. M. Tom."

Kamenev: "A stenographer (loyal communist) is necessary to assist the secretaries of the sessions. L. Kam."

(The words underlined in the foregoing text were so done by Trotsky and Stalin themselves.)

Why did I say that Stalin acted in bad faith? He underlined "regarding such questions" as if the debate on the note in question were ultra-secret. Since it was Politburo habit to treat virtually all matters before it as already secret, to distinguish those matters which could not be entrusted to the secretaries was absurd, impossible. On Trotsky's statement, "For Politburo members only," Stalin, to show how he completely disregarded

the advice of one member of the Politburo, gave the note to Nazaretian—
the very person not supposed to see it.

Stalin had to concede defeat on this. How good it would have been to
have his own men—Nazaretian and Tovstukha—as secretaries of the
Politburo! But it had not worked. There was always Bazhanov, who was
working out very well as secretary of the Orgburo and who would probably do just as well at the Politburo, but would he be Stalin's man? That was
the question. But the risk had to be taken.

On 9 August 1923 the Orgburo of the Central Committee decided:
"Appoint Comrade Bazhanov assistant to secretary of the Central Committee Stalin, and relieve Bazhanov of his functions as secretary of the
Orgburo." In this decision Stalin said nothing of my functions as secretary
of the Politburo. It was intentional. I was his assistant. As to designating a
secretary of the Politburo, it was his prerogative and he could name to it
anyone in whom he had confidence. (After me it was Malenkov, who had
to wait a long time before becoming his assistant.)

4. Stalin's Assistant and Secretary of the Politburo

Approval of the Politburo's agenda. The mechanisms of power. The Troika. *The Politburo's technical apparatus. OGPU messenger corps. Tamara Kazhanova's top secret. Stalin's secretariat. Nazaretian. Division of work. Kanner. House No. 1 of the Soviets. Fifth floor of the Central Committee building. Beginning to work with Stalin. Stalin's telephone tap. The $7,000,000 cavalry scam. Politburo sessions.*

In handing over to me the powers of secretary of the Politburo, Amayak Nazaretian said; "Comrade Bazhanov, you don't understand the importance of the position you now occupy."[1] In fact I only understood it a couple of days later, when for the first time I prepared the agenda for the next Politburo session.

The Politburo was the principal repository of power in the USSR. It was responsible for all major decisions respecting government of the country, as well as all questions of world revolution. At that time, the Politburo met two or three times weekly. The agenda for these routine meetings included a good one hundred matters for discussion, sometimes as many as one hundred fifty. In addition there were extraordinary sessions to handle urgent problems.

All segments of the government which had matters to submit to the Politburo sent them to me, at the secretariat of the Politburo. I would study them and put those with merit on the next Politburo session's draft agenda. I didn't put the agenda into final form until it had been approved by the *Troika*. That is where I suddenly discovered the real secret of the *Troika*'s power.

On the eve of a Politburo meeting, Grigory E. Zinoviev, Lev Borisovich Kamenev, and Stalin got together. At first these gatherings usually took place in Zinoviev's apartment. Later they mostly met in Stalin's office in the Central Committee. Officially they met to approve the agenda for the Politburo, an action not required by any statute or regulation. Either Stalin or I could have done it, but the *Troika* took over the function in order to operate as a secret government which decided—in advance—all important matters. Only four of us were present: the *Troika* and I. I would briefly explain the proposed agenda items. In principle the *Troika* was to decide only if a problem would be kept on the agenda for discussion in the Politburo meeting. In fact the *Troika* decided how each question should be resolved at tomorrow's session, agreeing even on what roles each would play in the discussion. My minutes included no such agreements, but in fact everything the Politburo was to decide was predetermined. There would be discussions in the Politburo session, but in effect everything had already been decided in the *Troika*'s tight little circle . . . sincerely discussed, with no holds barred, by these three real powers.

The *Troika* was, in fact, the real government, and my role as principal reporter and inevitable witness to all the secrets, all the behind-doors decisions, went far beyond that of mere secretary of the Politburo. Now I could understand the significance of Nazaretian's remark.

For two more years the *Troika* system worked perfectly. My reports and suggestions to the *Troika* had to be very brief, clear, and concise. It was soon obvious that the three members were very pleased with my work.

The secretariat of the Politburo was under my orders. There were ten or so staff, all loyal Party members, tried and proven. They worked from dawn to night, as late as midnight or 1:00 the next morning. There was even more chaos here than there was when I took over the Orgburo. The mountains of paper were bigger, all of it jumbled in a state of complete disarray. We could only rarely retrieve any particular document, and then only because of the almost unbelievable memory of one of the girls.[2] I started a complete reorganization, using my index and filing system. Within two or three months all was in order and we could find any document instantly. Officials of the Central Committee and section heads, who formerly found it useless to scratch around in the Politburo's "archives," now came willingly and were immediately served. More, they now began to ask their own sections to follow the Politburo's example. Shortly we were able to put all the staff on normal working hours, and soon they were proud of their work and their special mission: to handle, safeguard, and store all the secrets of the State, which passed through their hands daily.

Because all documents handled by my secretariat were "Especially" or "Absolutely" secret, there was a corps of special GPU messengers, carefully chosen, well armed, clad in leather from head to toe, to distribute and recover the documents. Carrying a document from the Politburo in a sealed envelope, they ignored all secretaries and doors and delivered the envelope to the addressee only.

If, for example, the recipient was Lev Davidovich Trotsky,[3] they would penetrate past his secretaries and his assistants, right into his inner sanctum, where they waited until he himself received it and signed on the envelope for it. They waited until the recipients—all members of the Central Committee—had read the document (and they had no right to copy them), and then they returned the document to my secretariat. There, unless it was destined for the archives, it was destroyed, and its disposition noted. This work was done by my ten-member staff, who also handled document production, printing, and reproduction, as well as other technical matters.

The Secretariat of the Politburo was on the fifth floor of the Central Committee building, on Staraya Ploshchad ("Old Square"). Politburo sessions were held in the Kremlin's Sovnarkom meeting room. My staff and I brought a precious cargo to the Kremlin for those meeting: Politburo documents for use in the meetings, including minutes of the last few Politburo sessions. Two armed chekists from the messenger corps accompanied us, looking tense. They were certain that no documents were more secret than these, and they would defend them with their last drops of blood. We were, of course, never attacked.

Among my staff was a young Georgian girl, Tamara Khazanova, very beautiful with lovely large black eyes. I'd never really had a big love affair up to this time, but luckily I held back. Tamara was as limited as she was beautiful. Some years later she became a fast friend of Stalin's wife, [Nadezhda] Nadia Alliluyeva.[4] It was not, however, a friendship of two women on the same level, like that of Nadia and Molotov's wife (Zhemchuvnina).[5] Tamara had a schoolgirl crush on Nadia and followed her about like a shadow. She was always at the Stalin apartment and helped with the children. When Nadia committed suicide and the children were left in care of the domestic servants, Tamara continued to care for them.

It seems to have been at this juncture that Tamara became, if one can put it this way, of particular interest[6] to Stalin. But she was stupid, and he soon couldn't stand her. She went from there to a secretarial job in the Party organ at the Central Trade Unions Council. Then she seduced Politburo member Andrei Andreevich Andreev who married her.[7]

When I started working in Stalin's office, his secretariat was still nominally run by Amayak Nazaretian. However, he took a long vacation right away and then was absent because of illness. He only returned for a short time at the end of that year (1923), when Stalin sent him over to work at Pravda with special instructions. (More on this later, since it caused a real scandal.)

Nazaretian, a highly cultivated, intelligent, kind, and self-possessed Armenian, worked with Stalin on Party matters in the Caucasus in the

early days and was one of only three who called Stalin [familiarly] "thou."
The other two were Kliment Yefremovich Voroshilov[8] and Ordzhonikidze. These three also called Stalin by his old Party pseudonym, Koba.[9]
But I felt that Stalin, already dreaming of making himself autocrat of all
the Russias, was irritated that his head of secretariat used his familiar
name. To him it was a disagreeable detail, and he got rid of Nazaretian at
year's end in an inelegant fashion. Their personal friendship stopped
thereupon. Nazaretian went off to the Urals as president of a regional
control commission, then back to Moscow to work in the Central Control
Commission. He was never again close to Stalin, who had him shot in
1937.

Another assistant to Stalin, Ivan Pavlovich Tovstukha, played an important role in Stalin's staff until his death in 1935. When I got there in
1923, however, he was off on an important mission for Stalin—forming
up the Lenin Institute. So only three of us were with Stalin full time: Lev
Zakharovich Mekhlis,[10] Grigory Kanner, and I. We split the work as
follows:

Bazhanov: Secretary to Stalin for Politburo matters
Mekhlis: Stalin's personal secretary
Kanner: Stalin's secretary for "dirty tricks"
Tovstukha: Stalin's secretary for matters that were "semishady."

This requires some explanation. My work and that of Mekhlis contained nothing hidden or underhanded about it. It was aboveboard. Specifically, all matters addressed to the Politburo went through my hands.
Mekhlis took care of all that was addressed to Stalin personally and
reported to Stalin on such matters. In effect I served the Politburo, and
Mekhlis served Stalin personally.

Officially, "Grisha" Kanner's functions were vague and were more
related to housekeeping or daily routine. He was overtly responsible for
security, housing, vehicles, the medical commission of the Central Committee, and the Party cell of the Central Committee—at first look, a lot of
trivia. But this was only the superficial part of his work. People could only
guess at the layers beneath. But I soon discovered the main lines of
Kanner's work. The man administratively responsible for the Central
Committee was the old chekist, Ivan Ksenofontovich Ksenofontov, a
former member of the collegium of the Extraordinary Commission for the
Struggle against Counterrevolution and Sabotage (vCheka). He and his
assistant Brizanovsky, also a chekist, worked under the orders of Kanner,
and under his orders only.

As soon as I was appointed secretary to the Politburo, Kanner and Ksenofontov declared that I must move into the Kremlin, or at the very least into the "First House of the Soviets." The "Fifth House of the Soviets," where I had been living, was mainly a transient quarters, and anyone could come and go there. But now the security people would have to watch over my precious person, they said. This was easy to do at the Kremlin, where people could only enter after filling out various forms and submitting to tight controls. At the "First House of the Soviets" there was also a control or security office and all visitors had to call in first and arrange for a pass, which had to be returned when they left.

They had a point. My work required me to bring rush work home, always ultrasecret Politburo documents. At the Fifth House it was not secure enough for that. So I agreed to move, but not to the Kremlin, where each step was watched and one couldn't sneeze without it being reported to the Kremlin. I moved to the First House, where at least there was a little more freedom. Kaganovich, Kanner, Mekhlis, and Tovstukha also lived there.

The Central Committee offices, located in 1922 and the first part of 1923 in the Vozdvijenskaya Road, now moved to a huge building on the Staraya Ploshchad. The fifth floor was reserved for secretariats of the Central Committee and our secret services. Arriving on the fifth floor, you turned left for the offices of Molotov and Rudzutak [also a Politburo member], their assistants, and the secretariat of the Orgburo. If you took the corridor to the right, the first door on the left opened into the offices of Kanner and Mekhlis. Past that office was a room in which there sat a beefy female chekist, Nina Fomenko,[11] a messenger and general cleaning woman who guarded the entrance to Stalin's office. Then there was Stalin's office. The door at the other side of Stalin's office led to the immense room where Stalin and Molotov held their frequent meetings. On the other side of this meeting room were Molotov's offices.

No one saw Stalin in his office without first going through Mekhlis. The chekist Nina Fomenko entered Stalin's office only if he rang for her. Even when Kanner or Tovstukha had to see Stalin, they telephoned him first to get permission. Only two people could go into Stalin's office unannounced: Mekhlis and I—he, of course, as personal secretary and I because I had to see him continually on Politburo business, matters of prime importance and urgency. From the start, I entered Stalin's office without regard to who was with him or what he might be doing at the moment, and I spoke to him without ado. He would interrupt his conversation or meeting to attend to whatever I brought to his attention. The affairs of the Politburo were accepted as being of the greatest urgency.

I had the same right (of entry and interruption) with all the secretaries of the Central Committee and all other high Soviet dignitaries. When it was necessary I interrupted no matter what meeting—for example Sovnarkom (the actual government). I went into the offices of Cabinet ministers without waiting or being announced, to break into no matter what on necessary Politburo business. That was my prerogative as secretary of the Politburo. I came only on Politburo business, of which nothing was considered more important and more urgent.

During the first days of my new work, I went in to see Stalin dozens of times a day, to report to him on documents addressed to the Politburo. But I soon observed that neither the content nor the outcome of these documents were of the slightest interest to him. When I would ask him what should be done about this or that matter, he would reply, "And what do you think should be done?" I would respond that in my opinion it should either be submitted for Politburo discussion or sent to some specific office of the Central Committee or maybe sent back for further research, coordination, or better presentation. Stalin would agree at once, "Very good. Do it."

I quickly concluded that I was seeing him often for no reason and that I should take more initiative myself. And that was what I did. The others in Stalin's offices explained to me that he read no documents and took no interest in any matters of government. I began to wonder what did interest him.

Before long, there was an unexpected answer to my question. I went into Stalin's office on an urgent matter, as usual without warning. I found him on the telephone—but listening, not talking. He simply held the receiver and listened. My affair was urgent but I didn't want to interrupt him so I waited politely for him to finish. But this went on some time: he listened, saying nothing. I stayed there and waited.

Finally, I observed with astonishment that he was using none of the four telephones on his desk. He was listening on an instrument of a type unfamiliar to me, that I hadn't seen before. Its wire disappeared into the drawer of his desk. I looked again at the four ordinary telephones. One was the internal Central Committee phone, which passed through a woman switchboard operator. The next two were "high" and "low" Kremlin phones, the former for the Kremlin offices, the latter for the use of senior officials and their families' apartments. These two were also handled by switchboard operators chosen by the GPU as well as the Kremlin services. The fourth phone was part of an automatic system (*vertushka*) installed on Lenin's orders. He had thought it dangerous to let the telephone "girls" listen in on important and secret conversations. A separate unmanned automatic system had therefore been installed, linking at first sixty, then eighty, then more people—all exclusively government officials. The system was to ensure the security of their telephone conversations. Having one of these automatic phones became the surest sign that you had arrived at the top. Only Central Committee members, peoples' commissars and their deputies, and of course Politburo full and candidate members had these phones.

But Stalin wasn't using any of the four phones. It didn't take long to realize that a phone "central" [tap] had been installed inside his desk. It enabled him to listen in on all the other officials who had automatic phones. Those others, of course, thought their phones were secure because no girl operators were involved. They spoke freely on their lines, and so Stalin could hear all their secrets.

Stalin raised his head and looked me right in the eyes, with a meaningful stare. He realized that I had understood what I was looking at. I would have discovered his secret sooner or later anyway, since I still came in without warning several times a day. His look conveyed a question: did I understand the consequences this discovery could have for me personally? Of course I did! In Stalin's struggle for power this was one of his most important secrets. It allowed him to listen to the private conversations of all those such as Trotsky, Zinoviev, and Kamenev with each other and so be aware of all their planning and thinking. It was a weapon of colossal importance. Among them all only Stalin could see; the others were blind. Certainly they realized for years that he knew their plans, their thoughts, their alliances, their opinions of him, and their intrigues against him, but they didn't know how he knew. For Stalin it was one of the most essential tools in his successful climb to the summit of power.

Clearly if I should ever make the slightest allusion to this secret, Stalin would wipe me out. I returned his stare, and neither of us spoke. It wasn't necessary. Eventually I made a sign to indicate I didn't want to disturb him, and I left the room. Stalin was doubtless sure I would keep his secret.

Thinking about it later, it was clear that at least one other person had to know about this, Mekhlis. He too went in to see Stalin regularly with no warning. I chose a propitious moment and told Mekhlis that I shared the secret, and that we must be the only two who knew it. Mekhlis indicated that he'd expected me to make this discovery, but that there was a third; Grischa Kanner, who had organized the technical side of the listening system. Thenceforth the three of us spoke freely among ourselves about this secret that we shared. I wanted to know how Kanner had organized it. At first he refused to speak, turning it into a joke. But soon his boastfulness got the better of him, and he began to relate the story. Bit by bit, it came out in all its details.

When Lenin had the notion to install the automatic system, Stalin undertook to get it done. As most of the instruments were to be placed in the Central Committee building [in the offices of] (the three secretaries of the Central Committee and those of the Politburo and Orgburo, their principal assistants, and the principal Central Committee section heads), the core of the system had to be in the building itself. In addition, it was technically best to locate it on the fifth floor where many of the recipients were located. The three secretaries of the Central Committee, and the secretaries of the Politburo and the Orgburo already accounted for seven instruments. So, the system central was installed in the vicinity of Stalin's offices.

The actual installation was done by a Czech communist, a specialist in automatic telephone systems. Kanner, on Stalin's orders, instructed the Czech to install a "control post" at which, "in case of a breakdown or malfunction, the lines could be tested and the problem found." This control system, on which one could listen on all the lines, was installed. I don't know who actually put it inside Stalin's desk, either Kanner or the Czech communist. But as soon as the installation was made and was working satisfactorily, Kanner telephoned Genrikh Grigoriyevich Yagoda[12] at the GPU, on Stalin's behalf, to say that the Politburo had received precise information and proof from the Czech Communist Party, that the Czech telephone technician was a spy. Knowing this, they had let him finish his installation. But now, he must be arrested and shot at once. The GPU was to receive the documents on the case later.

At that time, the GPU shot "spies" out of hand. Yagoda however was troubled because this case involved a communist. There might be repercussions. He called Stalin, just in case. Stalin confirmed the matter. The Czech was shot immediately.[13]

But Yagoda received no documents at all on the case. A few days later he telephoned Kanner who responded that the matter was not closed: Spies and enemies had infiltrated into the summit of the Czech Communist Party, and all documents on this case would forever be top secret and would never leave the Politburo's archives. Yagoda was satisfied with this explanation. It goes without saying that the "case" against the Czech was totally fabricated, and the Politburo archives contained not one document on the matter.

Now I had a problem. What to do? I was a Party member. I was aware that one Politburo member was spying on the others. Should I warn them? There was no doubt of what would then happen to me. Either I would be the victim of an "accident," or the GPU would fabricate for Stalin a dossier naming me a saboteur or an agent of British imperialism. In any event Stalin would liquidate me. One can obviously sacrifice one's self for a great cause. But this would be in vain . . . just to stop one Politburo member from listening in on the others? I decided that there was no hurry. I knew Stalin's secret; I would always be able to reveal it for a good reason. For the moment I saw no advantage to doing so. My six months in Orgburo had already dispelled quite a few of my illusions. I could clearly discern that a struggle for power was afoot, a struggle quite devoid of ethics. I had no particular sympathy for any of the competitors. If Stalin spied on Zinoviev, perhaps Zinoviev in turn was spying on Stalin. Who could tell? So I decided to wait and see what the future would bring.

During the beginning of my years as secretary of the Politburo, I spent a great deal of time reorganizing my secretariat. In sorting through the various files, I came across traces of stunning, interesting affairs. For example GPU reports on a continuing matter that was still unresolved. At the end of the Civil War the Politburo concluded that on the one hand the cavalry had played a decisive role in the war and therefore much attention should be given to its strengthening.[14] On the other hand during the war the raising of horses in the USSR had been completely destroyed. All horses—including those in stud farms—had been requisitioned by the armed forces, and most had perished at the front. In order to reconstitute the cavalry it was necessary to acquire purebred stallions and resume breeding and raising horses. But at that time—the end of 1920 and the start of 1921—not one country had yet recognized the Soviet regime. There was no normal commerce with any country or any way to deposit in foreign banks any sums to be used to buy goods. All such monies were blocked as a result of complaints by foreigners whose assets in the USSR had been stolen by the Bolshevik Revolution.

A way to get around the problem was found, not without difficulty. An operation was organized based on crooked businessmen who were sending overseas jewels stolen from Russian bourgeois elements by the Soviet powers. The plan was to buy the stallions in Argentina, under cover of a Swedish breeder. Then they would be shipped openly to north Sweden, where they would be taken across the poorly guarded Soviet border. Seven million US dollars were raised for the operation, but since no banks could be involved it was necessary to physically transport the money to Argentina. Obviously such a huge sum couldn't be trusted to crooked businessmen. The Politburo decided to send it with an old Bolshevik, a member or candidate member of the Politburo, in whom they had complete confidence.

They set him up with all necessary (false) papers, assured him of full protection along his voyage by agents of the GPU's foreign section, and the money was entrusted to him in large denominations. He left the USSR with his dollars, and at a stop along his way he suddenly disappeared.

An exhaustive GPU investigation determined that he had neither met with an accident nor been a victim of bandits. It was proved that he had carefully prepared his disappearance, and he had made off with the money. The Politburo ordered that he be found no matter what the cost. But the search was in vain; he had disappeared without a trace. In the GPU reports he was known by a pseudonym. I could have eventually found his true name by weeding through the Politburo files, but I didn't have the time. It would have meant piecing together who, among the original VIP Bolsheviks, had ceased to appear in documents or lists of Central Committee members, at the time indicated. But I never did it. I leave the solution of the mystery to Party historians or "Kremlinologists."

Politburo sessions usually took place in the Sovnarkom conference hall. Two tables faced each other in the long, narrow room, with red tablecloths on them. At one end was the Politburo president's chair, originally occupied by Lenin but now occupied by Kamenev, who presided over the sessions. The other members sat side by side facing each other, with a space between the two tables. Stalin was on Kamenev's left, Zinoviev on his right. Between Kamenev and Zinoviev a small table was set right against the larger table, and that was where I sat. On my little table was a phone linking me with my staff who waited in the next room. Persons due to appear before this session also waited in that room. When one of my staff called me, a small light went on. I would tell her who to send in for the next point on the agenda.

As each point was settled I would note its disposition on the file and pass it to Stalin, sitting facing me. Usually he glanced at it and gave it back to me, signifying "no objection." If the case was very important and complicated, he would pass it back to me via Kamenev who examined it and wrote "OK" [*d'accord*] in the margin.

The other members sat lower down the table than Stalin and Zinoviev. Nikolai Ivanovich Bukharin[15] was usually next to Zinoviev, then Molotov (still a candidate member), then Mikhail P. Tomsky. Next to Stalin there was usually Aleksei Ivanovich Rykov,[16] then Aleksandr Dmitrievich Tsiurupa.[17] Tsiurupa was not a member, but was deputy president of Sovnarkom and a member of the Central Committee. Dating from Lenin's time he sat in on all Politburo sessions more to keep informed of the decisions made than to participate in the discussions. He rarely spoke and above all listened.

Next sat Trotsky, with Mikhail Ivanovich Kalinin[18] sometimes behind him, sometimes behind Tomsky. At the end of the room, a closed door led to the next room, full of people waiting to appear before the session. Almost all the peoples' commissars and their deputies were there, in full force. At least a hundred agenda questions, involving almost all the ministries, were debated at each regular session. The government officials waited, milling about chatting, smoking, listening to stories invented by Karl Bernardovich Radek,[19] and using the occasion to resolve various interministerial matters. Only those persons convoked for a specific point were allowed into this waiting room, and they came on the run. The Politburo's time was precious. As each question was resolved, the person or persons brought in to assist were dismissed without ceremony.

Kamenev was an excellent president, guiding the discussions well, cutting short superfluous conversation, and quickly arriving at decisions. He kept a chronometer in front of him and marked down the time allowed each speaker, the time he began and ended the discussion. Stalin never presided, and in fact he wasn't capable of doing so.

During each session the members exchanged notes ceaselessly, on small pads headed "For the POLITBURO Session." One often remembers clearly things that happened for the first time. I have no clear recollection of the events in the hundreds of Politburo sessions for which I was secretary—they became routine. But I clearly recall my first session. It was to begin at ten in the morning. Ten minutes before that I was in my place, making sure that all was in order and that the members would have before them all necessary papers. At one minute to ten, with military precision, Trotsky came in and took his place. Three or four minutes later the three members of the *Troika* came in, one after the other, after obviously having got together just beforehand. Zinoviev came in first. He didn't look in Trotsky's direction, and Trotsky also pretended not to notice him and consulted the documents in front of him. Then came Kamenev, exchanging nods with Trotsky as he walked to his seat. Stalin was last, walking right up to Trotsky, shaking his hand with a theatrical gesture of friendship. I saw clearly the falseness of the gesture. Stalin was the sworn enemy of Trotsky and couldn't stand him. I remembered the words of Lenin: "Don't trust Stalin. He will accept dishonest compromises and will betray you." Indeed, as time went by I was to learn a great deal more about my boss Stalin.

The fact that the *Troika* members sat next to each other at the end of the table was very helpful in their conspiracy. They could exchange notes whose contents were shielded from the rest of the members and whisper comments or agreements to each other; for the time being the *Troika* functioned without problems.

Not only did Kamenev preside well, he did it with a joyful tone and often cracked jokes . . . a tone which apparently started with Lenin. Zinoviev half lounged in his chair, running his hands through his untidy hair, looking as if he had problems and was unhappy. Stalin smoked his pipe, often got up and walked the length of the table, standing in front of the speakers. He himself seldom spoke.

5. Observations of the Politburo Secretary

The German revolution. Enlargement of the Revolutionary Military Council. Internal Party liberty. Party bureaucracy and the intrigues surrounding it. Discussion. The Right Opposition and Trotsky on the "Left." Stalin's methods. Stalin's anti-Semitism. Poskrebyshev.

Fifteen days after I began work in the Politburo, I was present at an extraordinary session on 23 August 1923. It was an ultrasecret meeting devoted only to one subject: revolution in Germany. Present were the Politburo members and candidate members, as well as Radek, Georgy Leonidovich Piatakov,[1] and Tsiurupa. Radek, a member of the executive committee of the Comintern, presented a report on the revolutionary wave that was rising in Germany. Trotsky was the first to speak after him. "Leon Davidovich, perpetually fiery," as wicked tongues said, felt himself in his element and gave a vigorous speech, full of enthusiasm.

"Here, finally, comrades, is the tempest which we've been awaiting for so many years with impatience and which is to change the face of the world. The imminent events will have a colossal scope. The German revolution will bring collapse of the capitalist world. But we must see things as they really are. We are playing our whole hand. We must realize that what's at stake is not only the success of the German revolution but the very existence of the Soviet Union. If this revolution succeeds, capitalist Europe will not accept it and will try to crush it by force of arms. For our part, we must throw all our forces into the struggle, for the outcome of the battle will decide everything. Either we win, and the victory of world revolution is ensured, or we lose, and with it we lose the first proletarian state in the world as well as our power in Russia. We must therefore deploy considerable energy. Our preparations have been too slow. The German revolution is commencing. Don't you hear its brazen clang? Don't you feel how high the wave has risen? We must hurry lest the cataclysm catches us unprepared. Don't you feel that it's already just a matter of weeks?"

The Politburo shared none of Trotsky's enthusiasm. No, they'd neither seen nor sensed any of that. Certainly, the German revolution was a very serious matter, but they were not at all ready to link its success with the very existence of Soviet power in Russia. And then, were events in Germany really so pressing?

Zinoviev didn't think so at all. A matter of weeks? As usual, Trotsky's temperament was distorting things far away from reality. It would be nice if it were a question of months! Apart from that, with such serious problems, one must be prudent and act only after mature reflection. Without using clichés and vague terms, Stalin added in the same vein that for the time being there was no question of a revolution in Germany. In the autumn, the spring, or still later, perhaps!

Even though the Troika went to pains to show that it was not at all in agreement with Trotsky's predictions and in any event wouldn't let itself be influenced by him, it nonetheless held the same view that a revolutionary wave was rising in Germany. Various measures were decided upon to support the movement.

A commission of four members of the Central Committee was formed to direct work related to the German revolution. The members were Radek, Piatakov (deputy chief of the supreme National Economic Council), Iosif Stanislavovich Unshchlikht[2] (deputy chairman of the GPU), and Vasily Vladimirovich Shmidt[3] (peoples' commissar for labor). They went immediately to Germany on false travel documents to work there clandestinely.

Their functions were allotted as follows: Radek was to direct the Central Committee of the German Communist Party, and transmit to it Moscow's directives as if they were those of the Comintern. Shmidt, of German origin, was to direct the trade unions revolutionary cells organization, that is to say the factory committees which—once the revolution succeeded—would become soviets and at their extraordinary congress would proclaim soviet power in Germany. Piatakov was to coordinate all the work and ensure liaison with Moscow. Unshlikht was to recruit and organize armed revolutionary units and provide them with weapons. He was also responsible for organizing a German "Cheka" which was to annihilate the bourgeoisie and enemies of the revolution after the coup.

Lastly, the Soviet ambassador in Berlin, Krestinsky, was to finance the German revolution using Gosbank commercial funds deposited in Berlin for use in commercial operations.

From the start of his reporting from Berlin, Piatakov told of the pitiful condition of the leadership of the German Communist Party. According to him, the leaders were not up to the task, neither organizationally nor on the political level. They were convoked to Moscow, but not admitted to Politburo sessions. Zinoviev and Bukharin were responsible for them. The matter became complicated because, in addition to the official leaders (the Brandler group), which had been selected by the Comintern, there was another group of leaders which in effect had more weight: the Maslov— Ruth Fischer group.[4] They paraded their independence from the Comintern. That greatly displeased Zinoviev, who suggested even to the Politburo that it should send an ultimatum to Maslov: either accept a large sum of money and quit the party and Germany, or Unshlikht would be tasked to exterminate him. But Maslov held to his course and would accept no compromises.

While all this haggling was going on, we began to see that the German Communist party was absolutely unprepared for prompt and decisive action, and its work was limping along. In contrast, the Soviet embassy, consulates, and trade representation in Germany were moving quickly and in an exemplary fashion, undertaking very active and fruitful work. The Politburo shifted its focus to them, and Krestinsky became the fifth member of the Central Committee's commission. The embassy and the trade representation were charged with the purchase and delivery of weapons, as well as the principal organizational work. Inside Russia all communists of German origin or who spoke German were mobilized and sent to Germany to perform clandestine activities.

Piatakov's reports became more and more optimistic. Germany's economic situation was going from bad to worse, causing great discontent among the working masses. Clever and widely spread propaganda added oil to the fire, and the revolutionary wave grew rapidly. The Politburo had more and more frequent sessions to discuss all the various practical questions regarding support of the revolutionary work. Piatakov's reports were precise and detailed. It had been decided not to be stingy, and the funds assigned to the venture were enormous. The Troika's initial opposition to Trotsky was forgotten, and now everyone believed that the German revolution would take place tomorrow.

An extraordinary Politburo session was held at the end of September, so secret that only the Politburo members and I attended. No one from the Central Committee was admitted. The question was to select the date of the coup d'état in Germany. The 9th of November was picked.

The plan for the coup d'état was as follows: The workers were to demonstrate en masse in the streets on the anniversary of the October Revolution in Russia. Unshlikht's "red hundreds" were to provoke armed conflict with the police, to lead to repressive action and bloody clashes, and so to increase the discontent of the worker masses and produce a general workers' insurrection. Working on a prearranged plan, Unshlikht's detachments were to occupy the most important government departments and form a soviet revolutionary government composed of members of the German Communist Party's Central Committee. After that, an extraordinary congress of factory committees would proclaim soviet power.

The date fixed for the uprising was to be known to no one, even among the members of the Central Committee, CPSU. I prepared a minute on the session which said only this:

Proposal:	Decision taken:
Comrade Zinoviev's question	See special dossier.

That is all that was communicated to the members of the Central Committee in the form of minutes of the session. However, I noted the decisions taken as Politburo resolutions, and inserted it in my "special dossier."

A word about this "special dossier": There was a safe in my office whose only key was in my hands. In it were stored particularly secret resolutions of the Politburo, which could be known only to its members. Members of the Central Committee who wanted to know their contents had to ask the Politburo's approval, and only with that authorization could I show them the pertinent resolution. In fact, in all the time I worked in the Politburo, such a request never occurred.

But the 1923 German revolution failed. From October it was clear that we were too late and had poorly calculated the timing and that the revolutionary wave had reached its apogee and commenced to recede, although the work of organization and propaganda foresaw at least two or three months more. Soon, the revolutionary wave commenced to recede so rapidly that the Politburo had to face the fact that there was virtually no chance for a coup d'état and that it must be set forward to a more favorable time. Trotsky delivered a plethora of criticisms after the fact, pointed at Zinoviev and the Comintern for having waited so long and missing the boat. Zinoviev and Stalin, on the other hand, got out of it by accusing Trotsky of overestimating the acuteness of the German revolutionary situation, and, in the final analysis, it was they who were right. In the Comintern they heaped all the blame on the incompetent Brandler group,[5] and after lengthy internal bickering, this group was declared "rightist" in April 1924 and expelled from the party. Direction of the German Communist party was given back to the Maslov–Ruth Fischer group. But later, during the *Troika*'s struggle against Trotsky, the Maslov–Ruth Fischer group took Trotsky's side. They were quickly characterized

as Trotskyists and expelled from the party leadership, not without difficulty. In 1927, they definitively took over leadership of the Trotskyist
organization in Germany.

In September, the *Troika* decided to undertake its first serious attack on
Trotsky. Since the beginning of the Civil War, Trotsky had been the organizer and the permanent chief of the Red Army, and was peoples' commissar for the armed forces as well as president of the Revolutionary Military
Council of the Republic. The *Troika* planned to remove him from the Red
Army in three stages. First, the membership of the Military Revolutionary
Council would have to be enlarged and packed with Trotsky's adversaries,
so that he would be in the minority. Second, the Armed Forces Ministry
would be reorganized, getting rid of his deputy Efraim Markovich Skliansky[6] and replacing him with Mikhail Vasilevich Frunze.[7] The third step
would be to relieve Trotsky from his post as peoples' commissar for the
armed forces.

On 23 September, in a plenum of the Central Committee, the *Troika*
proposed enlargement of the Revolutionary Military Council. All the new
members, among them Stalin, were Trotsky's enemies. The significance of
the proposal was perfectly clear to Trotsky, and he made a thunderous
speech: the proposal was but a new link in the chain of corridor intrigues
mounted against him with the objective of removing him from the leadership of the Revolution. Having no wish to engage in a struggle against
these intrigues, and having one wish only—to serve the cause of the
Revolution, he proposed to the Central Committee that they release him
from all his titles and functions and permit him to sign up as a private
soldier of the imminent German revolution. He hoped that they would at
least not refuse him this wish.

Trotsky was serious, and it made the *Troika* ill at ease. Zinoviev spoke
in an obvious attempt to make the scene farcical. He proposed that he too
be liberated from all his titles and functions and be sent with Trotsky to
Germany as a soldier of the revolution. Transforming it definitively into a
comedy, Stalin solemnly declared that the Central Committee could in no
event allow two such precious lives to be risked, and he demanded the
Central Committee to deny departure for Germany of its "well-loved
bosses." This proposition was put to a vote right away, in all seriousness.
All this smacked of a well-rehearsed play, but then "a voice from the
people" rang out, or in other words the president of the Leningrad Executive Committee, Nikolai Pavlovich Komarov,[8] speaking with exaggerated
proletarian manners, asked, "I don't understand one thing. Why does
Comrade Trotsky put on such airs?" The words "such airs" made Trotsky

explode. He got up and said, "I request that you delete my name from the list of actors in this humiliating comedy." And he rushed for the exit.

That was the breaking point. The hall was deathly quiet. Trotsky, furious, decided to slam the door shut after himself, to make more of an impact.

The meeting was being held in the Throne Room of the Palace of the Tsars. The door was enormous, made of cast iron. To open it, Trotsky pulled with all his strength. The door moved slowly, solemnly. At that moment, Trotsky should have realized that some doors cannot be slammed shut. But in his excitement Trotsky had not realized this and he brought all his strength to bear. The door closed as it had opened, slowly and solemnly. Trotsky's intention was to underline, by his furious slamming of the door, the great chief of the Revolution's break with his treacherous comrades. But the result was different: a billy-goatee'd man, extremely irritated, set about an unequal combat with a heavy and obstinate door. The scene failed.

With this decision of the plenum of the Revolutionary Military Council, the fight between the *Troika* and Trotsky entered its overt phase. It was the main occupation of the trio during the last months of 1923. The principal political documents of this period were devoted to the fight, and they reflect it. That is why historians of the Party believe that it was undergoing a struggle between the majority of the Central Committee and the Trotskyite opposition. What was actually happening was quite different and much more complex.

To understand the true history of this era, some preliminary clarifications are necessary.

NEP—the recoil of Lenin from communism to a certain degree of market freedom and stimulation of a free economy—had brought about a rapid amelioration of living conditions. The peasants resumed planting, private sector commerce and manual trades commenced supplying the markets with goods long unseen, and the country was revitalized. Monetary reform began to replace billions of worthless notes with solid, stable golden rubles. But the bureaucratic public administration, long accustomed to the pervasive imperatives of communism, were unable to keep pace with the changes. Food supplies for the towns and their workers and employees were still very deficient. Discontent of the workers, the only class daring to express its feelings, took the form of a wave of strikes in the summer of 1923. There was an immediate reaction: creation in the bosom of the Party of "Workers' Pravda" and the "Workers' Group" of Pyotr Alekseevich Bogdanov and G. Miasnikov. These groups accused the Party

apparatus of bureaucratic degeneration and total disregard for the workers' interests.

During this epoch, political life existed only within the Party. The
country was divided into two camps. One consisted of the huge mass of
people without a Party, enjoying no rights at all, and entirely in the hands
of the GPU. This mass was crushed by the dictatorship and felt that it had
not only no political rights but not even legal rights. The concept of justice
had been abolished. There were tribunals, considered instruments of the
dictatorship and guided, in theory, by class consciousness and the requirements of class warfare, but in practice totally and arbitrarily governed by
little Party satraps. Further, these miserable tribunals could only judge
small affairs of common law or daily life. In all cases that were important
or fundamental, therefore considered to be in the political domain—in the
"sphere of the class struggle"—the arbitrary rule of the GPU was complete. Anyone could be arrested solely on the basis of suspicions known
only inside the GPU. People were shot by decision of an anonymous
"troika," which could also send people for ten years to an extermination
camp, known as "concentration camps." The entire population trembled
before this crushing terror organization.

By contrast the second camp, consisting of several hundred thousand
members of the CPSU, enjoyed considerable liberty. One could have his
own opinion, disagree with higher levels, and contest their decisions. This
"democracy within the Party" dated from the period before the Revolution, when it was a normal state of affairs in a Party whose members had
joined of their own free will. In that prerevolutionary time, there was also
a fierce fight for control of posts which had the right to dispose of Party
funds and press organs. The GPU was not yet in existence, and it was
necessary to win by one's powers of persuasion. Even Lenin didn't always
win, although the Party (and its fundamental character as a party of
professional revolutionaries) was his creation. Lenin was in the minority
more than once (losing at the same time control of the funds and the
presses); he got his majority back with difficulty, by means of alliances
that were awkward and not always pleasant. But this free competition
inside the Party created a long habit of liberty in the Party's bosom, which
still existed (and didn't disappear for several more years, after Stalin took
everything in hand).

Because political life was only possible inside the Party, social processes
taking place in the country could only manifest themselves indirectly,
through influence and pressure of the masses without a party, on members
of the Party. This was relatively easy as regards the working class since the
Party, impregnated with Marxist ideas, was continually reaching for con-

tact with labor. That led to rapid formation in the autumn of 1923 of "worker opposition" groups within the Party, and this in turn led to a vigorous reaction against them by the Party leadership. Fearing that Trotsky would capture this opposition for his own benefit, the majority of the Central Committee tried to take the initiative. Trotsky fiercely attacked the Party's bureaucracy during Politburo sessions. I well remember the scene when, staring at Molotov across the table from him, Trotsky made a cutting philippic against "the Party bureaucrats without souls, whose stone bottoms crush all manifestations of free initiative and free creativity of the laboring masses." Molotov, whose name Trotsky hadn't mentioned, should have kept quiet and acted as if the matter had nothing to do with him, or better, nodded to indicate a sense of approval. Instead, he declared while adjusting his pince-nez and stuttering: "We can't all be geniuses, Comrade Trotsky." It was pitiful, and I was embarrassed for Molotov.

An aside on how "history" is written: In 1929, I related the foregoing to the press. I was stunned when in 1932 I read in *Soviet Portraits (Sovietskie portrety)* by Dmitrievsky,[9] a Soviet diplomat who had fled the USSR, my piece in its entirety. But this was Dmitrievsky's version of what followed Trotsky's speech: "Molotov accepted the challenge. He smiled calmly. And said softly, slightly stammering as usual, 'We can't all be geniuses, Comrade Trotsky, and the strongest is he who wins.'" In fact, Molotov had added nothing of the sort. But to Dmitrievsky in 1932, Trotsky was a jewish revolutionary fanatic, while Molotov was a perfect leader of the new Russian political scene, that's to say a Russia embarked upon a course of patriotism and nationalism. Thus Dmitrievsky's fabricated addition.

In order to gain the initiative, the majority in the Politburo solemnly condemned the Party bureaucracy and immediately created a commission presided over by Dzerzhinsky, charged with clarifying the question of bureaucratism in the Party and the question of the sources of discontent among the workers. At the September plenum of the Central Committee, the Dzerzhinsky commission presented a report on politics in the Party, reducing the bureaucracy question to the fact that in many Party organs persons were nominated for jobs, rather than elected.

Their report on the "scissors' crisis" was more serious. The Party had set the price of industrial products too high, and of agricultural goods too low. It was a policy of rebuilding and developing industry at the expense of the peasantry. Strong discontent had resulted among the peasants, who felt they had been duped. They had been at liberty to sell their surpluses on the free markets, but the State, master of the great majority of the commercial apparatus, had obliged them to sell their wheat too cheaply and to pay too much for industrial products. The plenum directed the Politburo to take "practical measures" in the matter (i.e., they temporarily ignored the essential problem).

On 8 October, Trotsky sent the Politburo a letter apparently addressing these economic problems. In reality, he was violently attacking the Party's bureaucracy and stated that it was not the Party making these decisions; everything was under the yoke of the bureaucrats, the secretaries of the Party. At the same time, this letter began to be widely distributed in the Party by Trotsky's partisans. The *Troika* preferred not to act overtly and ordered the docile Central Control Commission to forbid circulation of Trotsky's letter, which the commission did on 15 October. But on that same day the Central Committee received what is called the "declaration of the forty-six," concerning the Party's internal management. This letter resulted from an alliance of two groups: the old group of "centralist democrats" with the principal role being played by Valerian Valerianovich Osinsky,[10] Vladimir Smirnov,[11] Yakob Naomovich Drobnis,[12] and Timofei Vladimirovich Sapronov,[13] and the recent group of Trotsky partisans led by Piatakov, Yevgeni Alekseevich Preobrazhensky,[14] Yosif Vikentievich Kossior,[15] and Bieloborodov.

As a matter of fact, the letters and declarations of the forty-six contained nothing extraordinary, and in no way did they reflect what was really going on in the depths of the Party. The Central Committee decided to get rid of the problem by a resolution, and at the end of October the plenum decreed that further discussion on all these matters was inopportune in the Party. In addition, to show that the Central Committee itself had been the first to rise up against the bureaucracy, a joint meeting of the Politburo and the presidium of the Central Control Commission was called for 5 November. It unanimously adopted a resolution on "Party building" which solemnly proclaimed the Party leadership's commitment to democracy inside the Party, and condemned just as solemnly bureaucratism in the Party. To explain all this to Party members, Zinoviev wrote an article entitled "The New Party Tasks," which confined itself to verbiage on reinforcement of internal Party life. It was published in *Pravda* on 7 November. The Politburo hoped for détente, but instead there were violent and incomprehensible reactions within Party organizations. In particular, in the numerous Moscow Party organizations, the voting ran not for the Central Committee but against it. In mid-November the Politburo decided to launch a discussion in the Party, to concentrate on an energetic campaign against Trotsky and in so doing to crush him as well as the opposition.

Now began the celebrated "unilateral discussion." In the media and at meetings of Party cells, the Central Committee mobilized all its forces against Trotsky and the "Trotskyite opposition." They were accused of all the mortal sins. The most astonishing thing about it was that Trotsky kept silent, taking no part in the discussion or replying to any of the accusations. He read French novels during Politburo meetings and, if one of the Politburo members spoke to him, he acted astounded.

I quickly deciphered this enigma, thanks to the multiplicity of information I was receiving as to what was going on in the Party. In the autumn of 1923, the "first" opposition was absolutely not "Trotskyist." In general it is wise to be very skeptical concerning the political image of the opposition in those years. Mainly what was involved was the struggle for power. The adversary was accused of deviation (to the left, the right, or in favor of the kulaks), or of underestimation of something, or overestimation, of forgetting something, of derogation of the precepts of Ilich, etc., whereas in reality all the charges were invented and inflated. Once the adversary was defeated, his policies which had just been called criminal, Menshevik, or kulak were adopted immediately and shamelessly.

Generally, Trotsky was, if one can put it that way, more "to the left" than the Central Committee; that's to say he was a communist of more substance. Meanwhile, the Central Committee had classed him with the "right" opposition. This was a sort of failed Thermidor ideology,[16] a completely spontaneous reaction which was developing in the Party, without program or chiefs. Neither Trotsky, "the forty-six," nor the Workers' Opposition were in any way leaders of it. It was an opposition to communism, principally on the part of intellectual and idealistic elements who had joined the Party in the first years of the Revolution. They were the first to see that their dreams of building a better society were only an illusion, that their faith in a revolution accomplished for the good of all had not been realized. Instead a new bureaucratic class had formed itself and had captured all the advantages, reducing the workers and peasants—for whom, supposedly, one had undertaken the Revolution—to slavery without rights. In brief, they were saying, "What did we fight for?"

This reaction had found neither leaders nor a program, and its only expression was in protests and heavy votes against the Central Committee. Trotsky right away divined that this opposition was rightist, but his position was difficult. Had he been an unprincipled opportunist and taken the head of this opposition, accepting its rightist policy, he would have had every chance (as was soon apparent) to capture the Party majority and win his victory. But that would have meant a turn to the right, a Thermidor, liquidation of communism. Trotsky was a 100 percent fanatic communist. He couldn't take that path. Nor could he declare himself overtly hostile to this opposition: he would have lost his weight in the Party, as much with the partisans of the Central Committee as those of the opposition. He would have been isolated, a general without an army. He chose to shut up and maintain an ambiguous position.

That was tragic because the opposition, born spontaneously, with no chiefs and no program, was obliged to accept Trotsky as their leader, imposed on them by circumstances. This brought him quickly to defeat.

Meanwhile, discussion and voting in the cells was passionate and went more and more against the Central Committee. Trotsky resolved to exploit the situation for his benefit and at the same time to give the opposition his views. On 8 December he sent a letter to the Central Committee. It was simultaneously read to the militants of the Krasnaya Presnia local, and published in *Pravda* on 11 December as an article entitled "A New Way." In it, he accused the Party summit of bureaucratic degeneration.

In mid-December the GPU timidly tried to warn the Politburo that in most of the Party organizations the majority was not for the Central Committee. I know that in the huge cell of the Central Committee itself, the majority voted against the Central Committee. I asked Izaak Abramovich Zelensky,[17] secretary of the Moscow Party Committee, the result of votes in his organization. I received a stunning report: the Central Committee had lost the majority in the Party organization of the capital city, the most important in the country. The provincial organizations were falling into line with the Moscow one.

When the *Troika* met to approve the Politburo's next agenda, I gave them Zelensky's report. It was an unexpected blow.

Naturally, they viewed this as a problem of primordial importance. Zinoviev made a long speech. It was an obvious attempt to find and to formulate the general lines of a political strategy, based on Lenin's blueprints. But he also wanted to inject himself into it and justify his leadership role. He spoke of the "philosophy of the times," of general aspirations (which he found in the general desire for equality), etc. Next, Kamenev spoke. He drew attention to the fact that the political process could only be expressed through the Party. Showing a real flair for politics, he guessed the opposition to be rightist. Lapsing into Leninist-Marxist jargon, he said the opposition reflected the rebirth of classes hostile to communism: wealthy peasants, businessmen, the intelligentsia. One must return to Lenin's policies respecting union between the workers and peasants.

During this summit discussion, Stalin kept quiet and pulled on his pipe. In truth, his opinion was of no interest either to Zinoviev or Kamenev: they were sure his advice was useless in questions of political strategy. But Kamenev was a man of great courtesy and tact. That was why he asked,

"And you, Comrade Stalin, what do you think of this question?" "What," asked Stalin, "of what question?" (In fact they had raised several questions.) Forcing himself down to Stalin's level, Kamenev said, "Of the question of capturing the majority of the Party." "Do you know what I think about this?" Stalin replied, "I believe that who and how people in the Party vote, is unimportant. What is extremely important is who counts the votes, and how they are recorded." Kamenev, who knew Stalin well, coughed significantly.

The next day Stalin called Nazaretian into his office and chatted with him a long time. Nazaretian left the office with a defeated expression. But he was a man who obeyed. The same day, by an Orgburo notice, he was appointed responsible for the section of the Party which oversaw *Pravda*, and he got to work.

Pravda received minutes and voting results from local organizations, especially those in Moscow. Nazaretian's work was very simple. If a certain cell had 300 votes for the Central Committee and 600 against, Nazaretian "corrected" it: "For the Central Committee, 600—against, 300." It was so published in *Pravda*. He did this for all the organizations. Naturally, a cell whose elections results were erroneously reported protested, phoning *Pravda* and asking for the section "Party Life." Nazaretian would politely respond and promise to verify immediately. The verification would show that "you are perfectly right, there was a regrettable error, the printers made the mistake. They're overworked, you know. The *Pravda* editors apologize. We will print a retraction." Each cell thought that its error was unique, for that cell alone, and was unaware that it had happened to most of them. Meanwhile, little by little the impression went around that the Central Committee was winning all along the line. The provinces became more prudent and began to follow Moscow, i.e., the Central Committee.

During this period, a tempest was unleashed in the Politburo. It's true, it was only a tempest in a teapot.

The fact is that Mekhlis and Kanner, needing help, had taken on assistants who had indeterminate duties (just as one could not define, in effect, the duties of Kanner himself). Kanner's assistant was a very amiable jew named Bombin. Everyone called him by the nickname Bombik. He was very nice, sang the Swan Song from Lohengrin very well, and carefully hid his links to the GPU. He hid them especially from me, for by then everyone knew of my bad relations with the GPU. Mekhlis had taken on two assistants: Makhover was administrative assistant for the Central Committee of the Komsomol. He soon reached retirement age and was transferred to the Party, where he became the devoted personal secretary of Ordzhonikidze just before the latter's suicide. Mekhlis's second assistant was Youzhak, a young jew with a round, bright red face.[18]

Nazaretian was a man of great detail. Not only did he "correct" the party voting results, he let Stalin know the real situation by sending him bulletins showing the real voting versus *Pravda*'s falsifications. Mekhlis took these bulletins in to Stalin. Now, this is how Stalin's secretariat discovered in a quite unexpected way that Youzhak was a hidden Trotsky-ist. The bulletins often lay on Mekhlis's desk. Youzhak snitched them and gave them to Trotsky, who kicked up a scandal in the Politburo. It was clear to all that Nazaretian was acting on Stalin's orders. The members of the Politburo, Stalin first of all, pretended to share Trotsky's rightful indignation. Stalin promised to start an immediate inquiry. This lasted a week, but during that time the objective was reached. The machine went into reverse, the majority passed to the Central Committee, and the opposition was defeated.

Stalin told the Politburo that the inquiry had exposed the personal culpability of Nazaretian, who was at once relieved from his post as Party section chief at *Pravda* and expelled from Stalin's secretariat. He was sent to a provincial post in the Urals, as president of a regional control commission. He would never forgive Stalin for not coming to his defense and for heaping all the blame on his head. He never again was close to Stalin, who had him shot in 1937. I don't know what happened to Youzhak, but I have no doubt that he didn't survive the 1930s. Stalin had a good memory and never forgot anything.

New details on Stalin kept coming to my attention. One day, I ascertained that he was anti-semitic, which told me many things about the next two years.

I learned this by chance. Mekhlis (a Jew) and I were talking. Stalin came out of his office and approached us. Mekhlis said to him, "Comrade Stalin, we've received a letter from Comrade Faivilovich. He protests, he's angry with the Central Committee. The Central Committee's policies are flawed, and so on." (I must add that Faivilovich was the fourth secretary of the central committee of the Komsomol, whose job it was to educate youth with the spirit of communism. But the leaders and members of the Komsomol were not yet Party members and had no right to discuss Party political problems, at least in the Komsomol cadre. All such tentatives were brutally stopped: "Where do you think you're going? It's too soon. You're not yet ready for such thing.")

Stalin exploded, "Who does he think he is, this dirty little yid?" Right away Stalin realized he'd gone too far. He turned around and went back into his office. I looked at Mekhlis curiously, "Well, little Leon, you swallow that?" "What, what do you mean?" He pretended surprise. "What do you mean, 'what?' You're a Jew, after all." "No," said Mekhlis, "I'm not a Jew; I'm a communist." It was a useful position. It enabled him to stay with Stalin until Mekhlis died, a loyal and devoted Stalinist providing his master with irreplaceable services.

I wondered how Stalin, being anti-semitic, could have two Jewish secretaries: Mekhlis and Kanner. I soon discovered that they had been originally employed for camouflage purposes. During the Civil War Stalin had led a group of partisans who detested Trotsky, his deputy Skliansky, and their assistants: the jews of the army commissariat. This caused suspicions in the party leadership that Stalin was anti-semitic. When he returned to civilian life, he wanted to dispel these suspicions and so he took on Kanner and Mekhlis—first in 1921–22 when he was nominal head of the Workers and Peasants Inspection Commissariat, then as his personal secretaries in the Central Committee secretariat. He never had reason to regret his choice. Kanner and Mekhlis were always his devoted assistants. But, just to be sure, Stalin had Kanner shot in 1937: he had been his confidant and executive in too many shady affairs.

All this business with the opposition happened at the end of 1923. There was an amusing sidelight: given that, during the in-Party discussions, the opposition had captured the majority of the Central Committee (CC) cell (it had 1,500 members; all the staff of the CC were communists), the question of staff chiefs came up. It was obvious that the secretary of the CC cell was an incompetent. He was a Party veteran but still an obvious imbecile. Kanner decided to replace him. But the choice of a new secretary for the cell was important, and he didn't dare to do it without approval of Mekhlis and me. He asked us, and we reflected on it. Mekhlis smiled, "We are a Party of workers. The CC cell contains only office employees, bureaucrats, and not one single laborer. According to Party strictures, we must have a factory worker, or at least a manual laborer. But there aren't any in the Central Committee." To amuse myself, I said, "Listen. There is a manual laborer in the CC." "Impossible; you invented that." "I assure you." "Then who is this bird?"

I explained to them that, when I worked for Molotov as secretary of the *Izvestia* of the CC, this pitiful journal arrived printed at the CC mail room, from where it was sent out to all Party organizations. There was a worker in this office who folded, stuffed, and sent off the *Izvestia* envelopes. He was a small bald-headed man and, I believe, not stupid. His name was Aleksandr Nikolaevich Poskrebyshev.[19] In the midst of general hilarity, it was decided to call him. He arrived, not aware of why he was needed in Stalin's secretariat. We chatted with him. He wasn't dumb, and he would be extremely docile. Almost by mischief we decided to propose him as secretary of the CC cell (and as the proposal came from Stalin's secretariat, it passed at once). Poskrebychev was a very obedient cell secretary, and he even ran too often to Kanner, looking for instructions.

But the joke of Stalin's secretaries again played a determining role in Poskrebyshev's career. In 1926, Stanislas Kossior[20] became the fourth secretary of the Central Committee (there were five then). Usually, the dignitary in this post trailed along behind him a long suite of confidants, "his men." Kossior wanted to show that he had no such group and didn't want one, and when asked whom he wanted as his deputy, he responded modestly that he'd leave the choice to Stalin's secretariat. Kossior, like Poskrebyshev, was small and bald, and they made a comic couple. Kanner, stifling his laughter, proposed to Kossior that he take on Comrade Poskrebyshev as his assistant. Kossior agreed.

So began the career of Stalin's future secretary. In 1928, Poskrebyshev quit Kossior's secretariat to become assistant to Tovstukha, and after the latter's death, in 1935, he replaced him as Stalin's assistant and head of the special sector. For eighteen years he was a loyal servant of Stalin, and ministers and Politburo members trembled before him. It's true that he committed the indiscretion of marrying the sister-in-law of Lev Lvovich Sedov[21] (Trotsky's son). But when his wife was arrested in 1937 on orders from a suspicious Stalin, he never flinched. He stayed at Stalin's side, never leaving him, until 1953. He was dismissed only a few months before Stalin's death and feared his execution. But Stalin did not have him executed.

6. At the Bolshevik Summit

Throughout the second half of 1923, Stalin's secretary Tovstukha
undertook a shady mission for Stalin that was of great importance in
the latter's fight for power.

Lenin was dying. The struggle for the succession put the Troika and
Trotsky at odds. The Troika members conducted lively propaganda
within the Party, presenting themselves as the best and the most loyal of
Lenin's disciples. As for Lenin, the official propaganda was making him
into an icon: the brilliant chief to whom the Party owed everything, whose
writings represented the gospel word, the truth revealed. In fact, there was
nothing that Lenin didn't write about, and one can draw almost no matter
what conclusions based on quotes from his work. For Stalin, however, one
portion of Lenin's writings held particular interest. During the quarrels
among the émigrés before the revolution, then during the revolution and
the Civil War, Lenin had occasion to make judgments about various
Bolsheviks, not so much in published articles as in letters, notes, and after
the Revolution when he ran the government, in all sorts of written remarks and office notes. Now it was possible to extract from old dossiers
violent condemnations by Lenin of various Party members, with a view to
publicizing it to ruin his career: "Just look at what Lenin had to say about
him!"

One can also extract a lot of things, not only from Lenin's writings but
from what his adversaries said about him in the heat of discussion. It's
enough to recall the polemics between Lenin and Trotsky before the
Revolution, when the former accused the latter of all the mortal sins,
while Trotsky wrote in anger that Lenin was a dishonest intriguer and
a professional profiteer [exploiting] the backwardness of the Russian

masses. And what couldn't be found in Lenin's personal notes about his colleagues and members of the government! If all that were assembled, what a weapon in Stalin's hands!

The Troika, in my presence, discussed how to do it. I could clearly see that Zinoviev and Kamenev thought only of the fight against Trotsky and his allies, while Stalin kept silent and thought of a much wider use for Lenin's dynamite. It was decided to suggest indirectly to David Borisovich Ryazanov that he make the requisite proposal to the Politburo. Ryazanov was an old Party member and was considered to be an eminent Marxist theoretician. He was director of the Marx-Engels Institute, and he rummaged passionately through the manuscripts and letters of Marx.[1] It was with pleasure that he proposed to the Politburo that the Marx-Engels Institute should become the Marx-Engels-Lenin Institute. The Politburo gave its approval in principle, but judged it necessary first to create a separate Lenin Institute, devoted for several years to Lenin's work and to assembling all the materials which represented it. Only later would the two institutes be merged. The Politburo decided that it must be done at once and, on 26 November 1923, it declared that the Lenin Institute would be the unique repository of all "original documents" of Lenin. By way of Party discipline and under threat of sanctions, it was ordered that all Party members possessing in their personal archives or those of the administrations, notes, letters, resolutions, and other documents written in Lenin's hand, must relinquish them to the Lenin Institute.

The Politburo resolution was well camouflaged. It had been adopted on the initiative of Ryazanov. Members of the Central Committee receiving the minutes of the Politburo session would think that a study of Lenin's works was afoot.

Tovstukha became assistant to the director of the Lenin Institute. For a long time already he had been working through the Politburo files, pulling out and sorting Lenin's notes. Consequently he disposed of a whole raft of documents which could be set aside for Stalin. Those of Lenin's notes which were not to Stalin's advantage disappeared for good. Those which were disparaging to all others were scooped up and classed by names. On Stalin's orders, any Lenin note injurious to any Party member could be sent to Stalin whenever the general secretary thought it necessary.

On 14 and 15 January 1924, the Central Committee plenum drew up the results of the discussion in the Party: the *Troika* noted with satisfaction that the opposition had been crushed. New steps could be taken in the fight against Trotsky, but these steps would be done progressively and with caution. First, several Central Committee members declared that things were not going well in the Red Army. The plenum created a

"Military Commission of the Central Committee . . . to study the situation in the Red Army," presided over by Sergei Ivanovich Gusev.[2] The members of the commission were chosen so that their conclusions could be predicted. The commission members included Unshlikht, Voroshilov, Frunze, and the docile Andreev and Nikolai Mikhailovich Shvernik.[3]

Right away after the plenum, the thirteenth Party conference (16–18 January) of "apparatchiks" (heads of local Party organizations), based on a report by Stalin, called Party bureaucrats to vigilance, indicating that "the opposition, directed by Trotsky, wants to break up the Party apparatus." The conference urged cessation of all the discussions.

Lenin died a few days later, on 21 January. One can make several interesting observations about the confusion that followed. Stalin was true to himself: he sent a telegram to Trotsky, who was in the Caucasus undergoing medical treatment, giving a false date for Lenin's funeral. As a result Trotsky thought he hadn't the time to get to the funeral ceremony, and he stayed in the Caucasus. That was why at the funeral, the *Troika* members presented themselves as Lenin's successors (whereas Trotsky hadn't judged it useful even to attend). They monopolized the speeches and eulogies at the ceremony.[4] As for me, I observed the various reactions.

The country's attitude toward the death of Lenin was ambiguous. One part of the population was content but hid it. For them, Lenin was the father of communism: he was dead; good for him! Another part of the population believed that Lenin was better than the other [communists] because, having seen the failure of communism, he hastened to recover some elements of normal life through his NEP, which would permit one to eat and to live reasonably. Most Party members were devastated, especially at the bottom. For them, Lenin was the chief, the recognized leader. They were a bit lost. What would one do without him?

Among the leaders, sentiment varied. There were those who were sincerely upset, like Bukharin, or Lenin's assistant Tsiurupa, who was very attached to him. Kamenev was a little saddened by Lenin's death; he wasn't devoid of human traits. Stalin, however, made a bad impression on me. In his heart he was extremely content at the death of Lenin, one of the principal obstacles in the way of his rise to power. In his office and in the presence of his secretaries, he was in an excellent humor and beaming. In meetings, he took on a hypocritical air, tragically stricken, making false statements and emphatic oaths of loyalty to Lenin. Watching him, I said, despite myself, "What a swine."

Stalin was as yet unaware of Lenin's explosive "Letter to the Congress." Krupskaya scrupulously followed Lenin's wishes. This letter was destined for the Congress to be held in May. It would be then that she would open the envelope and transmit Lenin's Testament to the Politburo. Kamenev had already heard of the Testament through Fotieva, who still worked with him as secretary of Sovnarkom, but he kept quiet.

Because of Lenin's death and the confusion that followed, Central Committee plenums were held more frequently. The first CC plenum of January was followed by an extraordinary plenum after his death, then still another one in January. At the month's beginning there had been all the nominations and personnel transfers in the USSR peoples' commissariats, but now the more important posts were to be redistributed. Who should replace Lenin as president of Sovnarkom? There was no agreement on this, either in the Politburo or in the *Troika* itself. The *Troika* members feared that if one of them were designated, the country would conclude that he was the definitive successor to Lenin as number one in the regime: a situation that was not to the other two's liking.

In the end they agreed on the nomination of Rykov. He was a political lightweight, and his post as head of government would be more decorative than substantive (like Kalinin, president of the Central Executive Committee, that is to say something like president of the republic but in reality with no power). Until then, Rykov was president of the Supreme National Economic Council.

However, the Council of Labor and Defense was reorganized as a result of the formation of the USSR. Kamenev was placed in charge of it, and effective direction of all the peoples' economic commissariats came under the Labor Council. This further diminished the importance of the post of president of Sovnarkom, now in Rykov's hands. The GPU was reorganized, becoming the OGPU with its power extended to cover all the USSR. Officially it was directed by Dzerzhinsky, but as he had been appointed president of the Supreme National Economic Council as well, replacing Rykov, the actual direction of the OGPU fell not to his first deputy chairman Vyacheslav Rudolfovich Menzhinsky,[5] but to the second deputy chairman, Yagoda, who had already established close relations with Stalin's secretariat (but not with me).[6]

The 3 February plenum of the Central Committee discussed problems of calling the next Party congress and, above all, heard a report of the Military Commission of the Central Committee. There was violent criticism, directed ostensibly against the Peoples' Commissariat of War but in fact against Trotsky. It was decided to "recognize the fact that, in its present form, the Red Army was not prepared for combat," and that reform of the army was indispensable.

Then a new plenum in early March brought another attack on Trotsky. His assistant Skliansky (whom Stalin hated), was dismissed, and the new composition of the Revolutionary Military Council was approved. The presidency remained with Trotsky, but Frunze was appointed to be his assistant and concurrently chief of staff of the Red Army. Trotsky's enemies—Voroshilov, Unschlikht, Andrei Sergeevich Bubnov,[7] and even Semyon Mikhailovich Budenny[8]—were brought en masse into the Revolutionary Military Council. The purely decorative post of specialist commander in chief, held by tsarist army Colonel Sergei Sergeevich Kamenev,[9] was abolished.

The *Troika* discussed what to do with Skliansky. Stalin proposed that he be sent to the United States, as president of the commercial mission (Amtorg). It was an important post. The USSR had no diplomatic relations with the United States, and therefore there was neither plenipotentiary nor commercial representation. There was only the Amtorg commercial mission, which, in effect, fulfilled the functions that would normally have been carried out by [diplomatic] plenipotentiary and commercial representatives. Amtorg served as a base for all clandestine activities [in and from the United States] of the Comintern and the OGPU.[10] Its commercial functions were equally important. After the Civil War it had been possible to restore to action the totally destroyed railway system, thanks to the purchase of a substantial number of locomotives in the United States. This was accomplished through a special commercial mission led, for form's sake, by Professor Lomonosov. The entire purchase was only possible because of the support of a group of powerful jewish financiers who were favorable to the Soviet Revolution. A great deal of skill and diplomacy had been necessary.

I was not the only one to be astonished by Stalin's suggestion. He detested Sklianksy (who hadn't stopped harassing him throughout the Civil War) even more than he hated Trotsky. Zinoviev couldn't stand Skliansky either. I recall that not long before this, at a Politburo meeting, during a discussion about Skliansky, Zinoviev scornfully said, "There's nothing more comical than these people from the provinces who imagine themselves to be great leaders." The jab was intended not only against Skliansky but against Trotsky too, who flushed but controlled himself. He threw Zinoviev a piercing look but kept silent.

Skliansky was appointed president of Amtorg and left for the United States. Soon after, a telegram arrived saying that he had been drowned in a boating accident on a lake. The imprecision of the accident report was striking: he had gone out in a boat and didn't return. A search found the boat keel up and his drowned body. There were no witnesses.

Mekhlis and I went at once to see Kanner and said in union, "Grisha, it was you who drowned Skliansky." He defended himself weakly, "Of course it was I. I'm blamed for everything." We persisted, but he went on denying it. Finally I said, "You know that in my position as secretary of the Politburo I must know everything." Kanner replied, "There are things it's better not to know, even for a secretary of the Politburo." Even though he had admitted nothing (everyone in Stalin's secretariat was more prudent after the Youzhak affair), Mekhlis and I were convinced that Skliansky had been drowned on Stalin's orders, and the "accident" had been organized by Kanner and Yagoda.

I got to know the Sverdlov family, which was very interesting. The older Sverdlov was already dead. He was an engraver from Nizhnii-Novgorod. A revolutionary spirit, he was in touch with all sorts of revolutionary organizations. His principal work was to make bogus seals or cachets so that clandestine revolutionaries could make themselves false documents. The atmosphere of his house was revolutionary, but the oldest son, Zinovy, had experienced a profound moral crisis and had broken all at once from the revolutionary circles, his family, and Judaism. His father cursed him according to the solemn Hebrew tradition, and he was then adopted by Maxim Gorky and took the name Zinovy Peshkov.[11] Following his own spiritual guidelines, Zinovy broke with Gorky's revolutionary entourage and left for France, joining the Foreign Legion to cut off his past life completely. When he learned a short time later that he had lost an arm in combat, his father asked anxiously, "Which arm?" Learning that it was the right arm, his joy was complete: according to the Hebrew malediction, a son cursed by his father shall lose his right hand.

Zinovy Peshkov became a French citizen, remained in the army and rose to the rank of full general. He had completely disavowed his family, and when I arrived in France and tried to give him news of his two brothers and his sister living in Russia, he replied that they meant nothing to him and he didn't want to hear any mention of them.

The second brother, Yakob, was in Lenin's party, a prominent member of the Bolshevik Central Committee. After the October Revolution he became Lenin's right arm. He was president of the Central Executive Committee, i.e., titular head of the Soviet Republic. His principal work was involved in organization and distribution of jobs. He was forming up what later became the apparatus of the Party, when he died of tuberculosis in 1919.[12]

The capital of the Urals, a city of one million persons, bears his name: Sverdlovsk. After Stalin came to power the city's name was not changed, although, as we will see, Stalin had personal reasons for not liking Sverdlov, and he never forgot reasons of that kind. Perhaps Ekaterinburg continues to be called Sverdlovsk because it is where the tsar and his family were massacred in July 1918, and part of the responsibility for this massacre was Yakob Sverdlov's. He was then nominal head of Soviet power, and on orders from Lenin (who neatly escaped all official responsibility), he advised the local Bolshevik authorities that he would leave the question of the fate of the tsarist family in their hands.

The third brother, Veniamin Mikhailovich Sverdlov, was not drawn to revolutionary activity. He emigrated to the United States and became the owner of a small bank. But after the Bolshevik Revolution, Yakob urged him to come home. Veniamin liquidated his bank and arrived in Petrograd. At that time Lenin was still under the influence of demagogic, wild ideas such as "Each cook must be able to govern the state." He applied his ideas by making absurd appointments to suit his propaganda. As we know, the ensign Nikolai Vasilievich Krylenko was appointed commander in chief of the armed forces, to annoy the bourgeoisie, while a semiliterate sailor was named head of the State Bank. A mechanic named Emshanov, who was not very educated either, was made minister of the railways.[13] Poor Emshanov made so many dumb errors in his ministry and got so confused himself that after a month or two he beseeched Lenin to relieve him from responsibilities that were beyond his capacities. Then Yakob Sverdlov proposed to Lenin that his brother, who had just arrived and wasn't even a communist, should have the job. And so it was that Veniamin Sverdlov became peoples' commissar for transport. After some time, he became convinced that he could do nothing in this job (which was later occupied with no greater success by Trotsky and Dzerzhinsky), and he was moved to the Presidium of the National Economic Council. Thereafter his career declined slowly but surely. He remained outside the Party, and it is astounding that his career wasn't instantly ruined when his brother died. But he remained, in the years 1923–25, a member of the National Economic Council, where he supervised the technical-scientific section.

Shortly before the war, Vera Aleksandrovna Delevskaya, a very young (I think she was seventeen) but very talented actress, joined the Moscow Art Theater. She was a great beauty. She had not yet had star roles, but she was passionately devoted to the Art Theater and lived only for it. This was not only Chekhov's theater but also Maxim Gorky's. A very revolutionary group was constantly revolving around Gorky. One day, one of his theatrical colleagues asked the naïve girl to provide a service: to hide some revolutionary literature. She knew nothing of this field, but she didn't dare to refuse. She did the job so maladroitly that the police immediately discovered everything. She was arrested and exiled. When the tsarist police exiled anyone, they paid them a salary to cover their food, lodging, and minimal needs. In fact, they lived freely but were watched by the police. This surveillance was in reality almost nonexistent and it was very easy to leave one's place of exile. But then you had to live clandestinely, which had certain inconveniences (I'm not really sure what, because in case of recapture, the fugitive was merely sent back into exile with no increase of the sentence). The tsarist police extended their solicitude for these faraway exiles to the point where they grouped them by party affiliations, sending Mensheviks to one place, Bolsheviks to another, and so on. This made it considerably easier for the exiles to pursue their Party activities such as meetings and debating over tactics and programs, writing articles for the Party press, discussing them, etc.

Vera Aleksandrovna, who, it seems, had hidden Bolshevik literature, was sent to a location where prominent Bolsheviks were detained, including three Central Committee members: Spandarian, Stalin, and Yakob Sverdlov. Stalin and Sverdlov were infatuated by the young and beautiful artist, and paid court to her. She rejected Stalin out of hand, for he was somber, antipathetic, and uncultivated. She preferred Sverdlov who was cultured and had been educated in Europe.

When he returned from exile, Yakob went back to his wife, Klavdia Novgorodtseva, and a son, Andrei, and his new and more important government functions. Vera Aleksandrovna found herself single again, but when Veniamin Sverdlov saw her they soon fell in love and got married. Their marriage lasted all the time I knew them.

The fourth brother, German Mikhailovich, was in fact their half brother. After his first wife died, the Sverdlov father had married a Russian, Kormiltseva, and German was their son. He was much younger (in 1923 he was nineteen) and had not participated in the Revolution. He was a Komsomol member, extremely intelligent and witty. I was four years older than he, and he attached himself to me: he came to see me often, and we were very close, but he was not aware of my internal evolution as I gradually became anticommunist. We spoke of everything except politics.[14]

The four Sverdlov brothers had a sister who married a rich man named Averbach and lived somewhere in southern Russia. They had a daughter and a son, Leopold, who as an adolescent was very bright but cheeky. Leopold arrogated to himself the job of chief of Russian literature, and for a while he undertook a strict chekist control over the literary milieux. He got there through his sister, Ida, who had married the celebrated Yagoda, head of the GPU.

Yagoda was, in effect, indebted for his career, in considerable part, to the Sverdlov family. He had not been a pharmacist at all, as the rumors (which he aided) had it, but had been apprenticed as a engraver to the Sverdlov father. Yagoda eventually decided to set up on his own as an engraver, and he fled the household having stolen all the tools and believing, quite rightly, that the old Sverdlov would not go to the police lest his revolutionary activity be revealed. But Yagoda was not successful in setting up on his own, and after a while he went back, head bowed, to the Sverdlovs. The old man forgave him and took him back in. Not long after that Yagoda, proving at least that he was consistent, again stole all the tools and made off.

After the Revolution all this was forgiven. Yagoda seduced Ida, niece of the head of state, and his career was thus considerably helped along. He now had his entrée to the Kremlin.

Yakob Sverdlov's widow, Klavdia Novgorodtseva, led a retiring life and didn't work. One day German Sverdlov came to see me and told, among other things, how Andrei (son of Yakob and Klavdia), now aged fifteen, had been wondering why one drawer of his mother's desk was always closed. When he asked her, she replied, "That's no affair of yours." Eaten up by curiosity, he seized an opportunity when she forgot and left the keys in the room, and he opened the drawer. He saw a whole lot of fake gems, resembling large diamonds. They had to be fake, he reasoned, for how could his mother have come to possess such a trove of real stones? He closed the drawer and replaced the keys.

German agreed with him: they were made of glass. Yakob Sverdlov was not a crook and could never have owned precious jewels. I was in agreement with German: the stones obviously had no value.

But I learned that the truth was quite another matter. Already, shuffling through Politburo papers, I'd learned that about four years before, in the period 1919–20, at the height of the crisis when the Soviet regime was hanging by a thread, a "fund of Politburo diamonds" had been selected from the state diamond holdings. These Politburo diamonds were destined to be used, in the event the regime lost power, by Politburo members to live on and continue their revolutionary activities. The files contained mention of orders to that effect, but nowhere was it revealed where the diamonds were hidden. There was not even a mention of this in the special dossier, filed in my own safe. Evidently it had been decided that only Politburo members would know the location of the cache. Now, I had unexpectedly found the answer. In the event they lost power, the only reasonable hiding place was with an individual in whom the Politburo had complete confidence but who, at the same time, played no political role and had a totally low profile. This explains why Klavdia Novgorodtseva didn't work and led an impeccable life and also why she didn't use the celebrated Sverdlov name, which could have greatly helped her in all sorts of small things; instead she continued to use her maiden name. So it was that she was the repository of the diamonds, although I don't believe it could have lasted long because year by year it became less likely that the Soviet regime would be overthrown.

I must add that Veniamin Sverdlov was put to death in 1937. Leopold Averbach was shot in 1938 along with Yagoda. I have no idea what became of Vera Aleksandrovna. More about German later.

My situation as Politburo secretary was quickly becoming more solid. At first Zinoviev and Kamenev had looked upon me with a certain mistrust: I was "Stalin's man." But they soon concluded that I was in the job not because of Stalin's patronage but because I had the talents the job required. During the first three or four weeks of my work, I maintained the previous modus operandi whereby at Politburo meetings Lenin, then Kamenev, formulated the Politburo's decisions and dictated them to the secretary, Glyasser. But soon I decided to use my experience with Molotov and the Orgburo, and formulate most of the decisions myself. When I did it with Molotov, not only did it save him a lot of time, but I was also able to help him considerably because he wrote slowly and with difficulty. Kamenev, on the other hand, was a brilliant president who expressed himself rapidly and with precision, so only time could be gained. I spoke to Kamenev, "I'm always very well prepared for our meetings; I know perfectly all the nuances of each proposal of the central administrative organs, including the significance and history of each matter. You don't need to dictate to me. I can formulate the resolutions myself exactly as they are supposed to be." Kamenev looked at me quite surprised, as if to say, "Young man, it seems you've taken a lot upon yourself." But he said nothing.

At the next Politburo meeting they discussed a complex problem of the national economy on which neither the Supreme Council of the National Economy nor the Gosplan nor the Peoples' Commissariat of Finance were in agreement. After lengthy discussion, Kamenev finally declared: "Well, as I see it the Politburo leans toward Rykov's viewpoint. We'll vote." In fact, the vote confirmed Rykov's position. After throwing me a brief glance, Kamenev said, "Good, we'll continue." He passed on to the next question on the agenda. Then it was like taking a difficult examination. I wrote out a long and complex resolution on the numerous and diverse aspects of the problem, as usual on folded cardboard cards, and passed it over the table to Stalin. He read it and silently passed it to Kamenev. The latter read it carefully, made not the slightest correction, and returned it to me with a movement of his eyes to signify "bravo." From then on we used my method, and the Politburo saved a lot of time previously wasted formulating resolutions. The habit had been to discuss amendments, proposed by members, to the text the president had formulated. Now, for the most part, the general sense of each resolution was established and adopted, and it was left to the secretary to write it up (under the president's control, certainly, but I must say that Kamenev almost never changed my text, even on the most complex matters).[15]

Obviously I had considerably complicated my work. I had to take care of the logistics of the meetings (see that the proper witnesses came in and that the Politburo members had all the documents they needed); watch to see that the Politburo didn't err in repeating former resolutions or making new ones that contradicted ones made recently (in which case I'd remind the Politburo); carefully follow the debating to be sure to understand all the nuances; and meanwhile write up the previous resolution. Watching how I handled all this, Zinoviev said, "Comrade Bazhanov is like Julius Caesar, he can do five things at once." I didn't know that Julius Caesar had this skill, but I certainly enjoyed Zinoviev's compliment.

I now rose another notch in my career as an "apparatchik." At a *Troika* meeting I said, "In the Politburo you adopt a large number of very good resolutions, but you don't know how, or even if, they are applied. I don't mean that we should create a supplemental control mechanism to watch over the execution of resolutions: all the Politburo's work is absolutely secret and we must not increase the number of persons who know these secrets. But there is a simple way to achieve such control, and that is to put it in my hands as Politburo secretary, as part of my general functions. Then I will contact the heads of the administrative organs responsible for the execution of Politburo decisions. No matter what the level from which this control comes, the simple fact of constantly reminding the heads that there's an eye in the Politburo continually watching the results of our resolutions can only have a beneficial effect." Kamenev and Zinoviev found my idea perfectly logical and gave their approval. Stalin kept quiet. He clearly understood how this would reinforce his power. His own assistant would exercise control over all the activities of the various ministries, and of the members of the Central Committee, greatly increasing Stalin's power. Stalin looked over at me with that same searching gaze which seemed to say, "It looks as if you'll go far."

Here's how I organized the control of the application of the Politburo's decisions. We prepared large notebooks. On the left page were pasted the text of each resolution, and on the right I put my remarks concerning the results of my control. I did all this work myself and answered to no one. I would take the internal government telephone [*vertushka*] and call the head of the unit charged with execution of a resolution. "Comrade Luna-charsky, Bazhanov here. On such and such a date the Politburo adopted this resolution. Tell me, please, what you have done to put it into action." And the comrade had to tell me, like a schoolboy. Because of the peculiarities of the Soviet system, and negligence and general confusion, only a small number of resolutions had been applied. Comrade Lunacharsky would explain to me in the most convincing manner that, even though few resolutions had been acted upon, neither he nor his minister was responsible. The responsibility fell upon others, or on "objective circumstances."

This system of control put me in a strange position, and I even came to represent a bit of a threat to all the top Bolshevik people, right up to the highest levels. It was a classic example of the power of the apparatus. I could accept an explanation and stop the matter right there. Or I could reject it and make a report to the Troika or the Politburo. Not that the Politburo would instantly act on my report and relieve the offender of his functions. Appointments and demotions were made for quite different reasons: the struggle for power and the corridor intrigues. But if one already wanted to rid himself of someone holding an important post, what better pretext than the report of the Politburo secretary complete with facts and proof showing that he had not executed the Politburo's decisions? I continued to effect this system of control during all the time I was at the Politburo.

I was young then, and energetic, and soon I found another interest. While I was secretary of the Orgburo I was present at the creation of the Supreme Council for Physical Culture and the general directives that were to govern the functioning of this organization. Even then I had been struck by the absurdity of this institution, but I was still too low-level an apparatchik to venture an opinion.

Physical culture was considered good for the health of the laboring masses, and it was to consist of collectively agitating their arms and legs. That was what they were trying to impose on the various workers' clubs, almost forcing them to participate. This program obviously interested nobody and was considered as boring and irritating as the study courses in politics which they had to take. According to the theoreticians of "physical culture," competitive sports was an ugly survivor of bourgeois culture. It developed individualism and was consequently hostile to the principles of collective proletarian culture. The masses were dying of boredom at the physical culture séances, and the Supreme Council led a miserable existence.

While I was secretary of the Politburo, I said to Stalin one day that "physical culture" was absurd, it was of no interest to the workers. We needed to return to competitive sports, and the masses would definitely love it. The representative of the Central Committee who was on the Supreme Council of Physical Culture was the chief of the Central Committee's propaganda section, and he, knowing the uselessness of this institution, had never set foot in it. If I were to be designated the Central Committee's representative, I would see to it that sports would replace physical culture. Stalin agreed. It was his custom always to agree with me on questions that didn't interest him at all (his only interest was power and the struggle to acquire it). I arranged to get myself appointed Central Committee representative to the Supreme Council of (unhappy wording) Physical Culture.

This Council was composed of representatives of a large number of institutions. Yagoda, incidentally, was there representing the OGPU. The work, however, was to be effected by a presidium of five people: the president was Nikolai Aleksandrovich Semashko, peoples' commissar for public health.[16] His assistant president was Konstantin Aleksandrovich Mekhonoshin, a representative of the War Ministry.[17] The other three members were myself representing the Central Committee of the Party, the young doctor Ittin, from the Komsomol Central Committee, and Senyuchkin, representing the Central Council of Trade Unions.

A plenum of the Supreme Council was called, and I presented a report urging that Council policy be changed from promoting physical culture to developing sports for the working masses. The former sports organizations, which had been destroyed or closed by the Revolution, would have to be reconstituted. The athletes, who had been chased out and scattered, would have to be reassembled and used as teachers and focal points of athletic activity. Then the working masses would have to be attracted.

Yagoda immediately objected. Before the Revolution, sports were mainly in the hands of representatives of the bourgeoisie; sports organizations were, and would again be, centers of counterrevolutionaries. It would be dangerous to give them ways to reunite, and anyway competitive sports were contradictory to collectivist principles.

I accepted the challenge, indicating that the new line adopted by the Central Committee was based on the principle of emulation, without which it would be impossible to awaken the workers' interest and get them to participate. The political tendencies of old athletes would in fact be of no consequence: soccer or the hundred-meter dash couldn't feed counterrevolution. Moreover, the Party's policy had always been to use specialists: engineers and technicians were for the most part from the bourgeoisie, but nevertheless they were used on a large scale in the national economy, just as the Red Army was created and was able to win, thanks to the use of former tsarist officers who were politically very far from the Party and even hostile to it.

The council was entirely on my side (it was, after all, the "line of the Central Committee"). When Yagoda again tried to say that the sports clubs would be nests of counterrevolution and would have to be surveilled very carefully, Semashko interrupted him, "That's your affair; it's nothing to do with us."

Things went along rapidly, the clubs developed, the masses were enthusiastic for sports. In the summer of 1924 the first Russian Olympiad was held (for light athletics), and it was very successful. I was its principal supporter, for all this captivated me.

The OGPU substantially complicated my work. They considered all old athletes to be enemies. I had to go to war against them to defend my athletes, who were not noted for their love of communism. Some had to be torn from the fangs of the OGPU. Anatoli Anatolievich Pereselentsev was the best Russian sculler: in 1911–12 he had won the European skiff championship, but he was "from the bourgeois classes." The OGPU hated him and tried to arrest him. He was saved when I intervened and threatened to bring the matter up to the Central Committee if the OGPU touched him or tried to manufacture a case against him. Until 1927 he survived under my protection. He knew it and was grateful. In 1927, when I was getting ready to escape overseas, I met him in a sports club and told him that I was going off to work in a distant province, and as he would have no one to protect him he would be devoured right away by the OGPU. I urged him to hide somewhere far away from Moscow, and he promised to act on my advice. I don't know what became of him.

Soon the Bolshevik leaders began to take an interest in sports, mainly for health reasons. Stalin and Molotov never paid sports any attention, but Kaganovich skied in winter. I often played tennis with Grigori Yakovlevich Sokolnikov, peoples' commissar for finances,[18] and with Izaak Isaevich Reingold, the director of his budget department. Sokolnikov's wife, Galina Iosifovna Serebriakova, also played with us on occasion. Sokolnikov was shot in 1941 in the Orel prison, and Reingold was shot earlier, in 1936–37. Galina was sent to a concentration camp. She returned after Stalin's death and wrote a bitter book about what she'd seen during her many years in exile.[19]

7. I Become Anticommunist

Lenin's testament. My career. I become an adversary of communism. The real Lenin. The dogmatists and the practitioners of communism. Marxism, the lie which permeates everything.

The Thirteenth Party Congress was near. Several days ahead, Krupskaya opened Lenin's envelope and sent the Central Committee the bomb which this Testament represented. When Mekhlis told Stalin the contents of Lenin's letter (which urged demotion of Stalin), Stalin emitted a stream of curses against Krupskaya and rushed to consult with Zinoviev and Kamenev.

At this time Stalin still needed the *Troika* badly. Trotsky had to be liquidated. Meanwhile Stalin's salvation was his alliance with Zinoviev and Kamenev. It had already been decided that Zinoviev would present the Central Committee's political report to the congress, thus appearing as the Party leader. To underline its importance and clout, the *Troika* decided to call the next congress, the Fourteenth, in its fiefdom, Leningrad (a decision that was postponed when the *Troika* broke up). But now, because of Lenin's Testament, it was essential for Stalin to have agreement from Zinoviev and Kamenev that Stalin would remain general secretary of the Party. Thinking, with amazing naïveté, that Stalin was no longer a threat because Lenin's Testament would considerably diminish his weight in the Party, they agreed to save him. The evening before the congress, on 21 May 1924, there was an extraordinary plenum of the Central Committee, called to hear Lenin's Testament.

The CC plenum was held in the meeting hall of the Presidium of the Central Executive Committee. Kamenev and Zinoviev presided on a small, low dais, and next to them was a small table for me (I was, as usual, secretary of the Central Committee plenum). The Central Committee members were seated in rows of chairs facing the dais. Trotsky was in the third row, next to the center, beside Piatakov and Radek. Stalin sat to the right side of the dais, facing it and the window, in such a manner that the Central Committee members couldn't see his face. I could, however, observe him very well.

Kamenev opened the séance and read Lenin's letter. There was silence. Stalin's face was somber and strained. Following a scenario prepared in advance, Zinoviev took the floor right away: "Comrades, you all know that Lenin's posthumous wishes, each word of Ilich's, is law for us. We have sworn more than once to accomplish what Lenin passed on to us. And you know perfectly well that we will do so. But we are happy to note that on one point it seems that Lenin's fears were not justified. You have all witnessed our joint work during these past months and, just like me, you have been able to see with satisfaction that that which Ilich feared has not happened. I speak of our general secretary and the dangers of scission within the Central Committee." (I've given the sense of his presentation.)

It was, certainly, untrue. The Central Committee members knew perfectly well that a split in the Central Committee had already taken place. Everyone kept quiet. Zinoviev proposed that Stalin be reelected general secretary. Trotsky kept silent also, but he showed his extreme disgust with the comedy by a vivid mimicry.

Kamenev, for his part, urged members to keep Stalin in the general secretaryship. Stalin continued to gaze out of the window, teeth clenched and features drawn. His career was at stake.

Because there was silence, Kamenev proposed to settle the matter by vote. Who favored leaving Stalin in as general secretary? Who was against? And who abstained? I looked down the rows, counting the votes and giving the totals to Kamenev. The majority voted in favor of Stalin, while the small Trotsky group voted against. There were some abstentions. I was busy counting the votes and didn't notice who abstained, which I much regret.

Zinoviev and Kamenev had won. If only they had known that they had thus prepared the bullets that were later to kill them!

Eighteen months later, when Stalin removed Zinoviev and Kamenev from power, Zinoviev asked bitterly, remembering this plenum and the way he and Kamenev had saved Stalin, "Does Comrade Stalin know what gratitude is?" Pulling his pipe out of his mouth, Stalin replied, "Certainly I know; it is a malady that afflicts dogs."

In addition to leaving Stalin as secretary general, the plenum decided not to read Lenin's Testament to the congress and not to distribute his text to the delegates. Instead, the heads of delegations were to convey it to their own delegates. The resolution of the plenum had been formulated vaguely on purpose, to allow delegation heads simply to tell their delegates what

Lenin's letter contained, as well as the plenum resolutions, without conveying the actual text of what Lenin wrote.

The history of the communist regime in Russia is so full of lies of all sorts that it is too bad that witnesses and participants in events who are more or less honest, make mistakes and add to the tangle of lies about the past. The story of Lenin's Testament, in particular, is already sufficiently scrambled. Trotsky, usually a reliable witness concerning facts and dates, committed a gross error when he related the history of the Testament.

In his book on Stalin, written in the last years of his life, Trotsky said, after describing the plenum at which the Testament was read, "Actually, the Testament not only failed to terminate the internal struggle, which was what Lenin wanted, but, on the contrary intensified it to a feverish pitch. Stalin could no longer doubt that Lenin's return to activity would mean the political death of the General Secretary."[1]

One can deduce from these lines that Lenin was still alive when his Testament was divulged. Since it was made public at the plenum which preceded the congress, Trotsky meant the plenum of the Central Committee of 15 April 1923 and the Twelfth Congress of 17–25 April 1923. But it is a gross error. The Testament was read to the CC plenum of 21 May 1924 (the Thirteenth Congress was 22 to 31 May 1924), which was four months after Lenin's death. It is easy to demonstrate that it was Trotsky, not I, who was in error. In the same passage of his book, Trotsky quotes me as a witness to the plenum: "Bazhanov, another former secretary of Stalin's, described the seance of the Central Committee at which Kamenev read the testament. 'Terrible embarrassment paralyzed all those present. Stalin, sitting on the steps of the rostrum, felt small and miserable. I studied him closely . . . etc.'" From these texts, one could only conclude that we were both at the same plenum. Although I was at the 1924 plenum, it was impossible for me to have been at the 1923 one, since I was not yet Politburo secretary. Consequently it is beyond doubt that the Testament was divulged at the 21 May 1924 plenum, after Lenin's death, and that Trotsky was mistaken.[2]

Zinoviev presented the political report at the congress. Just before the congress, he had asked me to prepare an analysis of the Politburo's work for the previous year, to be used in his report. I did it, classifying by categories the thousands of Politburo resolutions, and drawing certain conclusions—all very mundane and routine. Zinoviev used my work in his report, citing my name three times and thanking me for the work I had done. He had a hidden motive that I understood very well.

I had reached a very elevated point in my career. I've already related how, when I was first with Stalin, I went to him many times daily to seek his instructions. Then I soon became convinced that it was useless: nothing of this sort interested him. "And what do you think should be done? Oh, very well, do it." I got used to this quickly, stopped wasting time, and started doing things on my own initiative. The various government department heads had constantly to address questions to Stalin or the Politburo. They quickly understood that it was useless to query Stalin personally. Affairs of state didn't interest him. He didn't understand them well, didn't concern himself with them, and was capable only of giving purely formal answers. If asked how to solve a problem, he would reply disinterestedly, "Take it up with the Politburo; we'll discuss it."

Given that I had started to follow up on the resolutions of the Politburo and so was in constant contact with all department heads (via the famous Kremlin internal telephone system—*vertushka*), I quickly accustomed them to the fact that there was a secretary of the Politburo who understood all their problems. They would do well to bring their questions to me, for I could tell them how various matters were unfolding, advise them on Politburo policies, and guide them as to how best to proceed. Progressively I came to do what Stalin should have been doing. I would indicate to heads of departments, for example, that their questions had not yet been coordinated adequately with other central administration departments. Instead of taking it up uselessly with the Politburo, it would be better to do this or that. My guidance saved them time and effort, not only bureaucratically but in their conduct of affairs of state. I was consulted more and more, and finally I realized that I was definitely doing more than I was empowered to do.

I went to see Stalin and told him that I was going too far. I was taking too much responsibility and was in fact doing his work. He replied that the institution of assistants to the [three] secretaries of the Central Committee had properly been created, on Lenin's initiative, to relieve the secretaries of secondary matters so that they could concentrate on the essentials. I responded that in effect I was not undertaking secondary matters, but ones of primary importance. (I understood, of course, that for him affairs of state were not essentials; for him it was the fight for power, the intrigues, and espionage against his rivals and adversaries.) He answered, "You're doing fine. Keep it up."[3]

After this my career began to take an unusual turn (don't forget I was only twenty-four years old). To sum it up, Zinoviev and Kamenev recalled Lenin's words, "We are in our fifties, whereas you others are in your forties. We must prepare for our succession by comrades now in their thirties and their twenties." As I've already said, two men in their thirties had been named: Kaganovich and Mikhailov. Now, it was decided to name two in their twenties. They were Lazar A. Chatskin and I.[4] Officially we were, of course, told nothing. But Chatskin learned it thanks to Zinoviev's secretaries, whereas I learned it from Kamenev's secretaries, Muzyka and Babakhan.[5] The fact that Zinoviev had cited my name three times in the Central Committee political report took on new meaning.

Chatskin and I tried to get to know each other as best we could. He was a very intelligent young man, talented and cultured, from a very bourgeois Jewish family. It was he who invented the Komsomol and was its founder and organizer. Initially he was first secretary of the Komsomol central committee, then, imitating Lenin, who was never officially head of the Party, Chatskin hid in the corridors and directed the Komsomol [from behind the scenes] for many years, with the help of his lieutenant, Tarkhanov.[6] Chatskin was a member of the Komsomol central committee, which was officially directed by the secretaries of the Central Committee (whom Chatskin selected from among cadres who were not too bright). In 1924 Chatskin had already left the Komsomol due to his age, and was studying at the Institute for Red Professors. Later, he worked for the Comintern. He was shot during the Yezhovshchina purges, 1937–38.

Instead of giving me satisfaction, my shining career put me in a very difficult position. The problem was that during the year I had already worked at the Politburo, I had gone through a rapid and profound evolution which had run its course: I was becoming a convinced enemy of communism.

The communist revolution represented a gigantic upheaval. The rich and ruling classes lost power, their immense wealth was confiscated, and they were physically exterminated. The entire national economy came into other hands. For what purpose was all that done?

When I was nineteen and joined the Communist Party, there was no doubt in my mind, as with tens of thousands of adolescents as idealistic as I: the Revolution was undertaken for the good of the masses. It could not have been otherwise. To have admitted that a group of professional revolutionaries had crossed this sea of blood only to acquire all the riches of the country and the power to run it for their own benefit would have been sacrilege. We were ready to risk our lives, even to lay them down, for a social revolution for the good of the people.

It's true that during the enormous upheavals brought on by the Revolution and then the Civil War and the reorganization of society there were incidents that were profoundly foreign to us, even inadmissible. We explained those things as being inevitable ancillaries of the Revolution: "You can't make an omelette without breaking eggs." The people were savage, illiterate, uncultivated, and it was very difficult to avoid excesses.

And while condemning many things, we were unable to correct the situation: it was not our doing. For example, throughout the Ukraine, sinister rumors circulated about the red terror, while the idiots in the Cheka, often sadists and drug addicts, exterminated thousands of victims in the most ferocious ways. I thought it was due to unleashing the local rabble, criminals who had infiltrated into the organs of repression and who were taking advantage of their tremendous power, and that the heads of the Revolution were not involved and indeed were quite unaware of what was being perpetrated locally in the Revolution's name.

When I arrived in the Central Committee, I found myself at the center of all the information flow and said to myself that I would find the precise answers to all the questions to which a rank-and-file Party member could get no real answers. Even in the Orgburo I was close to the heart of the regime and I had understood many things. For example a group of "apparatchiks" were undertaking an energetic and systematic project, directed by Stalin, Molotov, and Kaganovich, to infiltrate the Party's central organs in order to achieve power. But that was only part of the story. I needed the complete answer to a more profound question: Was this being done in fact for the good of the people?

Once I became Politburo secretary, I had the opportunity to get the answer that I was searching for. These few men, who now directed everything, who yesterday made the Revolution and were still continuing it, how and why did they do it? For a year I observed and analysed the motives behind their activities, their goals, and their methods. There's no doubt that the most interesting thing would have been to start with Lenin, the founder of the Bolshevik Revolution, to know him, and to study him personally. But when I got to the Politburo he was already paralyzed and for all practical purposes he no longer existed. He was, however, still at the center of attention, and there was much to be learned about him from people who had worked with him these last years, as well as from the mass of secret Politburo documents that were in my care. Without difficullty, I dissected the hypocritical and untrue eulogies built up by the leaders, who made an icon of the "genius" Lenin and governed in his name as his loyal disciples and successors. It was not hard. I could see through Stalin's hypocrisy. In public he swore his loyalty to the genius of the master, whereas in fact he sincerely detested Lenin who was the principal obstacle on his road to power. In his secretariat Stalin was uninhibited, and it was clear from his intonations, his asides, and so on, what his real feelings were regarding Lenin. On the whole the others knew it also. For example, Krupskaya said shortly after, in 1926, "If Volodya were still alive, he would be in prison now."

Although playing "if" is only an exercise of the imagination, I have often wondered what Lenin's fate would have been had he lived another ten years. In that case, I am sure, he would have had to rid the political scene of Stalin in time (during the years 1923–24), but personally I doubt he would have done it. In 1923 Lenin wanted to remove Stalin from the post of general secretary for two reasons. First, because Lenin knew he was dying and was thinking not of his own primacy but of his heirs (which is why all considerations of his majority and his break with Trotsky were cast aside). Second, because Stalin, seeing that Lenin was finished, had passed all bounds of decency and had become insulting with Krupskaya and with Lenin. Had Lenin still been well, Stalin would never have dared to inflict such insults. He would have remained a docile and ardent partisan of Lenin, all the while creating his own majority in the apparatus until, at his chosen moment, he would have overthrown Lenin just as he did Zinoviev and Trotsky.

It is amusing to speculate on what might have happened afterward. Lenin would have been accused of all sorts of deviations and errors, and Leninism would have become a heresy just as Trotskyism did. It would have appeared, for example, that Lenin was an agent of German imperialism (which had sent him into Russia in a sealed train to undertake espionage and other clandestine activities), but that the Revolution succeeded despite this, thanks to Stalin who turned it all around in time, having seen through and expelled the "traitors and spies," Lenin and Trotsky. Lenin would no longer be the head of world revolution but a shady individual. Would that have been possible? Just look at the Trotsky example; he was made to seem, not the central figure of the October Revolution, not the creator of the Red Army, but simply a foreign spy. Why not the same with Ilich? He might even have been "rehabilitated" after Stalin's death, although Trotsky was not.[7]

Once I had begun to know what was in the authentic [Politburo] documents concerning the real Lenin, I was struck by one of the traits he had in common with Stalin. Both men had a maniacal lust for power.[8] All Lenin's activity had a leitmotiv: "Acquire power at no matter what price, and stay there the same way." One can imagine that Stalin aspired to power simply to benefit from it in the Ghengis Khan tradition, and he was uninterested in such other considerations as, "Why this power?" By contrast, Lenin wanted power in order to have in his hands a powerful and unique instrument to construct communism, and he wanted to keep power for the same end. I believe that this hypothesis is close to being correct. Personal requirements played less of a role in Lenin's case than Stalin's, in any event a different role.

I tried to sketch for myself a moral portrait of Lenin, not the "great, historic" Lenin depicted by communist propaganda, but the man as he really was. I was forced to conclude, from documents of unquestionable authenticity, that his ethical level was low. Leader prior to the Revolution of a small group of extremist revolutionaries, he was constantly engaged in incessant intrigues, disputes, and wrangles with other similar sects and in unsavory struggles to capture the finances and wring handouts from other socialist groups or bourgeois supporters. In order to get control of a tiny journal, he used any means including the defamation of a rival and disgusted Trotsky, who was much more pure and honest. Unhappily, the mores instilled by Lenin remained those of the Party leaders after the Revolution. I found them as much in Zinoviev as in Stalin.

And Lenin's greatness? It's agreed that when a man robs and kills another, he is a criminal. But when he robs a nation and kills tens of millions, he becomes a legendary and historical figure. How many contemptible and repulsive megalomaniacs who manage to take control of large countries become great men no matter what harm they've done to their own countries and others along the way?

I came to the conclusion that Lenin was a good organizer. The fact that he was able to come to power in a large country, if you look at it closely, demonstrates the weakness of his adversaries (the champions of revolutionary disorder), their ineptness, and their lack of political experience. The little group of well-organized Leninist professional revolutionaries appeared as a better adapted organization, indeed almost the only valid one, to avert general anarchy. Even for all that, I could find no particular genius of Lenin's.

Lenin's goals? Certainly to install communism. After they had taken power, Lenin and his Party went all out in that direction, and within three or four years it had resulted in a complete catastrophe. In later Party documents it wasn't represented as a failure to build a communist society but as a failure of "war communism." That's obviously untrue, the usual falsification, of course. It was communism in general that had failed in those years. How did Lenin react to this failure?

Lenin's official pronouncements display how he represented the turnabout of his Party in the face of this failure. What interested me was to find out what Lenin really thought about the failure. Obviously his real thoughts could only be known by his close entourage, especially his two secretaries, Fotieva and Glyasser, with whom he had worked daily. I wanted to question them on the subject.

At first it was not easy. I was, as far as they were concerned, "Stalin's man." But, after a few months, when I had been in touch with them daily as part of my work, I impressed them as being a "Politburo man" and only pro forma Stalin's assistant. Now I could gradually interrogate them about Lenin, and I was able to ask what Lenin had really thought about the NEP: did he believe that we were facing a failure of communist theory? The secretaries told me that they had asked Lenin this question, and he responded: "Certainly, we've failed. We thought to build a new communist society overnight, whereas it will take decades and even generations. So that the Party doesn't lose heart, lose its faith and its will to fight, we must tell it that our return to a market economy, to capitalism, is only a temporary step back. But between us, we must clearly see that the initiative failed, that one can't change in one fell swoop peoples' psychology and their age-old customs. We could have tried to impose by force a new way of life on the population, but then there was no guarantee that we would have held on to power in the ensuing Russia-wide butchery."

I've always remembered those words of Lenin's since, a few years later, Stalin began to effect that "PanRussian butchery" as he imposed communism on the people by force. It is now clear that success was possible, if one were not to be stopped by the cost in tens of millions of victims. It was possible to conserve power while doing it. Lenin was stopped by Kronstadt and the Antonov uprising.[9] Stalin didn't recoil in the face of the gulag archipelago.

An interesting detail. I wanted to know which were Lenin's favorite books. Glyasser told me that Gustav Lebon's *Psychology of the Masses* was one of them. I didn't learn whether Lenin used the book as a practical tool, necessary for influencing the masses, or if he had drawn from this remarkable book by Lebon the understanding that, despite Rousseau's naïve theories, the amalgam of old customs complicates life, and the mix of history and culture that constitutes the substrate of society can't be modified in one single move by the decrees of dreamers and dogmatists.

It was quite evident that Trotsky, just like Lenin, was a fanatic follower of communist dogma (but less flexible). His unique goal was also to install communism. The question of the good of the people could only have been seen by him as an abstract hope for a faraway future, if indeed Trotsky ever thought about it.

But in this respect one must mentally divide the masters of Russia into two distinct groups: the first was represented by Lenin and Trotsky, fanatic dogmatists. They led the country from 1917 to 1922, but then they were overtaken. Two other groups came to power and fought to stay there. They were no longer fanatic dogmatists but the practitioners of communism. One of the groups consisted of Zinoviev and Kamenev, the other included Stalin and Molotov. For them communism was a method to acquire and retain power. The Zinoviev and Kamenev group were simply practitioners of power who invented nothing new but were continuing in Lenin's footsteps. Stalin and Molotov were leaders of a group of "apparatchiks" who progressively assumed power for the personal benefit it would give them, and they are now commonly called the group of "bureaucratic degenerates" of the Party. The question of the peoples' welfare was not of interest to these two groups, who represented the present and the future of the Party in power, and indeed it would have been embarrassing to have raised the subject. From observing them daily, I concluded bitterly that the peoples' good was the least of their concerns. Even communism, for them, was merely a good method, above all not to be abandoned.

I had to conclude that the social revolution had not been undertaken for the people. In the best of cases (Lenin and Trotsky), it was only to pursue a theoretical dogma. In the intermediary case (Zinoviev and Kamenev), it was to acquire the special advantages of power for a minority. In the worst case (Stalin), it was usurpation of power by amoral criminals.

Let's look at the best case: the Revolution was effected to pursue Marxist dogma. But how did the Politburo view this dogma? From my first presence at Politburo sessions my attention had been drawn to the irony of the term "trained Marxist." It was clear that it really meant "garrulous oaf."

At times it was even worse than that. The Peoples' Commissar for Finances, Sokolnikov, who was undertaking monetary reform, submitted to the Politburo the nomination of Professor Yurovsky as member of the Narkomfin board and head of the department of foreign exhange. Yurovsky was not a communist, and he was unknown to the Politburo. One of the members asked, "I hope he's not a Marxist?" Sokolnikov hastened to reply, "No, oh, no. In the foreign exchange department one must know how to work, not chatter." The Politburo approved the nomination at once.

I tried to increase my knowledge of Marxist theory. It strikes you right away that the social revolution in Russia was done in contradiction to all the theories and predictions of Marx. Those predictions were also totally wrong in the "capitalist" West. Instead of crushing pauperization of the proletariat, we've seen constant and unprecedented growth in the standard of living of the masses. I recall, in that context, that according to the famous note Marshal Vauban wrote to King Louis XIV, at that time one-fifth of the French population was dying, not of illness or old age, but of hunger. Marx had absolutely not foreseen social revolution in Russia, where 85 percent of the population consisted of peasants and small landowners, and labor constituted just over 1 percent. (The official history of the Soviet Communist Party, volume IV, page 8, 1970, gave the 1921 Russian population as 134,200,000, of which industrial workers were only 1,400,000.)

To tell the truth, the more I got into Marxist theory, the more this gibberish which sought to represent itself pompously as an economic science, nauseated me. Still, I dug into it, beginning with Adam Smith, who in the second half of the eighteenth century and with the best of intentions, wanted to find a scientific basis for economics. His effort was at once premature and inopportune. Premature because the methods of exact sciences were only then beginning to take shape, and it was too soon to try to apply them to a field as complicated as the arena of economic phenomena. Inopportune because Smith applied to the analysis of economic phenomena the German idealistic and noumenonic philosophy of his time, not exact scientific methods. It was thus that Smith originated his labor theory of value, a crude and erroneous fruit of German philosophical concepts. What in fact is it that determines prices of goods? The search for the causes and real life consequences is not properly in the realm of philosophy. Price is a phenomenon. According to the philosopher, there is a hidden key: the noumenon. It is the value of products. Value is determined by the work, the physical labor expended in the manufacture of a product. Lucid observers disagree, of course, citing a thousand examples where it is not so, such as, machines which do identical work, or the price of a diamond found with no effort beside the sea, and so on. Smith corrected himself: value is not only a function of labor, but it is determined by the average amount of labor necessary for production. This theory, which was presented as scientific although it was totally false, is remarkable in one respect. It demonstrated that a flawed product of the human mind could cause millions of deaths. This abortion of Smith's began to live its own life as a theory. Smith was followed by Ricardo who drew all the logical conclusions from Smith's theory: if physical labor is the way in which wealth is created, how is capital generated? Obviously the capitalist doesn't pay his laborer the full salary due for his work, but he keeps a portion of it (the surplus value): it's the accumulation of this stolen portion that creates capital. Consequently, Karl Marx proclaimed, all capitalists are thieves and crooks, and all capital is wealth stolen from the workers. The proletarians of all countries must unite to recover by force that which was stolen from them.[10]

At first glance it seems quite curious that all this nonsense could be considered something scientific. According to him only workers created value, created useful things, products, and made the economy work. The efforts of scholars, inventors, engineers, entrepreneurs, being work that was performed by brain rather than brawn, were represented as creating nothing, as playing no role. Men have always had hands to work with, but enormous forward steps in the well-being of society and of the masses only became possible when wisdom and technology combined to put labor and machines together, to arrive at incomparably better results. But Marx held that if you don't work with your hands, you are a thief and a parasite. How ridiculous! Everything is upside down in this gibberish that is presented as science.

However, Marxism has been a potent factor in our society. One must again recall Lebon's formula: "Reason creates understanding; the spirit makes history." Marxist theory, producing nothing on the economic level, proved to be dynamite emotionally. To tell the poor and dispossessed, "You are poor and miserable because the rich have robbed, and continue to rob you," is to ignite a global fire, to raise such a wave of envy and hatred that only a sea of blood will extinguish it. Marxism is a lie, but a lie of extraordinarily explosive force. It was on this rock that Lenin built his church in Russia.

I soon understand all the nuances of the attitude of the communist leaders toward Marxist theory. As practitioners and pragmatists governing the state, they realized the complete uselessness of Marxism in the field of comprehension and organization of the economy. Thus their skeptical and ironic attitude toward "trained Marxists." Inversely, they appreciated greatly the explosive emotional force of this Marxism which brought them to power in Russia and would bring them to power over the entire world (they hoped, not without reason). In sum, as a science Marxism was nonsense. As a revolutionary tool to control the masses it was irreplacable.

Still, I wanted to verify even further their attitude toward Marxism. Officially, it was untouchable. It was only permitted to "interpret" Marxism and then only in the most orthodox way.

I often went to visit Sokolnikov, who had been a lawyer. He was part of the Zinoviev-Kamenev group, and he was unquestionably one of the brightest and most gifted Bolshevik leaders. Whatever job was given him, he executed perfectly. During the Civil War he commanded an army. As commissar of finances after NEP, he deftly effected monetary reform and stabilized the ruble, bringing the economy out of its Bolshevik chaos. After the Thirteenth Party Congress in May 1924, he was named candidate member of the Politburo. At the 1926 congress he took the side of Zinoviev and Kamenev and was the only platform speaker to urge removal of Stalin from the general secretaryship.[11] That cost him his job as peoples' commissar and his place on the Politburo. At the Fifteenth Congress [December 1927], when Stalin proposed his criminal collectivization policy, Sokolnikov came out against it and urged normal industrial development, starting with light industry.

One day in 1925 I visited Sokolnikov. He was at home, ill. In such cases, we spoke generally of finances and economics. But this time I had decided to take a risk and speak of Marxism. Without denying the Marxist revolutionary role, I focused on a critical look at Marxism. Starting with the fact that the theory was created nearly one hundred years before, and there had been many changes which meant that the theory should be updated, and since the Politburo was not using the outdated theory, I suggested, as a reasonable alternative, a fairly radical reform. Sokolnikov listened to my long discourse without making any objections. When I had finished, he said, "Comrade Bazhanov, there is much of value and of interest in what you've said. But there are taboos which must not be touched. I give you my friendly advice; tell nobody what you just told me." Obviously, I followed his advice.

I had to conclude that the communist leaders used communism as a method to have power, completely ignoring the interests of the people. While making communist propaganda, doing their best to ignite a communist explosion throughout the world, they did not at all believe in its theory. Therein was a key to help me understand another very important aspect of the question, one that had always bothered me.

In all the practice of communism, lies permeated everywhere and everything. Why? Now, I understood. The chiefs themselves didn't believe in what they proclaimed to be the gospel truth. For them it was just a means, and the goals were low, shameful. These lies which impregnated the system were not a fortuitous tactic but were the very essence of the regime itself.

According to Marxist theory, we had dictatorship by the proletariat. Seven years after the communist revolution, the entire population of the country, plucked and miserable, constituted the proletariat but without the slightest shred of power. The dictatorship had been established over the population. Officially we still had power in the hands of the workers and peasants. But it was evident, even to a child, that power was uniquely lodged in the Party, and even then only in the Party apparatus. The country was full of organizations of Soviet power, but they were only executors of the decisions of the Party apparatus. I was, also, a cog in this lying machine. My Politburo was the pinnacle of this power, but it had to be hidden from the entire world. Everything about it was rigorously secret:

all its resolutions, its lofty talk, its information, its documents, if divulged, would have led to severe punishment for the guilty.

Another illustration of the way in which lies permeated the system, was the trade unions. They were the official organs charged with defending the workers. In reality they were the mechanisms used to control and constrain, and their sole objectives were to force the workers to labor as much as possible and to squeeze out the maximum profits for the enslaving regime. All the terminology was false. Penal servitude was called "camps for reeducation through labor," and hundreds of media liars sang the praises of the glory of Soviet power, so wise and so humane, which reeducated through work the most implacable enemies of the state.

At Politburo meetings I often asked myself, "Where am I, at a meeting of the government of a large country, or in Ali Baba's cave at a meeting of a band of thieves?"

An example: The problems of the Peoples' Commissariat for Foreign Affairs always were first on the Politburo meeting agenda. Customarily the peoples' commissar, Chicherin, and his deputy, Litvinov, attended, and it was Chicherin who usually presented the report. He spoke timidly and with humility, hanging on each critical remark by a Politburo member. One could see right away that he carried no weight in the Party: before the Revolution, he had been a Menshevik. Litvinov, by contrast, had a disinterested and insolent attitude. He was a boor by nature and seemed to be saying, "I'm an old Bolshevik, quite at home here." In fact, he was an old friend and fellow émigré of Lenin's. His most famous prerevolutionary exploits involved shady financial maneuvers. For example, he exchanged in the West tsarist banknotes stolen by armed attack on the Caucasus treasury. The serial numbers were known to the Russian authorities, so Lenin tasked Litvinov to use his contacts outside the country to exchange them. Litvinov was arrested and jailed. The whole Litvinov family was apparently of the same stripe. His brother tried to steal from the Soviets through commercial transactions in France, profiting from his brother's position as deputy peoples' commissar, and the Soviets had to appeal to bourgeois French justice and show that Litvinov's brother was a thief and a crook.

Chicherin and Litvinov cordially detested each other. Not a month went by without my receiving a note marked "strictly confidential, for Politburo members only," from one or the other of them. In these notes, Chicherin complained that Litvinov was rotten, ignorant, a gross and crude animal who should never have been given diplomatic duties. Litvinov wrote that Chicherin was a homosexual, an idiot, and a maniac, an abnormal individual who worked only at night and thus disrupted all the efforts of the Commissariat. Litvinov added picturesque details such as the claim that the door of Chicherin's office was guarded all night by a OGPU internal security soldier deliberately chosen by the OGPU because he wasn't someone whose virtue one needed to worry about. The members of the Politburo read these messages, smiling, and the matter went no further.

Once, there was a discussion of foreign policy, concerning a forthcoming international conference. Litvinov said, "I propose that we recognize the tsarist debts." I looked at him with astonishment. Lenin and Soviet government had proclaimed dozens of times that one of the overriding principles of the Revolution was the refusal to pay foreign debts which had been contracted by Russia under the tsarist regime.[12] (The French bankers didn't suffer in the slightest, since they pocketed their commissions when the bonds were issued. Those who lost were the little people who had saved for their old age, trusting the bankers who had assured them there were no better investments.)

One Politburo member, one of the least shrewd, I believe Kalinin, asked, "What debts, those of the war or those from before it?" "Both," said Litvinov casually. "Where will we find the money to pay them?" Litvinov, with an insolent and scornful air, "Who said we would pay them? I'm speaking of recognizing them, not paying them." Kalinin didn't give up, "But to recognize them is to admit we owe the debt, and as a result must pay." Litvinov put on a weary look: how could anyone not understand such a simple thing? "No," he said. "It's not at all a question of paying anything." Now Kamenev became interested, "And how do we recognize them, not pay them, and not lose face?" (Kamenev, it must be said, had some regard for appearances.) "Nothing simpler," said Litvinov. "We declare to the entire world that we recognize our foreign debts. The well-intentioned imbeciles will trumpet that the Bolsheviks have changed, that we have become a state like the others, and so on. We garner the maximum [propaganda and bargaining] benefit. Then we send a secret directive to all local Party organizations: form associations of victims of the foreign intervention, and compile their claims. You understand that if we send out such a circular through Party channels, we can have claims by 'victims' of any amount necessary. But we'll be modest, and we'll run up a total slightly above the tsarist debts. Then when we begin our negotiations for payment, we'll show our own claims which will more than cover our debts, and we'll ask for the surplus."

The proposal was seriously discussed. The main difficulty came from the fact that Lenin's triumphal declarations of nonpayment were too fresh in peoples' memories. It was feared that the proposal would sow discontent among brother parties overseas. Kamenev even remarked in passing, "That was what Curzon called 'the Bolshevik baboonery.'" It was decided to postpone a decision on Litvinov's proposal.

Lenin with Krupskaya, ca 1923   Doyle Collection – Photography by Jeffrey S. Caldwell

Lenin (*L*) and Stalin in 1922   Doyle Collection – Photography by Jeffrey S. Caldwell

L. to R. Chicherin, Radek, and Litvinov in Geneva, 1922   Doyle Collection –
Photography by Jeffrey S. Caldwell

500 ruble banknote (1912) similar to those stolen by armed Bolshevik attack on the Caucasus Treasury (page 88)   Doyle Collection – Photography by Jeffrey S. Caldwell

СТРОГО СЕКРЕТНО

Пролетарии всех стран, соединяйтесь!

Российская Коммунистическая Партия (большевиков). ЦЕНТРАЛЬНЫЙ КОМИТЕТ.

Отдел _Бюро Секретариата._

14 АВГ. 1923 г. ___ 192__ г.

№ ____

Т.т. Кнорину, Бажанову, Комфонтову.

Выписка из протокола № 27 заседания Оргбюро ЦКРКП от 9/VIII-23 г.

Слушали:

С помощнике Секретаря ЦК т.Сталина.

Постановили:

Назначить помощником Секретаря ЦК т. Сталина т.Бажанова с освобождением его от обязанностей секретаря Оргбюро.

Правила о порядке хранения см. на обороте.

При ответах ссылаться на наш № число и отдел.

МОСКВА, Воздвиженка, 5. Коммутатор ЦК.
1-05-27, 1-05-28, 1-05-29, 1-05-30.

Bazhanov's appointment to Stalin's Secretariat in 1923   Doyle Collection – Photography by Jeffrey S. Caldwell

L. to R. Trotsky, Lenin, Kamenev in Moscow, 1920   Doyle Collection – Photography by
Jeffrey S. Caldwell

Zinoviev, ca 1922   Doyle Collection – Photography by Jeffrey S. Caldwell

Trotsky, ca 1920   Doyle Collection – Photography by Jeffrey S. Caldwell

8. Stalin's Secretariat. The Military.

Stalin's lists. Tovstukha and Mekhlis. The struggle for power continues. Trotsky is removed. Frunze, Voroshilov, and Budenny.

The Thirteenth Party Congress was over, and Tovstukha busied himself with a new "semishady" project: he gathered up all the documents from the congress "to study them." But soon it was clear that only certain documents interested him. He studied them with a chekist who was a graphology specialist.

When the delegates arrived for the congress, they presented themselves to the Mandate Commission which verified their credentials. They were then given delegate cards, with either voting or nonvoting rights. Each delegate had to fill out a long questionnaire by hand, which included several dozen questions. Every delegate had to submit to this questionnaire. During the congress, the Mandate Commission statistically analyzed the questionnaires, and at the end of the congress it presented a report on the number of delegates attending, classified by such things as their social class, age, sex, length of time in the party, and so on. Everyone understood the need for this lengthy but routine questionnaire.

But there was one detail they had not divined.

At the end of the congress the delegates voted to elect people to the Party's central organizations (Central Committee, Central Control Commission, Central Revision Commission). Beforehand, the leaders of the Central Committee had got together with the chiefs of the principal delegations (Moscow, Leningrad, Ukraine, etc.). This meeting had discussed the composition of the new Central Committee. The list of nominees was printed, and each delegate with a right to vote received a copy of it. The list was a voting ballot which was to be deposited in the urn when the secret vote was taken for the Central Committee elections. The fact, however, that there was only one list didn't mean that the delegates were obliged to vote for it. Party elections were involved, not election of soviets. There was still a certain amount of liberty in the Party. Each delegate had the right to strike out any name and replace it with one of his own choice (which, we note in passing, he had to do in his own handwriting). Then the votes were counted. There was little probability that those on the list would not be elected. That would have required an unlikely accord among the principal delegations. Whereas the entire list was elected, there was a wide disparity in the number of votes for each candidate. Among a thousand delegates, for example, the most popular ones would get 950 to 970 votes, and the less popular ones would not even get 700. This was known to and understood by everyone.

What was unknown, was Tovstukha's activity. It interested Tovstukha (i.e., Stalin) most to ascertain who had stricken the name of Stalin from his ballot. If just the name had been stricken, the voter would not have been identifiable. But he had to write another name in place of Stalin's, and that gave a handwriting sample of the voter. Comparing these samples with the questionnaires, Tovstukha and the chekist graphologist identified those who voted against Stalin and were therefore his hidden enemies. The time would come, in ten or so years, when they would receive a bullet in the back of the neck. Tovstukha was preparing the execution list. Comrade Stalin never forgot anything and never forgave anything.

To explain Tovstukha's work completely, I must go forward a bit. After the Thirteenth Congress, in 1925, 1926, and 1927, the same freedom existed within the Party. The fight against the opposition was carried out in the committees, Party cells, and meetings of organs and militants of the Party. Leaders of the opposition vehemently urged their partisans to be as active as possible to attack the Central Committee. In so doing, they would underline the strength and influence of the opposition.

I was astonished when, after the Fourteenth Congress [December 1925], Stalin and his new majority in the Central Committee did not oppose this freedom. It didn't seem to be in Stalin's manner of doing things; it would have been simpler to forbid discussions within the Party and to proclaim, by a resolution of the Central Committee's plenum, that such discussions harmed the Party and turned its efforts away from constructive lines, etc.

I knew Stalin well enough already, and so I guessed what he was up to. I was able definitely to confirm my theory during a conversation with Stalin and Mekhlis. The latter was holding in his hands the report of a local Party meeting, and he cited violent intervention by opposition elements. He was indignant and said, "Comrade Stalin, don't you think this goes too far, and the Central Committee is wrong in letting itself be discredited so openly? Wouldn't it be better to forbid it?" Stalin smiled, "Let them speak! Let them speak! The dangerous enemy is not he who shows his hand. It's the hidden enemy, whom we don't know, who is dangerous. We know all the people [in this report] and have files on them. The day will come when we'll settle accounts with them."

Now the second semishady work by Tovstukha. He composed, in his office at the Lenin Institute, long lists of the people who were so naïvely taking positions against Stalin. They were saying to themselves, "Today we're against, but tomorrow we might be for Stalin; freedom has always existed in the Party and it always will." They didn't understand that Stalin, in power, was giving them the opportunity to sign their own death warrants. Within a few years these lists that Tovstukha was compiling would be the basis for shooting people by groups, by hundreds, then by thousands. There is no limit to human naïveté.

How did I feel in the bosom of Stalin's secretariat, this place of such capital importance? I had not the slightest sympathy either for Kanner or for Tovstukha. I thought of Kanner as a dangerous serpent, and I had only strictly professional dealings with him. In view of my position he had to be amiable toward me. But I had no illusions: if Stalin wanted to liquidate me tomorrow, he would have Kanner see to it. Kanner would find the right method. For me, Kanner was a criminal and the fact that he was so necessary to Stalin was a reflection on "the boss," as Mekhlis and Kanner liked to call Stalin. Kanner was always happy and friendly in appearance. A small man, he always wore boots (I don't know why), and his curly black hair was like a sheep's fleece.

Ivan Pavlovich Tovstukha was a tall, very thin, tubercular intellectual. He died of tuberculosis in 1935, soon after they had begun to shoot the people on his lists. His wife was also tubercular. He was [now] thirty-five or thirty-six. Before the Revolution he had emigrated and lived abroad. He came back to Russia after the Revolution. In 1918, for some reason, he became secretary of the Peoples' Commissariat for Nationalities, of which Stalin was the commissar (without doing any of the work there). From there he went into the Central Committee staff, before Stalin became general secretary. In 1922, when Stalin became general secretary, he engaged Tovstukha in his secretariat. Tovstukha stayed there almost until he died, doing somewhat shady tasks for Stalin, as well as being (as I've said) assistant director of the Lenin Institute and later the Marx-Engels and-Lenin Institute.

In 1927, after I had left the secretariat and Mekhlis had gone to study at the Institute of the Red Professorate, Stalin made Tovstukha his principal assistant. At that time Stalin's secretariat included a "special section" directed by Poskrebyshev, who replaced Tovstukha when the latter died. Yezhov directed the "cadres [personnel] section" of Stalin's secretariat; he continued Tovstukha's lists and, a few years later when he headed the OGPU, he shot those on the lists and embarked the country in a new sea of blood—on instructions, of course, of his boss, the great and brilliant Comrade Stalin. Malenkov became secretary of the Politburo and assistant to Poskrebyshev in the "special section." Later, Malenkov replaced Yezhov as chief of the cadres section.

As Stalin consolidated his personal dictatorship, so his secretariat played an increasingly important role. The day came when the president of the Council of Ministers or a member of the Politburo had less weight than Stalin's secretary, who could always get in to see the dictator.

Tovstukha had a sinister personality: he looked up at you from under his brows and coughed a lot. He had only one lung.[1] Stalin had complete confidence in him. Tovstukha treated me with caution ("after all, this young man is making a brilliant career for himself"), but he could never forgive me for having taken his place and that of Nazaretian as Politburo secretary and for staying at the center of things while he was compelled to undertake unsavory work for Stalin in the corridors. He tried to bite me once. He asked Stalin (in my absence but in front of Mekhlis who told me), "Why does Bazhanov carry the title of secretary of the Politburo? It is you, Comrade Stalin, who is the secretary of the Politburo. Bazhanov has the right only to have the title of technical secretary of the Politburo." Stalin responded evasively, "Certainly it is I, elected by the Central Committee, who is the responsible secretary of the Politburo. But Bazhanov does very important work and frees me from a large number of tasks."

I didn't like Tovstukha, a shady character, an intrigant, envious, ready to undertake the most ignoble missions for Stalin.

Leon Mekhlis was the same age as Tovstukha. After the Civil War he went into the Peoples' Commissariat for Workers' and Peasants' Inspection, which Stalin headed (but where he did nothing). He left in 1922 to become Stalin's secretary in the Central Committee staff. Mekhlis was more honest than Kanner and Tovstukha; he avoided shady tasks. He put on the useful mask of a sincere communist, but I don't believe much in that because he was an opportunist, ready to bend to any wind. I was not mistaken, for as things developed, no crime of Stalin's bothered him. He served Stalin loyally to the end of his days, all the time pretending to believe in Stalin's superiority. He was actually Stalin's personal secretary, and like a good opportunist he was ready to accept any charge and obey every order. He tolerated my success and did his best to establish friendly relations with me. In 1927 Tovstukha forced him out of Stalin's secretariat and he went to study for three years at the Institute of the Red Professorate. But in 1930 he demonstrated to Stalin that *Pravda,* the Party's central news organ, was not doing its job to explain the role played by Stalin's personal direction of affairs. The latter immediately appointed him editor in chief of *Pravda,* and there he rendered Stalin an inestimable service. *Pravda* set the tone for the entire Party and its organizations.[2] Mekhlis vaunted the great and ingenious Stalin's qualities, and his benign direction, daily in *Pravda's* pages. At first this produced a strange impression, as nobody in the Party, particularly those who knew him well, considered Stalin a genius.

In 1927 I visited the Party cell of the Institute of the Red Professorate several times. It was the preserve of young Party arrivistes who strove not so much to study and improve their qualifications as to calculate on which horse they should bet to further their careers. I teased them, saying, "I don't understand one thing. No one among you is writing a book on Stalinism. I'd like to see the state publishing house which wouldn't publish it right away! More, I guarantee that at most one year later, the author will be a member of the Central Committee." The young careerists made faces, "What? On Stalinism? Well, you're a true cynic." (I must note that I said this in pure bravado, since I was already a convinced opponent of communism and was preparing my defection.)

In 1927 "Stalinism" still seemed something immodest. By 1930 its time had come and in edition after edition of *Pravda* Mekhlis set the tone for the Party: "Under the wise leadership of our great and brilliant guide and master, Comrade Stalin. . . ." It was obligatory to repeat it in the Party cells. After two years of this work, people could no longer speak of Stalin either in the Party or in the country, without adding the epithets, "great and ingenious." Later, other zealots invented many different expressions: "Father of the people" . . . "the greatest genius of humanity," and so on.[3]

In 1932 Stalin took Mekhlis back into his secretariat. However, Tovstukha was more his man: he inserted him [Tovstukha] increasingly into Party organizations. Before World War II he was chief of the political directorate of the Red Army. Then he became peoples' commissar for state control. During the war he was a member of various army and army group war councils, where he conducted himself like a true Stalinist: he devoured the lives of Red soldiers as if they were of no account. After the war he was again peoples' commissar for state control. He died in his bed the same year as Stalin.

Stalin's secretariat grew and took on more and more importance. But still Stalin's principal battle for power had not been won. Zinoviev and

Kamenev had just saved him in May 1924, and he was already asking himself how to betray them.

There was an amusing incident at the Thirteenth Party Congress. To show the country that the workers were grateful to the Party for its wise direction, there were brought on to the scene for the first time delegations of non-Party persons. In the following years this fraudulent spectacle was to become frequent. To start off, a delegation of unaffiliated workers was brought in from the well-known Moscow Trekhgornaya Textile Factory. A woman with a tireless tongue had been coached, and she spoke grandly from the congress rostrum of the wise direction of the great Bolshevik Party and of the fact that "we, the unaffiliated workers, approve and completely support the Party leaders," and so on.

The event, however, had a goal other than her simple intervention. It must be emphasized that the country was being run by new bosses. Until now, the word had been "long live Lenin and Trotsky." Now it was necessary to show that the masses were following the leadership of these new bosses. Whereas the good woman had been well coached and had apparently understood everything, there was a misunderstanding: "In conclusion," she said, "long live our chiefs, Comrade [she hesitated slightly] Ziniviev, and . . . [after a moment's reflection, and turning toward the presidium] excuse me, I think it's Comrade Kaminov." The congress roared with laughter, especially Stalin, while Kamenev, in the presidium, smiled sourly. By the way, the organizers hadn't even considered including Stalin among the "chiefs." It would have seemed ludicrous.

Meanwhile, since Trotsky hadn't personally intervened against Stalin either at the congress or at the CC plenum before it, Stalin conceived a tactic: Zinoviev and Kamenev had been used by him to distance Trotsky. Why couldn't Trotsky be used to weaken Zinoviev and Kamenev? Stalin tried, but it didn't work.

On 17 June Stalin presented a report to a special course run by the Central Committee for county committee secretaries. In it, he stated quite clearly to his future "apparatchiks" that the dictatorship of the proletariat was giving way to dictatorship by the Party. At the same time, without naming them, he leveled his guns at Zinoviev and Kamenev, accusing them of various errors.

Zinoviev reacted with great vigor. He called an immediate conference of Party leaders (the Politburo and the twenty-five members of the Central Committee), at which he and Kamenev bluntly raised the question: not only was the attack against them out of order but they considered Stalin's thesis of the "dictatorship by the Party" to be a signal error. The conference, obviously, condemned Stalin's thesis, as well as his intervention against the other two members of the *Troika*. Stalin saw that he'd gone too fast and made a mistake. He offered to resign his general secretaryship. However, the conference saw it as a manifestation of goodwill and didn't accept his resignation.

Zinoviev and Kamenev had, on the other hand, understood Stalin's tactic in respect to Trotsky, and they intensified their efforts against the latter, urging his expulsion from the Party. But there was no majority in the Central Committee for the expulsion of Trotsky. Zinoviev tried to carry the fight into the arena of the central committee of the Komsomol, which suddenly urged expulsion of Trotsky. But the Politburo fell back on its own dogma: it was not the Komsomol's place to interfere in politics, and they applied sanctions by removing fifteen or so Komsomol leaders from their posts.

It is amusing that at that time, in the Central Committee, Stalin slowed down the attacks against Trotsky by Zinoviev and Kamenev. By contrast, in the Comintern, where Zinoviev ruled, a resolution was voted "on the Russian question" against Trotsky at the Fifth Comintern congress in June/July 1924. As a result the Bulgarian Vasily Petrov Kolarov,[4] who had particularly distinguished himself by his attacks against Trotsky, was promoted by Zinoviev to the post of general secretary of the Comintern executive committee.

From then until the end of 1924 there was a period of calm in the fight against Trotsky. The summer was very dry, and the harvest very poor. In August there was an uprising in Georgia. The Politburo discussed what policies should be taken in respect to the peasantry. In truth, the Politburo didn't know what to do in this regard. They wanted to industrialize the country. But at whose expense? (The method of approaching the problem was very Bolshevik: in order to accomplish something, someone had to be plucked.) The orthodox communists, led by Preobrazhensky, proposed "a primitive socialist accumulation" at the peasantry's expense. The Politburo hesitated. The discussions of the problem at the October Central Committee plenum brought no solution, despite the adoption of thundering declarations on "turning to confront the countryside." Should the land be seized and, by means of collectivization, the peasants forced into kolkhozes? It was recalled that, recently, in one of his last articles on "cooperation," dictated 4 to 6 January 1923 and published in *Pravda* at the end of May, Lenin had spoken of the question of kolkhozes, but he foresaw free consent. At the Central Committee plenum of 26 June 1923, this had been discussed and Lenin's directive adopted. At that time, however, neither Zinoviev nor Kamenev expected much to come of the sovkhozes and kolkhozes, while Stalin as yet had no opinion on the subject.[5]

At the end of the year the fight against Trotsky suddenly resumed its role as the central theme of Party life. Stalin had renounced his idea of using Trotsky against his allies, and Trotsky had written his book *1917*, in the preface of which, entitled "The Lessons of October," he violently attacked Zinoviev and Kamenev, demonstrating that their attitude in October 1917 (when, as we know, they opposed the armed coup d'état) was by no means an isolated phenomenon, and these men had none of the qualities of leading revolutionaries. Trotsky's "Lessons of October" was published as a newspaper article. After this, Zinoviev and Kamenev again proposed to Stalin that they make peace and collaborate. Stalin hastened to accept, and the *Troika* was reconstituted for a while. At that moment, Stalin was going through a crisis of doubt about his strength. He knew he'd made some mistakes when he switched his struggle to the arena of political strategy, where he was weak. The Georgian uprising, a direct result of his Georgian national policy, was on his mind. It was at this time that Stalin realized that it was not via grand political strategies that he would win over his rivals but by selecting his own men to give him a Central Committee majority. Until that was done, he must maneuver carefully and put things off until he was ready.

Zinoviev, on the other hand, vociferously urged definitive elimination of Trotsky. During the January 1925 plenum of the Central Committee, Zinoviev and Kamenev proposed exclusion of Trotsky from the Party. Stalin opposed this, playing the role of conciliator. He persuaded the plenum not only to keep Trotsky in the Party, but to keep him in the Central Committee and the Politburo. It's true that the plenum condemned Trotsky's interventions and his political views, but the important point was that the moment had arrived to rid the Red Army of him. His replacement had been ready for a long time, in the person of his assistant, Frunze. The latter was not particularly Stalin's man, but Zinoviev and Kamenev liked him, and in the course of long *Troika* sessions on the subject Stalin accepted the nomination of Frunze to replace Trotsky as peoples' commissar for war and president of the Revolutionary War Council, with Voroshilov as assistant.

After the Civil War Voroshilov was named (over protests by Trotsky) commander of the North Caucasus secondary military zone. Stalin wanted him moved up, and by the time of the CC plenum, Voroshilov was commanding one of the most important military zones, Moscow. Stalin proposed to the plenum that Trotsky be given a warning. If he didn't stop his factional infighting he would be expelled from both the Central Committee and the Politburo. Having stripped him of his post as peoples' commissar for war, the plenum named him president of the Glavkontsesskom [Central Concessions Committee] and of the special conference for the Supreme Council on the National Economy, responsible for the quality of production.

These nominations were at once comic and provocative. As the head of Glavkontsesskom, Trotsky had to discuss with Western capitalists the industrial concessions inside the USSR which had been proposed to them. In fact, we at the Politburo had known for some time that these concessions were nothing more than crude traps. The concessions proposed to Western capitalists had terms that appeared to be very appealing and advantageous. The provisions of the agreements were respected while the concessionaires were bringing their equipment and materiel to the USSR, installing it, and getting their projects going. Then, using various tricks (of which the authorities had many), the concessionaire was maneuvered into a position where he couldn't abide by the terms of the concession. He was then denounced, and his imports and the enterprise became the property of the Soviet state. (I will set forth later in detail one such case involving Lena-Goldfields, for it is a story which had unexpected and amusing consequences.[6]) It was for this purpose that the concessions gimmick had been created. Trotsky was not the man to engage in such dishonest operations, which was doubtless why he had been appointed to the job.

He was even less suited to the job of supervising the quality of Soviet factory production. A brilliant orator and polemicist, superb leader in difficult or critical situations, it was absurd to expect him to watch over the quality of trousers or Soviet nails. At first, he tried conscientiously to accomplish the job the Party had given him. He created a commission of specialists, toured several factories with them, and presented the results of his study to the Supreme National Economic Council. Not surprisingly, there was no followup to his recommendations.

Frunze took over as minister of war. He had, in May 1924, become a candidate member of the Politburo, along with G. Y. Sokolnikov and F. E. Dzerzhinsky.

Frunze was an old revolutionary, a famous commander in the Civil War, and a talented military man. Very prudent and reticent, he gave me the impression of a card player with a good hand who doesn't show his cards. He spoke rarely at Politburo meetings and then only on military matters.

Since 1924, as president of the Central Committee's commission responsible for studying the condition of the Red Army, he had declared to the Politburo that the Red Army, in its present form, was absolutely incapable of fighting. It was more a collection of bandits than an army, and it should be completely dissolved. That was, in fact, what happened, in the strictest secrecy. Only the cadres were kept: the officers and non-commissioned officers. A new army was formed in the autumn, based on peasant conscripts. During all of 1924 the USSR was virtually without an army. It seems that the West was unaware of this.

Frunze's second important change was to achieve removal of the political commissars in the army. They were replaced by political assistants to the commanders, responsible for political propaganda but without the right to interfere in command decisions. In 1925 Frunze completed all this by making personnel appointments and switches that placed competent military men at the head of military districts, corps, and divisions. These men were selected on the basis of their military qualifications, not their devotion to the Party.

By this time I was already secretly anticommunist. Looking at the lists of Frunze's senior officers, I asked myself, "If I were in his place, and anticommunist, who would I have selected to run the army?" I would have had to respond to myself, "The same men." They were a group who would have been perfect for a coup d'état in case of war. They were, of course, in appearance merely excellent military officers.

I never discussed this matter with Stalin, and naturally I had no wish to draw his attention to it. But when the occasion presented itself I asked Mekhlis if he had heard Stalin say what he thought of the new military appointments. I asked it innocently, "Stalin is always interested in military matters." "What does Stalin think? [He replied,] "Nothing good. Look at the list: men like Tukhachevsky, Kork, Uborevich, Avksentiev, are they good communists? They're good for an 18 Brumaire, but not the Red Army."[7] I wanted to know more, "Is that your opinion, or Stalin's?" Mekhlis puffed himself up and said conceitedly, "His, and mine too, of course."

Stalin had a rather enigmatic attitude toward Frunze. I was a witness to the discontent he expressed during the *Troika*'s frank debate on this nomination. But to Frunze's face he was very friendly and never took issue with his proposals. What did it mean? Was it perhaps a repeat of the Uglanov story, which I'll get into later? That would mean that Stalin, while pretending to be against Frunze, Zinoviev's protégé, had in fact concluded a secret alliance with him against Zinoviev. The latter didn't seem to me to be dissembling. It was not his style, and he had nothing in common with Stalin.

The mystery was only solved in October 1925, when Frunze had almost completely recovered from an ulcerous stomach (which he'd contracted in prison before the Revolution). Stalin manifested an extreme concern over his health, "We aren't taking care of the precious health of our best militants." The Politburo virtually forced Frunze to have an operation to get rid of the ulcer. Furthermore, the doctors didn't consider the operation dangerous.

I saw this with quite a different perspective after I learned that the operation was organized by Kanner, with the Central Committee physician Pogosiants.[8] My fears were fully justified. An anesthetic Frunze's heart couldn't tolerate was subtly used for the operation. He died on the operating table, and his wife, convinced that he had been murdered, committed suicide soon after. Everyone knows *Tale of an Unextinguished Moon*, written on this subject by [Boris] Pilniak [well-known Russian poet—see chapter 2], who paid dearly for it.

Why did Stalin organize Frunze's assassination? Was it only to replace him by his own man, Voroshilov? I don't think so: a year or two later, when he had supreme power, he could have made that change without difficulty. I believe that Stalin shared my impression that Frunze saw himself as a future Russian Napoleon. He eliminated him right away, and later shot the others of Frunze's group—including Marshal Tukhachevsky.

In his book on Stalin, Trotsky categorically rejects my interpretation of the Frunze affair, but he distorts my thinking. He attributes to me the theory that Frunze was leading a military plot. I never wrote anything like that, especially since it's obvious that at that time no plots were possible in the USSR. I wrote that Frunze, in my view, was no longer communist, that he'd become a military man to the marrow of his bones and was waiting for his hour to come. But there was no question of a plot.

It was not worth discussing with Trotsky: he was notable for his astonishing inability to assess people, and a naïveté not less astonishing. Speaking of him later, I will cite facts in this regard.[9]

So it was that Voroshilov, after Frunze's death, took over command of the Red Army. After the Fourteenth Congress, in January 1926, he also became a member of the Politburo. He was a very mediocre person, who had placed himself in Stalin's footsteps during the Civil War and who always supported Stalin during the fight against Trotsky's skilled hand. His lack of intelligence was notorious in the Party. The students of the history section of the Institute of Red Professors used the joke, "All universal history is divided into two very distinct groups: before Voroshilov, and after him." He was always a docile assistant of Stalin's and was kept on, for cosmetic reasons, for a while after his master's death.[10]

All members of Stalin's Civil War military group were promoted, but it's hard to find a single competent soldier among them. However, well-orchestrated propaganda made some of them celebrated, for example Budenny.

He was a very picturesque figure. A typical cavalry sergeant of the tsarist army, good horseman and swordsman, he began the Civil War at the head of a band of cavalry fighting the Whites. Formally, a group of communists manipulated the band, which grew and had some victories. The cavalry was at that time the tanks of today. Suddenly Moscow, interested in cavalry, singled out Budenny.

At this time Trotsky had issued his call, "Proletarians, to horse." It was quite comic for its emphasis and lack of realism. The men from the steppes made good cavalry, as for example the Cossacks who were born horsemen. One could even use peasants on horseback, for even if not trained horsemen they knew horses and could handle them. But an urban worker, a proletarian, was useless in the cavalry. Trotsky's call to horse was ridiculous.

As a sign of their interest, Budenny received presents from Moscow: an automobile and a Party card. A little uneasy, he showed them to the leaders of his band, "Here, fellows," he said. "Moscow sent me a car and this." He put the Party card on the table, carefully, as if it were a fragile Chinese vase. The men reflected, then decided, "The car, Semyon, take it. A car is a good thing. And 'that' (the Party card), put it away somewhere: at least it doesn't eat any bread." And that's how Budenny became a communist.

Budenny's band soon became a brigade, then a corps of cavalry. Moscow sent him some commissars and a good chief of staff. Even though he was promoted to commandant, Budenny never interfered with the command or with operations. When the staff asked his advice on a projected operation, he would say, "You take care of it. My thing is to saber."

During the Civil War he "sabered," and he obeyed Stalin and Voroshilov, who had been placed over him. After the war he became something like inspector of cavalry. One day they decided to have him attend a meeting of the celebrated Politburo. I remember perfectly this amusing event.

During the Politburo session, the time came to discuss a military question. I had the military men waiting to testify brought in, among them Budenny. He came in on tiptoe, but making a lot of noise with his heavy boots. The passage between the table and the wall was wide, but his whole posture displayed extreme fear of knocking over or breaking something. He was shown a chair next to Rykov and sat down. His mustache stuck out like a cockroach's. He stared straight ahead and obviously understood nothing that was said to him. Here was the famous Politburo which people said had the power to do anything, even transform a man into a woman. Meanwhile we had finished the military matter. Kamenev said, "We have finished with strategy. The military men are free to go." Budenny stayed seated, not understanding such subtlety. Kamenev, however, was also a dummy. He should have said, "OK, Comrade Budenny, forward march." That would have been clear. But Stalin said, with a large gesture of hospitality, "Stay, Semyon, stay." So Budenny stayed, eyes goggling, staring right ahead, while two or three other problems were discussed. Finally, I explained to him that it was time to go.

Later, Budenny became a marshal, and in 1934 he even got into the Central Committee. It's true that it was Stalin's captive Central Committee, and, if he'd had a sense of humor, Stalin could have aped Caligula and made Budenny's horse a member of the Central Committee. But Stalin didn't have a sense of humor.

I must add that during the German-Soviet war the incompetence of Voroshilov and Budenny was so evident from the first operations, that Stalin had to send them to the Urals to train reserves.

9. Stalin

Stalin. His character. His qualities and faults. His career. His amorality. His attitude toward his staff and toward me. Nadia Alliluyeva. Yashka.

It is time to speak of Comrade Stalin. By now I knew him well, in fact, very well.

Stalin's physique is well enough known. But on no portrait does one see that his face was scarred by smallpox. The face was without expression. He was of medium height, he waddled, and he continually sucked on his pipe.

Some authors have affirmed that one of his arms functioned poorly. His daughter Svetlana said that he moved his right arm with difficulty, whereas the old Bolshevik Boris Zakharovich Shumiatsky wrote in the Soviet press that Stalin couldn't bend his left arm. To tell the truth, I never noticed anything like that. I frequently saw him make large gestures with his right arm, bending and unbending it. In the final analysis, I never saw him do any physical work. It's possible that his left arm was in bad shape, but I never had occasion to observe it.[1]

He led a very unwise life, sedentary, without sports or physical work. He smoked a pipe and drank Kakhetinskoye wine. In the second half of his reign, he spent all his evenings at table, eating and drinking with Politburo members. It was astonishing that, given such a life, he survived to seventy-three years of age.

Always calm, he disciplined himself well. He was extremely secretive and vindictive and never forgave or forgot anything. He would even avenge himself after twenty years. It was very difficult to find any redeeming qualities in his character; for my part, I never found any.

Myths and legends slowly grew up about him. For example, his extraordinary willpower, his firmness, and his decisiveness. It was a myth, for by nature Stalin was a very prudent and hesitant man. Very often he didn't know what to do or how to do it, but he didn't show it. I often saw him hesitate, preferring to follow events rather than direct them.

Was he intelligent? He wasn't stupid or devoid of native common sense, both very useful for him.

For example, various matters of state were discussed at Politburo sessions. Stalin had little education and couldn't contribute usefully to the problems being discussed. It was a difficult situation, but his astuteness and his common sense permitted him to find an adequate solution: he would listen to the debate, and when he saw that the majority were in favor of a solution, he would speak out and propose in a few short phrases that the majority position be adopted. He did this in simple terms, so that his ignorance was not clearly manifested. For example, he would say, "I think Comrade Rykov's proposition should be adopted; that of Comrade Piatakov will never work, comrades, it will never work."

The result was that, even though Stalin was simple and spoke poorly, everything he proposed was adopted. Not understanding his ploy, the Politburo members began to see in Stalin's interventions a hidden (even mysterious) wisdom. Personally, I was not duped by this. I could see that he had no systematic thinking process. He simply searched for the opinion of the majority.[2] He would propose today something which didn't fit at all with what he had proposed yesterday. I knew that he understood state problems poorly, from private conversations with him in the Central Committee offices. But the Politburo members were seduced by him and ended by ascribing to his proposals a sagacity that didn't exist.

Stalin was uncultured. He read nothing and was interested in nothing. Science and scientific methods were beyond him and anyway of no interest. A poor orator, he spoke with a strong Georgian accent. His speeches were thin in content; he spoke with difficulty, searching for words and looking at the ceiling. In reality he wrote nothing; his "works" consisted of his speeches and interventions on various subjects. Later, based on stenographic records, his secretaries wrote the text (which he himself never read, since in his view it was their job to produce his books and articles). Usually it was Tovstukha who did this work for him.

Stalin never said anything witty. In all the years I worked with him, I only heard him once try to be funny. Tovstukha and I were chatting, standing in the office of Mekhlis and Kanner. Stalin came in, looking very serious and solemn. He raised the index finger of his right hand, and we shut up, expecting something very important. "Tovstukha," said Stalin, "My mother had a beak of a nose just exactly like yours. But it didn't wear pince-nez." After which, Stalin turned and went back into his office. Tovstukha gave a little servile laugh.

Stalin was indifferent to art, literature, and music. From time to time he went to the opera, preferably to hear *Aïda*.

Women didn't interest him. His own woman was enough for him, and he paid scant attention to her.

He had only one passion, absolute and devouring: lust for power. It was a maniacal passion, that of an Asian satrap of long ago. It occupied him entirely and was the unique goal of his life.

Certainly this passion was useful in the fight for power, but at first glance it's hard to explain how Stalin managed to achieve dictatorial power with such limited means.

Let us look at the steps in his ascent. It will surprise us even more to see how his defects served him better than his capabilities.

At the start he was merely a small provincial revolutionary propagandist. Lenin's professional revolutionary Bolshevik group suited Stalin perfectly. One didn't have to work there like everyone else did, and one could live on the Party's treasury. Stalin was never attracted to hard work. That entailed risk: you could be arrested and sent to the North under police surveillance. For social democrats, the repression didn't go further than that.

The authorities were much harsher with Socialist Revolutionaries, who threw bombs. In exile, the tsarist authorities provided the necessities, and one lived freely within the confines of a small town or a village. You could escape, but then you were an outlaw. By contrast, the leaders had a much more comfortable life than the simple propagandists. Lenin, Martov, and so on lived in Geneva and Paris: the chiefs refused to risk their precious persons.[3]

Outside Russia, the leaders spent their time raising money for themselves as well as the Party. Funds were obtained from friendly political parties (which gave parsimoniously and with bad grace) and bourgeois do-gooders. For example Burevestnik (i.e., Maxim Gorky),[4] who was one of the leaders of the Moscow Arts Theater, helped the comédienne Andreeva seduce the millionaire Savva Morozov, whereupon a flood of gold poured into Lenin's treasury via Andreeva. But there was never enough. The Anarchists and a group of Socialist Revolutionaries found a way to procure the funds they needed: quite simply, they robbed capitalists and banks. On the other hand the Socialist Democratic parties, who had long played the role of respectability and often participated in the government, categorically rejected this practice. The Russian Mensheviks also rejected it. Lenin too made a statement of rejection but without enthusiasm. Stalin, for his part, quickly understood that Lenin was pretending and that he would be happy to have money even if it did come from robbery. Stalin participated actively in the recruitment of a number of Caucasian bandits, who had to be simultaneously converted to Bolshevism. The best recruit of this type was Kamo Petrossian, a robber and cutthroat of great courage.[5]

Several armed robberies by the Petrossian band filled the party coffers, to the point where the only problem was to launder the money for onward passage. Lenin accepted the money with delight. It was Comrade Stalin who organized the holdups by the Petrossian band, but he was careful not to participate himself.

In this regard, one wonders if Stalin was a coward. It's hard to answer the question. No case in all his life can be cited where he proved his physical courage, neither in the Revolution nor in the Civil War, where he always commanded from the very rear, nor in peacetime.[6]

Lenin was extremely grateful to Stalin for this activity, and was not opposed to his advance in the Party hierarchy: for example, to bring him into the Central Committee. However, it couldn't be done at a Party Congress where the delegates would say, "The fact of organizing armed attacks for the Party is very good, but not reason enough to make a Party leader of him." Lenin found a workable solution. In 1912, Comrade Stalin was "co-opted" into the Central Committee without election. Insofar as he was from then on in exile until the Revolution, the question of his Party status was not posed. After the February 1917 Revolution, he returned from exile as an old member of the Central Committee.

Stalin, as it is known, played no role whatsoever either in the "second" Revolution (February 1917) or in the October 1917 Revolution. He was in the shadows, waiting. Shortly after taking power, Lenin appointed him to run two Peoples' Commissariats which he expected to disappear quite soon. The first was that of the Workers' and Peasants' Inspection, a stillborn child that Lenin expected to merge into the Central Control Commission—which was eventually done. The second was the Commissariat of Nationalities [Narkomnats], which was also to be eclipsed and its functions transferred to the Central Executive Committee's Council of Nationalities. What Lenin thought of Stalin was illustrated in the discussion which took place in a meeting when Lenin nominated him to be peoples' commissar of nationalities. When Lenin proposed his nomination, one of the participants proposed another candidate, showing him to be an intelligent and perceptive man. Lenin interrupted, "We don't need an intelligent man for that; we'll send Stalin."

Stalin was a peoples' commissar on paper only, for he almost never set foot in his commissariats. On the Civil War fronts his anarchistic activities were very debatable, and during the war with Poland, when the offensive against Warsaw failed because he and his army didn't execute the orders of the commander in chief, his activities were downright nefarious. Stalin's real career began at the moment when Zinoviev and Kamenev, wishing to grab Lenin's heritage, organized a campaign against Trotsky and chose Stalin as their necessary ally in the Party apparatus. But Zinoviev and Kamenev failed to understand one very simple thing: the Party apparatus was headed toward power, spontaneously and automatically. Once installed at the head of this machine, all Stalin had to do was to keep himself there and be carried to the top. It must be noted that Stalin had understood that the machine would carry him up, and he did what was necessary to take advantage of it.[7]

One is naturally led to conclude that, until 1925, Stalin's faults played a much more important role in his career than his merits. Lenin brought him into the Central Committee, into his majority there, because he feared no competition from this man of little culture or political stature. It was for this same reason that Zinoviev and Kamenev made Stalin general secretary of the Party: they considered him politically insignificant, seeing him as a useful assistant, not a rival.

Without any exaggeration, Stalin was a completely amoral man. Lenin was amoral himself, rejecting with contempt on his own behalf and for his professional revolutionaries, all the moral qualities which, in our Christian civilization's traditions, we hold to be the required cement that makes reasonable life viable in human society: honesty, loyalty to one's given word, tolerance, sincerity, etc. According to Lenin all that was bourgeois morality that must be rejected: the only morality was whatever served the social revolution, or more accurately, whatever served the Communist Party. Stalin showed himself to be a pupil who had surpassed his teacher. Studying his life and comportment, it is hard to find human traits. The only thing of that sort I was able to discern, was a certain fatherly attachment to his daughter Svetlana. And that was only up to a point. Other than that, I could find nothing.

Stalin's coarseness was quite natural and resulted from his lack of culture. In fact he could control himself very well and was only boorish when he judged it unnecessary to be polite. I made some interesting observations in his secretariat. He was not wittingly crude with his secretaries but, for example, if he rang and Fomenko (the orderly) was not there (perhaps she would be taking documents somewhere), and instead Mekhlis or Kanner responded to his bell, he would say one word: "tea," or "matches." His assistants called him [formally] "you" and "Comrade Stalin," but he called Tovstukha, Mekhlis, and Kanner [familiarly] "thou." I was the only one he called more formally "you," yet I was the youngest one of all. He showed no affection whatsoever for his staff, but he appreciated them in proportion to their usefulness. All of them provided him with substantial services: Kanner and Tovstukha for semicriminal affairs, and Mekhlis, whom he didn't appreciate so much at first, to make him "great and brilliant." I was also very useful in my role as Politburo secretary, but his attitude toward me was not the same as it was toward the others. They were "his" men, devoted and adhering to their posts. By contrast I didn't show either respect or attachment for Stalin, and thus I was something of a mystery to him. I didn't make special efforts either to hold on to my job or to share in the power structure.

Only once did he try to be crude with me. It was at a Politburo session. As usual I had transcribed a resolution on a cardboard card and passed it across the table to him, and after reading it he would return it to me. Not being in agreement on a point (which was of no concern of mine) with the other members, he was angry and wanted to show his bad humor. He could think of nothing better than to fling the card across the table, rather than hand it to me. My reaction was immediate. I threw the next card at him, just as he had done. He look at me astonished and ended his game right then.

He completely ceased to understand me one fine day when, having lost the desire to be a useful cog in the Politburo machinery, I told him that I would like to go to work at the Peoples' Commissariat for Finances. (Sokolnikov had proposed to me that I head the economic and finance bureau of the commissariat, which had replaced the advisory committee of the tsarist Ministry of Finance.) Stalin was amazed. "Why?" Obviously I couldn't give him my real reason, so I replied that I wanted to become expert in the economic-finance arena. He responded that I could do it while continuing my work, and the work would benefit from it. "In addition, the Party has given you a very important task, with great responsibility; there's no reason to give it up." So I worked at the Finance Commissariat (of which I'll speak later) as well as my Politburo job. To Stalin, for whom power was everything, my indifference to it was an enigma. He knew that in me he had something he couldn't understand. Perhaps that's why he was always completely polite with me.

In those years, the 1920s, Stalin led a very simple life. He always wore an ordinary outfit, of a military cut, with boots and a military cap. He had neither the taste for luxuries nor the wish to enjoy the pleasures of life. He lived in the Kremlin, in a small and simply furnished apartment, where palace servants had lived before. Whereas Kamenev, for example, with his new understanding of cars, had a splendid Rolls Royce, Stalin was content with a Russo-Balt (an old Russian model) that was powerful but old and modest. (There were hardly any usable roads then, and one virtually had to stay in Moscow; if one left town, only the Leningrad road was passable.) Like the other Bolshevik leaders, Stalin had almost no money problems. They all had everything without money: apartment, car, train travel, holidays at spas, and so on. Their food was prepared in the Sovnarkom canteen and taken to their residential apartments.

Routine Politburo meetings began in the morning and went until lunchtime. When the Politburo members went to eat, I would stay in the meeting hall, formulating the resolutions on the last matters discussed. Then I would to to Stalin's apartment. Usually he was at table with his wife Nadia and his oldest son Yashka (from his first wife, née [Ekaterina] Svanidze).[8] Stalin would look over my cards, and then I would go to the Central Committee offices to finish my minutes.

The first time I found him at table, he poured a glass of wine and offered it to me. "I don't drink, Comrade Stalin." "A glass of wine does no harm, and it's a good Kakhetinskoye wine." "I've never drunk alcohol, and never drink it now." Stalin was amazed. "Well, then, drink to my health." I refused to drink his health, and he never offered me wine again.

Often Stalin left the Politburo sessions but didn't go straight home. He would walk around in the Kremlin, continuing a conversation with one of the other members. In such cases I had to wait. That was how I got to know his wife Nadia [Nadezhda Sergeevna] Alliluyeva, whom I called simply Nadia and with whom I had a friendly relationship.

Nadia didn't resemble Stalin in any respect. She was a very fine, honest woman. She wasn't pretty, but she had a pleasant face, open and sympathetic. She was about my age but seemed older and at first I thought she was several years older than I. She was, of course, the daughter of the St. Petersburg worker, Alliluyev, at whose house Lenin hid before the October 1917 Bolshevik insurrection. She had by Stalin a son, Vasily (then five) and a daughter, Svetlana, three years later.

When I got to know Nadia, I had the impression that she was surrounded by emptiness. At that time she had no female friends, and men dared not approach her. If Stalin suspected anyone of paying court to her, it would be most dangerous for him. I got the impression that the wives of near-dictators lack the most basic human contacts. In any event, we quickly became friends. At that time I was completely absorbed in a love affair and had no intention of chasing after Nadia. Slowly, she told me what her life was like.

Her family life was miserable. Stalin was a tyrant at home. Having constantly to hold himself back with strangers, he didn't stand on ceremony at home. Nadia told me more than once, sighing, "This is the third day he says nothing, speaks to nobody, and doesn't reply when you speak to him. What a difficult man to live with!" However, I tried to avoid conversations bearing on Stalin. I already knew him for what he was. Poor Nadia, apparently, was only now discovering that he was amoral and inhuman, and she didn't want to believe what she was learning.

One day Nadia disappeared, and I learned that she'd gone to spend the last months of her pregnancy with her parents in Leningrad. When she returned, she said to me, "Admire my little treasure." The treasure was about three months old, a wrinkled little ball: Svetlana. As a sign of special confidence, I was allowed to hold her in my arms (not long, fifteen seconds—men are so clumsy!).

After I left Stalin's secretariat I met Nadia only rarely and then by chance. When Ordzhonikidze became president of the Central Control Commission, he engaged Nadia as his third secretary. The first secretary was Trainin, a debonnaire giant. I met Nadia for the last time one day when I went to see Ordzhonikidze. We had a long and amiable conversation. She had blossomed working for Ordzhonikidze, where the atmosphere was agreeable and the boss a warm man. He took part in our conversation. He and I called each other "thou," although it bothered me a bit because he was twenty years older. In fact he called everyone for whom he had the slightest warmth, "thou." I never saw Nadia again.

Her tragic end is known but probably not in all its details. She had been studying at the Industry Academy. Despite its pretentious name, it simply gave review courses and general instruction to local communists; former workers, and peasants who were now directing industrial enterprises and who, for lack of education, were having trouble discharging their duties. The year was 1932, when Stalin had set into motion his gigantic meat grinder of forced collectivization. Millions of peasant families were sent to extermination camps. The students at the academy were from the provinces and had seen this dreadful annihilation of the peasantry with their own eyes. Learning that the new student was Stalin's wife, they kept quiet. But little by little it became apparent that Nadia was a good and compassionate woman in whom they could have confidence. Tongues loosened, and she was told what was happening in the countryside, whereas prior to that she'd only read the pompous and lying Soviet newspaper accounts of brilliant victories on the agricultural front. Nadia was horrified and told Stalin what she'd learned. I can just imagine how he reacted, for in their discussions he used to call her an imbecile and an idiot. Stalin told her that her information was false, kulak counterrevolutionary propaganda. "But all the witnesses say the same thing." "All of them?" Stalin asked. "No," she replied. "There's one who says it's all false information. But he's visibly lying, from fear; it's the secretary of the academy cell, Nikita Khrushchev." Stalin remembered this name. Later, during another domestic conversation, Stalin told Nadia that her information was wrong and asked for the names of her sources. Only that way could their stories be checked. She gave him the names.

If she had ever doubted what sort of a man he was, this was the last time. All the students who had taken her into their confidence were arrested and shot. Thunderstruck, Nadia finally realized with whom she had made her life and, doubtless, what communism really was. She killed herself. (I was not, of course, a witness to this, but have reported what I understand of her suicide, based on information that has come to us.)[9]

As for Comrade Khrushchev, it was from this moment that his brilliant career began. Next time there was an election of local committee members and secretaries of the Moscow Party organization, Stalin told the Moscow committee secretary, "You have an excellent militant, the secretary of the cell at the Industrial Academy, Nikita Khrushchev. Name him local secretary." At that time, Stalin's word was virtually the law, and Khrushchev immediately became Krasnaia Presnia secretary, I believe, and then soon after secretary of the Moscow committee. So began Nikita Khrushchev's rise to the very top.

Yakob, Stalin's son by his first marriage, lived with his father. I don't know why, but he was never called anything but Yashka. He was a very reserved and taciturn individual, self-effacing. He was probably four years younger than I. He had a very surprising peculiarity, classifiable as neurotic deafness. He was always deep in thought. You could speak to him, and he didn't hear, having an absent air. Then, all of a sudden, he would realize that he'd been addressed, and he understood perfectly well. Stalin didn't like him and bullied him endlessly. Yashka wanted to study, but Stalin sent him to a factory as a laborer. The boy detested his father with a profound, hidden hatred. He always tried to pass unnoticed and played no role until the war. Mobilized and sent to the front, he was captured by the Germans. When the Germans proposed to exchange him for an important German general, Stalin replied, "I have no son." Yashka remained a prisoner and was shot by the Gestapo during the German retreat.[10]

I almost never saw the son that Stalin had with Nadia; Vasily. He was a young child at the time. As an adult he became an alcoholic. The story of Svetlana, on the other hand, is well known. Like her mother, she understood what her father and communism were, and she fled abroad. This was a serious blow to communist propaganda ("What a regime; Stalin's own daughter couldn't stand it and got out").

Summing up all that's been said about Stalin, it is clear that he was an amoral man with criminal tendencies. However, I believe that the Stalin case poses another, much more important problem: how could such a man exercise all his criminal tendencies, exterminating millions with impunity, for a quarter of a century? There's only one answer. The communist system created Stalin. The communist system incites hatred and calls for extermination of whole classes and entire groups of the population, creating a climate where the leaders can present their actions as a struggle against imaginary enemies: class enemies, counterrevolutionaries, saboteurs. Every failure of their absurd and inhuman system can be blamed on the works of their pretended enemies and used to maintain forever their repressions, liquidations, and the stifling of thought, liberty, truth, and human sentiment. On such a field, the Stalins of this world can flourish with ease.

When the leaders of the system realized that they too must also live with a pistol against the neck, they decided to loosen the vise slightly but not too much. They made sure the essentials of the system didn't change. That is what happened after Stalin.

10. Trotsky

Trotsky's qualities. Orator. Brave man. Poseur. Organizer. Narkomput. Red Army. Theoretician. Theory of permanent revolution. Socialism in one country. The fundamental problem. Trotsky's "non-Bolshevism." Socialism, the wolf. Trotsky's naïveté.

When Trotsky wrote about me, he was almost always unfair. He called me anticommunist, therefore an enemy, a "reactionary," and by the Bolshevik code one must have nothing to do with me. I don't want to throw mud back at him, but will try to describe him objectively.

Of all the Bolshevik leaders, Trotsky impressed me as the most important and the most talented. However, to be just, it must be noted that he was not talented in every field, and alongside his great qualities there were great flaws.

He was an excellent orator but of the revolutionary stamp: a fiery agitator. He could select and use the exact word he wanted, speaking with much ardor and enthusiasm, and thus inflaming his audience. He could also control himself, and he spoke seriously and with restraint at Politburo sessions, where emphasis wasn't necessary.

He had a very biting pen and was a talented polemicist, full of flair and character.

He was a brave man who accepted all the risks that went with his revolutionary activities. In 1905, for example, when he presided over the St. Petersburg Soviet of Workers' Deputies, he was courageous and provocative to the limit and left the rostrum to go directly into prison, then to exile.

The story of the "thesis of Clemenceau" of 1927 is even more illustrative. By then Stalin had assumed total power, and was continually finding new hidden enemies in his fight to destroy the opposition. At the Central Committee's plenum of November 1927, where Stalin eventually proposed his expulsion from the party, Trotsky said, inter alia, addressing the Stalin group (I'm giving the gist of his words), "You are a bunch of bureaucrats without talent. If one day the country should be threatened, if war breaks out, you will be totally incapable of organizing the defense of the country and of achieving victory. Then, when the enemy is a hundred kilometers from Moscow, we will do what Clemenceau did in his time: we will overthrow this incompetent government. There will be one difference in that whereas Clemenceau was content to take power, we, in addition, will shoot this band of contemptible bureaucrats who have betrayed the Revolution. Yes, we'll do it. You too, you'd like to shoot us, but you dare not. We dare to do it because it will be an absolutely indispensable condition for winning." These words, of course, reveal great naïveté and incomprehension of what Stalin was, but one must salute such courage.[1]

Trotsky's temperament, his courage, and his energy unquestionably made him a man for crises, when he would assume command and go for broke. That is why his role was of key importance during the October Revolution. He was the irreplaceable executive of the Leninist plan to take power. Stalin was hiding somewhere. Kamenev and Zinoviev recoiled before the risk and came out against it, whereas Trotsky went all the way and took over. Lenin, incidentally, didn't show much courage: he accepted his entourage's arguments right away, hastening to hide so his precious life wasn't at risk. In the same manner, after the abortive insurrection of July [1917], Lenin hid right away, whereas Trotsky didn't run and was put in a Kerensky prison.

One of Trotsky's serious defects was that he was a poseur. Convinced that he would live in History (with a capital H), he never stopped posing for that History. It didn't always succeed. At times it was justifiable in light of the role he played in seeking world socialist revolution. In the Civil War, for example, when Soviet power was hanging on a thread: "We'll lose, but with a door slamming that will shake the entire world." That, too, was a pose for History. Sometimes his posing was less justified. It was still understandable when he was addressing his Red Army on parade, standing on a machine gun carriage. But less so when he struck poses that were misplaced or ridiculous, and yet he didn't see it. I gave an example earlier, citing the time when he tried to slam the huge door at the Central Committee plenum.

Although Lenin certainly guided Civil War strategy more than Trotsky, the latter undoubtedly played a very large role in organizing the Red Army. In addition, he grew on the job. This trait was shared by many other leaders, intelligent men who quickly progressed and taught themselves how to run the country, organizing the fight and the economy. Leonid Borisovich Krasin,[2] Sokolnikov, and Syrtsov, for example, became better statesmen year by year. Even those less talented rose and learned in the school of hard knocks. Kalinin, for example, whom Lenin brought into the Politburo partly to achieve his majority and partly to have at hand a man who knew the rural scene and peasant psychology, made significant contributions in this field. When, however, he tried to participate in debates that required knowledge and sophistication, he made such dumb statements, at first, that Politburo members couldn't help smiling. But, after two or three years, Kalinin had become much more intelligent. He had come to understand a lot of things and, having good common sense, often made sage comments and was no longer the group's comedian.

Although he was capable and learned a lot by undertaking administrative work, Trotsky made mistakes. After the Civil War transport was totally destroyed and the railway men, working for almost no pay, had to raise vegetables and search for food in the countryside to avoid starving to death. They had no time to work the trains, which ceased running. Lenin appointed Trotsky peoples' commissar for transport (not without an ulterior motive, to place him in a ridiculous situation). Trotsky made a pathetic appeal when taking up his duties: "Comrade railwaymen! The country and the revolution are wasting away for lack of transport. Let us die at our posts, but make the trains run!" His appeal had as many exclamation marks as destiny allows for any office worker during his whole life. The comrade railwaymen preferred not to die at their posts but continued to eke out an existence, which required them to raise potatoes and seek food in the countryside. The trains didn't run, and Lenin, having achieved his goal, relieved Trotsky from his post as commissar for transport.

It is beyond doubt that in the first period of the organization of the Red Army by Trotsky, there were only slogans and speeches, committees of soldiers, election of commanders, confusion, demagogy, and banditry. Trotsky quickly realized that one can not create an army without a minimum of military knowledge and a minimum of discipline. He called upon specialists, former tsarist army officers. Some were won over by promotion to higher ranks, others were simply mobilized, and they were obliged to perform under strict supervision by political commissars. As for discipline, he had to fight all through the Civil War against such people as Stalin and Voroshilov. Trotsky himself learned a lot and transformed himself from propagandist to organizer. But he was still unable to reach great heights in this arena. Without taking the transport scandal into account, he created nothing effective when it came to fighting for power. In the field of organization, mediocrities like Molotov beat him all along the line. Trotsky believed that the most important thing in the political struggle was grand political strategy, long-term political strategy in the realm of the struggle of ideas. There he followed Lenin, whose schemes and formulae he copied. Even there he showed his comparative weakness, for Lenin also was occupied by long-term political strategy, but he assigned no less importance to matters of organization. (In the 1917 Petrograd insurrection, organization played a greater role than politics.)

Another of Trotsky's weak points was his lack of substance as a theoretician and thinker. He was more of a fanatical believer. First he believed in Marxism, then in its interpretation by Lenin. His faith was profound and unshakable. He never manifested doubt or hesitation as to the dogma. He was unable to capitulate except in the face of his Party, which he believed to be the perfect instrument of universal revolution. He never recanted his ideas and believed in them fanatically to the end of his days. Men of this ilk become the world's Saints Francis of Assisi, Peter the Hermits, Savonarolas, but also the Trotskys and Hitlers. Neither theoreticians nor thinkers, such fanatics influence the destiny of humanity far more than do pillars of reason and of wisdom.

It isn't easy to make sense of Trotsky's principal political ideas because of the mass of lying accusations launched at him first by the partisans of Zinoviev, then those of Stalin, and finally those of Stalin's heirs. In any event, already at that time when the fight was going on inside the Party and I was a witness, the falseness and the deceit of most of the conflicting views were as obvious to me as they were to all the Bolshevik leaders. They sought to win the fight and take power, while not giving the impression of a squabble among crabs in a basket. Rather, they sought to demonstrate that the fight was on an elevated ideological level, that the divergencies of opinion were of extreme importance and that the future of the Revolution hung on their solution. Instead, they were generally a battle of words. In particular there were many fruitless and tendentious discussions on Trotsky's famous theory of "permanent revolution" as opposed to Stalin's theory of "building socialism in one country." In fact Trotsky's idea was that the October Revolution in Russia had opened a period of universal social revolution which would explode in other countries as well. Never losing sight of this goal, communist Russia was to be made into a permanent base to support and carry out preparatory revolutionary work in other countries. That didn't mean that while pursuing the objective of world revolt, one would pay no attention to what was happening inside Russia. On the contrary, according to Trotsky communism had to be actively established in Russia, but he thought (and Lenin agreed completely before the Revolution) that an isolated revolt in Russia would not long survive pressure from the "capitalist" countries who would try to crush it by force of arms.[3]

It is quite evident that although Trotsky was chased out, assassinated, and condemned as anathema, this general idea of permanent world revolution has always guided Russian communism, continues to guide it, and will always be the fundamental strategic line of communism.[4]

It's true that with the press of events and with experience, Russian communists had to rethink some of the initial pessimistic views of Lenin and Trotsky. In the face of good sense, not only did the leaders of the major "capitalist" countries fail to overthrow Russian communism by force of arms but, when threatened, Churchill and Roosevelt did all they could to save communism, thus betraying Western civilization and giving half the world to the main global menace to humanity. It was, in effect, very difficult to foresee such a degree of betrayal and of political cretinism. In this respect I take the part of Lenin and Trotsky: their hypothesis was based on the concept that they were dealing with normal and sensible adversaries. I am compelled to quote the excellent Russian poet Georgy Ivanov:

> "If one tells you of all the world's imbeciles
> Who hold humanity's future in their hands . . .
> If one tells you of all the world's rotters
> Who enter history crowned with laurels. . . ."

The discussions on Stalin's theory of "socialism in one country" have just the same deceitful quality. Wishing to seem in ideological disagreement with Trotsky, early in 1925 Stalin accused him of "not believing" in the possibility of building socialism in one country, Russia, where the communist revolution was already a fact. Unhappily, at that moment (March 1925) the quarrel between Zinoviev and Stalin was resumed. Zinoviev couldn't tolerate Stalin's incursions into the field of general strategy. He found Stalin's efforts to play theoretician and strategist ridiculous. There were altercations, and Stalin avenged himself by showing Zinoviev that a majority in the Central Committee had the advantage over no matter what strategy. The plenum rejected Zinoviev's theses, which were destined for the executive committee of the Comintern, for puerile reasons: the war of words. It had nothing to do with the "definitive" victory of socialism. In April Zinoviev and Kamenev redoubled their attacks on Stalin's socialism in one country. It was not acceptable that Stalin should try to be strategic head of the Revolution. At the end of April Stalin convoked the Fourteenth Party Conference, where this matter was discussed at length.

But this was another war of words. Could socialism be built in one country only? In the final analysis it was a matter of whether the enemy would overthrow it by force of arms. Eight years after the Revolution one could already see that, for the time being, nobody had such intentions. Should socialism in one country become an article of faith? If so, in what sense? Or should one just plan, for the time being, to strengthen one's forces and wait to see what would happen? In reality, such considerations had no importance. Once engaged against Stalin the Zinoviev group spilled buckets of ink to show that he was not a revolutionary, that he had abandoned world revolution, that he had become occupied with just local matters, etc.

In addition to all this, which was artificial, there were also (of course) problems of great importance. The most important in the years 1925–26, was whether or not the NEP should be continued. Should there be peaceful cooperation between capitalist elements (with their free markets, profit motive, and economic liberty) and the communists, or should the country go back to the policies of 1918–19 and install communism by force? The lives of millions of people would depend on which road the leaders chose.

In practice, rural Russia was the main question. Should the peasants and their economy be given the possibility of slow economic evolution, without ruining them? Or should they be crushed without pity? (In Marxist theory they were small proprietors, hence an element of the petite bourgeoisie.) The question was also one of whether it was attainable. Lenin feared that the government would lack the necessary force to do it, and so he preferred a gradual solution, with voluntary entry of the peasants into the kolkhoz collective farm system. Later, with Stalin, a gigantic police apparatus (supported by the army) achieved such strength that it was possible to create a system of labor camps enveloping all of Russia.

There was disagreement on which way to go. Bukharin and Rykov, based on their practical experiences, believed Lenin's NEP should be pursued. In April 1925, at a meeting of Moscow militants, Bukharin made his famous declaration according to which "collectivization is not the high road leading to socialism." He said that the economy of the peasants should be developed, even proposing that the peasants should be told to enrich themselves. In fact the choice was either to follow a humane road, using good sense (therefore not the communist road), or to start a communist butchery. It's significant that the most competent leaders—Bukharin, Sokolnikov, Krasin, and Syrtsov—had understood (like Lenin before them) that the failure of communism was evident and that they had to return to common sense. The fanatics like Trotsky, the dishonest and scheming power seekers like Zinoviev, and those without any morality like Stalin, were in agreement, for different reasons, in deciding to install communism by force.

It wasn't done, however, in one move. In 1925 the Zinoviev clan wasn't opposed to Bukharin's viewpoint. It took the 1926 distancing of this clan from power for it to turn about and defend Trotsky's thesis of superindustrialization alongside pressure on the peasants. As for Stalin, he didn't delve far into theory but instead subordinated everything to his own conspiracy. After he had eliminated Zinoviev and Kamenev in 1926, he upheld against them Bukharin's position, and he stayed in this posture until the end of 1927, meanwhile crushing the Zinoviev-Trotsky bloc. At the end of 1927 he decided to get rid of the old Politburo members: Bukharin, Rykov, and Tomsky. Then he reassumed, quite shamelessly, the entire policy of Zinoviev and Trotsky, a policy he previously hadn't ceased to condemn. He came out for forced industrialization and forced collectivization, including crushing the peasants. When the December 1927 Congress finally gave him a solid and unshakable majority in the Central Committee (the reward for years of indefatigable work), he adopted this policy, got rid of the old Politburo members, and serenely took the road to his brand of communism, climbing over mountains of corpses.

In effect the paths of Stalin and Trotsky had come together. Trotsky was also a consistent communist: devoid of common sense.

In his Testament Lenin had mentioned that Trotsky "was not a Bolshevik" (but he counseled not to reproach him too much for this). He meant that before the Revolution Trotsky had never belonged to Lenin's party of professional revolutionaries. Arriving in Russia after the February Revolution, Trotsky first adhered to the "mezhraiontsy" [Interdistrict] group and in the summer of 1917 he finally led them into Lenin's organization.[5] It's a great compliment to Trotsky that he wasn't a Bolshevik before the Revolution. The members of Lenin's Bolshevik group were steeped in intrigue, quarrels, and calumny. They were a collection of amoral parasites. Trotsky couldn't stomache their mores. He even refused to live as Lenin did, on the Party treasury and the grace of bourgeois well-wishers. Trotsky earned his own living as a journalist. I recall seeing his articles before the war in *Kievskaia Mysl (Kiev Thought)*. Being by comparison an honest man, he didn't accept Lenin's peculiar morals. Although he was fanatical and intolerant in his faith, Trotsky wasn't bereft of normal human sentiments: loyalty to friends, sincerity, elementary honesty. So, in effect, he was no Leninist Bolshevik. When I got to know him better, I was amazed that he was the son of a peasant. Strange as it may seem, in the 1880s there were still Jews who worked their land and lived on their own labor as peasants. It was so in his father's case: he was a good peasant, and therefore by the barbarous Bolshevik terminology, he was a kulak. He worked hard and lived well. We can only guess what effect this proximity to the land and nature had on Trotsky.

For me, Trotsky represented an important human problem. I was moving away from communism, but I still thought about it and tried to find answers to certain generic problems, the following one in particular.

The struggle between communism and the old Christian civilization has filled our epoch. As far as I can see, until twenty centuries ago, during the Roman empire, man treated his fellow man like a wolf. Then came Christianity, which proposed that man organize society so that people are friends and brothers, not wolves. That's the main social message of Christianity, apart from its very important religious aspect. During twenty centuries, well or badly, these ideas crept into the human conscience as the ideal to which one must aspire. The pure socialist idea in its true form, not Marxist, was similarly generated by Christianity. But man's nature is nasty, and the slow evolution of these ideas didn't stop the twentieth-century advanced Christian nations from mutually exterminating each other. Communism and Marxism are the direct negation of the Christian ideal: they harbor murder and violence, and mass extermination becomes law. Once again man is a wolf. The Communist Party itself, the apparatus destined to create this new society of socialism with a wolf's muzzle, is built on the principle of a wolf pack. There are no friends or brothers, only "comrades." What is a comrade? It is he who runs beside you (as wolves do) but only up to a certain point. He may march beside you for twenty years, join you in combat and adversity, but if you break the wolf pack law or if, for one or another reason, you cease to suit him, he will jump on you and tear you to pieces instantly with his fangs. He is neither friend nor brother but merely "comrade" and no more. That's the nature of the Communist Party.

Why would communism reject so categorically the idea of friendship and brotherhood among people? Why establish this kingdom of wolves? How did it succeed and survive? These doubts troubled my fairly inexperienced youth. Perhaps the concept of brotherhood was an absolutely unattainable utopia, a lovely dream from Galilee but still just a dream, condemned by history?

I know that man has always been a crude animal and an aggressor, over the centuries a soldier, hunter, savage nomad, and finally farmer, but always fighting against danger: enemies, nature, wild animals, and his neighbors. He has always killed. The Christian message is better received by women, who by their biological nature perpetuate the race and tend to like and care for the weak. All woman's life is a sacrifice for her young and thus is closely linked with the Christian idea of love and compassion. I'm convinced that Christianity was spread by the iron legions of Rome thanks to women. Violence is perhaps more man's arena, the wolf's world, in which communism is so successfully established.

Take Trotsky, a convinced and sincere man. When the communists set out to turn the world upside down in order to suppress exploitation of man by man, it was quite evident that it was a delusion. As soon as they could, without any shame, they replaced what they called capitalist exploitation (they said labor was not sufficiently paid for its work) by a socialist exploitation beyond labor's imagination. It no longer was a matter of underpayment but of free labor by millions of captives and their inhuman extermination. Trotsky, sincere and faithful to his ideals, understood that it was all a fallacy. How then could he have been with Lenin in the instigation of terror, the organization of "armies of workers," of iron discipline where refusal to work could mean instant execution?

Trotsky had human qualities. He was a good husband and father. He loved his children, who in turn admired him, were devoted to him, and followed him blindly. I knew his daughter Zina who resembled him greatly. She was a fragile, thin, tubercular girl, as impassioned as her father. He was her whole life, and of course she perished in Stalin's prisons.

Another Trotsky trait always surprised me: his astonishing naïveté and incomprehension of people. One would think that he'd spent his entire life dwelling on abstractions without ever seeing living people as they really are. In particular he never understood anything of Stalin, although he wrote a long book about him.

In 1930, already in France, I wrote of the expulsion of Trotsky from the USSR that I was very surprised and didn't recognize my Stalin, whom I had studied so carefully. It would have been much more Stalin's style to handle Trotsky as he did Frunze. Stalin disposed of an infinite number of ways to poison Trotsky. Not directly, for that would have been obvious, but indirectly, by a virus, a culture of microbes, or radioactivity. Then to have him buried in Red Square with pomp and ceremonious speeches. Instead, he banished him. I ended my exposé as follows: "It's not easy to understand why Stalin didn't follow his usual habits, which are so much part of his character. In the final analysis it's perfectly possible, however, that he will find it more convenient to have Trotsky assassinated outside the USSR."

I wrote that in 1930. In 1940 Trotsky's last work, his book on Stalin, was not completed due to his death. He had the time to write 584 pages of his book.[6] At the end he wrote, "A propos my expulsion in February 1929,

Bazhanov wrote . . ." He then quoted a half page from my book, and continued, "When Bazhanov's book appeared in 1930, I thought it was merely a literary exercise. After the Moscow trials, however, I took it more seriously." He then put forth the [false] hypothesis that I had heard something about this matter during my time in Stalin's secretariat, which I had left in 1926. It would then have been clear to me in 1930 that Stalin would, when he wished, have him assassinated. The advent of World War II made it urgent, yet Trotsky only "took it seriously" a short time before his murder. Even then, he had to believe that I had heard talk of it in 1926. That is why I say that Trotsky had an astonishing naïveté and incomprehension of people and understood nothing of Stalin.[7]

11. Members of the Politburo

Zinoviev. Kamenev. Rykov. Tomsky. Bukharin. The "Rehabilitation." Kalinin. Molotov.

During three years, Grigory Zinoviev was the number one figure of the communist movement, and then for the next ten years he descended slowly toward the basement of the Lubyanka [State Security headquarters], where his days ended. He succeeded Lenin in the position of leader but wasn't accepted as the real leader by the Party. One might think that this hastened his defeat, but in the reality of the struggle for power, victory or defeat was determined by other factors than popularity or perceived superiority. Among these were some very important factors, not widely understood even now, which I'll discuss later.

Zinoviev was an intelligent and cultured man: a nimble intriguer, he was a graduate of the prerevolutionary Leninist Bolshevik school. More or less a poltroon, he shrank from the risks of clandestine activity and until the Revolution almost all his work was outside Russia. In the summer of 1917 he wasn't enthusiastic about the risks of a revolutionary insurrection and he took a position against Lenin. After the Revolution, however, Lenin soon forgave him, and early in 1919 made him head of the Comintern.

From then on Zinoviev prudently cast himself as Lenin's student and disciple. This posture was also useful in his drive to succeed Lenin. However he didn't rise to the challenge of the situation in any way: not in political theory, or in politics, or in organizing the struggle. As a theoretician he accomplished nothing. His efforts of 1925–26, when he declared the philosophy of the time to be the search for equality, didn't fit communism's objectives or practices and were received by the Party with indifference. In the field of grand political strategy he subordinated everything to the tactics of the power struggle, rejecting vehemently everything Trotsky said. When he was forced from power, Zinoviev adopted Trotsky's (precisely opposite) views in order to join with him against Stalin. In the domain of organization Zinoviev was only able to make himself master of Leningrad, the second capital. That was not, however, enough to succeed. He also had the helm of the Comintern, but that was even less important. Whoever was boss in the Kremlin could appoint whomever he chose to run the Comintern. (Later, Stalin even had Molotov doing it for a while.)

When he proposed Stalin for general secretary of the Party, in the spring of 1922, Zinoviev thought that the posts he himself occupied at the Comintern and in the Politburo were far more important than that of the Party general secretary. It was an error and showed lack of understanding of the process then taking place whereby power in the Party was being concentrated in the hands of the apparatus. One thing in particular should have been very clear to the men engaged in the power struggle: to win that power you had to get a majority in the Central Committee. The Central Committee was elected by the Party congress. To win that meant having behind you a majority of the delegates to the congress from regional organizations. These delegates were selected, more than elected, by leaders of local Party apparatuses: the provincial committee secretary and his closest colleagues. Thus to select and place your people as provincial committee secretaries and in other local leadership posts was to obtain a majority in the congress. That was the work that Stalin and Molotov had been doing systematically for several years already. Their work didn't go smoothly everywhere. In the Ukrainian central committee, for example, where several provincial committees were represented, it was difficult and complicated. They had to shuffle people around, get rid of some, replace others, and then put Kaganovich in as first secretary of the Ukrainian central committee to restore order by making additional personnel changes so as to harness the undisciplined Ukrainian militants. By 1925 the bulk of that work had been done. Zinoviev, who should have comprehended the sense of Stalin's work earlier, understood it too late.

At the 1924 Congress Zinoviev presented for the second (and his last) time the Central Committee's political report. Several days before the Congress he still didn't know what he was going to say. He asked me if I could work up for him an analysis of the past year's work of the Politburo. I did so, presenting it in the form of notes on the most important segments of the Politburo's work during the year. I never thought of it as more than an unpretentious collection of raw material. To my utter astonishment Zinoviev took these documents and practically made his report from them: "Comrades, during the past year we've been working on this and that problem, and we've accomplished this and that . . ."

I was stupefied. A real chief would have focused on the key problems of life in the country and progress in the Revolution. Instead, his report was superficial. By chance my documents served as the framework for this accountant's kind of report. From this I was sure that Zinoviev lacked not only depth but range. It is difficult to say why but Zinoviev was not liked in the Party. He had faults: he liked the perquisites of his position. He always had his claque around him. He was a poltroon, a schemer without political weight. Those around him weren't worth much more, and some were much worse. The popular characterizations doing the rounds among Party leaders about him (and Stalin too) weren't favorable: "Beware of Zinoviev and Stalin. Stalin will betray you and Zinoviev will abandon you."

He shared a common trait with Lenin and Stalin: a fevered thirst for power. It wasn't the devouring passion that it was with Stalin. Zinoviev liked the good things of life, but power was of great importance to him; not at all like Kamenev, who had little ambition.

To his misfortune Kamenev was in Zinoviev's shadow and was led by him into all his political conspiracies. Kamenev was a good man, undemanding, and with quite a "bourgeois" character. Although he was an old Bolshevik, he wasn't a coward. He accepted the risks that go with revolutionary work and had been arrested several times. He was exiled during the war and only liberated by the Revolution. That was when he fell back into the orbit of Zinoviev and followed him everywhere, especially against Lenin's plan to take power. Kamenev proposed a coalition government in alliance with other political parties, and he resigned. However, he was soon back with Zinoviev, directing the Moscow Soviet, then becoming one of Lenin's best economic assistants. When Lenin was ill, he directed all economic affairs. Zinoviev brought him into the *Troika*, and for three years Kamenev replaced Lenin as head of all administrative organs: he presided over the Politburo, Sovnarkom, and the Council of Labor and Defense.

He was an intelligent, educated man with the skills of a good statesman (today we'd say a good technocrat). Had there not been communism he could have been a good socialist minister in a "capitalist" country. His wife was Trotsky's sister, Olga. His son, Liutik, while still young was already clearly on the road to being in the Party's "decomposed bourgeois" group: drunks, young actresses, and those who took advantage of their family position. There were still some idealists in the Party, and they were indignant. One play was even produced in a Moscow theater, *The Son of the Peoples' Commissar*, which mocked Liutik Kamenev. According to several sources it wasn't hard to divine about whom the play was written. The propaganda section of the Central Committee telephoned

Kanner to get instructions, and Kanner asked Stalin what should be done about the play. Stalin replied, "Let it go on playing." Kamenev, however, brought the problem of prohibiting this play, which discredited a Politburo member, to the *Troika*. Zinoviev said it would be best not to draw attention to it. By prohibiting the play, Kamenev would be admitting that it referred to him. Zinoviev recalled the story of *Messieurs Obmanov*, a novel by the revolutionary writer Aleksandr Valentinovich Amfiteatrov, which grossly libeled the Tsar's Romanov family. Although the text contained a mass of details by which it was clear of whom the author wrote, the Tsar thought it unwise to recognize it was about his family by banning it, so it circulated freely. "Thank you, Henry," replied Kamenev (alluding to Shakespeare), "we know how that ended" (quoting himself). It was decided not to interdict the play but rather to use whatever pressure was necessary to have it withdrawn from the repertoire.

In the field of intrigues, trickery, and tenacity Kamenev was altogether weak. Officially he was master of Moscow: the capital was considered his fiefdom, as was Leningrad considered to be Zinoviev's. Zinoviev had organized his clan in Leningrad, putting his own men in key posts, and he had the second capital of the country well in hand. By contrast Kamenev knew nothing of such techniques, had no clan, and kept his place in Moscow by force of inertia. We'll soon see how he lost it (along with all the rest).

Olga Davydovna was head of VOKS (the department of foreign cultural relations). This organization subsidized Soviet authors who wrote for foreign publication—trusted people like Mayakovsky and Ehrenburg—and foreign authors who came to admire the Soviet Potemkin villages, as well as other "intellectual" revolutionary writers.[1] Her organization resembled a great big mise-en-scène for the theater [we'd now call it disinformation], and Olga did very well at it.[2]

Among the other members of the Politburo neither Rykov nor Tomsky were leaders, nor did they pretend to be. Before the Revolution Rykov was a clandestine activist in Russia and joined Lenin in exile. He became interior minister after the Revolution, but the position didn't suit him at all. The Revolution demanded a Cheka which shot people, whereas Rykov was a peaceful, talented, and intelligent technocrat. He became president of the Supreme National Economic Council and, after Lenin's death, nominal chief of government. He had a weak point, however: he liked to drink, and the population started calling vodka "rykovka," which irritated him. When drinking in his small circle of Soviet dignitaries, he would say with his usual stutter: "I d . . . don't k . . . know why they c . . . call it rykovka." He had no special gifts or flaws, but incontestably he had common sense. That is why he was lost when Stalin undertook his horrible collectivization. Despite his customary restraint and his caution, he couldn't accept such destruction of the peasantry and of agriculture. He went into [open] opposition against Stalin, which led to the basement of the Lubyanka. He was brought down in 1938, with all the humiliating farce that Stalin so enjoyed heaping on his victims before he exterminated them.

Tomsky was head of the Soviet trade unions. He came into the Central Committee in 1919, the Orgburo in 1921, and the Politburo in 1922. He was a prudent member of the Central Committee and played no part in the fight for power; he went over to the winning side when it was clear who had won. He had a disability: he was hard of hearing. When a problem of particular interest to him was discussed at Politburo sessions, he would place himself squarely in front of the speaker. He was as insignificant a man as was the institution he led in the Soviet system. Even though he was on Stalin's side, the day came when he was an embarrassment to Stalin because he was an old Bolshevik from Lenin's time, aware of everything about Stalin. Despite all his exterior signs of submission, privately Tomsky didn't perceive Stalin as having any qualities of "great and wise" chief. Although he remained outside the opposition and its intrigues, in 1936 Stalin decided to liquidate Tomsky as well. He didn't, however, follow in the footsteps of other Stalin victims: when they came to arrest him, he shot himself.

Bukharin was one of the most capable members of the Politburo. Keen and witty, he was greatly liked in the Party. Lenin, in his Testament, characterized him as the Party's favorite. Bukharin was an old Leninist who lived in Lenin's entourage in exile but was able to stay out of most of the intrigues and internecine quarrels. He was above all a writer, a journalist, and a publicist. Editor in chief of *Pravda*, he made it into a journal that constantly set the tone of the Party line. A longtime member of the Central Committee, he didn't achieve Politburo candidate membership until 1921, as a result of the Tenth Congress. Then he was third candidate, but the following year the Eleventh Congress made him first candidate. He was in effect a member, however, because of Lenin's absence due to illness. After Lenin's death he was elected a full Politburo member.

Bukharin was wrongly considered by the Party to be a dogmatist and an academic. In truth he was neither dogmatic nor a theoretician. During the two first years of the communist regime he thought (along with all the other leaders) that a new communist society was being built. As he was a good popular writer, he wrote a book exposing all the nonsense in Marxism: *The Economy of the Transition Period*. Then, in collaboration with

Preobrazhensky, he wrote the very popular *ABC of Communism,* which enabled the whole Party, in particular the young members, to learn what communism was. In effect these works contained what all the leaders were saying then, including Lenin. But when the rapid failure of communism became evident and Lenin had to install NEP, the other leaders had the advantage of not having written such books. Bukharin and his premature communist society had to be disavowed and the two books, repurchased on the sly, were gathered up and destroyed. That was why Bukharin had the label dogmatist and theoretician pinned on him, whereas in fact he had simply had bad luck. He was a writer, setting down what others thought and said. The political wind had changed, but whereas spoken words are gone, written words remain. Bukharin came out of it with a reputation of fabricating theories which didn't survive reality.

Bukharin was intelligent and capable. He never came out with Marxist absurdities at Politburo sessions, but to the contrary he spoke with good sense, pertinently and with spirited intellect. He kept his profound aspirations to power well hidden. In this respect he was an apt pupil of Lenin, whose teachings had not been without use to him. However, during the period when everything was decided by capturing the Party apparatus, he had no chance to play any but a secondary role with the possibility of participating in the conspiracies of the other Party leaders. In any event the first, difficult choice between Zinoviev and Stalin was no problem to him: he skipped over this step lightly and allied himself with the winner.

At the Institute of the Red Professorate, a hotbed of young Party opportunists who were intent on knowing which horse to back, the majority favored Bukharin. They were drawn to his talent. Trotsky also had talent, but he was clearly beaten. Zinoviev wasn't considered a chief, and Stalin had neither their respect nor their confidence. A group of young Party members, cultivated and often very bright, formed around Bukharin. For the several years while Bukharin was in the upper leadership, many of them were recruited into the cadres because of their excellence: chiefs of the propaganda and the press sections of the Central Committee, editors of *Pravda,* heads of history or Soviet philosophy sections, and so on. They included people like Sten, the Slepkov brothers, Astrov, Maretsky, Stetsky, Karev, Lominadze, Pospelov, Mitin, etc., known as the Bukharin group. For several years they set the line for the media, but when Bukharin fell they were sacked mercilessly. In 1932 most of them were expelled from the Party, and in 1937–38 they were shot.[3]

Because he hadn't taken Zinoviev's side in the decisive struggle of 1925–6, Bukharin was rewarded with Zinoviev's place in the Comintern. For Stalin this was a temporary assignment. It displeased him that a

Russian member of the Politburo should head the Comintern. Strictly speaking the Comintern was the supreme organ of world communism and so, in principle, was more important than Stalin. Soon Bukharin was replaced by Molotov, more docile, and then by the Bulgarian, Georgy Dmitrov.[4]

It is to Bukharin's credit that he didn't accept Stalin's butchery: starting the march toward communism by destroying the peasantry. Bukharin could have joined the new boss's chorus, along with Molotov and Kaganovich, especially as he had no sympathy for the Trotsky-Zinoviev opposition. He saw no great difference between their policies and those of Stalin. When Stalin definitively chose the route of abolition of NEP and destruction of the peasantry, Bukharin took a firm position against him. Then Stalin distanced him from power, and Bukharin went into the opposition. However, even though Stalin's partisans branded him a Trotskyite, the alliance was never a fact. Bukharin remained as far from the Trotsky-Zinoviev bloc as he was from Stalin's policies. For many years Stalin persecuted Bukharin only moderately and didn't expel him from the Central Committee until 1937. His turn came, however, in March 1938, when he too went down to the Lubyanka basement, after the usual Stalin parody of justice.

The 1976 reader of the official history of the CPSU has the right to be astonished. Stalin was knocked off his pedestal years ago, and Stalingrad has been Volgograd for a long time. Why then haven't the inept and absurd accusations against Bukharin and a large number of other leading communists been cleaned up? Especially since a certain number of Party personalities have been "rehabilitated," with public acknowledgment that the accusations against them by Stalin's underlings were false.

Here is the reason why some have been "rehabilitated" and others not.

The Party has established once and for all the principle that it is never wrong and always right. It never waivers from this principle, and all its history is based on that.[5] Let's look at the case of Bukharin, an important and competent Party personality. Suppose that at important decision-making moments he gave useful and sensible advice to the Party. That would have been rejected by the various Party congresses and conferences, as well as by the Central Committee plenums. In other words the assembly of Stalin's henchmen, trembling before him, adopted decisions which he dictated. Those became "decisions" of the various congresses and conferences. Had Stalin required diametrically opposite decisions, the meetings would have given them to him by voting his line with "enthusiasm" and "ovations without end." Consequently to pretend that those decisions were made by the congresses or the conferences is pure fiction. Both the

Party leaders and the historians know this very well. However, among the many types of lies on which the Communist Party is built and lives, this one has its place. Its aim is to reinforce the principle that the Party is always right and never wrong. No matter that it was not then a Party but rather a collection of frightened lackeys and terrorists who jumped to Stalin's tune. It was the Party's infallible decision to follow its own lies. Bukharin was opposed to this and so he was anathema to them and will always remain an enemy in Party history. Read it. It explains endlessly that Bukharin was always wrong, always made mistakes, always agitated against the Party, etc. It's true that they've revised the more absurd diatribes against him, for example where second-rate hack writers and "historical" film script authors like Eisenstein depicted the wise and ingenious Stalin striding majestically through history's pages while the little, ignoble traitor Bukharin ran behind him squeaking, "We must take care of the kulaks, or we're lost . . ." The style has changed, but the rehabilitation of Bukharin, requiring admitting that he was ignobly calumnied, will always be impossible.

For the same reason it is impossible to rehabilitate all important members of the Party against whom Stalin-era Party sessions adopted resolutions.

In contrast, let's take the cases of army marshals M. N. Tukhachevsky, Vasily Konstantinovich Blucher, and Aleksandr Ilich Egorov.[6] They were outside Party life and played no role in it. Stalin judged it useful to shoot them, so he had them labeled spies, like Trotsky, for the Germans, Japanese, or others. But the congresses and conferences of the Party didn't accuse them of any deviation. So, when the time came to admit that Stalin had gone a bit too far in his cult of personality, there was no reason not to rehabilitate them. There had been a mistake (by Stalin, or Yezhov, or another), but it was a human error or a mistake by a government organ, not a Party error. So the matter could be revised and the Party's infallibility was not in question.

That's how those Party members who weren't highly visible in the opposition can be rehabilitated, while it's absolutely impossible to rehabilitate others such as Trotsky and Zinoviev. The founder of the Red Army and the first president of the Comintern will continue to figure among the foreign spies and enemies of communism.

If this should ever change, and one fine day it becomes possible in the Party to say and write the truth about these people, there would be every reason to judge that it is no longer a communist party.[7]

A few words on the two other candidate members of Lenin's Politburo: Kalinin and Molotov.[8]

There's not much to be said about Kalinin. He was an absolutely colorless personality, an "all-Russian starosta" [respected village elder] decoration whom Lenin mistakenly brought into the Politburo. The other members tolerated him but had no respect for him. He fulfilled his decorative duties at official functions, but he never tried to exercise independent judgment. He simply obeyed those at the top. In order to have incriminating documents on hand against him in time of need, the OGPU sent him young ballerinas from the Bolshoi Theater, with prior approval from Kanner. For lack of experience, Kalinin was content with the most third-rate conquests. The OGPU organized them against him purely out of zeal, for they had no use whatsoever. He never dared to go up against the established power. Even later, when Stalin was undertaking the massive peasant exterminations, Kalinin, who knew the countryside well, merely grumbled. The rest of the Politburo, used to him, paid no attention. In sum he was afraid and insignificant, which is why he was able to survive the Stalin era and die in his bed, even earning a change in the name of the town of Koenigsberg to Kaliningrad. In 1937 Stalin ordered his wife arrested, but Kalinin did nothing.

I've spoken abut Molotov already. He played a very important role in the ascent of Stalin to supreme power. He himself didn't aspire to the top position, although he came very close to it. In March 1921 he was elected executive secretary of the Central Committee and candidate member of the Politburo. For a year he had all the apparatus of the Central Committee in his hands, but in March 1922, when Zinoviev organized the *Troika*, the latter wanted Stalin in charge of the Central Committee and appointed him general secretary. This pushed Molotov back down a rung, as second secretary of the Central Committee. Zinoviev's formula was that he wished to get rid of Trotsky, of whom Stalin was a ferocious enemy. Zinoviev and Kamenev preferred Stalin, so Molotov not only bowed to them but became a loyal Stalin lieutenant forever. Later, Molotov avenged himself delightedly on Zinoviev and Kamenev. On Trotsky also, whom he disliked because Trotsky lived in an abstract world and made of Molotov the incarnation of the "degenerate Party bureaucracy."

From then on Molotov always followed Stalin's lead. He handpicked the apparatchiks, the territorial and provincial committee secretaries, and worked to create Stalin's Central Committee majority. When Stalin needed him, he became president of Sovnarkom and of the Council for Labor and Defense, later, head of the Comintern and even foreign minister.

It's worth noting that Stalin used the same technique on Molotov as he used on a large number of his other assistants: he had his wife arrested, while Molotov wasn't himself disgraced. Stalin did the same with Kalinin and Poskrebyshev, as we've already seen. Molotov's wife was Jewish. Under the Party name [Polina] Zhemchuvnina ("Pearl") she had the important Party job of running the perfume industry. Stalin had her arrested and exiled, an exile that was much more brutal than the tsarist ones. Molotov waited for her patiently and without question, but that's not at all surprising. What is remarkable is that after Stalin's death she returned from exile and they both remained loyal Stalinists. Molotov disapproved the destalinization program of Khrushchev. Kaganovich, Malenkov, and Molotov were convinced Stalinists, and at the first opportunity (1957) they tried to overthrow Khrushchev. They lost, and it cost them all their jobs in the Party hierarchy from which they were definitively cast out.

Why did Molotov support a return to the Stalin methods? Was it nostalgia for the time when they had the power of Ghengis Khan and everybody in the country trembled and was afraid to speak? Perhaps he made a more realistic assessment. To maintain itself, the communist regime has need of violence, of a gigantic police apparatus, of a system of terror. The stronger the terror, the more secure is the regime. In the Stalin epoch people were even afraid that a heretical thought might come into their heads, and there was no question of even the slightest action against the regime.

Khrushchev loosened the screw and people began to think, to speak, to dissent. Where could that lead? In Stalin's time there were no such risks.

Perhaps Molotov is a good example of what communism does to people. I worked with him a lot. He was a very conscientious bureaucrat, not brilliant but an extremely hard worker, calm and in command of himself. He was always kind and amiable with me. He was always very polite to people, never gross or arrogant or cruel and showed no desire to humiliate or crush anyone.

Ten years later, Stalin wasn't happy approving by himself the lists of people to be arrested and jailed or shot. He arranged, cautiously, that the lists went through the hands of Molotov and Kaganovich. Molotov signed them under Stalin's signature. If a name caught his attention, he might write next to it, "V.M.N. [*Vysshaia mera nakazaniia*]." That meant supreme punishment measure. It was enough to send the person to be shot.

Was it mimicry of Stalin? Was Molotov drunk with power . . . to write three letters and man is destroyed? How many thousands of assassinations did this peaceful bureaucrat approve on those lists, without the slightest remorse? Maybe he thought it would have been safer to return to Stalin's way of doing things.[9]

Put a man in Stalin's hands, raise him in a society where men are wolves toward each other, and he will watch millions die in atrocious suffering with indifference. Form a simple bureaucrat in a system with humane values, and he will work all night to find a way to help peasants who've had a bad harvest. The contrast of how men act was often in my mind when I was in the high Bolshevik strata. For Molotov I have a special sentiment.

Fifty years after I was a witness to all that passed at the Bolshevik summit, of those who saw it all only Molotov is still alive. Even Kaganovich wasn't at the summit in the 1920s, which is the era I'm addressing. Only Molotov was at the very top for the next thirty years after I left. But he can not write or publish a single line on this subject that would disagree with the official lies.

He is now [1976] eighty-six years old and after having walked with Stalin on top of millions of cadavers, he will probably die peacefully in his bed, doubtless without even thinking that he had an unpleasant life.[10]

12. Stalin's Coup d'Etat

First trip abroad. The Economic and Finance Bureau of the Peoples' Commissariat of Finances. Kondratiev. The year 1925. The struggle between Stalin and Zinoviev. Preparation for the Congress. The Congress. The coup d'état. Another ramification of the coup d'état.

In addition to my Central Committee work, I worked at the Supreme Council for Physical Culture and at Narkomfin (the Peoples' Commissariat for Finances). At the Supreme Council it was more like entertainment than work. I participated in Presidium meetings and ran two sections: in summer, light athletics, and in winter, skiing and ice skating. The work in the Presidium posed no problems. The president of the Supreme Council, N. A. Semashko (also peoples' commissar for public health) was an intelligent and cultivated man with whom it was easy to work. More than that, he understood very well that he had to hew to the Central Committee's line, and it was I who set that line. N. V. Krylenko, former army commander in chief, then a bloodthirsty procurator of the (Russian) republic, now peoples' commissar for justice, attended the Presidium meetings. He was a fanatic chess player, so we put him at the head of the chess section. That was why he came. While we discussed other problems and he had nothing to do, I would start a game with him on a piece of paper, noting each move down. But after seven or eight moves he could no longer play without seeing a board. So he would take a small traveling set out of his briefcase and use it. Semashko would look reproachful, but it wasn't possible to drag Krylenko, who hated losing, from his chess game.

The winter sports section gave me the occasion to make my first trip abroad. Because Soviet skates and skis were still of very poor quality, it was decided to buy some in Norway. The council asked me to go there for a short time, and see what should be purchased. In December 1924 I made a brief trip, which impressed me greatly. It was my first time abroad, and I found a normal, humane life that was totally different from Soviet life.

The three Scandinavian countries in which I traveled, Finland, Norway, and Sweden, had something unknown in Soviet Russia. The people were extremely honest and frank. I couldn't get used to it right away. In Norway I wanted to visit the Oslo area. Near the capital is the Holmen-kollen, much used for winter sports and hiking. I went up it with a Soviet embassy employee as guide. It was not very cold, and as we were warmly dressed, the climb made us too hot. My guide took off his heavy woolen sweater, put it on a rock beside the trail, wrote something on a piece of paper and set a stone on top to keep it down. I asked him what he was doing. "I'm too hot," he said. "I'll leave my sweater here and pick it up on the way back. "Well, you can say good-bye to it," I said. "No," said he. "I've left a note which says this sweater isn't lost, please don't touch it." I thought it a strange farce. The trail was crowded, and we came back down two hours later. The sweater was still there. My guide explained that here nothing was ever stolen. If there were a theft in town, it usually turned out to be by a sailor from a foreign ship. In the Finnish countryside there weren't even locks on the doors. Theft was unknown.

In Sweden, on a Sunday, I was with Soviet Embassy Counselor Asmus and his wife Koroleva. They had just arrived from Russia with their seven-year-old son. A workers' protest demonstration against something passed in front of the embassy, well-dressed, dignified people, walking calmly and deliberately. The little boy of seven watched for a long time through the window, then asked his mother, "Where are all these bourgeoisie going?"

On the way home, I crossed the Soviet frontier at Beloostrov, thirty kilometers from Leningrad. The conductor reminded us, "Citizens, you are already in Soviet Russia. Watch your baggage." I was watching the countryside through the window. I had a glove on one hand, and I put the other one on the seat. An instant later I discovered my second glove had already disappeared.

I returned to Soviet life. At Narkomfin there were regular and large expenses for new electric light bulbs. There was a great shortage of light bulbs in Russia, and the Narkomfin employees were snitching them and taking them home. Peoples' Commissar Sokolnikov found an ingenious solution: he asked the factory to etch on each bulb "Stolen from Narkom-fin." The thefts stopped at once.

I came back from Scandinavia with the strange impression of having stuck my head out of the window and breathed fresh air.

In contrast with the Supreme Council for Physical Culture, my work at Narkomfin was serious and it interested me a lot.

Before the Revolution, the Ministry of Finance had a committee of the best specialists in finance, mostly professors. Sokolnikov created a Narkomfin bureau of economy and finances, which replaced the committee. The bureau was divided into an institute for economic research and an institute for applied economics. He invited the best specialists to participate, mostly members of the former committee. There were no Marxists or communists among them. Sokolnikov created good working conditions for them, and their advice was much appreciated. Based on their advice, a complex and difficult monetary reform was brilliantly undertaken. A solid gold–based ruble was created and national finances put in order. This bureau was supervised by Narkomfin collegium member Professor Mechislav Genrikhovich Bronsky.[1] When I asked Sokolnikov if Bronsky really was a professor, he replied smiling, "Anyone can represent himself as a professor, until he's proven wrong." Bronsky was a very cultivated and erudite Polish Jew, a former émigré who had been in exile with Lenin and had been a journalist. He had very little Bolshevik spirit and no administrative talent. He did little to supervise the bureau. His principal occupation and the only one that interested him was editing a thick monthly magazine entitled *Socialist Economics*. Bronsky claimed, probably with reason, that it was the best economic review in Soviet Russia. He also directed the daily *Finance Journal*. He left the bureau to its own devices, and things weren't working well. Sokolnikov asked me to take it over. He thought my Politburo experience in economics would enable me to bring the bureau's activities more in line with daily practical economics. In fact, insofar as they were far from the organs which made practical decisions, the bureau's professors had a tendency to do more abstract theoretical work than applied work.

I was already anticommunist when I took the job. All the professors were in fact anticommunist also, but they considered me an enemy who was loyal to the regime. Even more amusing was that they thought they could do something useful for the country while working with the regime. I was better informed than they about that.

In any event the fact that they'd been given a young communist as their boss was viewed as a serious menace to their freedom and independence. The director of the Economic Research Institute came to see Sokolnikov on their behalf and said they planned to quit Narkomfin because they couldn't work for a young communist who, simply because of his age, could not command their obedience. Sokolnikov smiled and said, "If you wish, we'll discuss it in a month. You're quite wrong about your new boss."

After the first two weeks everything changed. The old, very experienced professors who had been advisors to the tsarist ministry of finance, Genzel, Sokolov, and Shmelev, discovered with astonishment during institute meetings that not only did I know in depth all the economic and fiscal problems but I had a great advantage over them: I knew what solutions were politically acceptable to the government. Thanks to my Politburo work I knew how the work should be directed in practical terms. At meetings of the Institute for Applied Economics I provided useful indications as to how the work should best be oriented. Even in their own fields, where they considered themselves unequaled experts, I was in fact on a par with them. From the first meeting I urged better market estimating by forecasting seasonal changes in the usability of roads for horsedrawn transport, one of the more effective means of predicting the markets for food products. In addition we got along very well because the local Party cell and Party authorities, wishing to keep an eye on these "suspect experts" so as to demonstrate their communist vigilance, were watching them very closely. I was an authority figure to the local communists because of my Central Committee status, so I was able to chastise them and make them leave the professors in peace.

Two weeks later Shmelev told Sokolnikov that the work was going very smoothly and they wished to withdraw their objections to their new chief.

I also developed excellent rapport with Bronsky. He was a very likable man, with almost no sympathy for Bolshevism. He lived in part of the large apartment where Veniamin Sverdlov and his wife lived, whom I visited a lot.

One of the nicest of my new subordinates was the director of the Institute of Applied Economics, Professor Nikolai Dmitrievich Kondratiev. He also worked in the agricultural section of Gosplan, the state planning committee. He was a prominent scholar, a man of considerable intelligence. He created the institute, and his understanding of the evolution of the national economy and his advice on it were of great value to Narkomfin and other government organs dealing with the economy. His work, of course, was also based on the naïve illusion that it was possible to collaborate with the Bolshevik regime. "They" couldn't be complete idiots; they must surely understand that experts and competents were useful and even necessary. Like the other expert advisors to Narkomfin he believed in the value of his work and he didn't understand the barbarous nature of communism.

He soon learned with what he was dealing. At Gosplan he wanted to introduce a reasonable agricultural policy. He started from the basis that if one wanted to increase agricultural production, it was unwise constantly to stir up the parasites and hangers-on against the diligent working peasants (the target of the Bolshevik rural "class war"). Instead, they should be allowed to work peacefully.

However, the Gosplan communist cell, with no Bazhanov to hinder it, took on Kondratiev. Stories went around that he favored renouncing the Bolshevik struggle in the countryside, that his cronies wanted to back the kulaks. There was an uproar. Rumors flew, articles appeared in *Pravda,* and a crusade against "Kondratiev's men" was declared. Little communists of no weight tried to make their careers thanks to their "vigilance in discovering and unmasking a hidden class enemy." Poor Kondratiev, not given the chance by *Pravda* to respond to all this press persecution, was shaken. The Narkomfin cell wanted to go after him too, taking their lead from *Pravda,* but I wouldn't let them. I explained that all this was a problem of Gosplan's agricultural section, a problem of a solely agricultural nature, whereas at Narkomfin Kondratiev worked on quite different problems: applied economics, which had no connection with his political ideas about the peasantry. Here, his work was useful and irreproachable, and he must be left in peace. As long as I was at Narkomfin they didn't dare persecute him. He was, however, already being watched on a national level. After collectivization was put into effect, agriculture was ruined, production fell off, and there was famine. Then, in line with established communist custom, enemy scapegoats had to be discovered and blamed for the problem.

In 1930 the OGPU "discovered" the absolutely absurd chekist invention "the party of the toiling peasantry." This mythical party was led by Kondratiev, assisted by professors Chaianov[2] and Yurovsky (the latter being a Jewish specialist in foreign exchange and monetary circulation who had never had anything to do with peasants or the peasantry). The OGPU was flattering: the Party had one or two hundred thousand members. A show trial was prepared to tell the country that the lack of bread was due to sabotage perpetrated by Kondratiev and his supporters. Poor Kondratiev would, of course, have to admit all his crimes to the court. At the last minute, however, Stalin decided it wasn't sufficiently convincing. He canceled the trial and ordered the OGPU to condemn the leaders and members of the "party of the toiling peasantry" by means of a closed verdict pronounced by a troika of three chekists. They were sent to a Soviet extermination camp. That's how Kondratiev, a great sage and remarkable man, perished. He died mostly because he was a victim of the illusion that he could work with the communists and the Soviet regime, doing something useful for the country. Alas, for him it was a profound error. The regime used people like him while they were useful, then exterminated them brutally when the regime wanted to find a scapegoat upon whom to pin responsibility for their destructive, senseless, and absurd Marxist policies.

The year 1925 saw the power struggle between Zinoviev and Stalin. The *Troika*, temporarily reestablished to conduct the fight against Trotsky, was definitively dissolved in March. During April Politburo meetings Zinoviev and Kamenev violently attacked Stalin's theory of "building socialism in one country." The *Troika* didn't meet again, and Stalin alone approved the agenda for each Politburo meeting. For several months the Politburo functioned as a collegiate body, outwardly under the direction of Zinoviev and Kamenev. This apparent leadership was especially due to Stalin's customary reticence at meetings, a result of his lack of knowledge about most of the problems discussed. Kamenev, still in his old job at the head of the entire national economy, was very involved because economic problems occupied much of the Politburo's time. Trotsky made a show of participating in the current work, and a precarious peace reigned in the Politburo.

Stalin wasn't sure that the majority of the Central Committee members would follow him, so he waited for the next congress and didn't try to fight it out in the Central Committee plenary sessions. He did his clandestine preparatory work and not only didn't force things but did all in his power to delay the congress. In summer, as usual, the political scene was quite calm. In autumn, however, Trotsky published his brochure *Toward Socialism, or toward Capitalism?* This reopened his fight against the majority of the Central Committee which, in turn, began to divide up. Zinoviev wished to keep his role as political leader, so he responded with his article *Leninism*, introducing his theory of the philosophy of equality. At the start of October the Politburo had to fix the date of the congress and decide who would present the Central Committee's political report to the congress. It was resolved to have the congress in mid-December, and on a proposal by Molotov, the Politburo majority voted that the political report be given by Stalin. Zinoviev and Kamenev had lost their majority in the Politburo. They immediately requested a discussion, but in the Central Committee plenum that took place right afterward, it was apparent that all Stalin's preparatory work had borne fruit. The plenum confirmed that Stalin would give the political report, and it refused to open the discussion that Zinoviev considered his main chance. In addition the plenum presented itself as attributing the greatest importance to "Party work among the poor peasants" and, to move along the campaign against Zinoviev and Kamenev, simultaneously condemned all deviations "against the poor peasants [*bedniaki*]," deviations to the right (the kulak variants) and to the left (those who opposed the middle peasants [*seredniaki*]). On the basis of this resolution the Party apparatus set out to persecute the "new opposition" without surcease. As usual, before the congress, the Central Committee was required to publish the provisional theses developed for the congress, upon the basis of which it would open its deliberations. Stalin and Molotov completely sidestepped all such discussion (Stalin feared political debate), and replaced them with a simple "study in depth" of the resolutions of the October plenum. It was on the basis of this study that the congress would have its elections. Only on 15 December did the Central Committee plenum ratify the theses destined for the congress, which opened 18 December.

In December the various Party organs and meetings began engaging in polemics. Election of delegates to the congress, which took place early in December in the territorial and provincial Party conferences, decided in advance the composition of the congress and thus the defeat of Zinoviev. Being unable to control the entire local Party apparatus (which only Stalin and Molotov could do, in the bosom of the Central Committee), Zinoviev and Kamenev counted on the support of the three most important ones: those of Moscow, Leningrad, and the Ukraine. Kaganovich, sent in his role as secretary of the central committee of the Ukrainian communist party, did all that was necessary down there to ensure that the Ukrainian organization was lost to Zinoviev and Kamenev. By contrast Zinoviev had the Leningrad organization well in hand even though Stalin had managed to remove Leningrad committee secretary Pyotr Zalutsky, who had taken a position against him too soon and too violently. Zalutsky had accused Stalin, Molotov, and their majority of "thermidorean degeneracy," but Grigory Eremeievich Evdokimov, secretary of the northwest bureau of the Central Committee, was the right-hand man of Zinoviev and had the Leningrad organization behind him.

The passing of the most important organization—Moscow—to Stalin's side was a totally unexpected and catastrophic blow to Zinoviev and Kamenev. The treachery of Nikolai A. Uglanov, recruited with skill and timeliness by Stalin, was at the root of this about-face.

I've already related how, at the end of 1923 when the right opposition broke out, the Politburo was unhappy with Moscow Party committee first secretary Zelensky. During the summer of 1924 the *Troika* agreed to appoint him first secretary of the Central Committee's Central Asian bureau. The whole *Troika* thought him unfit for the Moscow job. The question then was who to place at the head of the Moscow organization, the Party's most important one? Kamenev, having as usual little interest in organizational matters, left the initiative to Zinoviev. Stalin would have preferred Kaganovich for the job, but Zinoviev, then still calling the shots as number one, wanted his own man as secretary of the Moscow commit-tee. He proposed Uglanov for the position. The matter came up before the Politburo at a session which I, as usual, attended.

In 1922 Uglanov had worked with Zinoviev in Leningrad. He was devoted to Zinoviev, and the latter insisted on him as the candidate for first secretary of the Nizhnii-Novgorod provincial committee. It was the early days of the *Troika*. Stalin was still not raising his voice on every issue, and he had to accept the nomination. Right afterward, however, Stalin and Molotov started to work on Uglanov. One day in the summer of 1924 I was looking for Stalin and found him in the room that separated the offices of Stalin and Molotov. They were there with Uglanov, who went pale when he saw me and looked very agitated. Stalin reassured him, "It's Comrade Bazhanov, secretary of the Politburo. Don't be afraid, we have no secrets from him. He's aware of all our activities." Nevertheless Uglanov had trouble calming down.

I understood at once what was afoot. The evening before, when Zinov-iev had proposed to the *Troika* that Uglanov run the Moscow organiza-tion, Stalin had asked if he was up to the job of running this key organ. Zinoviev insisted that he was, whereupon Stalin pretended to be against and accepted the decision with bad grace. In reality Uglanov had already been worked over by Molotov, and what I had interrupted was a secret pact against Zinoviev being concluded between Stalin and Uglanov.

Abiding by the pact, Uglanov played a double role for eighteen months, assuring Zinoviev and Kamenev of his loyalty and, during the second half of 1925, of his hostility toward Stalin. In fact he had selected and formed up the cadre he needed and, at the 5 December conference of the Moscow Party which preceded the congress, he suddenly switched to Stalin's side, taking with him all the Moscow Party leaders, bag and baggage. It was the final blow that sealed Zinoviev's defeat.

The events of the Fourteenth Congress that December are known. Stalin presented a drab, boring political report. The Leningrad delegation requested that Zinoviev help present the report, and that was agreed upon but it changed nothing. The entire congress, except for Zinoviev's Lenin-grad delegates, voted docilely for Stalin. Kamenev's report on "problems of building today's economy" was withdrawn. Apart from Zinoviev, the opposition had the votes of Kamenev, Sokolnikov, Evdokimov, and Mi-khail Mikhailovich Lashevich only. (Evdokimov was shot in 1936, and Lashevich committed suicide in 1928.)[3]

Even in the heart of the Leningrad delegation there were those who hastened to switch to the winner's side. Among them were N. M. Shver-nik, Leningrad committee secretary; Moskvin, assistant to the secretary of the Central Committee's northwest bureau, and N. P. Komarov, president of the executive committee of the soviets of Leningrad province.

Trotsky remained silent at the congress and watched the downfall of his principal enemy, Zinoviev, with malicious pleasure. Four months later, in April 1926, Zinoviev and Kamenev came to Trotsky, hat in hand, to join him in forming a new opposition bloc.

The congress elected the new Central Committee. Its majority was for Stalin, and he became the Party chief. The real Stalin era didn't begin right then, however, since it wasn't possible to change everything all at once. Trotsky, Zinoviev, and Kamenev were reelected to the Central Committee. Then, starting at the first Central Committee plenum after the congress, in January 1926, all sorts of organizational changes were made. Kamenev was removed from his position as head of the national economy, his post as president of the Council on Labor and Defense, and his vice presidency of the USSR Sovnarkom. Also, he was demoted from full to candidate member of the Politburo. Rykov replaced him as president of the Council on Labor and Defense. The Politburo was enlarged, Molotov and Kalinin going from candidate to full membership. Voroshilov came straight in as a full member, and Trotsky and Zinoviev kept their seats. In addition to Kamenev and Dzerzhinsky, who was already a candidate member, new candidates were Rudzutak, Uglanov (to reward him for his deception), and Grigory Ivanovich Petrovsky (the official head of the Soviet regime in the Ukraine). Stalin was reelected general secretary with Molotov as second secretary, Uglanov third secretary, and Stanislas Kossior fourth secretary. Stalin appointed Sergei Mironovich Kirov (former Azerbaijan central committee secretary) to be Leningrad central committee secretary.

The year 1926 was marked by progressive elimination of the "new opposition." The world knew that there had been a change in direction of communist Russia and of world communism. But few people understood that Stalin had executed a veritable coup d'état that brought in entirely new people to rule Russia and communism. I will explain.

Before the Revolution the Jews of Russia, whose rights were limited, were mostly in the ranks of the opposition. Young Jews furnished a large number of the cadres in revolutionary parties and organizations. Jews had always played an important role in the leadership of these parties. The Bolshevik party was no exception to this rule, and almost half its Central Committee members were Jews.

After the Revolution all the principal levers of power were quickly concentrated in this group of Central Committee Jews. Doubtless there was at play a Jewish habit from the secular diaspora, of sticking tightly together. The Russians didn't have this custom. In any event all the central power positions were in the hands of Jews: Trotsky, Red Army head and the second political figure (after Lenin); Sverdlov, official head of state and until his death Lenin's principal assistant; Zinoviev, head of the Comintern and simultaneously all-powerful chief of Leningrad, the second capital; Kamenev, Lenin's first assistant in Sovnarkom, effective head of the Soviet economy, and supposedly chief of the principal capital, Moscow. Thus, whereas they had less than half the Central Committee, the Jews had much more power and influence than the non-Jews.

This situation lasted from 1917 to the end of 1925. At the Fourteenth Congress Stalin not only removed from central power the Jewish Party leaders but took a decisive step toward removing Jews entirely from the central power structure. At the next congress, two years later (December 1927), Trotsky, Zinoviev, and Kamenev were expelled from the Party.

Thereafter very few Jews were elected to the new Central Committee. Jews never got back into the ruling circle, with a very few exceptions. There were always Kaganovich and Mekhlis, openly asserting that they didn't consider themselves Jews. In the years that followed, Stalin allowed a sprinkling of Jews to become candidate members of the Central Committee, the more docile ones like Yagoda who were obedient to his orders. Later, however, he had them shot as well. During the last decades no Jew has been brought into the Central Committee. Since the death of Mekhlis in 1953 and the removal from the Central Committee of Kaganovich in 1957, there is (I believe) only one Jew, Dymshits, a candidate member of the Central Committee, among four hundred members and candidate members.

Stalin's coup d'état, consisting as it did of removing forever from power the predominant Jewish group, was undertaken cautiously and without appearing to mount a coup against the Jews as such. First, the fact that power passed to a Georgian gave no appearance of a Russian nationalistic reaction. Second, it was always proclaimed that the struggle against the opposition had involved only ideological differences. Zinoviev, Kamenev, and their supporters were eliminated because they'd believed in creating socialism in one country in a different manner.

Not only were these appearances well kept, they were later confirmed in two significant ways. On the one hand Stalin didn't pursue his removal of the Jews from the ruling circles all the way to the bottom. For several years Jews remained in lesser positions. On the other hand when mass executions of leading Party cadres started in the mid-1930s, there were an equal number of Jewish and non-Jewish victims.

One might look at this and suppose that as Stalin got rid of his competitors in his drive for power, the fact that they were Jews was just coincidental.

I cannot accept this for two reasons.

Firstly, because Stalin was anti-Semitic. When he had to hide it, he did it well and it only showed through rarely in cases such as that of Faivilovich, mentioned earlier. From 1931–32 on, he had serious political motives to hide it. Hitler, an avowed anti-Semite, had come to power in Germany, and foreseeing possible conflict with him, Stalin didn't want to generate Jewish hostility against himself.

This ploy turned out to be very useful before and after World War II. When it became superfluous in 1948–50 Stalin changed the Party line to a virtual declaration of hostility against the Jews. Only his unexpected death saved the Russian Jews from extermination. His anti-Semitism was, in fact, confirmed by his daughter Svetlana. She recounted how he sent her Jewish suitor to forced labor and how he became cool toward her when she married another Jew. The story of the "Doctors' Plot" is also well known.[4]

Secondly, when I observed the preparations for the Fourteenth Congress, I could see that Stalin's basic direction followed a very specific line. The composition of the Party had been changing significantly since 1917. The Jews were then a relatively important group in the Party. They were artisans, merchants, and intellectuals, infrequently from labor and not at all from the peasantry. After 1917 the Party recruited considerably, bringing in workers first and later peasants. Little by little the Jews were submerged by numbers but retained their high positions which now gave the appearance of a small, privileged class. Discontent slowly grew in the Party on this score, and Stalin was able to make use of it skillfully. When the Jews broke into two rival factions, Trotsky versus Zinoviev, Stalin was able to undertake a clever, camouflaged operation. He gave Party positions to the discontented, those kept in second-level jobs by the Jewish leaders. Officially they were selected for their firm anti-Trotskyism, but they were also anti-Semitic. I watched closely in those years how Stalin and Molotov chose the Party committee secretaries in the provinces and regions. All were to become members of the Central Committee or maybe the Politburo. All aspired to eliminate the group of Jewish leaders and take their places. The necessary terminology rapidly took form, as the Stalin center gave the new Party line to the apparatus: true communists were those from the worker and peasant classes; the Party must become more a "workers' party"; to join the Party and progress in it, social origin played an ever-growing role. This was reflected in the Party's new statutes. Jewish leaders, intellectuals, merchants, or artisans by origin, were now merely considered sort of fellow travelers. By the end of 1925, under cover of war against the Trotsky faction, the necessary cadres were already in position to spring the coup against the second Jewish faction, that of Zinoviev and Kamenev.

All the militants looking toward Party jobs, having helped Stalin mount this coup, occupied the newly empty positions with pleasure.

In 1947–48 the game began to show but with caution, first in the form of a campaign against "Zionists," then against "cosmopolitanites," and finally by requiring the nationality "Jewish" to be printed in their passports, which definitely placed the Jews in the special category of internal enemies.[5]

It's very significant that the Jewish world diaspora did not understand Stalin's anti-Jewish policy until World War II. Whereas Hitler made no bones about his blatant anti-Semitism, Stalin hid his. Until the Doctors' Plot Jewish public opinion thought it not possible for the communist regime to be anti-Semitic, and even that plot was attributed to Stalin personally. Many more years were needed to convince them that Stalin's successors saw no reason to modify his policy.[6]

Radek invented a large number of Soviet and anti-Soviet anecdotes, and I was privileged to hear them from his own mouth. His stories reflected the political situation of the time. Here are two of them, on the problem of Jewish participation in the ruling circles.

Two Jews are reading a newspaper in Moscow. The first says, "Abraham Osipovich, they've appointed one Briukhanov peoples' commissar of finances. What's his real name?" Osipovich replies, "But that is his real name." "What," the other exclaimed. "Then he's Russian?" "Yes, he's Russian." "Well," says the first Jew. "These Russians are truly an extraordinary nation. They manage to infiltrate everywhere."

When Stalin had rid the Politburo of Trotsky and Zinoviev, Radek asked me one day, "Comrade Bazhanov, do you know the difference between Stalin and Moses? You don't know? Moses got the Jews out of Egypt, and Stalin got them out of the Politburo."

It may seem a paradox, but to the ancient religious and racist forms of anti-Semitism there has been added another, Marxist anti-Semitism, which appears to have a secure future.

13. OGPU. The Essence of Power

The OGPU. Dzerzhinsky. The OGPU collegium. Yagoda.
Wanda Zvedre. Ana Georgievna. What to do? The regime's
power evolution. Its essence.

The OGPU. Those initials mean a great deal to a Russian.

When I joined the Communist Party in 1919 the Bolsheviks were in control of my native town. On Easter Day the communist daily appeared with a banner headline: "Christ is born again." The director of the newspaper was a young, debonnaire Jewish communist from our region whose name was Sonin (true name, Krymerman). I was very pleased by this example of religious tolerance, even of goodwill, and I thought it a communist trait. Several months later the chekists came to town and began to shoot people. I was indignant and quite naturally classified the communists in two categories: the good ones who wanted to create a better society and the others who represented evil, hatred and cruelty, sadism, and murder. It took me quite a while to realize that this distinction was naïve and false and that it was the system, not the men, which was the problem.

During the time which followed in the Ukraine, I learned a lot about the bloody terror unleashed by the chekists. I arrived in Moscow very hostile to the Cheka, but I had practically nothing to do with them before I started work in the Orgburo and the Politburo. There I met Latsis and Peters, who were both simultaneously members of the Central Control Commission and of the GPU collegium. They were the same well-known Latsis and Peters who had on their consciences mass shootings in the Ukraine and in other regions during the Civil War. Their victims numbered in the hundreds of thousands. I expected to find them fanatic assassins, sinister, and lugubrious. To my great surprise these two Latvians were nothing more than common thugs, obsequious and officious rascals, looking for ways to foresee the wishes of the Party leaders. I feared that upon meeting them I wouldn't be able to stomach their fanaticism, but there was no trace of fanaticism in them. They were bureaucrats whose function was to kill people, and they were very preoccupied with their careers and their personal well-being. They hung on every gesture from Stalin's secretariat. My hostility toward the Cheka turned into disgust for its leaders.

Felix Dzerzhinsky, GPU president, wasn't such a simple case. An old Polish revolutionary, head of the Cheka since its formation, he continued to be its official head until his death. However, he played a small part in its activities after Lenin's death, because he became president of the Supreme National Economic Council (replacing Rykov who went off to preside over Sovnarkom). From the very first Politburo session where I met him, his appearance and his way of expressing himself were disorienting. He resembled Don Quixote and spoke like a man convinced of the soundness of his ideas. I was surprised by his old jacket with its patched elbows. It was absolutely clear that he took no advantage of his position by using it for material benefit. At first I was equally amazed by the vehemence of his discourses. One got the impression that he took very much to heart the problems of Party and state. His ardor was in contrast to the cold cynicism of the Politburo. Later, however, I had to modify slightly my opinion of Dzerzhinsky.

During this period there was within the Party a freedom which didn't exist in the rest of the country. Each member of the Party was able to defend his viewpoints. Discussion of all sorts of problems was just as free in the Politburo too. The opposition, such people as Trotsky and Piatakov didn't hesitate to take positions diametrically opposed to the majority view. Even within the majority itself problems were freely discussed. Many times, for example, Sokolnikov would speak out against Politburo resolutions concerning the national economy, saying, "You're sabotaging my monetary reform program; if you adopt this resolution, you can relieve me of my duties as peoples' commissar for finances." Krasin, on problems of foreign policy and commerce, while he was commissar of foreign commerce, openly accused Politburo members of knowing nothing about the matters under discussion, and he would lecture them on the subject.

I soon noticed that Dzerzhinsky observed those in power, and if he ardently defended a position, it was invariably one that the majority had adopted. In addition, his vehemence was believed by the Politburo members to be an affectation, hence unseemly. When he spoke the members looked aside, fiddled with their papers, and were visibly embarrassed. Once Kamenev, presiding, said dryly, "Felix, you're at a Politburo session, not a public meeting." As if by a miracle Felix, rather than trying to justify his ardor, instantly switched to a simple, prosaic, calm tone. At one *Troika* meeting the subject of Dzerzhinsky came up and Zinoviev said, "He has, of course, angina pectoris but he uses it a bit too much for it to be effective." I must add that when Stalin brought off his coup d'état Dzerzhinsky started to defend Stalin's positions with as much ardor as he had defended those of Zinoviev and Kamenev when they were in power.

My overall view of Dzerzhinsky was that he never wavered one iota from the majority line even when one could sometimes hold a different opinion. It was beneficial for him, and when he defended the orthodox line with suffocating ardor, wasn't Zinoviev right to point out that he took advantage of his angina pectoris?

This was in 1923, when I was still a communist, and it made a very bad impression on me that the head of the OGPU should feel the need to project an aura of sincerity and honesty. Yet he was beyond reproach in that he never used his position for personal benefit, and in this regard he was a completely honest man. Doubtless part of the reason the Politburo kept him on as the official OGPU head was so that he would not allow his subordinates to abuse their situations too much. Temptation didn't lack at the OGPU, which had the power of life and death over the disenfranchised masses. However, I don't believe that Dzerzhinsky effectively fulfilled this role. He stayed far away from his immense organization, and the Politburo contented itself with the fiction of what was wanted rather than the reality of what was going on.

Dzerzhinsky's first deputy was V. R. Menzhinsky, a Pole also. He had a strange illness of the spinal cord and was an aesthete who spent his time lying on a couch and directing, also very half-heartedly, the OGPU's work. As a result second deputy G. G. Yagoda was in fact the OGPU chief.

Right at the start I quickly understood the position of the Party leaders, from the very frank discussions within the *Troika*. Holding as it did the entire population in a grip of terror, the OGPU could have become too powerful. The *Troika* deliberately kept Dzerzhinsky and Menzhinsky in charge where they did not really run the organization, while charging Yagoda with the practical running of it. Yagoda had no weight in the Party, was considered to be of little account, and was very aware of his total dependence on the Party apparatus. The OGPU had to be always completely subservient to the Party and have no pretensions to power.

This tactic was easy to put into effect, and the OGPU remained under Party control. The Party leaders, however, who were only interested in relations between the OGPU and the Party, were completely indifferent to the general population, which was thus delivered into the arbitrary hands of the OGPU. While these leaders fought for power internally, the OGPU built a very effective barrier against the population, forbidding all political activity. Consequently all threats to the Party's power were suppressed. The leaders slept peacefully, unconcerned that they had given limitless possibilities to the OGPU to squeeze the masses more and more in its gigantic stranglehold.

The first time I saw and heard Yagoda was at a Politburo session to which he was one of those called to attend. While waiting for others to arrive, Yagoda was chatting with A. S. Bubnov, who was then still head of Agitprop (the Central Committee's propaganda organ). Yagoda was boasting that the OGPU information network, slowly covering the entire country, was developing very well. Bubnov replied that the principal asset of this network was Party members, who must always be OGPU informants, whereas the OGPU selects its informants among non-Party members from those closest to and most devoted to the Soviet regime. "Not at all," responded Yagoda. "We can make anyone collaborate with us, especially those hostile to the regime." "How so?" asked Bubnov. "Very simply," said Yagoda. "Who wants to starve to death? No matter what their level of resistance, people chosen to be informants eventually cooperate. We can make them lose their jobs, and they can't be hired elsewhere without approval of our secret organs. This is especially true of women with children, who have to capitulate rapidly." Yagoda made a detestable impression on me.

The rest of the top level of the OGPU, a band of scoundrels under Dzerzhinsky's umbrella, consisted of the old chekist Ksenofontov, former member of the Cheka collegium and now responsible for Central Committee administration, who executed all Kanner's shady missions, and Latsis, Peters, and Grigory "Grisha" Belenky, the insolent and brazen OGPU collegium secretary.[1]

It was at just this time that the stationmaster of Podolsky came to Moscow to see me. He was a man of great integrity, married to one of my aunts. He had known me since I was in high school and called me "thou" despite my position, while I always called him "you." He was quite demoralized and had come to ask my advice and help. The local OGPU people in the railroad system had requested him to be a secret collaborator, to spy on and denounce his colleagues. No doubt they'd assessed him as an easy mark: he had a wife and children and he had a gentle disposition. But he refused. The local chekist put his cards on the table: you will be fired, you won't get a job elsewhere, and when your wife and children begin to die of hunger, you'll have to accept.

His visit was to ask what he should do. Fortunately, being an "apparatchik" of senior rank I was able to help. I wrote on Central Committee letterhead to the local railroad chekist head, asking that my relative be left in peace. The letterhead worked, and he wasn't bothered again. This incident showed me clearly the system Yagoda was using to blanket the country with his network of informants.[2]

Not long afterward I tangled directly with Yagoda at a meeting of the Supreme Council on Physical Culture. Being the Central Committee representative to the council, I was easily able to apply a line opposed to that of the OGPU. Yagoda was beaten and humiliated. In addition, having a strong aversion toward the leadership of the OGPU, I didn't hide my hostility to them, which alarmed them greatly. They found it most disturbing to have Stalin's assistant and the Politburo secretary as an enemy. They wondered what to do and finally decided to come out openly and officially against me, which would permit them to counter my attacks. Naturally, they knew I could be dangerous because of my closeness to the *Troika*, the Politburo, and the Central Committee staffs. They decided to benefit from Stalin's extreme distrustfulness. Yagoda sent him a letter in the OGPU collegium's name stating that the collegium wished to warn him that in their unanimous view I was a hidden counterrevolutionary. Unfortunately they had as yet no proof but were basing it on their intuition and experience as chekists, and they felt it their duty to warn the Central Committee. Yagoda signed the letter.

Stalin handed me the letter and said, "Read." I read it. I was twenty-three, and Stalin, who considered himself a great judge of people, watched me very carefully. In my youth, had there been any truth in it, I would have become confused and tried to justify myself. On the contrary, I smiled and silently gave Stalin back the letter. "What do you think?" he asked me. "Comrade Stalin," I replied. "You know Yagoda. He's a scoundrel." "Even so," Stalin said. "Why write this?" "For two reasons, I think. He wants to sow doubt about me. On the other hand, we tangled in the council, where as Central Committee representative applying its policy line, I arranged that we not take his nefarious ideas into account. He's not only after revenge, but he knows I have not the slightest respect or liking for him, so he wants to cast suspicion in advance on everything I might say about him to you and the other Politburo members."

Stalin found this explanation perfectly plausible. Furthermore, knowing him, I didn't doubt for an instant that this turn of events pleased him greatly: the Politburo secretary in open warfare with the OGPU ensured that they would watch me closely and report to him the slightest thing. On the other side, I would watch them closely and let him know of any slight infraction in the OGPU collegium.[3]

On this basis my relations with the OGPU were established. From time to time Yagoda informed Stalin of their certainty about me, and Stalin sent me these reports with indifference.

I must also note that I was happy with Yagoda's first denunciation because his open hostility saved me from danger in one regard. The OGPU could easily have arranged for me to be done in—in a car crash, killed during an armed robbery (by bogus bandits), etc. After declaring its open hostility against me, however, the OGPU could no longer resort to such measures, for now Yagoda would pay with his life in the event I were harmed.

Shortly before this letter, the following occurred: Groups of Central Committee employees wishing to study foreign languages had been formed. I participated in the English and French groups. I got to know a young and charming Latvian girl in the English group, Wanda Zvedre, who worked in the Central Committee staff. I was unattached, and Wanda and I were lovers, both seeing it as an uncomplicated, agreeable adventure. She was married to an important chekist, with whom she lived in the Lubyanka apartments reserved for senior OGPU officials. Wanda usually came to my place, but one day she invited me to hers. I was curious to see how the OGPU leaders lived. I went there one evening after work. She explained that her husband was on official travel and asked me to spend the night. I thought it suspicious, since I could easily be shot by her angry husband returning "unexpectedly" from his mission. I refused, citing an urgent work load as my pretext. I didn't mistrust Wanda but rather the OGPU, which could have used the incident.

After Yagoda's letter the possibility of an accident or an assassination motivated by jealousy disappeared. I was openly at war with the OGPU, and everyone knew it. Stalin was used to it and wasn't bothered at all by incidents such as that involving Anna Khutareva.

I had a fellow student friend at the Higher Technical School, Pavel "Pashka" Zimakov. He had no interest in politics and didn't join the Party. Upon the death of his father, his mother Anna Georgievna married a very rich man, Ivan Khutarvo, who owned a large fine cloth factory in the Moscow suburbs. During the Civil War Khutarov went to the south to escape the Bolsheviks; then in 1924 he left Russia to live at Baden, near Vienna. His wife stayed behind with four young children, and as the wife of a "capitalist" she led a poor and difficult existence.

Pashka Zimakov told me his mother wished to see me. I went there and learned that in all innocence she had asked a doctor of some friends for a medical certificate attesting that her health would benefit from a cure in the Baden waters. Armed with the certificate, she asked her local soviet administrative section for a passport to go abroad for medical attention. The official read it. "You want a passport to go with your four children?" "Yes." "You must be crazy, citizen, or else you're pretending to be." "Why? I simply want to be cured." "Good, come back in a month."

The paperwork went to the OGPU, which started an investigation. It was learned that this bourgeoise had the gall to ask authority to escape abroad to rejoin her husband, a White guard and a capitalist. A month later, when she returned to the administration, they asked her into an adjoining office, where three chekists undertook a preliminary interrogation. It was clear that they knew everything about her husband, even that he lived at Baden. They asked, "Are you trying to make fun of us?" The poor woman had an idea that was supposed to save her. "You know, I'm not in the Party and I know nothing of politics; but if an important Party member were to guarantee my return?" "Who is this important person?" they asked sarcastically. "He's Stalin's secretary," she replied. "What? What kind of a joke is this? Are you insane, citizen?" She replied, "But I assure you he'll stand guarantee for me." They looked at each other, then said, "Good, bring his letter and we'll continue this conversation."

I was enchanted by Anna Georgievna's incredible naïveté and said to her, "You really want me to guarantee that after a month of the cure you and your four children will return to Russia?" "Yes." "But," I said, "you're going to join your husband in order to stay there and not come back?" "Yes." It was charming. "Here, you understand, with the children I can't make ends meet. My only way out is to rejoin my husband." "All right," I said. "Give me the paper, and I'll sign it." "And I," she replied, "will pray to God for you all my life."

Afterward, everything went smoothly. Yagoda received a report on my guarantee. I can just imagine with what malice he rubbed his hands together. He issued the passport at once, and Anna Georgievna left for Austria with her children. As expected, when a month later the Soviet consulate reminded her that her visa had expired and she must return, she replied that she was renouncing her Soviet citizenship and would remain abroad as an émigré.

That was what Yagoda was waiting for, and at once Stalin received a report detailing how Bazhanov had helped a bourgeoise flee abroad. "What's this story?" Stalin asked me, giving me Yagoda's denunciation. "Comrade Stalin, I did it to verify just how stupid Yagoda is. If she was a bourgeoise who wanted to escape abroad, and if he knew it, why did he give her a passport and let her go? And if there was, on the contrary, nothing wrong with her departure, what can he find to accuse me of? Yagoda is ready to go to any lengths to make trouble for me, and he doesn't understand how ridiculous he makes himself look." This is where things stood: Stalin paid no further attention to the matter.

I quickly understood the OGPU's power over the masses, who belonged to no Party and were totally at its mercy. It was also clear why no personal liberty could exist under the communists. Everything was nationalized. Everyone had to work for the state in order to live. The least liberty of thought, the slightest desire for personal liberty, and you were threatened with losing your job, hence your means of existence.

All about stretched the vast secret informant system. Everything was known, everyone was in the OGPU grip. While it accumulated this power and began to establish the enormous gulag empire, the OGPU informed the Party summit as little as possible of what it was doing. The camps developed, forming a huge system of extermination, and the Party was informed that a clever method had been devised to obtain slave labor for the five-year plan at the expense of the counterrevolution. In addition, the camps were to "reeducate through labor." I got the impression that the Party leaders were happy to have this OGPU barrier between them and the population work perfectly, and there was not the slightest wish to know what was happening in the basement. They were all happy to read the official verbiage in *Pravda* about how the steel sword of the revolution (the OGPU) watched with eternal vigilance over Party conquests.

I tried at times to talk to Politburo members about the fact that the population was completely under the uncontrolled power of the OGPU. This conversation interested nobody. I realized that, by happy chance, my suggestions were attributed to my hostility toward the OGPU. Otherwise I would have been suspect of "intellectual weakness, lack of true Bolshevik vigilance against enemies," etc. Through constant and prolonged indoctrination, the minds of communist Party members were oriented in a definite direction. Not only was he who read and understood (the sterile and boring) works of Marx a Bolshevik but also he who chose to surveille and persecute possible enemies without respite. The OGPU's activities never stopped developing and increasing, as if that were normal. Since the essence of communism is to hold the population by the throat, how then could the OGPU be reproached for accomplishing this task to perfection? I finished by realizing definitively that the problem wasn't so much that the OGPU people were dregs but that the wolfish system encouraged and permitted these functions to be performed by scum.

I have often said that Yagoda was a criminal and a scoundrel. His role in the creation of the gulag is so well known that it seems impossible to say something positive about this individual. There was, however, an episode in his life that greatly pleased me, an episode that speaks in his favor.

It occurred in March 1938, when Yagoda was subjected to the parody that was his "judgment." The prosecutor was a creature of human appearance: Andrey Yanuarievich Vishinsky.[4]

VISHINSKY: "Traitor Yagoda, have you never, during the course of your ignoble criminal activities, felt the slightest regret, the slightest remorse? And at this moment, before the proletarian tribunal, have you not the slightest regret for the awful crimes you committed?"

YAGODA: "Yes, I regret. I regret greatly. . . ."

VISHINSKY: "Listen, comrade judges. The traitor Yagoda shows regret. What do you regret, Yagoda the spy and criminal?"

YAGODA: "I much regret. . . . I regret greatly not having had the lot of you shot while I had the power to do it."

Yagoda, who had himself organized a long series of similar trials, hadn't the least illusion about the outcome of his own "judgment."

My personal situation was paradoxical. The OGPU detested me. Stalin, suspicious to the point of mania, paid no attention to the OGPU denunciations of me, and all the secrets of power remained in my possession. For my part, I had begun to study ways of helping to overthrow this regime.

I had no illusions about it. The masses couldn't overthrow this slave regime: the day for street barricades had long since passed. The regime possessed not only tanks but a huge police system with incredible power. The leaders would stop at nothing to retain power. Unlike Louis XVI, who wished to avoid shedding his subjects' blood, these men would shed whatever was necessary.

Change could only be brought about at the summit, in the Central Committee. That was, however, almost impossible. It would take people—hiding their anticommunism—who would become a majority in the Central Committee. I knew all the communist leaders and couldn't see among them people ready to take such action.

And I? An enemy of communism, I was aware of all its secrets and I was present at all meetings of the Politburo and plenums of the Central Committee. I still worked on occasion at the laboratory of the Higher Technical School, and I could have made a bomb using nitric acid and glycerine. To have taken it into a meeting hidden in my briefcase would have been simple since no one ever asked what I was carrying. But clearly that made no sense for me. Another Central Committee and Politburo would have been elected, and it would have been neither better nor worse. You can't kill a system with a bomb. Nor was there any hope in the factionalism at the top. Trotsky was as 100 percent communist as Stalin. To create and organize a group in the heart of the Bolshevik summit was hopeless: someone would have reported it to Stalin. Clandestine activity was impossible in my case because of the constant close OGPU watch on me, hoping to find something against me.

What to do, then? One thing only: continue to hide my views and pursue an anti-Bolshevik career with the hope of eventually succeeding Stalin and then changing everything. History proved that that wasn't out of the question either. Malenkov, who followed me as Politburo secretary, in fact realized the first step in this direction. He succeeded Stalin, becoming number two in the country when Stalin died: first secretary of the Central Committee and president of the Council of Ministers. He was a good pupil of Stalin and a stalinist, but the second part of my program to change everything was alien to him.

I, however, rejected this program. I knew Stalin, and I saw where he was going. For the moment he had moderated things, but he was a cruel and amoral Asiatic satrap. How many more crimes would he commit against the country, in all of which I would have to participate? I knew I couldn't do it. To be close to and with Stalin, one had to develop within oneself to the highest degree all the Bolshevik traits: amorality, lack of friendship, lack of human sentiments. One had to spend one's life as a wolf. I didn't want to. What then remained for me to do in the country? Be a cog and help the machine run? I didn't want that either.

There was only one solution: to leave the country. There I would perhaps find a way to fight against this wolfish socialism. But it wasn't that simple.

First I had to quit the Politburo, Stalin's secretariat, and the Central Committee. I made the decision to do it. Stalin refused to let me go. It was not because I was irreplaceable. For Stalin there was no such thing as irreplaceable or indispensable people. What bothered him was that I knew all his secrets, and if I left he would then have to make them known to my replacement.

I sought Tovstukha's help to leave, and he was pleased I wanted to go. He wanted to take over the entire secretariat, but while I was the Politburo secretary I had all the important functions, and the apparatus of the Politburo was my domain. He was not himself capable of being Politburo secretary, but my departure would enable him to take over the Politburo secretariat and reorganize it to make himself its boss. It happened this way. When I went on my summer vacation I was replaced by Timokhin, Orgburo secretary. Lera Golubtsova, Malenkov's cunning wife who worked at Orgaspred, used her relations with German Tikhomirnov (Molotov's second secretary, of whom I spoke early in this book) to have her husband appointed temporary secretary of Orgburo. After having assessed Malenkov, Tovstukha decided to take him into the Politburo as recording secretary, that's to say secretary solely for the meetings. A stenographer was assigned to help him. The apparatus was supervised by Tovstukha and Malenkov's functions were limited. Control over execution of Politburo decisions was abolished after my departure, since it was too closely associated with my person. Malenkov had no access to Stalin's secrets at first or for many years after. They remained entirely in Stalin's hands, a change which suited Stalin better.

Once installed at the Politburo, in permanent contact with its members and always close to Stalin, Malenkov's career made slow but sure progress. He was a 100 percent loyal Stalinist. In 1934 he became Stalin's assistant, in 1939 secretary of the Central Committee, in 1941 candidate and in 1946 full member of the Politburo. For the two years prior to Stalin's death he was his principal replacement as first secretary of the Central Committee and president of the Council of Ministers. He was apparently number two in the country and Stalin's heir. After Stalin's death, however, the Politburo didn't accept him as successor, and he kept only the job of president of the Council of Ministers. Three years later when he tried to oust Khrushchev, Malenkov lost his power and became head of an electric plant somewhere in the provinces.

After I left the Politburo I stayed on, nevertheless, in Stalin's secretariat, although I did as little there as possible. I pretended my main work was at Narkomfin. However, until the end of 1925 I continued to supervise the secretariat of the diverse Central Committee commissions, especially the permanent ones. They didn't want to let me go for a long time because the work required good knowledge of the substance of their past activities. It was only at the end of 1926 that I quit the Central Committee definitively.

Stalin was indifferent to my departure. It was amusing that, after my departure, nobody knew if I was still part of Stalin's secretariat or if I had gone. Even then I might have come back, as others did, including Tovskuha who seemed to have left for the Lenin Institute but who came back and was better entrenched than before. I knew that I had left definitively, and I was even preparing to quit the country.

I was already seeing things with the eyes of a defector. I was drawing up a balance sheet.

I had known many Bolshevik leaders. Among them were talented, honest men, I had noted with amazement. I had no doubt of their unenviable future, since they weren't cut out for the system. (In all honesty the other communists were also headed for a poor future.) The decent ones had been drawn into this immense machine by mistake, as I had, and now were cogs in it. Now my eyes were open, and I could see what they couldn't: where the development of the application of communist doctrine was inevitably leading.

I saw the evolution taking place, the paths of development of the regime and its apparatus, as comprising two distinct questions. First, the mechanism of power, its veritable inner mechanism, not what was presented as the power structure for tactical reasons. After Lenin's group of professional revolutionaries had obtained power and with it all the assets of the country, they needed a huge administrative apparatus and, consequently, a large number of Party cadres. The Party doors were thrown open, and intensive communist propaganda easily attracted many people. The country was politically virgin territory: the first words of propagandists, delivered to simple folk who had never thought about politics, came like a revelation that suddenly opened their eyes to all of the important problems. All other propaganda was forbidden and was suppressed as being counterrevolutionary. The Party grew rapidly, thanks to these naïve and credulous people who came to work in the various organs of power: civilian, military, economic, organized labor, and so on. At the center was Lenin's group, directing the many institutions and organizations. In theory they governed by the intermediary of the organs of power which, as far as the public was concerned, was called Soviet power: the peoples' commissariats, the executive committees, and their sections and ramifications. They were numerous, however, and the center had to run not only them tightly but also all that which was outside their jurisdiction: the Cominterns and Profinterns, the army, the media, the labor unions, the propaganda machinery, the economy, etc. Such control was only possible through the Central Committee, which brought together all the principal leaders. But the Central Committee was unwieldy and hard to manage, so a small supervisory group was needed: the Politburo, which replaced Lenin and his closest assistants (Sverdlov and Trotsky), who had governed during the first years. The Politburo elected in 1919 quickly became a veritable government. At first it didn't change things for Lenin and his small group, merely making it easier for them to exercise legal power. As before, direction passed down through the organs called Soviet power. There was little change in this scenario during the Civil War. The Party apparatus was an embryo which provided services but didn't govern. Things began to change when the Civil War ended successfully and a real Party apparatus was formed and began to expand rapidly. Centralized directions, under the Politburo, slowly took shape regionally through the Central Committee's regional and territorial bureaus, and in the provinces through the provincial committee bureaus. The secretaries of the latter installed themselves in charge and began to become the masters of their provinces, in place of the presidents of the provincial executive committees and the various representatives of the center (the capital). The new statutes of 1922 gave definitive form to these changes. It was the start of the period of "power of the secretaries." In Moscow, Lenin, not the Party general secretary, directed everything. When Lenin was forced by illness to relinquish the reins in 1922, the Politburo, without Lenin, became the center of power. The fight for succession began. Zinoviev and Kamenev, who had taken over, thought they could sleep peacefully since they had the Politburo in hand. Stalin and Molotov saw further ahead. The Politburo is elected by the Central Committee. If you have the majority of the Central Committee with you, you can elect any Politburo you like. Select your people for provincial committee secretaries, and you have the majority in the congress and so in the Central Committee.[5]

Zinoviev didn't want to focus on that. He was so absorbed in his struggle to defeat Trotsky that he didn't notice Stalin's work of infiltrating the Party apparatus (work that went forward during 1922 through 1925). The country was run by the *Troika* from 1922 through 1924, then in 1925 when the *Troika* was dissolved, governance was reassumed by the Politburo. Starting in January 1926, after the December 1925 congress [the Fourteenth], Stalin harvested the fruits of his long labor: he had his Central Committee and his Politburo. He became the leader but still not all-powerful, for the Politburo members still carried weight in the Party, as did the members of the Central Committee. During the struggle in Moscow, however, the power of the secretaries was definitively established in the provinces. The first secretary of a Gubkom (Party provincial committee) was the all-powerful master of his province. All problems concerning the province were resolved in the Gubkom office. It was no longer the Party which governed the country but its apparatus.

What next? Where were we going?

I knew Stalin well: now he was on the right track to reinforce his personal power. In theory his overthrow was only possible by action of the Party congress, and as soon as all power was concentrated in his hands he would cease to convene congresses. Then there would be only one power in the country: not the Party, or its apparatus, but Stalin, he alone. He would then govern using those he judged most useful, whether it be the Politburo or his secretaries.

What would be the future of all those militants the Party had absorbed after the Revolution, of whom we've spoken earlier? We can pose this question again after looking at the second problem.

The second problem concerns the essence of power and its evolution.

When you understand the personalities of Lenin or Stalin, you're surprised by their maniacal lust for power, to which everything else was subordinated in both their lives.[6] In reality there was little that was particularly astonishing in this thirst for power. Lenin and Stalin followed their Marxist doctrine, and their way of thinking determined their entire existence. This doctrine called for overturning all of society, mandatorily using violence as their means. Violence that was brought about by an active and organized minority, with an obligatory condition: preliminary seizure of power. That was their alpha and omega. You can do nothing, according to their doctrine, without first seizing power. You can do everything and change everything, once power is in your hands. It was on this basis that their lives were built. Power went into Lenin's hands, then Stalin's, not only because they sought it but also because in the Party they represented the most striking incarnations of this Party doctrine. Power, that was all: the beginning and the end. That was the reason for Lenin and Stalin to exist. Everyone else had to obey them.

Power seized by an active minority using violence can only be retained by this minority through the exercise of violence against the vast majority. The minority (the Party) only understands the use of force. The population can be hostile to the regime the Party installs, but the authorities won't fear this hostility and will only act to change things (e.g., Lenin and the NEP) when they believe that their police grip on the country isn't strong enough and there's a risk they'll lose power. When the police terror system has the entire country in its grip, you can apply that violence as you wish (e.g., Stalin's collectivization and his terror of the 1930s) and force the country to live according to the Party's prescriptions, even if the cost is millions of victims.

The essence of power is violence. Upon whom? According to the doctrine, first against the class enemy: the bourgeois, the capitalist, the landed proprietor, the aristocrat, the former officer, the engineer, the priest, the rich peasant (kulak), those who think independently and haven't adapted to the new regime (counterrevolutionaries), the White guard, the saboteur, the social traitor, the parasite aides of the class enemy, the ally of imperialism and reaction, etc. Once these categories have been liquidated and are empty, new ones can be created: the average peasant can become the kulak's ally, the poor peasant an enemy of the kolkhozes and consequently a saboteur of the building of socialism. The worker who lacks enthusiasm can be an agent of the class enemy. And inside the Party there are deviationists, factionalists, Trotskyists, opposition of the right and left, traitors, foreign spies, lascivious vipers: one must endlessly destroy, shoot, and make people stagnate in prison and concentration camps. That is the essence and the tragedy of communism.[7]

In the beginning of the Revolution hundreds of thousands joined the Party believing in the creation of a better society. Little by little (not very quickly) it became clear that all that was based on deception. But the believers still believed. When terrible things were done, they blamed savage and ignorant executives: the leaders meant well, and one must fight to correct the errors. How? By protesting, by joining the opposition and fighting within the Party. But the path of opposition within the Party was doomed to fail, and all these believers slowly became what the authorities called class enemies (or agents of class enemies). All these believers were condemned and went into the huge communal meat grinder that Comrade Stalin had so skillfully built for them.[8]

The Party (especially the cadre leaders) slowly divided into two categories: those who exterminated, and those who were exterminated. Naturally, those who cared above all for their skins and their well-being tried to enter the first category (not all were successful, the meat grinder took everyone who fell into its hands). Those who believed in something and sought a better life for the people, fell sooner or later into the second category.

That doesn't mean, obviously, that all the profiteers and all the scoundrels would be chewed up. It does mean, however, that most of the Cheka executioners fell into the mill, largely because they were a part of it. It also means that all the people who were more or less honest, who still had a conscience and humane sentiments, inevitably perished.

My job as Politburo secretary put me in contact with all the Party leaders. I must note that among them were many decent, cultivated, competent, and even talented people. I'm not judging them definitively, merely recording what I observed at that time. The devil had pushed the engineer Krasin, a talented organizer, into the Lenin group of professional parasites. I've rarely met a better administrator than Syrtsov, who understood everything with remarkable speed. And the work of the lawyer Brilliant (Sokolnikov) came close to perfection.

Others were less well endowed, but they were honest, agreeable, and well-meaning. Ordzhonikidze was straight and honest. Rudzutak was an excellent worker, modest, and honest. Stanislav Kossior kept, despite everything, his naïve faith in communism: but when the Cheka arrested him and he refused, in spite of extreme torture, to agree to false charges against himself, they brought in his fifteen-year-old daughter and raped her in front of him. His daughter killed herself, and Kossior, broken, signed all they wanted him to.

I had excellent rapport, pleasant and friendly, with almost all the Party leaders. I can't even reproach the conscientious Stalinist bureaucrats, Molotov, Kaganovich, and Kuibyshev. They were always very amiable with me.

Yet this same Sokolnikov ordered mass executions in south Russia during the Civil War, when he commanded an army. And Ordzhonikidze did the same in the Caucasus.

The wolf doctrine, and peoples' faith in it, are terrible. It is only when you understand all that well, and know those people well, that you see what they inevitably became under a doctrine that preaches violence, revolution, and the extermination of "class enemies."

Photomontage of Bolshevik leaders, ca 1919   Doyle Collection (From early Soviet media
sources) – Photography by Jeffrey S. Caldwell

L. to R. G. Serrati (Italy), Trotsky, A. Rosmer (France), P. Levi (Germany), Zinoviev, Bukharin   Doyle Collection (From 1920 German Communist Party document) – Photography by Jeffrey S. Caldwell

L. to R. Stalin and Lenin, ca 1922   Doyle Collection – Photography by Jeffrey S. Caldwell

Lenin with Moscow Crowd, ca 1921   Doyle Collection – Photography by Jeffrey S. Caldwell

Trotsky and daughter Zina, ca 1925   From: "Trotsky," King, Ryan & Deutscher, Basil Blackwell, Oxford, 1986

Kalinin, Sverdlov, Kollontai, and Lenin
Eric Baschet Editions, undated, Paris? (ca 1926?)

From: "Russie 1904–1924, La Revolution est La,"

Trotsky's French passport photo, 1915   Doyle Collection – Photography by Jeffrey S. Caldwell

L. to R. Stalin, Lenin, Kalinin, ca 1921   Doyle Collection – Photography by Jeffrey S. Caldwell

Lenin, ca 1920
Doyle Collection –
Photography by
Jeffrey S. Caldwell

L. to R. Kalinin, L. Kaganovich, Ordzhonikidzr, Stalin, and Voroshilov, 1930
Doyle Collection – Photography by Jeffrey S. Caldwell

14. Last Observations. Fleeing the Socialist Paradise.

Literature. Mayakovsky. Eisenstein. Competition with "bourgeois sportsmen." Voyage to Norway. First effort to escape. Alenka. Impossibility of leaving by normal means.

In June 1925 the Politburo decided to bring literature under control. A Central Committee commission was formed, which adopted a resolution, "The Party's policy in the realm of literature." The core of this resolution, which the Politburo ratified, was that "there is no neutral literature" and that Soviet literature had to be a vehicle for communist propaganda. The composition of the commission was amusing. It was presided over by M. V. Frunze, commander in chief of the Red Army (who had never before been accused of any connection with literature) and included Anatoly Vasilievich Lunarcharsky and Iosif Mikhailovich Vareikis.[1] The latter was not very sophisticated. As secretary of a provincial committee (Voronezh, I think) he wrote an editorial in the local Party journal which attacked the latest opposition, ending his articles with a quote from Aleksandr Aleksandrovich Blok's Scythia, which was directed at the opposition, "You will hear your skeletons crack, in our delicate and heavy paws."[2] At a Politburo session Zinoviev cited this case as an example of unparalleled stupidity of an apparatchik. That was enough for Stalin to appoint Vareikis head of the press section of the Central Committee, a post he held for a long time.

Having become at heart an émigré, I would have much liked to get to know the best writers and poets of the country, who had never accepted communism, and for whom I had profound respect: Anna Andreyevna Akhmatova,[3] and Mikhail Afanaseyevich Bulgakov.[4] Alas, I had decided to flee. Contact with me could cause them many difficulties after my departure. By contrast I could freely have contact with communist writers [hacks], who risked nothing.

Obviously I didn't know V. V. Mayakovsky of the first period, pre-

revolutionary and embracing futuristism. The encyclopedias all assert
that he became a Bolshevik in 1908. He was fourteen that year. Judging
from his poetry before the Revolution, he was in any event well along the
road to becoming a professional revolutionary and true Bolshevik. He
wrote that he was much interested in a way to:

> . . . return and empty,
> With neither guilt nor malice,
> The pockets of his neighbor.

In precisely the same way, he had already formulated the customary
attitude toward work of a professional revolutionary:

> And when one speaks to me of work, on and on,
> As if he were grating horse-radish with a rusty rasp,
> I reply, taking the other gently by the shoulder:
> Do you still take a card when you have a five?[5]

I made the poet's acquaintance in the second period, after the Revolution, when he was thrusting poetry toward communism with determina-
tion and spirit, his Party card in hand. There was a purge in the Party in
1921 that Mayakovsky dubbed "the purge of contemporary poetry." It
was his way of mocking, not without humor, the poets not touched by the
grace of communism. At that time I was a student at the Higher Technical
School. The "purge" took place in the Polytechnic Museum. The public
was almost exclusively composed of students. He undertook his "purge"
in alphabetical order, starting with Akhmatova, who he said had never
seen in the Revolution anything but that "all was pillaged, sold, betrayed."
When he arrived at Blok, who had died soon before, a student yelped,
"Mayakovsky, for the dead—*aut bene, aut nihil.*" "Yes, yes," said Mayakovsky. "That's what I want to do; I'll say of the dead something
completely insignificant but which, at the same time, characterizes him
very well.

"At the time of which I [Mayakovsky] speak, I lived on Gorokhovaya
[street], in Blok's neighborhood. We planned to cook some blinis,[6] and
since I had no desire to cook, I bet that while the blinis were cooking I
would have time to go to Blok's and bring back a volume of his poems
with a dedication. I hurried over to Blok's and started to flatter him (you
know how well I do that) and asked him for one of his books with his
dedication. He took a volume and went to the next room where he sat and
thought. Ten, twelve minutes . . . and I had my bet and the blinis [to worry
about]. I poked my head around the door and said, 'Aleksandr Aleksandrovich, just write anything, no matter what.' Finally he wrote something. I seized the book and ran home. I had won my bet. I looked to see

what Blok had written, 'For Vladimir Mayakovsky, about whom I think a lot.' And it took him seventeen minutes to do that!

"For me, it was simpler. The poet Aleksandr Borisovich Kusikov,[7] who was then present, asked me for a book with a dedication. With pleasure. I immediately took the complete works of Vladimir Mayakovsky and wrote:

> People have all sorts of tastes, good and bad,
> Some appreciate me, others appreciate Kusikov."[8]

I met Mayakovsky later. He undoubtedly had talent, but he was cynical and really crude. During the NEP he had composed, for money, publicity slogans for Soviet commercial organizations. Carried away by this genre, he wrote similarly for his friends and acquaintances.

He couldn't stand the poet Iosif Pavlovich Utkin.[9] The latter was reciting, at the House of Poets, his latest, fully orthodox poem. When he finished and it was time to applaud, Mayakovsky's deep bass was raised, "Go on trying, go on trying, Utkin. You're becoming another Gusev." (Gusev was a Central Committee member and at that time supervised the committee's press section.[10])

I met Mayakovksy for the last time at VOKS (the department of foreign cultural relations), where I'd gone to see Olga Davydovna Kameneva. They were letting the poet go abroad to fill up his coffers; but they weren't allotting him enough foreign exchange to please him, and he was expressing his unhappiness in terms that weren't always literary.

I also met Sergey Mikhailovich Eisenstein, who is wrongly and persistently called a genius by West European progressives. I first met him in 1923 when he ran the "Proletkult" theater. He had just produced a play by Aleksandr Nikolaevich Ostrovsky which was a real spectacle: the text had almost nothing of Ostrovsky in it. The actors were buffoons, stiffly strutting as if they were puppets on strings, making political and antireligious propaganda. Not only the direction but also the text were Eisenstein's, and unhappily, there was nothing to commend the show unless it were his Bolshevik orthodoxy.

For example, to make antireligious propaganda, they brought out, on a huge dish, a comedian dressed as a mullah who sang to the tune of the well-known Russian song *Allah Verdy*:

> Judas was a good merchant;
> He sold Jesus and bought galoshes.

I had already gained the impression that Eisenstein had considerable respect for the commercial talents of Judas. Eisenstein himself manifested no other special gifts.

After having turned to the cinema and learned from Agitprop what was needed then ("We have no revolutionary propaganda films; make some"), Eisenstein produced *The Battleship Potemkin,* a rather banal propaganda film. All leftist (are there any rightist ones?) western film producers and writers pronounced it a masterpiece (if it was "revolutionary" it went without saying that it was a masterpiece). I went to the premiere, which, unless I'm mistaken, was at the Meyerhold Theater and not in a movie house. I found myself, by chance, next to Rudzutak, and afterward we exchanged impressions. "Certainly, it's very pedestrian propaganda," Rudzutak admitted. "But it's a long time now that we've waited for a one hundred percent revolutionary film." The instructions had been executed, and everything was in order in the film industry: brutal soldiers, ignoble tsarist police, and valiant sailors—the future "pride and glory of the revolution."

All Eisenstein's career after that was spent in shameless toadying. While the satrap Stalin was consolidating his power, Eisenstein produced *The General Line* (for the uninitiated: the wise line of the *general* secretary of the Central Committee, Comrade Stalin), by which all Russia would prosper under the brilliant leadership of the Chief. It should be noted that there was still opposition at that time, in the years 1928–29, and it was possible not to be a boot-licker. Bukharin and Rykov were loudly protest-ing against Stalin's extermination of the peasantry, while the genius Stalin hurried to unearth the rare professional boot-lickers. The summit of Eisenstein's toadying was attained with *Ivan the Terrible,* which was, it seems, accepted abroad at face value. It was, of course, produced to glorify and justify Stalin's terror. History repeats itself: the real Ivan the Terrible, supposedly on behalf of Russia the Great, impaled and decapi-tated his boyars. Stalin shot his, also accusing them of treason against their country. The only goal of all this ignominy was that Eisenstein wanted to save his own skin (which he did). But during all his life he was a coward and the lowest of toadies. He could have gone elsewhere and saved his neck otherwise. During the 1930s he was allowed to go to Hollywood, then to Mexico to make revolutionary films. He could have saved his life by staying abroad, but he preferred to go back and grovel prone before Stalin's executioners.[11]

At the end of 1925, the Supreme Council on Physical Culture received an invitation from Norway to send a team of speed skaters to the world ice skate racing championships. At that time Russian skaters were probably the best in the world. Until then, in line with the dogma of "Sportintern," which organized all the revolutionary workers' sports competitions, com-petition between "bourgeois" and "red" sportsmen wasn't acceptable. I decided it was time to change all that.

Sportintern was run by Nikolai Ilich Podvoisky.[12] In government circles his name was usually accompanied by the epithet "old fool." Before the Revolution he was in the military, but a Bolshevik. During the October Revolution he was part of the Petrograd Military Revolutionary Committee, which directed the insurrection. Thanks to that he considered himself an historic personage. Because of his stupidity and incapacity to do the slightest useful work, the authorities always had a hard time finding a proper slot for him. Finally they appointed him head of "Vsevobuch," an organization charged with giving military training to the civil population. Podvoisky was very mortified and offended: he wanted a real leadership position. When Sportintern was created he was placed at its head, which somewhat satisfied his amour propre.

While Podvoisky was still at Vsevobuch, Yagoda started his career there as head of the organization's administrative services. He didn't stay long, however. Profiting from the fact that he was related to Yakob Sverdlov, Yagoda transferred to the OGPU, where he was also head of administrative services, and that was where he found his real niche. Yagoda remained on good terms with Podvoisky and had a great deal of influence over him.

In particular, he had convinced Podvoisky that the red workers' organizations should never compete with "bourgeois" sportsmen because that would bring bourgeois demoralisation to the revolutionary workers' circles. Sportintern published this as an instruction and it was accepted by foreign communist parties as being a directive from Moscow. Consequently, it was rigorously applied.

The committee which organized the skating championships knew that, but they thought the world championship wouldn't be valid unless the Russians, the best skaters, were there. That was the motive behind their invitation.

At a meeting of the Supreme Council on Physical Culture, I insisted that the invitation be accepted, despite Yagoda's opposition. Podvoisky threw a fit: "You will undercut all our policy line." The secretary of Sportintern, Hans Lemberg, dashed over to the Comintern to get their opinion. Lemberg was the same Russian of German extraction, with blue eyes, with whom, as I said earlier, I was on guard duty five years earlier during the Kronstadt Iusurrection. In 1924, when I was already Politburo secretary and a member of the presidium of the Supreme Council on Physical Culture, I met him on a sports field. We have spoken of my belief that we should reconstitute the old sports organizations and develop competive sports. He accepted the idea warmly. So, to neutralize the stupid and obstinate Podvoisky somewhat, I got Lemberg appointed secretary of

Sportintern. However, he showed himself to be a traitor and an intrigant, and he went over right away to the side of Podvoisky and Yagoda.

At the Comintern, however, they abstained from these discussions and replied to Podvoisky and Lemberg that the matter should be resolved by the Central Committee. They would have addressed the Central Committee in vain, for I would have got my viewpoint adopted. Yagoda, therefore, chose the following way around it. The disagreement between the two presidents of the Supreme Council and of Sportintern, Semashko and Podvoisky, was represented as a conflict between two department heads, and Podvoisky asked the Central Control Commission to arbitrate the dispute. Since the presidium of the Central Control Commission included the chekists Peters and Latsis, friends of Yagoda and members of the OGPU collegium, Yagoda counted on the Central Control Commission finding against Semashko for having involved himself in the business of an international organization, outside his jurisdiction.

The day before the commission meeting I went to see Stalin and said, "Comrade Stalin, I represent the Central Committee on the Supreme Council on Physical Culture. We have a conflict with Sportintern. We believe that the workers' sports organizations can compete with bourgeois organizations, and Sportintern is against. Tomorrow the Central Control Commission will examine the dispute. I'd like your advice." Stalin responded, "Why not? We're in competition with the bourgeoisie wherever we can be, in the political and economic fields, why not in the sports field? It's obvious. Only an idiot wouldn't understand." So I said, "Comrade Stalin, let me cite your opinion tomorrow at the Control Commission meeting, just the way you stated it." Stalin replied, "Go ahead."

The next day our problem was examined by the Central Control Commission, with Gusev presiding (instead of Yaroslavsky who, sly little coward, excused himself: the matter was unclear and ticklish, and one didn't know who was behind the two disputants). Podvoisky explained the heart of the matter and the reason for the dispute, then Semashko gave the viewpoint of the Supreme Council. Yagoda supported Podvoisky. Mekhnochin (representing the war department at the Supreme Council) supported our viewpoint. Little by little all the interested participants gave their advice. I kept quiet. Gusev constantly glanced at me, visibly waiting for me to give my advice. I didn't speak, however. Finally he couldn't stand it and said, "It would be very interesting to know the thinking of the Central Committee's representative at the Supreme Council." I replied, "I don't need to explain my viewpoint. It's the same as that of the other presidium members." "But the audience would, perhaps, like to know what Comrade Stalin thinks on the subject?" "Yes, of course. I raised the question with Comrade Stalin yesterday. He replied as follows, authorizing me to quote him exactly: 'Why not? We're in competition with the bourgeoisie in all fields: why not in the field of sports? Only an imbecile wouldn't understand.'"

Yagoda became scarlet. The members of the Central Control Commission took on a satisfied and intelligent look, and Gusev quickly said, "Well, comrades, I think the problem is clear and that everyone will agree if I declare that Comrade Podvoisky is wrong, and that Comrade Semashko has quite rightly defended a position in perfect agreement with the Party's line. No objections?" There were none, and the session ended there.

Semashko and the presidium of the Supreme Council asked me to go to Norway as captain of the Soviet skating team, because there would be delicate negotiations with the Norwegian Communist Party. We would have to explain the change in Sportintern's policy. In Scandinavia, sports, especially winter sports such as skiing and skating, play a very important role. I accepted and went to Molotov to get him, if he would, to have the Orgburo pass a resolution designating me captain of the team.

We were to leave in a day or two, and it was time to face all my problems squarely for I had decided that this was an opportunity to go abroad and stay there, kicking the dust of the socialist homeland from my feet.

However, my problems were considerably complicated by romance. I had but one love in Soviet Russia. She was called Alenka Andreeva, and she was twenty. Her father was a general, and directed the Putilov Arms factory. During the Civil War he fled the Reds and went to southern Russia, taking his wife and daughter. There, he literally starved to death at the end of the Civil War, while his wife went mad. Their daughter of fifteen years, Alenka, was brought back to Moscow by a Komsomol group going to attend a congress. She was assigned to the Komsomol and became a permanent employee in their central apparatus. She was extremely pretty and intelligent, but after all she'd been through, her nervous stability left something to be desired.

When she was seventeen the secretary of the Komsomol Central Committee, Comrade Pyotr Smorodin, fell in love and asked her to marry him, which she did. She came to the Party Central Committee as a technical employee at age nineteen, and that was when I met her. Our relationship caused her to leave Smorodin, but we didn't live together. I lived at House No. 1 of the Soviets, and she lived next door in the building assigned to leaders of the Komsomol central committee. She had a room there, and lived near all her accustomed colleagues.

Our romance lasted a year and a half, but Alenka never knew of my political evolution and didn't doubt that I was an exemplary communist. It was impossible to tell her of my intention to escape abroad, so I devised the following stratagem.

Several months beforehand, I arranged her transfer from the Central Committee to Narkomfin, where she was employed as secretary of the Institute for the Study of Economic Crises. This work pleased her and greatly absorbed her. I invented a mission for her in Finland, to gather documents on monetary reform that her department supposedly very much needed. I had Narkomfin approve this mission, and I hoped it would be similarly approved by the OGPU (Yagoda signed service passports for trips abroad), since she would be in Finland when I was in Norway. I planned to meet her on my way back, in Helsinki, and only then tell her that I would be staying abroad, giving her the choice of staying with me or returning to Moscow. Were she to decide to return she would run no risk: the fact of returning would show that she hadn't shared my counter-revolutionary opinions and wasn't an accomplice to my departure.

A day went by, and my team was ready. They were three skaters: Jakob Melnikov, then the world's best skater, especially over short distances (500 meters); Plato Ippolitov, very strong over medium distances (1,500 meters); and the young Red Army soldier Kuchin, a distance expert (5,000 to 10,000 meters). We had to hurry and leave, or we would arrive too late for the championships at Trondheim. But my passport hadn't been signed by Yagoda. I telephoned the OGPU and could learn only that my passport was in Comrade Yagoda's office waiting for him to sign it. I tried telephoning him, but he wouldn't answer, even on the automatic telephone. I quickly understood what was going on. Yagoda was delaying it on purpose, to make our trip a failure. If we didn't leave this very day, we would arrive too late at Trondheim, and that was what Yagoda wanted.

I went to see Molotov and explained that by delaying us Yagoda would make our trip fail. I reminded Molotov that I was leaving in accord with a decision of the Central Committee's Orgburo. Molotov telephoned Yagoda: "Comrade Yagoda, if you think you can in this way sabotage a decision of the Central Committee, you're making a mistake. If Comrade Bazhanov's passport isn't in my office in fifteen minutes, I will send this matter to the Central Control Commission, accusing you of deliberately sabotaging decisions of the Party's Central Committee."

Molotov said, "Wait here, Comrade Bazhanov. It won't be long." In effect, ten minutes later an OGPU courier arrived with a thunder of boots. "For Comrade Molotov, extremely urgent, for his hands alone, return receipt requested." The envelope contained my passport. Molotov smiled.

We left that same day, arriving in Oslo the evening before the championships. We weren't able to reach Trondheim, however: the last trains of the day had already left and no airplanes were available—they were already there. We had to content ourselves with competing against a second ranking workers' team. However, my team's times were better than those of the world championships, and the newspapers argued over who had gained the moral victory.

The Soviet ambassador to Norway, Aleksandra Mikhailovna Kollontai, invited the general secretary of the Norwegian Communist Party, Peder Furuboten, to the embassy where I explained how and why Moscow had decided to change the Sportintern policy.[13] Kollontai told Furuboten exactly what my position was in the Party Central Committee, and in one fell swoop all possible objections were removed.

Sports played an incomparably greater role in the Nordic countries than they did in the USSR. The newspapers published numbers of photographs of our team, as well as me as captain. We were always together, at the skating rink, talking mainly with sign language, with other athletes including the charming fifteen-year-old doll, Sonja Henie.

That night I decided to attend the opera to hear how the Norwegians interpret *Carmen*. The fact that I don't understand a word of Norwegian didn't bother me, as I knew *Carmen* by heart.[14] During the first intermission I went to the foyer, stopping in front of a column. I wasn't dressed for the opera, but people recognized me from the newspaper photos: "It's the Soviet team captain." A charming young lady, accompanied by two very respectable and well brought-up young men, passed in front of me. They discussed something, the young men politely disagreeing. Suddenly I understood: she came up to me and began to talk. She spoke French and English, and we opted for French. At first we spoke of my team and of skating. Then she started asking me all sorts of questions about the Soviets, their policies, their literature. I tried to answer ambiguously, to be witty and to crack jokes (because I was planning to stay abroad [and didn't want to risk being recalled home]). She was very taken with our conversation, and we pursued it during all the intermissions that followed. I noticed that old and respectable people passing in front of her paid great respect to her. I asked her what she did. Did she work? No, she lived at home with her parents and was a student. The evening was very pleasant.

The next day, when I arrived at the embassy, Kollontai said, "Better and better! Now we're wooing royal princesses." I replied to her in Bolshevik manner, "How could I know she was a royal princess? It wasn't written on her." A report was made on the matter, and Stalin asked me, "What's this about a princess you courted?" But there were no repercussions.

I returned with the team via Finland. I had hoped to find Alenka in

Helsinki. Alas, she was in Leningrad and had asked that I telephone her when I arrived. I called, and she told me that she'd not been able to leave because Yagoda had refused to sign her passport.

The situation was very embarrassing. If I stayed abroad she would be considered my accomplice, who hadn't succeeded in fleeing with me, and the poor girl would have been shot even though she hadn't the faintest idea I would escape. I had to decide right away. If I went back, she wouldn't have any more problems. I put my effort to escape on hold and got on the train to return to Soviet Russia. Yagoda had already had the time to present Stalin with a report concerning my intention to emigrate with the woman of my choice. As usual, Stalin gave me the file with an air of indifference. I shrugged my shoulders: "It's become a mania with him." In any event my return left Yagoda looking like a fool. It was demonstrated that, since I'd returned, I had no intention of escaping. Possible humane motives for my return were inaccessible to the thinking of Stalin and Yagoda and wouldn't even have occurred to them.

It was now clear that if I wished to flee, I couldn't take Alenka. I had no choice but to leave her so she wouldn't be at risk. It was most difficult and disagreeable, but I had no alternative. On top of that I couldn't explain my real reasons to her. She was a proud girl with self-esteem: from the first signs of coolness on my part she accepted our separation without explanations. By contrast the OGPU, which hadn't stopped probing into my affairs, decided to profit from the situation. One of her friends, Genka, who worked at the OGPU unknown to Alenka, was instructed to undertake a mission which she did very well, "You know why he left you? He's got another sweetheart. What a swine," etc. Little by little they turned Alenka against me, persuaded her I was a hidden counterrevolutionary and made her decide (in accord with her communist duty) to accuse me of camouflaged anti-Bolshevism before the Central Control Commission. Yagoda was counting on his men Peters and Latsis, who sat on the collegium of the Central Control Commission. For that, however, they would need Stalin's prior agreement, and it wasn't worth asking him cold. Fate, however, came to their rescue. This was already the spring of 1926, and Zinoviev, Kamenev, and Sokolnikov were in the opposition. I still saw Sokolnikov, but it didn't embarrass Stalin because I worked at Narkomfin and there were all sorts of reasons to see him on official business. But Kamenev asked me to come and see him. Since January 1926 he was no longer a member of the Politburo, merely a candidate member. I saw no reason against going, although I didn't know what he wanted of me. I went. Kamenev tried to get me to come over to the opposition. I responded with bitter remarks about the divergences of the program he was developing: I wasn't born yesterday and could see that it was a fight for power, not a real difference of views. The OGPU reported that I'd gone to see Kamenev, and Stalin changed his attitude toward me, accepting that I should be convoked by the Central Control Commission, where Alenka's accusations would be heard. A woman with whom you've had an affair can tell some interesting secrets about you. (Certainly, according to the Soviet-Stalinist custom, I should have gone to report to Stalin about my meeting with Kamenev, but that system of espionage and denunciation disgusted me profoundly and I didn't do it.)

At the Central Control Commission, Alenka in effect talked only nonsense. Accusations concerning my counterrevolutionary tendencies went no further than the fact that I habitually said, "our customary Soviet madhouse" and "our Soviet bordello." I said that often, in fact, without a second thought. The people I said it to usually smiled respectfully: I was one of those dignitaries who could allow themselves to criticize Soviet practices. When Alenka was finished, I spoke up and begged the collegium of the Party not to judge her too severely. She was a devoted Party member, she said what she really thought was true, thinking that she was performing her duty as a communist and not that she was slandering a man from whom she was separated. It was amusing. In accusing me, she wanted to have me expelled from the Party, which was for me the equivalent of a bullet in the nape of the neck. And here was I, defending not myself but my accuser. Yaroslavsky, presiding, asked me what I would reply to the content of the accusations. "Nothing," I replied, with a wave of the hand. The collegium made as if to reproach me severely for having arranged a trip abroad for Alenka, but I paid no attention to it. I knew it was all for show and they would have to ask Stalin what decision they should come to. That was why, the next day, I went to Stalin and, among other things, raised the subject of the Central Control Commission as if it were nothing (merely the action of a woman scorned), then told him in passing that Kamenev had tried in vain to convert me to the opposition. Stalin was reassured and no doubt replied to Yaroslavsky's question as to what resolution in my regard the Central Control Commission should produce, that they should leave me alone, for the affair was never followed up.

Howbeit, it wasn't quite that way. The matter left a mark, and I've long been surprised that Stalin, with his customary suspicion, let it go on so long. In the spring of 1926 I tried to arrange another trip abroad, intending to stay there. By now I was completely at ease as far as Alenka was concerned. After all the accusations she had hurled at me, she was not a risk. If the OGPU were to accuse her of anything, she need only reply, "I told you he was a counterrevolutionary, but the Central Control Commission didn't believe me. Now you see I'm right." They would have had nothing to say to that.

I had written a work on the foundations of the theory of economic crises. This type of work didn't yet exist in world economic literature. I pretended to have urgent need for documents from the Institute of World Economy in Kiel, Germany (they were in effect very valuable), and I planned a Narkomfin journey of several days for myself in Germany. There were two possibilities: either to request Orgburo approval for the trip, which seemed pompous for such a small matter, or to go straight to Stalin and ask if he saw any objections. I went to see him, asking his approval for a short trip to Germany to do document research. His response was unexpected and heavy with implications: "Why, Comrade Bazhanov, do you endlessly want to go abroad? Stay in house for a while."

That meant that I could no longer travel abroad under regular conditions. At last, all the OGPU attacks against me had sowed suspicion in Stalin. "If Bazhanov stays abroad? He's full of state secrets, like dynamite. Better he stays here in house."

About three months later I made another indirect effort, fixing things so I wouldn't be obviously involved. In the Narkomfin collegium there was a problem concerning Professor Lyubimov, the Soviet financial agent in France. He was not a Party member, they had no confidence in him and suspected him of feathering his own nest as well as doing Soviet business. How was he to be replaced? One member of the collegium said, "Comrade Bazhanov could go there, perhaps, and straighten things out." I pretended not to be happy with that: "If it's not for long, maybe." Peoples' Commissar [Nikolai Pavlovich] Briukhanov supported the idea, and spoke of it at the Central Committee. Since the proposal was greeted with silence, I assumed that he tried to raise it with Molotov (or maybe Stalin) and was given the same reply: "Let him stay home."

Now there was no question of my being able to leave by normal means. However, I felt myself completely an émigré inside my own country, and I decided to flee by whatever means possible.

First, it was necessary that they forget me a bit, that I not see Molotov and Stalin too frequently. I had already slowly quit the Central Committee, simply by avoiding working there. Now I would have to work at Narkomfin for about a year, so that people would become used to seeing me working peacefully in my corner. During that time I would organize my departure.

Alenka had finally consoled herself, and she went back to her Smorodin. Due to his age Smorodin had left the Komsomol and was trying to educate himself, but despite all his efforts he got nowhere. His head wasn't made for the sciences, and he entered the Party apparatus. There, it was doubtless less necessary to have a brain, and he was promoted to be Leningrad Party committee secretary and candidate member of the Central Committee. He was shot in 1937. Poor Alenka fell into the Stalin grinder at the same time as he and finished her young life in the OGPU basement. Their daughter Maya, still a child, was too young to be shot, but after the war when she was older (in 1949, I think), she was sent to a concentration camp, from which she eventually came out alive.

15. Preparing my Escape

The Financial Publishing House. A finance correspondence course. Larionov. In central Asia. Good-bye to Moscow. Blium-kin and Maksimov. Ashkhabad. The secret section of the Central Committee in Turkestan.

Once I had quit the Central Committee, I had a lot more time. At Narkomfin I was in charge of the *Financial Journal*. It was a financial daily, specializing in economic and finance problems. Newspaper technology interested me a lot, as did that of the printing plant. There was a lot to learn there. Directing a newspaper didn't present any difficulties for me: I knew to perfection the regime's financial policies, and the replacement of Sokolnikov by Briukhanov had changed nothing.

In addition, I took on the direction of the Financial Publishing House, which published literature on economics and finances and employed 180 people. At the first meeting of the leadership of this enterprise, which included the chiefs of the various sections—operations, budget, editorial, and so on, plus the Party cell secretary and the president of the local trade union committee—I tried to understand what the enterprise's activities were. To all my questions, however, the leaders replied with tiring verbiage about vigilance, the Party line, and when I requested facts and figures, silence. Each person being questioned eventually turned to a very old man, modestly seated at the end of the table: "Comrade Matveyev! Give us the figures, please." And Comrade Matveyev would furnish the necessary figures. After an hour I was convinced that I was in front of an assembly of parasites who did nothing, knew nothing, and whose main occupation was working up intrigues, denouncing people, and carefully watching the Party line. I sent them away and closed the session. I asked Matveyev to remain behind, alone, to give me some figures. Comrade Matveyev was a man without a party, a specialist who made himself as inconspicuous as possible, but he was the only employee of the enterprise who knew everything and understood the work. His title was technical advisor. After half an hour, I had a clear and precise picture of the working of the enterprise. I was amazed at his unparalleled competence and asked him, "What did you do before the Revolution?" Embarrassed and inwardly cowering, Comrade Matveyev said he had been a bourgeois and an editor, and that he had edited these same economic and financial journals, of which he practically had the monopoly in Russia. His enterprise had been just about the size of ours. I asked him how many people were employed. Still embarrassed, he told me that he had no personnel. Then how did he manage? He did it all himself, with a helper who was both secretary and typist. That was all. What sort of building? No building, he worked in a small room behind his office, where the typist also had her little table. And he did the work now done by 180 parasites, who occupied a huge building. For me, that was a symbol representing the entire Soviet system.

I was completing my work on the theory of economic crises, trying to establish fundamental bases for the theory. Bronsky persuaded me to publish the work in his thick journal *Socialist Economy.* The peoples' commissar for public education let me know that he considered this work as a doctoral thesis, and the National "Plekhanov" Economic Institute of Moscow, which was inaugurating a chair on the theory of economic crises, invited me to accept a professorship. As it turned out I didn't stay there long, only the spring of 1927. After that I left Moscow for the free world, via central Asia.

I abandoned the bureau of economy and finance because I feared that Narkomfin could keep me because of the work, whereas I wanted to leave. So I invented an activity which would enable me to be my own master and which I could quit whenever I wanted. This is how it was done.

The peoples' commissariat for finances had need of tens of thousands of highly skilled employees for positions as inspectors of finance, comptrollers, banking experts, etc. The people who had occupied these posts before the Revolution, normally university graduates, had been chased out, shot, or left the country. There was a great shortage of workers of this type. On the other hand the new "class" policy meant that only persons of proletarian origin could get a higher education. Most of them were uneducated and unprepared for higher education, since they lacked even secondary schooling. Those young people who did have a secondary education weren't permitted to enroll for higher education, since they were mostly from nonproletarian backgrounds. Thus, they couldn't be recruited as specialists in finance. What to do? Narkomfin tried to organize, in Leningrad, courses to train the employees already occupying these posts. The courses of one year cost a great deal of money, since the students as well as the professors and support personnel had to be fed and housed.

Owing to the Soviet system this brought with it a mass of constantly growing trade union committees, clubs, cells, propaganda organizations and economic services, for administration, maintenance, budget, and so on. Only about a hundred trainees of dubious quality were turned out by the courses. Narkom official Briukhanov asked me to go to Leningrad to inspect the project and report my conclusions as to results. I did this and learned that substantial funds had been wasted. In addition, results were a drop of water in the sea of requirements for specialists in the department.

I saw a solution and said to Briukhanov, "Nikolai Pavlovich, lend me ten thousand rubles from Narkomfin funds and I'll organize correspondence courses. They will be self-financing, and I'll repay the money in two or three months. I'll train the thousands of finance officials you need, and it will have cost you nothing. But we can't have students of proletarian origin. The courses will open doors to young people who are now barred from jobs because of their social origins. What do their origins matter, as long as you have them." Briukhanov was intelligent and he agreed on the spot. I got my ten thousand—ruble loan.

I organized central economics and finances courses right away. In Russia, however, correspondence courses were almost unknown. In 1912–13 there had been such courses in general education in Rostov-on-the-Don, but they were stopped by the war.

I began by writing a little volume of a hundred or so pages explaining correspondence courses, which I had published by Financial Publishing House. It cost eighty kopeks and was astonishingly successful. One hundred thousand copies were sold in three months. It helped prepare the success of my course.

My personnel were as few as possible: Professor Sindeyev, my assistant, and former staff-captain Budavey.[1] Both were without party and were effective. I invited the country's best finance specialists to participate: the forty-nine leading professors, whom I knew well through my work in Narkomfin's economic and finance bureau. The courses were divided into four parts, which I parceled out to the appropriate specialists to put together a study course. The professors wrote up their courses, which were printed and sent out to the students. The students sent back written homework, which the professors corrected and returned with comments. The courses lasted two or three years, depending on which part of the program, and ended by examinations. The students who passed received diplomas giving them the right to work in Narkomfin as inspectors of finances, banks, and as comptrollers, etc. The students paid three rubles per month for everything, the course documents and the professors' work.

Seven thousand students signed up the first month. I accepted them all. Of the 21,000 rubles received, I paid back his 10,000 to Briukhanov. I paid the professors very generously, and they were happy and worked willingly. All were competent, and there wasn't a communist among them. Narkomfin was equally happy, for its lack of cadres at last being resolved.

At this moment the OGPU arrested my chief of the course on credit, Chalkhushyan.[2] A State Bank advisor, he was a great credit expert. Being in need of money, he made the mistake of selling an old painting to a Japanese diplomat. He was unaware of the mortal danger this represented under the Soviet regime. A poor little woman in tears, dressed in black, came to see me: his wife, asking my help. What could I do? Given my own relations with the OGPU and the fact that I was no longer at the Central Committee, my intervention could only make it worse for him. I ran a great risk telling her this frankly, but she wouldn't understand. She had heard it said that I was a Party luminary. I told her I couldn't explain, but that it would be clear to her in a few months (by then I'd have escaped). I took the phone, gave her an earpiece to listen, and called Prokofiev, head of the economic section of the OGPU. I spoke as if it were not an intercession in favor of Chalkhushyan: "Comrade Prokofiev, you've arrested my chief of credit section. What's it about?" "I can't tell you, Comrade Bazhanov. It's an OGPU secret." "But Chalkhushyan is doing urgent work on my courses: he's finishing up the study program for the section. In any event I need to know if it's serious or not. If you've arrested him for something minor, just to frighten him, and intend to release him soon, then I can wait a bit. But if it's a serious matter, then I'll have to replace him by another." Prokofiev advised me to replace him, it was serious.

Chalkhushyan didn't leave prison. The OGPU accused him of economic espionage on behalf of the Japanese. He was shot.

The courses worked very well. I stayed with them until the summer of 1927. Since I was my own boss in this affair and intended to quit Moscow, I named German Sverdlov as the director, to replace me. Two years later, already in Paris, I had the pleasure of reading in *Izvestia* an announcement about my courses, signed by the director, German Sverdlov. So, the course carried on [without me].

During the summer of 1927 I vacationed in the Crimea. Before leaving I received a Central Committee circular from the OGPU alerting all responsible Party workers that they must be careful. A dangerous terrorist was loose in Moscow. I learned in the Crimea that the terrorist had thrown a bomb in a meeting of the Moscow Party committee, killing and wounding dozens. Later, I met the terrorist in Paris and Berlin. He was a charming and unsullied young man named Viktor Aleksandrovich Larionov.[3]

At this time (1927) the head of the Military Union, General Aleksandr

Pavlovich Kutepov,[4] was fighting against the Bolsheviks. Young men and women, vowing to sacrifice themselves, went to Russia to throw bombs after the example of the old Russian revolutionaries. They weren't, however, aware of the power of the new and gigantic Russian police apparatus. They were supposedly aided by a strong and substantial anticommunist organization known as "The Trust," but in fact this trust had been organized by the OGPU. All its safehouses were known and all its collaborators were chekists. Terrorists crossing the Soviet frontier fell directly into OGPU clutches and were shot.

The Paris offices of the Military Union, where Kutepov worked, were in a house belonging to Tretiakov, a Russian capitalist and president of the Russian commercial and industrial association.[5] Nobody knew that Tretiakov was an OGPU agent who had placed a microphone in the wall of Kutepov's office. Everything that happened in this office was immediately known to the OGPU. They were aware well ahead of the details of the terrorists who were sent into Russia.

Tretiakov continued to work for the OGPU until 1941. He betrayed Kutepov, who was kidnapped by the Bolsheviks. He also helped General Skoblin organize the kidnapping of Kutepov's successor, General Miller.[6] When the Germans took Minsk in 1941, it was so rapid that the OGPU had no time to remove or destroy their files. Sorting through them, the Russian translator found a note from Moscow: "As our agent in Paris, Tretiakov, said . . ." The Germans shot him, but the reasons why he had worked for the OGPU for twenty years remained unclear.

Viktor Aleksandrovich Larionov and another young terrorist crossed the Russian-Finnish border, each at his own spot, carrying precise instructions. Larionov's friend fell at once into OGPU's hands and perished. Larionov was utterly confused, forgot or got everything mixed up, and once across the border he got completely lost. He traveled blind (which saved him) and came to a railroad line. He took a train to Leningrad, carrying his package with a bomb. He slept in railroad stations and ate bread. He learned from newspapers that there was to be a meeting of the plenum of the Party committee. It was August and hot. Windows were open at the street-level meeting hall. He threw his bomb through a window and disappeared. He got to the frontier and by a miracle got across, returning to France. From there he was expelled on a demand of the Soviets and lived in Germany until the war. I saw him again in Germany [1941].[7]

Upon my return from the Crimea I started the last stage of preparations for my escape.

I had to cross the border illegally, since I was unable to get an official permit for legal travel. Where to cross? My research was at first discouraging. The Polish frontier was completely closed, with rows of barbed wire and guards with dogs everywhere. The OGPU had done its best to ensure that the frontier was impenetrable. It was equally impossible to flee into Rumania, where the Dniestr River, itself the boundary, was watched day and night. The Finnish frontier, through woods and tundra, was much more difficult to guard. However, my mere approach to it would be sufficient proof that I was planning to escape the socialist paradise.

Studying the map, I noticed that in Turkmenistan the inhabited area was a thin ribbon between a sand desert and Persia. The capital, Ashkhabad,[8] was only some twenty kilometers from the frontier. There had to be a legitimate way to approach the frontier from there. I didn't yet suspect that the difficulties of fleeing via Persia would occur well after the frontier, as explained later. I decided to escape at that point. First I had to get to Turkmenistan, which was under the Central Committee's Central Asia Bureau.

I turned over my correspondence courses to German Sverdlov, then went to ask the Central Committee's Orgraspred to transfer me to the Central Committee's Central Asia Bureau. Even though I knew everything and everybody at the Central Committee, I was faced with a big problem. According to the grades of senior militants, I was in a category so elevated that Orgraspred couldn't accommodate me without approval of Orgburo. They asked me to submit a resolution on my departure for Orgburo approval, but I didn't want that. I explained that I didn't want to risk that an Orgburo member would name me to a vacant senior position that might not suit me. I suggested they phone Molotov and ask if he objected to my going to work in central Asia. If not, they could simply send me based on his approval. If he objected, I would go and get him to change his mind. They did this, and luckily Molotov, already sick of seeing me stubbornly reject Central Committee positions, replied, "If he wants to so badly, let him go." So I received orders assigning me "for a senior appointment, at the disposition of the Central Committee's Central Asia Bureau."

I arrived in Tashkent armed with this order and presented myself to Isaak Abramovich Zelensky, secretary of the Central Committee's Central Asia Bureau. He was the same Zelensky who as first secretary of the Moscow committee had gone over to the opposition in the autumn of 1923. The *Troika* had thereupon decided that he wasn't up to the demands of the Moscow organization, the country's most important, and they sent him to central Asia.

My arrival astonished him and perhaps made him uneasy. What did it mean? Was I Stalin's spy? I explained that I had abandoned my career at the center because I felt completely cut off from life and had decided to work in a local organization.

"Perfect," said Zelensky. "We'll appoint you my assistant and the man responsible for the Secret Department of the Central Asia Bureau. You'll organize it. I've heard how you organized the Politburo apparatus." I replied, "Comrade Zelensky, let's be frank. I didn't leave my position as Stalin's assistant and Politburo secretary in order to become yours. I want to work at the grass roots level, as far away as possible, in a forgotten corner. I know Ibragimov, secretary of the Turkmenistan central committee, from our Central Committee days. Send me to him." Zelensky accepted quickly, and I got a new mission order: "At the disposition of the central committee of Turkmenistan."

From Tashkent I returned to Moscow, without going to Ashkhabad, to say good-bye to my friends. I'd no idea whether I would ever return to my country.

I not only wanted to say good-bye to my friends but also to think about how my escape could cause them the least possible trouble. After my escape the OGPU would try to find out if I'd been part of some anticommunist group and with whom I'd been in touch. My friends would be at great risk. I had two types of friends. There were those I saw often and overtly, our friendship publicly known. These were German Sverdlov, Mounka Zorky, and two or three others. They had no idea that I was anticommunist, and the OGPU would understand that if I'd been politically linked to them I would never have been openly their friend. They ran no risk. There were others, however, who had undergone the same [political] evolution as I. I had been most careful with them the last years, seeing them only officially and only for business reasons. They would run a serious risk from the OGPU.

My friends gave me the following idea: "When you're abroad and are writing about Moscow and communism, make as if you became anticommunist not when you were at the Politburo, but two years earlier, before you went to work at the Central Committee. It won't change the value of your message; what's important is the precision of your eyewitness account. The OGPU will jump on your claim at once, saying that they had quickly sniffed out your counterrevolutionary ideas. Then, looking for the organization you were linked to, they'll follow a false trail. If you were already anticommunist before, when you came to Moscow and got to the Central Committee, you would have had to hide your opinions carefully from everyone, and each of us could as easily have been duped just as you duped the Politburo. The trail they will then follow leads not to Moscow but to your native town."

It wasn't a bad idea. They could search Moghilev as much as they wished and would never find my "organization." They would probably suspect my friends from the last years of high school: Mitka Anichkov who joined the White Army; Yury Syrbul, a Moldavian from Bessarabia, in Rumania, known as a fierce anticommunist. They were not at risk, and the OGPU would have followed a false lead. I promised to do this, and did so. I regretted it a lot later, as I'll explain further on.

At this point I'll digress on the matter of Comrade Bliumkin, the same Bliumkin who killed German Ambassador to Moscow Count Mirbach during the 1918 uprising of the Left Socialist Revolutionaries, in an effort to sabotage the treaty of Brest-Litovsk.[9]

In 1925 I still saw a lot of Mounka Zorky. That was his Komsomol nickname. His real name was Emmanuel Lifschitz. He supervised the press section of the Komsomol central committee. He was an intelligent, amusing, and witty young man, but he had a weakness: he had a panicky fear of dogs. When we were walking together and some inoffensive tyke came along, he would take my elbow and say, "Listen, Bazhanov, let's cross to the other side. You know I'm Jewish and I don't like to be bitten by dogs" [sic].

Once we were walking along Arbat Street, near an old and luxurious bourgeois house, he said, "I must leave you. On the third floor of this house there's an OGPU apartment. Yakob Bliumkin lives there. No doubt you've heard of him. I have an appointment with him, and he's waiting for me. In fact, come with me. You won't regret it. He's the kind of fool they don't make any more. When we get there, since he's waiting for me, he'll be in a red silk dressing gown, smoking an oriental pipe a yard [*aksin*] long, a volume of Lenin's work in from of him (I've checked, it's always open at the same page). Come on."

I followed, and it was just as he said: the dressing gown, pipe, and Lenin's book. Bliumkin was pretentious and vain. He was convinced that he was an historic personage. Zorky and I mocked his conceit: "Yakob Grigorievich, we went to the museum of the History of the Revolution. One wall is devoted to the assassination of Mirbach and to you." "Yes? I'm delighted. What's on the wall?" All sorts of newspaper clippings, we told him, and photographs, documents, and quotes. At the top, clear across the wall, is a Lenin quote: 'We need the powerful intervention of the iron battalions of the proletariat, not the hysterical extravagances of the degenerate petit-bourgeoisie.' All that was our invention: Bliumkin was greatly moved but he didn't go to the museum to verify our joke's authenticity.

Bliumkin's first cousin told me that Mirbach's assassination didn't happen quite as Bliumkin recounted it: when they were in Mirbach's office, Bliumkin threw his bomb and jumped in great haste through the window, but he was hung up by the seat of his pants on the railings outside, in a very uncomfortable position. The marine who was with him killed Mirbach without hurrying, unhooked Bliumkin, put him in a truck, and drove off. The marine was killed soon after on a Civil War front, and Bliumkin was declared an outlaw by the Bolsheviks. He soon passed to their side, however, betraying the Left Socialist Revolutionaries. He was accepted into the Party and the Cheka and became famous for his part in the bloody suppression of the Georgian insurrection. Later his Cheka career took him to Mongolia, where his excessive shootings caused even the OGPU to recall him. The silk robe and the pipe were souvenirs of Mongolia. The OGPU didn't know what to do with him, and they kept him in reserve.

When he showed me his apartment of four huge rooms, I asked, "You live here alone?" He replied, "No, I live with my first cousin Maksimov. He takes care of housekeeping." Maksimov was introduced to me. He was, like Bliumkin, from Odessa. Maksimov was his Party name, which he'd no right to have since in Odessa, where he joined the Party, he was quartermaster of a cavalry regiment and sold stolen oats for his own profit. He was expelled from the Party and the army. His real name was Arkady Romanovich Birger. He lived with his cousin, and Bliumkin was trying to get him a job. It wasn't easy because nobody wanted to hire a man expelled from the Party for selling state property.[10]

"You have two unoccupied rooms, whereas German Sverdlov lives in a little apartment with his brother Veniamin, and has no room to himself. He would be comfortable here, with you." "The brother of Yakob Sverdlov? He's welcome and can come today."

That was how German Sverdlov came to live at Bliumkin's.

From the moment Bliumkin went to work at the OGPU, he boasted that he knew me. Yagoda jumped on it, "Yakob Grigorievich, there's a job for you. Bazhanov detests the OGPU, and we suspect him of not being one of us: unmask him. It's a very important mission."

Bliumkin tried, but two or three months later he told Yagoda that he could see no possibility of seeing me more often or getting to know me better, and he asked to be relieved of the mission. He offered another solution: his cousin, who saw a lot of German Sverdlov, could find out about me from the latter, whom I saw a lot. The idea was approved and Maksimov was brought before Flekser, head of the OGPU administration. Maksimov had found his niche: to spy on me and report to the OGPU, which he did until the summer of 1927.

Not knowing what to do with Bliumkin, the OGPU tried to use him against Trotsky. In 1925 Trotsky visited factories with a commission charged with controlling quality of production. Bliumkin was integrated into the commission, and despite his naïveté Trotsky had no doubt that Bliumkin lacked qualifications to be on the commission. The first time a subcommission under Bliumkin visited a factory and Bliumkin wanted to report on it to a meeting of the commission, Trotsky, presiding, interrupted, "Comrade Blumkis is the eye of the Party here, in the field of vigilance. We don't doubt that he performed his mission. We will hear reports from experts who were part of the subcommission." Bliumkin said with a vexed air, "First, I'm Bliumkin, not Bliumkis; you should know the history of the Party a little better, Comrade Trotsky. Secondly . . ." But Trotsky rapped his fist on the table: "I didn't recognize your right to speak." Bliumkin was a bitter enemy of Trotsky by the time he left the commission. To make use of his hatred for the opposition, the OGPU tried him against Kamenev in 1926, when the latter was peoples' commissar for commerce (Narkomtorg). Bliumkin was appointed his counselor, and Kamenev's secretaries were convulsed with laughter at the work of this "counselor." They showed me a serious written protest by Bliumkin, who wrote Kamenev unhappily, "Comrade Kamenev! I ask you, where am I, what am I, and who am I?" They had to recall him from there also.

Bliumkin found his real vocation when the OGPU sent him to the Near East. We will meet him there, later.

When I was saying my good-byes in the autumn of 1927 Maksimov was very sad. My departure was losing him easy work for which he was well paid. I decided to play a game on him. I knew he was reporting to the OGPU about me, but he didn't know I knew. I had learned from my experience with the Soviets that if I thought the enemy wanted information about me, the best approach was to furnish it myself. That way I could choose what I gave them, and that's what I did. I related to German Sverdlov, who had no suspicions, what could be given to the OGPU without damage to me, and Maksimov passed it along to them.

I met Maksimov at German's before my departure and asked him, "What's your work situation?" "Not good, as in the past." "Would you like me to take you to central Asia?" He answered that he'd come with pleasure but could only give me a definite reply tomorrow: he was involved in some sort of negotiations. I understood very well that he was going to rush over to ask the OGPU what to do. They replied that it was perfect, he should go along and supply them with reports on me. That's why Maksimov came with me to Ashkhabad.

Upon my arrival I went to see Ibragimov, first secretary of the Turkmenistan Central Committee. I knew him from my time as Politburo secretary, when he was chief instructor at the Central Committee and thought of me as a bigwig. He was astounded to see me. His first idea was that I'd come to take his place. I disabused him and explained that I wanted to work at the grass roots level. "Appoint me, to start off, head of the Secret Department of the Central Committee (the job I'd refused to take with Zelensky). I'll be under your orders, and it'll be clear I'm not about to take your place." It was done.

Several days later I said I was an enthusiastic hunter, but for big game only (I must note that I hate hunting). I telephoned Dorofeev, commander of the Forty-sixth Frontier Troop Detachment of the OGPU, who guarded this section of the frontier, and asked him to send me two rifles and passes for Maksimov and me. I received them immediately.

For two or three months I studied the situation. Maksimov, for whom I'd arranged a small job, sent reports on me regularly to Moscow.

Ibragimov was a fine man, and we established excellent rapport. I ran the Secret Department of the Central Committee, running the secretariat at meetings of the bureau and at plenums of the Turkmenistan central committee, and soon found myself at the center of all the secrets, but now on a small local level. I often saw Ibragimov and questioned him about Persia. I was concerned that the railroad, our main communications link, ran right along the Persian border. In case of war the Persians would easily be able to cut this line. Ibraghimov laughed and asked what our Forty-sixth Frontier Detachment was for. I replied that I was thinking of the army. He responded, "Do you recall history? When there was a revolt in Tehran, a hundred years ago, and our ambassador Aleksandr Griboyedov[11] was killed, the tsar sent a hundred or so Cossacks from Russia and they reestablished order. Don't think things have changed much since then."

Another time I asked, "With the frontier so close, aren't there cases of escape?" "On the contrary," he replied. "It's very rare. The frontier is certainly long, and it would be very difficult to guard its entire length. But to approach the frontier you have to make your way to some inhabited place, and that's where permanent surveillance is concentrated. Nobody can pass without being seen." "Good," said I. "But that doesn't apply to Party members. A responsible activist can reach the frontier and cross it without difficulty. Have you had such cases?" "Yes," said Ibragimov. "But they pose no problem. We recapture them in Persia and bring them back here." "And the Persian authorities?" "They close their eyes, as if nothing had happened."

That wasn't very comforting. To cross the frontier was easy, the difficulties came afterward. Well, I would risk it.

I explored the frontier. Twenty or thirty kilometers from Ashkhabad, in the mountains, was Firusa, the [Turkmenistan] central committee rest house. Several of us from the central committee went there one Sunday to hunt. I went deep into a gorge, thinking I might already be in Persia. I realized that it wasn't a good place to cross. At the head of the gorge one could come across a border post where they might say, "Comrade, this is Persia. What are you doing here? Go back!"

From the map I picked Lotfabad,[12] forty or fifty kilometers from Ashkhabad. It was a railroad station and two kilometers away, across fields, was a Persian village of the same name. I decided to cross the border on 1 January 1928. The fact that I'm alive to write this is because I chose the 1st of January to cross.

16. Escape. Persia. India.

Crossing the frontier. Persia. First attempt. Moscow requests extradition. The Cheka at work. Agabekov. Khoshtaria and Teimurtash. Across Persia. Duzdab. India. MacDonald and Lena-Goldfields. Departure for France.

The evening of 31 December, Maksimov and I left to go hunting. Maksimov would have preferred to stay and bring in the New Year in cheerful company, but he was reluctant to annoy his patrons (the OGPU) by not following me everywhere. We went to Lotfabad by train and presented ourselves right away to the chief of the border post. I showed him our passes giving us the right to hunt in the frontier zone. He invited us to participate in their New Year celebration, out of politeness. I replied that I had come to hunt and preferred to sleep and leave early next morning, fresh and ready, and also they would certainly do some drinking, and being a teetotaler, I would be poor company. So, we went off to sleep.

Early the next morning we headed straight for the Persian village. After one kilometer, in an open field, I saw an old pole which marked the frontier. The border post showed no signs of life: they were all dead drunk. Maksimov understood none of the region's topography, and was prepared to believe that we'd already put one foot into Persia. We stopped there for lunch.

Having eaten, I got up. We each had a rifle, but I still had all the cartridges. I said, "Arkady Romanovich, this is the border marker, and that is Persia. You do what you like, but I'm going to Persia, and I'm quitting the socialist paradise forever. The glorious building of communism will continue without me." Maksimov was lost. "I can't go back. I'd be shot for having let you go." I offered him, "If you want, I'll take you with me to Europe. But I warn you they'll come after you just as they'll chase after me." Maksimov decided he had no choice, and he followed me into Persia.

We eventually found the local authorities in the village. They stated that our case was well beyond their competence, and they sent a courier to the administrative center, twenty kilometers away. The courier returned that evening with word that we should go to the center. However, the local authorities categorically refused to arrange our travel by night, and we had to sleep in Lotfabad.

Meanwhile, informants of the Soviets had crossed to the border post to inform on our escape. They were unable to report it until the morning of 2 January, as everyone was still drunk. By then we'd already left for the administrative center and were almost there. There is no doubt that, if it hadn't been the New Year, a Soviet army detachment would have crossed the frontier after the first night and taken us back. My career would have finished thus.

Another amazing stroke of luck was waiting for me at the administrative center: Pasban, the district chief.[1] Compared with all the other local functionaries, who were fearful, lazy, corrupt, and indifferent to everything, he was intelligent, energetic, and helpful. He had been trained in a German school during the world war.

He was to send to us to Meshed, capital of the province (Khorassan). He explained to me that between us and Meshed were mountains three thousand meters high. There was only one road; it went partly around the mountains, and near Ashkhabad it cut across the mountains through a deep gorge, passed near the village of Quchan,[2] and then turned left for Meshed. To send us to Meshed by the vehicular road would be to send us to certain death: from this day on the Cheka had a car on watch along the road. They would seize us and take us back to Soviet Russia. Our only chance would be to go straight through, across the mountains. There was no road anywhere there. There were footpaths, used sometimes in summer by the inhabitants. But now in winter everything was covered with snow and the paths were impossible to find. We had to try it. The Bolsheviks wouldn't dare to tackle the mountains. We would be given guides and mountain horses. Whereas we couldn't depend on the guides, we could have full confidence in the horses to find the way.

A caravan was organized, and we started off. Our voyage across the mountains, with snow, avalanches, potholes and steep slopes, lasted four days. Our little mountain horses, shaggy and intelligent, saved our lives twenty times. They climbed incredibly steep slopes like cats, slipped unexpectedly beside precipices and yet quickly let themselves fall on their bellies to stop the slide, four legs wide apart. Finally we arrived in the Meshed Valley on the fifth day, exhausted. We came out onto the high road in the suburbs. A truck came along, acting as a bus. We got in and had time to sit in the rear. Two chekists boarded right after us, but they had to sit in front of us. They apparently thought we were armed, and didn't dare do anything. We arrived in Meshed, and the bus took us to the hotel. They explaining that it was the only European-style hotel in town. The natives lodged in caravanserais.

We were very tired and dreamed of good beds. Before going to bed we ordered coffee in the hotel restaurant, but when it was served and my companion was about to drink it, I stopped him: the coffee smelled strongly of bitter almonds—the odor of potassium cyanide. We forgot the coffee and went up to our room. The hotel director, an Armenian named Koltukhchev, explained that there was only one room available and took us to it.[3] It had neither lock nor bolt; they were "being repaired." I saw empty rooms, but Koltukchev insisted they were booked by guests. We quickly barricaded our door with chairs, and lay on real beds with delight.

Our sleep didn't last long. We were awakened by violent knocking on the door: "Police!" We protested, but they took us to the central police station (*Nazmiye*), explained that it was for our own good. The chief of police, a rough, curt functionary, spoke no Russian. He took us into his office and disappeared. His deputy, a very nice Persian who had studied in Russia and spoke Russian well, told us what was happening. It seemed our arrival in Meshed had caused a great disturbance among all the Soviet organs there. Police informants, watching the Soviets, saw Soviet military agent Pachayev hand another Soviet agent (Koltukhchev, the hotel director) a revolver and something else (doubtless poison).[4] Foreseeing what was about to happen, the police mounted an ambush near our door. Koltukhchev came in the night with his revolver to kill us (he had been promised immediate safe haven in Soviet Russia afterward), but he was arrested at our door, and we were taken to the police.

The next morning I was received by the governor of Khorassan, an old Persian, cunning and phlegmatic. He knew no Russian, and we talked through an interpreter. I told this person, "Please tell the governor that Persia, like all civilized countries, obviously gives asylum to political refugees . . ." Instead of interpreting, he asked me, "Who told you Persia is civilized?" I replied, "It's of no interest who told me, translate my words." He scratched behind his ear. "The governor may think you're mocking him." "Anyway, go ahead and translate what I said."

Having heard me, the governor replied that he couldn't make a decision in my case. The government would have to decide, and he would send them a detailed report concerning me. While waiting for a response from Tehran, all necessary steps would be taken to guard my security.

We were moved into the offices of the chief of police. The building resembled a square Middle Ages fortress, with only one entrance. The deputy to the chief of police showed me a group of savage Kurd horsemen who were camped in the square in front of the police headquarters. They had been hired by the Soviets, and their mission was to grab me when I came out, to slit my throat, and to take off. The police, however, knew this, and I went out very little and then only with a strong escort.

The discussions in Tehran went on and on, the deputy police chief keeping me up to date. Negotiations were taking place between Tehran and Moscow, which was requesting my extradition, hence the delay.

During the last few years three or four matters were always in contention and being negotiated between Persia and the USSR, neither party ready to cede its proper rights. Included were fishing grounds in the Caspian Sea frontier zone, where there is a lot of caviar; several oil fields; and above all the exact border, since that would determine who got the very oil-rich frontier zone. Stalin was willing to cede to Persia all these assets in exchange for my extradition, and it seemed that the government was ready to give me up. My charming Persian told me this with profound embarrassment.

Simultaneously the OGPU was doing its work. On 2 January, finally awake, the frontier guard post had alerted Ashkhabad of my escape. The phone to Moscow went to work, and Yagoda became unusually energetic: Stalin ordered that I be assassinated or brought back to Russia, no matter what. A unit was sent into Persia, to await me (in vain) on the Quchan Road. Georgy Sergeyevich Agabekov, OGPU *Rezident* in Persia, flew from Tehran to Meshed, where he received substantial resources with which to organize my assassination. Various preparations were completed (Agabekov related it all in his 1931 book). When all was ready, Agabekov was suddenly told by Moscow to stop. He didn't understand why and was very discouraged. He was unaware that Moscow, via another channel unknown to him, had received assurances that I would be delivered up.[5]

Agabekov's later history is not without interest. In 1930 he was sent by the OGPU to Turkey, replacing Bliumkin. At that time he strongly suspected that if he were recalled to Moscow, he would be shot. In addition, he was going through the great love of his life: he had fallen for an English girl, to whom he had confided that he was a chekist and a Soviet spy. The girl was horrified and returned to England. Agabekov quit his chekist post and followed her, using false documents. The girl's parents told all this to the authorities, and Agabekov had to leave for France. There, it became evident that he'd broken with the Soviets. Upon Soviet insistence, he was expelled from France, where he had come with false papers. Belgium gave him asylum, and he wrote a book: *The Cheka at Work*, which appeared in

Russian and French. The book contains a chapter ten to fifteen pages long, which details how he was going to assassinate me. In 1932 I met him in Paris. He had the appearance and the psychology of a typical chekist.

He settled in Belgium, and Baron Vergulst, Belgian police chief, told me how the police had used him as an expert consultant on Soviet espionage. On one occasion arranged by the Soviets, a Belgian diplomatic courier fell into Soviet hands for an hour. The Belgian authorities were reassured: all the envelopes in the diplomatic bag were retrieved intact, closed and still sealed. "But the OGPU read them anyway," said Agabekov. Vergulst said it was impossible. Agabekov thereupon proposed that they pick a document, seal it in an envelope, and leave it with him for half an hour. It was done. Agabekov took the package and went off alone. Half an hour later he returned the package intact to Vergulst, to whom he described exactly the document's contents.

The Cheka pursued Agabekov. In 1937, during the Spanish Civil War, the Bolsheviks found his weak point. He had remained an unscrupulous chekist and wasn't above making a profit for himself on paintings sold by the Reds, who had stolen them from churches or bourgeois owners. Using this situation, the Bolsheviks lured him to the Spanish border, let him complete two quite profitable operations, then caught him in a trap on the frontier during the third operation. He was assassinated, and his body, abandoned in the mountains on Spanish soil, was only found some months later.

My kind police deputy came to see me, completely shaken. The Tehran government had ordered me transferred to the capital, preparatory to handing me over to the Bolsheviks.

It was time to go over to the attack.

Before the Revolution there existed in Persia the Russo-Persian Bank. From what they told me in Ashkhabad, the future shah was then serving in the armed guard of the bank. After the Bolshevik Revolution the bank ceased to function, but with NEP, Russian commerce with Persia resumed, and all transactions went through this bank, which had a virtual monopoly. A man called Koshtaria, who had established excellent relations with the Soviets, directed the bank. He came to Moscow often, where he was received by the director of the State Bank, then Piatakov. During one of his visits, Koshtaria asked Piatakov, "Would your government like to have one of the most important Persian government ministers, a personal friend of the shah, become your agent—for a large sum of money, of course?" Piatakov replied that it was a very attractive concept, but what were the conditions? Koshtaria spelled out the financial conditions for such collaboration, but insisted that no one other than Piatakov and the Politburo be made aware (he was evidently well informed on the real mechanics of Soviet power). Piatakov asked, "Not even the OGPU?" Koshtaria told him that above all the OGPU should not be told. That was condition number one. If the OGPU were aware, sooner or later one of its people would escape and tell the tale, which would cost the minister and Koshtaria their lives. Piatakov promised to report to the Politburo.

He did so, the conditions were accepted, and the principal of security was respected: the existence of this agent was made known only to the Politburo, to Piatakov who was the go-between, and of course to me as Politburo secretary. That was how Court Minister Teimurtash, a personal friend of the shah, became an agent of Moscow. He was paid by very clever means, according to Piatakov: Koshtaria bought a huge property through a strawman, but the apparent buyer didn't have the necessary funds. The Russo-Persian Bank loaned the missing amount. The apparent owner defaulted on interest and principal payments. The Bank proposed that Teimurtash purchase the property for the loan amount, but even that small sum wasn't required: Koshtaria sold a small part of the property to cover the debt. It seems that that was how the operation was managed, and Teimurtash became a rich man.

Moscow didn't bother him with trifles. He provided reports only on the most important Persian government problems. Now, however, when it came to turning me over, he was mobilized to use his influence to convince the Persian government to benefit from the high price Moscow was offering.

After being informed of my coming departure for Tehran, I waited until it was Friday, the Moslem equivalent to our Sunday: the government offices were closed, and everyone was resting. I asked to see the chief of police, but he was away in the countryside. I asked for his deputy, who came. I asked to see the governor of Khorassan urgently. He too was away, which is what I wanted. Since it involved a matter of extreme urgency and I wanted to impart a very important secret to the authorities, I asked to see the commandant of the military district of Khorassan (the *emiliachker*) immediately. He sent back word that he was waiting for me.

I knew that he had studied at a Russian military school before the war, spoke Russian well, and although Persian he was a Russian officer [by training]. In addition, he was close to the shah.

I told him I knew (as he also did, no doubt) that the government was bringing me to Tehran and, it seemed, intended to turn me over to the Bolsheviks. I thought that he wouldn't approve of this. He replied that it was a political matter which concerned the government, whereas he, a military man, was not involved.

I asked him for a favor, "During the trip, I'll doubtless be escorted by an armed guard picked by you." The *emiliachker* confirmed that I would be accompanied by an NCO [noncommissioned officer] and four soldiers. "Can you choose that all five be illiterate?" He smiled. In Persia 80 percent of the population was illiterate so that was no problem, he promised me.

"Now, let's go to the very important matter, on which I wished to see you. I ask you to go quickly to Tehran, to see the shah personally, and tell him privately that the Court Minister Teimurtash is a Soviet agent." "That's absolutely impossible. Teimurtash is a very influential member of the government and a personal friend of the shah." "Nevertheless, it's true." I gave him all my proof of it.

Next day the *emiliachker* flew to Tehran and reported it to the shah, who ordered an inquiry to verify my statement. The inquiry completely confirmed it. Teimurtash was arrested and brought before a court martial charged with a crime against the state. He was condemned to death.

Several days later Maksimov and I left by car with an NCO and four soldiers. The road went south, and forty kilometers from Meshed it divided: to the right to Tehran, and straight ahead it went south to Duzdab, on the Indian frontier.[6] I told the NCO to go south. He was astounded, "They told me we're going to Tehran." "They told you that to fool the Bolsheviks; we're going to Duzdab." Disoriented, the NCO didn't know what to do. I asked, "Do you have a mission order?" "Yes." He took an envelope from his pocket. "Look," I said. "The envelope is addressed to the authorities in Duzdab. Read it." "But I don't know how to read." "Have one of the soldiers read it." They were all illiterate. "Well, I'll take responsibility. We'll go to Duzdab."

For four days our overloaded, valiant Dodge proceeded on what passed for a road. As the Persians say, "God lost the road, but the chauffeur found it again." We passed paths, fields, dry riverbeds, and finally arrived at Duzdab. The armed soldiers were very useful. Along the road various bands would gladly have relieved us of our baggage, but the sight of armed soldiers cooled them right away.

When he received the envelope addressed to the Tehran authorities, or perhaps to the military authorities, the governor of Duzdab most likely understood nothing. I asked him to let the soldiers go, as they weren't involved and I had given them the order to go to Duzdab. He replied that he would have to wait for instructions from Tehran, and meanwhile he put at our disposal a small, isolated house. Since it was general opinion that telegrams in Persia traveled by camel, I thought the governor's correspondence with the capital would give me enough time to prepare the next stage: crossing the Indian frontier, which I planned to do without Persian permission, obviously.

I was, however, wrong to think we had plenty of time. The next day after our installation in the little house, while we sat on a bench discussing the situation, a car suddenly drew up before the house, and two men who looked like chekists, armed with revolvers, got out. We ran back into the house in record speed. The chekists apparently thought we would shoot at them, for they got back into the car just as quickly and took off in great haste. Had they known we had no weapons, things would probably have gone very differently.

In any event, it was clear we had to hurry. There was a British vice-consul at Duzdab, whose main activity (I was told) was to purchase Persian carpets and send them to England duty-free. I was also told that the Bolsheviks had organized his information service for him. When I wanted to see him, he refused to receive me. Later, in India, we learned that his Bolshevik informants had told him we were German agents.

Before us was the immense Baluchistan frontier, which the Persians didn't watch at all. It wasn't surveilled because across the border was the Baluchistan desert, dry and burned by the sun. A local, half-savage tribe provided some form of surveillance for the British.

We had to find a way. I chatted with merchants in the Duzdab market, asking who among the local Hindu businessmen was the man in whom the British placed their confidence. They told me. I asked him to take me to the Baluchi tribe that guarded the frontier on the other side, which he did, by car, that night.

I quickly reached an understanding with the Baluchi chieftain. He equipped a caravan comprising three or four warriors and several camels, and we started across the Baluchi Desert. I must note that when we left the Soviet paradise, we didn't have a kopeck in our pockets. Thus far, we had traveled at the cost of His Majesty the Shah; from now on, it was at the cost of His Gracious Majesty the King of England. Anyway, neither I nor the chieftain had any doubts on this score.

It was so hot that we could only travel at night. On top of that, camel-riding twists up your intestines, and it was preferable to go mostly on foot. Maksimov, my traveling companion, had a run in with a female camel, whom he brutally kicked in the muzzle. The camel didn't respond, but on the road she got behind Maksimov's camel and there, staying back two or three meters so he couldn't kick her, she spat at him with great skill. She was indifferent to his Soviet vocabulary. This third trip, by strange coincidence, lasted four days, just as had the first two, on horseback across the mountains, and by car from Meshed to Duzdab. The fifth day we reached a railroad station, where I spoke to the English local resident.

My English left a lot to be desired, and I don't know what he understood of my explanations, but he sent a long telegram to Simla. The next day the railroad car in which the viceroy and his ministers usually made official trips, came to fetch me. After the camels, it was a very nice way to travel. I particularly appreciated the bathroom and the cook who respectfully asked what menu we would like. (I didn't learn until 1977 that our successful entrance into India was not so much because of my initiatives as the effective actions of my unknown guardian angel, Mr. Skrine, British consul at Seistan.)

The Indian winter capital was at Delhi, but in summer it was so hot that the English had built a summer capital at Simla, at 3,000 meters altitude in the Himalayan foothills. It was an artificial town, purely administrative. The only other inhabitants were service personnel and merchants.

We were well received by the English and were lodged in a nice hotel. After our journey our clothes were disreputable, and the English found an elegant way to solve the problem. An examination session in the Russian language was taking place at the headquarters of the British Indian army, for staff officers. I was invited to be examiner and the fees paid for this were enough to buy Maksimov and me new suits, as well as provide pocket money.

We got to India in early April. Correspondence with London started and lasted a very long time. The local authorities understood that I represented a mine of information of all kinds on Soviet Russia and that I didn't intend to keep these secrets to myself. On the contrary, I judged it my duty to make them known to all adversaries of communism. Since, however, the local authorities couldn't utilize my information, they preferred that more qualified people in London exploit this mine, and they left me in peace.

I had lots of spare time. I felt secure and walked in the Simla area. Once, entering a Buddhist temple, there was a tribe of monkeys whose chief, to my astonishment, offered me his hand. Surprised by such politeness, I gave him mine. The mystery cleared up: he looked in my hand for a gift of food, which these sacred monkeys were in the habit of receiving from visitors.

I had discussions about my onward travel to Europe, with the chief of the intelligence service in India, Sir Isemonger.[7] He too was a source of astonishment to me, but an agreeable one. He was a perfect gentleman, absolutely honest. This, despite the fact that his work was espionage and counterespionage, the work of our OGPU. I was astounded at the difference between this gentleman and the scum of the OGPU.

Waiting for news from London, I read and, insofar as the heat permitted, played tennis.

Sir Isemonger explained with difficulty why the correspondence with London was taking so long. I understand that the government was moving the matter slowly because the British Labor party, led by James Ramsay MacDonald and very procommunist at that time, intended to use my case to embarrass the government, especially in parliamentary debates. The government wanted to avoid this and so delayed things by all possible means.

I had a great urge to throw a bucket of cold water on the ardent procommunism of MacDonald and the Labor party, and I had the means to do it. I wasn't sure, however, that it would serve its purpose if I gave the information to Isemonger, so I held back until a better moment. This is what was involved:

When the Soviets were executing the dishonest policy of concessions, the British Lena-Goldfields Company was among those that took the bait. Before the Revolution the company had owned well-known gold deposits on the Lena River. The October Revolution deprived them of the deposits. The deposits were no longer exploited, and the equipment was destroyed. Under NEP the Bolsheviks proposed that the deposits be exploited by concession. The company negotiated, and the Bolsheviks proposed enticing terms. The company had to bring in all necessary new equipment, dredges, etc., and organize production. The terms were very advantageous since the company could keep almost all the ore, selling only a portion to the Bolsheviks, and then at the world price. The Bolsheviks had stipulated in the agreement that production must be over a certain minimum, a small monthly total, and if production was under this amount the agreement would be void and all equipment would belong to the Soviets. The Soviet authorities had explained that their goal was to have maximum production, and they wanted to protect themselves against the possibility that, for one or another reason, the concessionaire might freeze production. The company, also interested in maximum output and having no intention to freeze production, agreed readily to the logic of the point and accepted it.

Sophisticated and expensive machinery was brought in, English engineers organized the operation, and full production began. When Moscow decided that the moment had come, directives went out by Party channels and "suddenly" the workers "revolted." At a general assembly they demanded that the English capitalists augment pay, not by 10 or 20 percent but by twenty times, which was of course impossible. This demand was accompanied by other equally absurd and impossible ones, and a general strike was declared.

The company's representatives hurried to see the local Soviet authorities, who explained that in Soviet Russia the workers were in power and were free to do what they judged to be in their best interest. In particular, the authorities absolutely could not become involved in a conflict between labor and management; a friendly negotiated solution with the labor union was recommended. Such negotiations were fruitless, of course, since a secret directive from Moscow had bidden the union to accept no compromise. The company representatives hurried to the central authorities, where the response was the same: here, the workers were free to fight to defend their interests as they saw them. The strike continued, time went by, and there was no production. Glavkontsesskom invoked the output clause, the agreement was declared void, and the company lost everything it had brought in.

Finally the Lena-Goldfields Company understood that it had been truly taken and turned to the British government. The problem was discussed in Parliament. The Labor party and its leader MacDonald, very much pro-communist then, rejoiced during the debate that there was finally a country where labor could bring guilty capital to its knees, where the government defended labor.

After the debate, the British government sent a note to the Soviet government. The note was discussed at a Politburo session. The response, obviously, was along the same lines as before, that the Soviet government could not intervene in conflicts between labor and management, that Soviet labor was free to do what it wanted, etc. During the discussion, Bukharin stated that he'd read British newspaper accounts of the debate in Parliament. "The most remarkable thing," said Bukharin, "is that these cretins in the Labor party have taken our arguments at face value. That imbecile MacDonald came out with a fiery speech totally justifying us and condemning the company. I propose that we send Comrade MacDonald to be secretary of the Party committee at Kyshtym, and appoint Misha Tomsky prime minister in London." Since the discussion was becoming farcical, Kamenev, presiding, brought things back to a serious level. He interrupted Bukharin and, half joking, said, "The proposal must be reduced to writing, please." Deprived of the privilege of speaking, Bukharin, unbeaten, wrote on a piece of paper: "Decision of the secretariat of the Central Committee of the Communist Party of the USSR . . . (date) . . . Appoint Comrade MacDonald secretary of the Party Committee of Kyshtym, paying for his trip, along with Comrade Urquart. Appoint Comrade Tomsky prime minister in London, simultaneously awarding him two starched collars."[8]

The document passed from hand to hand. Stalin "voted" in favor. Zinoviev: "No objection." The last to "vote" was Kamenev, who noted, "To be promulgated." I put the paper with my documents.

For this to be published in the press would be a hard knock against those mindless procommunists and MacDonald. For the time being I couldn't see how it could be done judiciously. One day, however, while waiting for a free court, I was sitting with a red-haired Irishman, a chance tennis partner. He knew who I was and questioned me about Soviet Russia. Within five minutes I realized he was extremely intelligent, full of ideas, and very well informed on Soviet Russia and Soviet affairs. I asked other players who he was, and they said he was O'Hara, interior minister of India. This, then, was my man for the Bukharin paper. I told him I had something important to tell him, and we agreed to meet the next day.

At his office I showed him the paper, translating it and explaining its meaning. "Will you give this to our government?" I replied that that was my intention. "And can you write an explanatory note relating how this came about?" "Certainly." "You've no idea what a service you'll be doing for Great Britain," said O'Hara. The document, accompanied by my explanations, left for London.

Afterward I found not the slightest trace of the story either in the Indian or the French press. I had expected the British government to exploit it by giving it to the press, but it never appeared.

Later, in France, I met with the assistant to the chief of the [British] intelligence service (who wanted my expertise in unmasking fabricated Politburo minutes being sold by the OGPU, mentioned later). I spoke to him of the document I'd given to O'Hara and said it would be a pity for it to mold in some desk drawer. He knew nothing about it but promised to ask his chief when he was in London. Some time later he returned from London and told me what had happened.

Once it arrived in London, the document had been transmitted directly to the prime minister. Instead of sending it to the press, he acted much more effectively. He called in the chief of the Intelligence Service and said, "Ask for an audience with the leader of the opposition, Mr. Ramsay MacDonald. Give to him, into his own hands, this document I've just received. I believe that since this document concerns Mr. MacDonald personally, it must be given to him personally." That is what the chief of the Intelligence Service did.

The document had a terrible effect on MacDonald. He wasn't a brilliant man, but he was profoundly honest. He was the creator and the uncontested leader of the British Socialist party. He had complete confidence in Russian Bolshevism and supported it in a convinced and unselfish manner. Now he knew what Moscow thought of him, and he knew it from a document of unquestionable validity. He reacted by distancing himself for a while from politics and retreating to his native Scotland. Then, having digested all this, he became an equally convinced anticommunist and strove to lead his party in his footsteps.

It was, in the event, not easy. When he broke with Russian communism only a minority faction of the party followed him. It did, however, permit formation in Great Britain of a national coalition government during the serious economic crisis of 1931. The minority faction of MacDonald's Labor party and the conservatives together had a majority of the Commons. The conservatives invited MacDonald to become head of government. It was a government without precedent: the Tories and Socialists united on the basis of anticommunism! Later, through a severe fight inside the Socialist party, MacDonald slowly managed to move the majority from pro- to anticommunism.[9]

My stay in India became longer and longer. Then I learned that there was a misunderstanding. In early August I became impatient, concluding that I was being led around by the nose, the real reason for the delay being hidden from me. I expressed my doubts to Isemonger. My suspicions bothered him, and to end my doubts he showed me secret correspondence about me between the Ministry of Indian Affairs and the viceroy. The secret, which he shouldn't have given me, was that the English sustained the myth among Indians that the viceroy was a man of great importance and power. In reality he was merely decorative, subordinated to the Minister of Indian Affairs. That didn't interest me. I could see by the correspondence that there was always concern that the opposition could cause problems about my case in Commons, because the British government was asking the right to give me asylum in Great Britain. Yet I had never indicated the slightest wish to go to England. "What?" said Isemonger. "Yet since our first talk you've asked to go to Europe." "Europe, yes. England, no." In speaking of Europe, I had not realized that for the English in India, going to Europe meant going to England. All my difficulty came from that.

I assured him I'd not the slightest intention of going to England. Where did I want to go? "To France." "Pity you didn't say so right away. You'd have been there long ago."

In fact, while still in Moscow, I'd selected from an old *Nenashev* guidebook the hotel I wanted to stay in in Paris. Not knowing the city and supposing that in Paris, like Moscow, it would be more interesting to be in the center of town (quite wrong, of course), I had chosen the Hotel Vivienne on the rue Vivienne, close by the Opera and the Bourse.

Events moved rapidly after that. The British government asked the French government to give me asylum in France. The French accepted, and their consul in Calcutta issued me a permanent residence visa. In mid-August 1928 Maksimov and I boarded the P & O steamer *Maloja* in Bombay. After two weeks the 25,000-ton ship brought us to Marseille. I took the train for Paris, arriving at the Gare de Lyon, where I said to the taxi driver—exulting in a moment I'd dreamed of in Moscow, "Hotel Vivienne, rue Vivienne."

This charming passage appears in Teffi: "One hot day in July 1921, an individual sporting a battered jacket and an old hat came out of the metro station onto the Place de la Concorde. He squinted against the hot July sun, rapped his fingers on the parapet, and said: 'All this, it's very nice, but what to do? What to do?' It was thus that the Russian emigration began."

17. Exile. Finland. Berlin.

*Emigration. Articles and book. The Politburo minutes. Besse-
dovsky's escape. Bliumkin and Maksimov again. Finland.
Mannerheim; the Russian Popular Army. Berlin. Rosenberg and
Leibbrandt. Last meeting with Leibbrandt.*

What was I to do? For me, there was no problem. The entire Soviet
system was founded on lies. I had to tell the truth about it, unmask
what Moscow so carefully hid, especially the mechanisms of power and
the events I had witnessed. Above all, it must be published in the émigré
press.

At that time (1928–29) two émigré dailies were published in Paris:
Vozrozhdenie (Renaissance) and *Poslednye novosty (Latest News)*. Both
were anti-Bolshevik, but they had quite different policies. *Renaissance*
was a rightist paper, implacably hostile to communism. *Latest News* was
a leftist publication whose director was Pavel Nikolaevich Miliukov,
former foreign minister of the Provisional Government, a pillar of the
Russian intelligentsia and a political nothing. From one issue to the next,
its readers were assured that Russia was evolving toward a normal regime,
that the Bolsheviks were in fact no longer Bolshevik, and that if communism wasn't yet totally overtaken, it soon would be, etc. All that was false
and very stupid.[1] I couldn't write for that paper. I would write a series of
articles for *Renaissance,* then write a book in French. It soon became clear
that it would be very difficult to get my essays published in the French
press. The leftist French press sympathized with the "Socialist avant-garde
experience" in Soviet Russia and tried its very best to smother what I
wrote. And since I described events I had witnessed with scrupulous
accuracy, Moscow, knowing they couldn't deny any of my writings,
joined in the plot to maintain silence. Neither *Pravda,* nor *l'Humanité,*
nor any other communist press so much as mentioned my name. Once
Romain Rolland tried, in ignorance, to write a polemic against one of my

articles, but he received a severe rebuke from the communist leaders for having mentioned my name.

The editors were the same. My book [*Alvec Staline dans le Kremlin*] wasn't published until 1930, and then with important excisions. What I was writing didn't appeal to anybody. At that time the left didn't want to attack the avant-garde socialist countries, and the rightists, with unprecedented blind incomprehension, thought it outstanding that communism and anarchy in the world had removed Russia from the ranks of the great powers. My predictions that communism had a substantial future, that world civil war had commenced, and that communism represented the principal present danger for humanity were considered to be the exaggerations of a partisan Russian émigré, a young émigré who wanted to teach experienced political experts their jobs.

I wasn't satisfied with my book, either. It was not only because the cutting had removed a number of my conclusions, leaving only an account of what I'd seen, but also for personal reasons. I had had to honor the agreement I'd made with my friends in Moscow and write that I was anticommunist before starting to work at the Central Committee. It had given me the appearance of a sort of James Bond adventurer who had penetrated the enemy fortress with courage and cunning, whereas in reality it wasn't at all like that.[2] I had simply not been able to discuss my real self and my political evolution. That was why in the end the book didn't interest me. On top of that there were many things I hadn't been able to discuss: people who had stayed in Russia and would have been at grave risk if I'd mentioned their names or referred to them.

Now that many years have gone by and conditions have changed, I can relate all that I witnessed and how things really went.

Some time after my arrival in France, a representative of the British Intelligence Service came to ask for my expertise. Gaiduk (obviously a pseudonym, not his true name), OGPU representative in Riga, was selling Politburo minutes to the British who, thinking them authentic, were paying dearly for them. In actual fact Gaiduk had never seen real Politburo minutes and was fabricating them according to his own concept of them. The British knew even less than he about the subject. I had, however, written so many of them that I was able to establish beyond doubt that the British were buying fakes. They thereupon stopped doing so.

At this time I was living in Paris, at the hotel. One day there was a knock at my door. "Come in," I said. It was a man with a very chekist look, who introduced himself calmly, "I am Gaiduk, the OGPU representative in Riga. I've come to see you because the British are buying, through me, Politburo minutes. Obviously, you are better able than anyone else to determine if they are real. I know that the future of my operation depends on your conclusions. I won't hide from you that this brings in a lot of money to me. If your judgment is that they are real, then I'll share with you half of what they give me." I responded, "I'm amazed that before coming you didn't ask your organization for information about me. They would have told you that I'm not for sale, which would have saved you this trip." "Mr. Bazhanov," said Gaiduk. "You're a new émigré. Right now you're publishing articles, and everything goes well. Believe my own experience. In a year, all that will change and you will have difficulty earning the bitter bread of the émigré. By contrast, if you accept my proposal you'll earn enough in six months to permit you to live at ease the rest of your life."[3]

I asked him, "Mr. Gaiduk, have you seen "Topaz," the latest play by Marcel Pagnol?" No, Gaiduk wasn't interested in the theater. "Well, in this play there's a passage in which an old, respectable-looking man visits a municipal councilman trying to blackmail him [the councilman]. After their conversation, the councilman asks him to leave but without turning his back on him, since the temptation to kick his bottom would be too strong. I ask you the same: go, but don't turn your back. I would be terribly tempted to help you out with my foot." Gaiduk was imperturbable. "If it would please you, go ahead." But at the door, he stopped, "You will greatly regret not having accepted my proposal."

He was mistaken. The money was unimportant to me, since I care little for what can be bought with it. The poverty of émigrés never frightened me. On the contrary, I greatly appreciate what money can't buy: friendship, love, and keeping one's word.

Some time after my arrival in Paris, which went unheralded, the escape of Grigory Zinovievich Bessedovsky from the Soviet embassy in Paris made a great clamor.[4] Soviet Ambassador to Paris, Valerian Savelievich Dovgalevsky,[5] had been on sick leave for a long time and had been replaced by Counselor of Embassy Bessedovsky. One day, in order to escape arrest in the embassy, the latter fled by jumping over the garden wall. For a month the press was ecstatic over this unprecedented case: an ambassador who had escaped his own embassy by jumping over the wall! No one knew the real reason for his flight: Bessedovsky had no reason to reveal it himself, and the British government knew but chose to be silent.

An adventurer on a grand scale, Vladimir Bogovut-Kolomiets, often visited the Soviet embassies in London and Paris.[6] He undertook large-scale commercial, banking, and other transactions for the Soviets. This was the period when the world economic crisis was becoming a real catastrophe. Bogovut had an idea: propose to the British that they offer the Soviets a substantial loan. The Soviets were undertaking their five-year plans for industrialization but were seriously hindered by lack of foreign exchange to buy goods abroad. Bogovut wanted the British to give the Soviets, for several years, the requisite machines and industrial materiel under a long-term loan agreement. In so doing British industry would have work and would surmount the crisis. For their part the Soviets would have to cease their revolutionary activity in the British colonies, especially in India. Bogovut was not a philanthropist, and he wanted all this to pass through him, giving him a 1 percent commission. Given the enormous amount of the loan, it would have made him a multimillionaire for the rest of his days. However, he couldn't put his plan into effect alone, and he persuaded Bessedovsky to participate.

The scenario was prepared as follows. Bogovut, who had his entrée everywhere, was to let the British government know that Moscow would like such a loan but didn't want to take the risk that negotiations would fail; therefore, the approach was being made through Bessedovsky's Paris embassy, not the ambassador in London, and must be conducted in the greatest secrecy. Only after an agreement was concluded, would it become official and public.

The British government was very interested and to conduct the secret negotiations with Bessedovsky, they sent an entire delegation to Paris including two ministers, one of whom was Sir Samuel Hoare. The delegation discussed the loan in detail with Bessedovsky. He warned them that absolute secrecy must be kept until an agreement was concluded: if London were to query Moscow, the reply would be that Moscow had made no proposal, and negotiations would be broken off. The delegation returned to London full of optimism. Samuel Hoare, however, didn't share their optimism. He said it was all a bluff, without serious content. He was, he said, a Jew himself and he knew his fellow Jews well: Bessedovsky was of a type not to be taken seriously, one mustn't believe a word he said. Hoare proposed that Moscow be asked for official verification.

In the end the Cabinet came around to his position, and the British ambassador in Moscow was instructed to request confirmation from Chicherin. Chicherin replied that he knew nothing of any loan negotiations but would ask a higher level (the Politburo). He appeared before the Politburo complaining bitterly that he had been placed in a ridiculous situation: negotiations with the British were going on, yet it had been judged not necessary to tell him, the foreign minister. The Politburo reassured him: there was no question of such negotiations. It became clear that Bessedovsky was engaged in an illegal enterprise. Chicherin recalled him to Moscow. Since there had been no further word from the British,

Bessedovsky understood that the game was up. Using the pretext that he was ill, he declined to return to Moscow. Chicherin called a special meeting of Soviet ambassadors to Western Europe, as a means to get hold of Bessedovsky. Once again Bessedovsky refused. The Politburo lost patience and charged Isaak Anshelevich Roizenman, a member of the Central Control Commission, with the task of bringing Bessedovsky home, dead or alive.[7]

Roizenman was furnished with appropriate credentials and went to Paris, where he showed his credentials to the chekists who, posing as concierges, guarded the entrance to the embassy: "From now on I am the boss here, and you obey only my orders. In particular no one leaves the embassy without my authorization." The chekists asked, "Not even Comrade Ambassador?" "Above all not the ambassador." Then, having fully briefed the first secretary, Roizenman installed himself in the ambassador's office and called for Bessedovsky. He scolded Bessedovsky brutally and informed him that he would immediately be taken back to Moscow, by force if necessary. The latter, understanding how badly it would go for him, ran for the exit, but the chekists barred the way and threatened to shoot if he tried to go out. He turned about, remembering a ladder left against the garden wall by the gardener. Using it, he climbed atop the wall and jumped over.

He then went to the local police station and asked the commissioner to liberate his wife and son, still in the embassy. The commissioner telephoned the Foreign Ministry. The general secretary of the ministry replied that the embassy enjoyed diplomatic immunity but that in this case the police could enter the embassy, acting on the ambassador's request. The wife and son were liberated. Bessedovsky asked for asylum, and the police hid him away carefully. Several days later the mailman brought a summons: Bessedovsky was to return to Moscow and face a tribunal on charges of treason. Moscow simply wanted to let him know that he couldn't escape the OGPU, which even knew the secret place where he was hidden.

The press had made so much noise about the Bessedovsky affair that the OGPU didn't try to kill him but instead strove to make all the trouble possible for him.

I met Bessedovsky from time to time between his escape and the start of World War II, mainly for security reasons. In those years he was, as I was, menaced by the OGPU, and we exchanged information on the danger they represented. He was writing for the newspapers and hadn't yet begun to fabricate stories, although his writings were superficial and full of fabrications. When we met he would question me about Stalin, his secretariat, the

Politburo members, and the Central Committee apparatus. I had never made a secret of my knowledge in this field, so I told him what I knew. Later, he used all this information in his writings, suitably disguised as his own knowledge.

I met him again after the war, when I was engaged in technology and was no longer involved with politics or the media. Bessedovsky said he was in journalism. Several fabrications appeared at that time: "The notes of Captain Krylov," "Soviet generals speak to you," and "Memoirs of General Vlassov." They were supposedly written by Cyril Kalinov and Ivan Krylov, who in fact never existed. I was not interested in this dubious, third-class literature; I read none of it and didn't know who was the author. But in 1950 a book appeared by the French journalist Delbar, *The Real Stalin.* I didn't know Delbar, but I recalled that he'd collaborated with Bessedovsky. I was interested and read the book. It was full of lies and inventions. I realized at once that it was Bessedovsky's work. Things I'd told him earlier about Stalin and other Party leaders figured in the book, but completely distorted, full of lies, and in effect an insult to the reader. In addition there was frequent mention that such and such a detail (usually false or invented) had been given to the author by a former member of Stalin's secretariat. This cast a shadow on me, since there were no other former members of Stalin's secretariat in exile. Reading the book, a specialist in Soviet affairs could be led to believe I was the source of Bessedovsky's documents.

I requested an explanation. He didn't deny having written it all and having mocked his readers. When I threatened to denounce his fabrications in the press, he replied that the book was signed by Delbar, and Bessedovsky was not officially involved: if I attacked him, I could be charged with defamation.

I requested him never to show his face to me again, and that was the last I saw of him.

About 1930 extensive personnel changes took place in the OGPU. In particular [Meier Abramovich] Trilisser, head of the foreign section, was replaced by [Stanlislav Adamovich] Messing.[8] As a result of personnel changes, the character of the organization's work abroad changed. Trilisser was a fanatic communist, who recruited his people from among equally fanatic communists. They were dangerous people who stopped at nothing. Such operations as the attack on the cathedral in Sofia (when the King of Bulgaria and all the government were inside) and the kidnapping of General Kutepov were typical. By 1930 these cadres were being dispersed; many of them favored Trostky and the opposition, and Stalin had no confidence in them. Messing brought in new cadres, peaceful bureaucrats. They did their best, it's true, but above all they gave the appearance of doing their best, and they had no desire to run any risks. When an operation was risky they always found objective reasons against its realization. Although in 1929 I was once again the object of an attack (this time in the guise of an automobile accident), the year 1930 marked the end of the most dangerous period for me.

In 1929 Bliumkin, who had been appointed to Turkey as OGPU *Rezident,* came to Paris to organize another attempt against me. In selecting him, the OGPU knew that he knew me personally and that I was in touch with his cousin Maksimov, whom I'd brought to Paris. Bliumkin found Maksimov, who had gone to work like everyone else after reaching France and had conducted himself reasonably for two years. Bliumkin persuaded him that the OGPU had forgotten about him long ago but that it was very important to them to find out if Bazhanov had left behind a network in Moscow, with which he was in touch. If Maksimov would go back to work for the OGPU, watch Bazhanov, and elicit information from him on his contacts and if possible organize his assassination, he would be pardoned and well paid. Maksimov accepted and once again generated reports about me. A year later, he tried to have me killed but in a manner to avoid any risk himself. The effort failed, but it was absolutely clear that he was again working for the OGPU. He hastened to disappear from my view. In 1935, in Trouville, I bought a Russian newspaper and learned that the refugee Arkady Maksimov had fallen or been pushed from the first platform of the Eiffel Tower. The paper speculated it was suicide. It's possible, but for me it remains a mystery.[9]

When Bliumkin himself returned from Paris to Moscow and related what he'd done to organize an attempt against me, Stalin found it useful to push, in advance, the rumor that I had been liquidated. He did it to teach others not to escape: "We never forget, we have a long arm and, sooner or later, it will reach the fugitive."

Bliumkin went to Turkey from Moscow. But his hatred for Trotsky had long ago evaporated. He made contact with the opposition and agreed to deliver some secret documents for Trotsky (who was then in the Prinkipo Islands) [Kizil Adalar, or Princes Islands, 10 miles S.E. of Istanbul]. He was called to Moscow on the pretext that he was to report on his mission, and was arrested and shot.[10]

The next attempt against me wasn't until 1937. A Spaniard, doubtless an anarchist or communist, tried to stab me as I was returning home, as I did each evening, after having left the car in the garage. This effort showed how the work of the OGPU had degenerated. The OGPU agents didn't want to run any risks themselves: they had undoubtedly told the miserable

Spaniard that I was a Franco agent or something like that. It was typical of how the OGPU settled old accounts in Paris at that time.

But there were more complicated cases, as for example the assassination in the Bois de Boulogne of the former Soviet functionary Navashin. During the Spanish Civil War, a whole class of "leftist" villains lived off the situation. In Spain, the Reds [Republicans] robbed churches, monasteries, and the bourgeoisie and brought their booty to France for sale. Many shady "leftists" helped them, and the largest share of the proceeds stayed in the pockets of middlemen. The Spanish Reds used the rest of the money to buy necessities which were in short supply in Red Spain. A band of thieves directed by Navashin undertook the following operation: using some of the Red money, they bought canned and other goods which were in spoiled or poor condition and at rock-bottom prices. These goods were loaded into boats and sent to the Reds. At the same time, the band informed Franco agents in Paris the names of the boats and their itineraries. Franco had a navy, whereas the Reds didn't have one. The boats were sunk by naval shell fire. All one could do was to raise one's hands to heaven and procure another boat, at substantial profit. Once, however, the captain had navigational instrument problems and followed a completely unexpected route. Because of this he wasn't intercepted by a gunboat and reached a Red port. The cargo was unloaded, and the fraud was clearly visible. Navashin was stabbed to death.

In 1939, at the very start of World War II, I had an amusing incident. For several years I had kept up to date a substantial information file on Soviet Russia. It was a great help in my journalistic writing, although it required systematic reading of the Soviet media, which took too much time. I decided to sell it for that reason and received much more money for it than I had expected. During the summer of 1939 I went to vacation in Belgium, at Ostend, and since the danger of war was in the air, I took all my money with me. In Ostend it rained several days in a row, and I decided to go to the Côte d'Azur, where it's always good weather in summer. I left my money in the vault of an Ostend bank in order not to carry it in hotels. I enjoyed the sun and the sea and didn't even read newspapers. One day, going out to swim, I saw notices on walls with two small flags. It was mobilization and consequently war. I had hardly got back to Paris when war began. The Belgian frontier was immediately closed and, along with all other visas, my permament Belgian visa was canceled. After two or three days it began to look as if this ridiculous situation would go on a long time: all my money was in Belgium, and I couldn't go there.

The solution was to take the bull by the horns. I drove toward Belgium.

The French roads were deserted, and I could go at full speed: all private cars had been hidden because the army requisitioned vehicles it met on the roads. They only requisitioned certain models and types of vehicles, but the public was unaware of such military secrets and, to be safe, didn't go out at all. At the French frontier I came to a French customs building outside which several gendarmerie officers were sunning themselves. I spoke to the senior one, a captain, and explained that I wanted to retrieve my money from Belgium. The officers laughed good-naturedly, "You must be from the moon. Don't you know it's wartime and the frontiers are closed? On top of that, you want to take your car. Don't you know that no vehicles can leave France without special authorization from the commander of the military district?" I waited until they'd finished laughing and said, "Captain, I ask you, as an officer: I give you my word of honor that I shall return in twenty-four hours." I had hit a sore point. The gendarmerie officers had always secretly suffered because the army officers didn't treat them as equals in terms of their code of honor. The captain replied, "In any event the Belgians won't let you pass." "I'll handle the Belgians." He gave up: "Try it."

The Belgian border post was five hundred meters farther. From there, they telephoned the chief of the Belgian police, Vergulst, who knew me personally, and I got into Belgium. I met with considerable luck in the streets of Brussels: my car was one of the very few with a Paris license plate, and passersby thought I'd come from France on an important mission. I got to Ostend, recuperated my money, and returned to France the next day. At the border the captain jumped to his feet and pointed me out. His fellow officers had made fun of him for twenty-four hours, saying I was a German spy who'd been unmasked and was trying to escape with nothing to lose so I'd chosen a gendarmerie border post to talk my way around.

The captain shook my hand and all but thanked me for returning.

During all the years before the war I'd done my best to fight against Bolshevism, but I'd never enjoyed getting involved with trifles and insignificant matters. That was why I took no part in émigré political life, which was noisy and unproductive.[11] All emigrations divide into a multitude of dark little kingdoms which compete and dispute with each other. I kept out of all that. When the Soviets attacked Finland, it became clear that I had acted wisely. I was the only man opting to act in regard to that war, and all the principal émigré organizations supported and applauded my action. A letter was sent to Marshal Mannerheim asking him to put his full confidence in me and promising him that these organizations would back me with all their means. The letter was signed by the Union of

Former Russian Combatants, by the newspaper *Renaissance,* and even by the president of the Council for the Monarchy (despite the fact that I'd never had any contact with the monarchy). Mannerheim invited me to Finland.

I assumed that the population under Soviet rule dreamed of being liberated from communism. I wanted to form a popular Russian army composed solely of volunteers from among Russian prisoners of war: they were not so much to fight as to convince Soviet soldiers to come over to our side and to liberate Russia from communism. If my viewpoint on the state of mind of the population was valid (and since this was after the nightmares of collectivization and the Yezhov terror, I supposed it would be), a thousand men would start a snowball going to Moscow, gathering force as they went, until we would reach Moscow with fifty divisions [of deserters from the Red Army].

In those days French public opinion was entirely with heroic little Finland. The French authorities favored my operation and quickly helped me through various formalities: the head of the political department of the Ministry of Foreign Affairs accompanied me to the Ministry of War so that all the paperwork could be done at one time, and a general in the ministry wished me luck.

I flew to Finland in early January. I arrived in Stockholm without incident, via Belgium, Holland, and Denmark. From Stockholm to Finland we had to cross the gulf of Bothnia in an ancient civilian aircraft at the end of its useful life. Before taking off we had to sit in the aircraft a long time, waiting. The Finns had no military aviation, whereas the Soviets had a strong air force and ceaselessly bombed Finland with impunity. Soviet patrols flew over the gulf, and we had to wait until a patrol had passed and was far enough away. Then we rushed aloft and flew at full speed, hoping that the Soviets didn't suddenly turn about, for in that case we'd have been reduced to dust.

All went well, and we were approaching the Finnish coast. Sitting at a window, I suddenly saw tongues of flame under the wing. I didn't know what it meant and showed it to the passenger seated in front of me. I later made his acquaintance; he was Finnish Minister of Economy Enkel, who had been in Western Europe arranging for equipment for Finland. He indicated by signs that he didn't know what it meant either, but by then we were landing. On the ground we asked the pilot if it were normal for flames to spout from that spot under the wing. The pilot laughed: had flames been coming from there, we would now be at the bottom of the Gulf of Bothnia, not talking to him. All we could do was shrug our shoulders.

Marshal Mannerheim received me 15 January at his headquarters at San Michele. Of all the politicians I had seen in my life, he made the best impression on me. He was a veritable giant of a man who held all Finland on his shoulders. The entire country followed him without reservations. He had been a cavalry general, and I was ready to meet a military man, not one so well versed in politics. I saw a man of great honesty and great purity, capable of solving all political problems.

I briefed him on my plan and its motives. He responded that it was worth trying: he gave me permission to interview prisoners in a camp of five hundred men. "If they rally to you," he said. "go ahead and organize your army. But I'm an old soldier, and I doubt that these men, after escaping an inferno and surviving almost miraculously, will agree to return to the inferno of their own accord."

There were two fronts: the principal front of Karelia, forty kilometers long, where the communists poured in one division after the other. The troops marched on mountains of cadavers and were exterminated to the last man. No prisoners were taken there. There was a second front: from Lake Ladoga to the White Sea, where everything was covered by a meter to a meter and a half of snow. There, the Reds attacked along the roads, and the same thing happened repeatedly: a Soviet division penetrated in depth, the Finns encircled it and destroyed it in bloody combat. There were very few prisoners, and it was those whom I found in the camps. In effect, they'd been saved as if by miracle.

My meeting with Mannerheim soon brought us to other subjects: the war, and social and political problems. It lasted an entire day. As I've said, all Finland had its eyes fixed on Mannerheim and expected its salvation from him. He was in a rather uncomfortable position, since he had to rely on men who in fact relied completely on him to find solutions to his country's principal social, economic, and political problems. I was from the outside, and I had experience in the heart of the Soviet government. More, I had always been greatly interested in such problems. That's why he wanted to talk with me about his problems. That day the Soviets bombed San Michele three times. The chief of staff came to ask Mannerheim to go down to the air raid shelter. Mannerheim asked me if I wanted to go down. I preferred to stay; the bombing didn't bother me. So we went on talking. The chief of staff looked at me almost with hatred. I understood: one bomb on our house and Finland's resistance would have ended. Everything depended on the old marshal. But at that moment I was already a military man, about to command his own army. I had to show the marshal that I wasn't afraid of bombs.

Just what I expected happened in the Soviet prisoner camps. They were all enemies of communism, and we spoke the same language. The result was that out of five hundred men, four hundred and fifty volunteered to fight Bolshevism. Of the remaining fifty, forty told me, "I'm with you a hundred percent, but I'm frankly afraid." I told them, "If you're afraid, I don't need you; stay in the POW camp."

All those men, however, were soldiers. I needed officers, but I didn't waste my time with Soviet officers taken prisoner. From my first contact with them I had seen that two or three semichekists, semi-Stalinists among them had already had the time to form a cell and terrorize their fellow officers. The least gesture would be reported to Russia, and their families would pay with their lives for their transgressions. I decided to recruit officers among the White émigrés. The military union put their Finnish section at my disposal. I chose only career officers, but it took a lot of time to orient them and get them into political rapport with their soldiers. They spoke different languages, and I had to make great efforts to get the officers to find the right tone to establish good relations with the men. In the end it worked out, but there were numerous other problems. For example, armies live by regulations and sets of automatic reactions. Our army had to have new regulations, not Soviet army ones, and we had to create them out of whole cloth. Something as simple as how people addressed each other had to be resolved. *Comrade* was the Soviet form. *Mister* was inappropriate and politically impossible. So we adopted the term *Citizen,* with which the soldiery were sufficiently familiar, and for officers, *Citizen commander.* For me it was *Citizen commander in chief.*

There was another psychological problem. My officers, Captain Kiselev, Captain 2nd class Lugovoy, and the others, were career officers. They were full of respect for my political power, but they had difficulty conceiving how a civilian could command them in combat. In combat, everything depends on the firmness of spirit of the commander. Would I have enough? They weren't sure of it. I knew it because in our exercises captain Kiselev addressed me as "Mr. Bazhanov," not as "Citizen commander in chief." Chance also solved this problem.

We worked in Helsinki, on the fifth floor of a large building. Soviet aviation bombed the city several times daily. It was winter and the clouds were very low. The Soviet aircraft climbed to a great altitude over Estonia, then some thirty kilometers from Helsinki they throttled back and glided down silently. Suddenly they would come out below the clouds, and one heard their motors and their bombs at the same time. We had no time to go down to the shelters, so we just went on working.

The aircraft flew over our building. We heard the "z-z-z" of the first bomb, then its explosion. Another "z-z-z" and an explosion very close by.

Where would the third fall, on us or beyond? I used the occasion and kept on speaking calmly. My officers were all ears. The third "z-z-z" came, but the bomb fell beyond us. Everyone breathed a sign of relief. I looked at them coldly and asked if they had completely understood what I had been explaining. Captain Kiselev replied, "Yes, Citizen commander in chief." Thereafter they had no doubt that they could count on me in combat.

Everything that could have been done in two weeks, took almost two months. Transfer to another camp close to the front, and organization, all went along at a snail's pace. Soviet air bombed the rail centers daily with impunity. By evening each railroad station was a nightmarish scene of rails and ties twisted in all directions, next to deep bomb craters. Each night everything was repaired, and the trains rolled all night, one way or another. But they couldn't move in daylight for fear of being decimated. Our army was organized by the first days of March, and we started moving to the front. The first detachment to go was captain Kiselev's. The second followed in two days, then it was the turn of the third. I closed the camp, to leave with the remaining detachments. I had the time to learn that the first detachment was already in action and some three hundred Red soldiers had come over to our side, but before I could verify this, the morning of 14 March, I got a telephone call from Helsinki. General Walden (Marshal Mannerheim's representative to the government) told me the war was finished. I was to stop all operations and come to Helsinki.

I reached Walden the next morning. He told me the war was lost and an armistice had been signed. "I called you to come urgently, so that you can quit Finland right away. Obviously the Soviets are aware of your activity, and they will undoubtedly request your extradition. We can't give you up, and if we arrange for you to leave Finland later on, the Soviets will learn of it and accuse us of duplicity. Don't forget that we're in their hands now, and we must avoid anything that will aggravate their conditions for peace, which will be hard enough as it is. If you leave now, we'll say you're no longer in Finland when they ask for you, and it will be easy for them to verify the date of your departure." "But my officers and men? How can I abandon them?" "Don't worry about your officers, they are all Finnish citizens and so they run no risk. As for any soldiers who wish to return to the USSR against our advice, we can't stop them, it's their right. Those who wish to stay here will be considered as volunteers in the Finnish army, and will have all the rights of Finnish citizens. Your action here won't put them at risk: we'll take care of them."

All that seemed perfectly just and reasonable. I went by car to Turku, arrived in Sweden the same day, and got back to France without problems. I presented a report on my action in Finland, first to the representatives of émigré organizations, and second to meetings of Russian staff officers. One meeting took place at the chief of the first section of the military union, General Vitkovsky's: those present included Admiral Kedrov, former ambassador Maklakov with his hearing horn, and even one of the Grand Dukes—Andrey Vladimirovich if I'm not mistaken. Soon after, the battle for France began, and in June [1940] the Germans entered Paris.

I lived peacefully in Paris for almost a year. In mid-June 1941 a German in uniform came unexpectedly to see me. At that time they were all in uniform, and I understood little of their stripes and insignia: I think he was something like a major. He told me that I must report right away to an organization on the avenue Iéna. What for? He didn't know, but his car was at my disposal and he could take me there. I replied that I preferred to change and get ready, and in one hour I would get there on my own. I used the hour to ask Russian friends what was this institution on avenue Iéna. It seems it was Alfred Rosenberg's Paris headquarters.[12] What could they want of me?

I arrived and was received by a man in a general's uniform, who told me that the German government wanted me in Berlin urgently. My papers would be ready in a few minutes. There was a night train to Berlin, and a sleeper had been reserved for me. Why had I been called to Berlin? He didn't know.

I had to decide before evening if I'd go to Berlin or not. If I didn't, it would mean that I would have to get away, over the Spanish border. On the other hand, the invitation had been extended in very polite terms. Why not go and see what it was about? I decided to go. In Berlin, they met me at the station and took me to the National Socialist [Nazi] Party's Central Committee building. I was received by Chargé d'Affaires Deringer, who quickly arranged all logistical matters (hotel, ration and other cards, restaurant, etc.).[13] Then he announced that they would fetch me at 1600 hours, to meet Dr. Georg Leibbrandt. Who was Dr. Leibbrandt? First deputy to Rosenberg.[14]

I was received by Leibbrandt at 1600 hours. He was a "German Russian" who had been schooled at the Kiev Polytechnic and spoke Russian as well as I. He began by telling me that our meeting had to remain completely secret, as much because of the subject we were going to discuss, as the fact that I was a known anticommunist. If the Soviets were to learn I was in Berlin, they would start protest notes and other unpleasantness, which it was best to avoid. As he was speaking, a man in uniform and boots, looking just like the huge portrait of Rosenberg on the wall, came out of the next office. It was indeed Rosenberg, but Leibbrandt didn't introduce me. Rosenberg leaned on the table and started to talk with me. He too spoke Russian well. He had studied at the University of Yuriev (Derpt) in Russia, but his Russian was slower and he had to search for words now and then.

I expected the usual questions on Stalin and other Soviet leaders, as I was considered a specialist in such matters. In fact these questions were asked of me, but in a very special context: if war suddenly started tomorrow, what did I think would happen at the summit of the Communist Party? A few more questions like that, and I understood clearly that war was only a few days away. The conversation quickly focused on my person. What did I think of this question, of that problem? I didn't understand why I was of such interest to Rosenberg and Leibbrandt. I told them frankly that I didn't agree with their ideology, that in particular their brand of ultranationalism was a very poor tool in the fight against communism. That was just what the communists wanted: it would draw one country up against another and have them fighting each other, when in fact the war against communism required unity and collaboration among all the civilized world. My rejection of their doctrine didn't cause a bad effect, and they continued to ask personal questions of me. When they had at last finished, I said, "From all that's been said here, it's clear that very soon you will go to war against the Soviets." Rosenberg said hastily, "I didn't say that." I told him that I had enough political experience that I didn't need it served on a plate and the food chewed for me. I asked permission to ask a question, "What is your war policy?" Rosenberg didn't understand my question very well. I specified, "Do you intend to make war against communism or against the Russian people?" Rosenberg asked me the difference. I said, "The difference is that if you make war against communism, that's to say if you liberate them from communism, the Russian people will be on your side and you'll win the war. But if you make war against Russia and not against communism, the Russian people will be against you and you will lose the war."

Rosenberg made a face and said that the worst profession of all was to be a political Cassandra. But I responded that in this case one could predict what would happen. Russian patriotism was prostrate on the ground, and for a quarter century the Bolsheviks had trampled on it. Whoever revived it would win the war. If it was the Germans, they would win: if Stalin, he would win. Finally Rosenberg said that they had a führer who established their war policy, and for the moment he, Rosenberg, didn't know what it was. I took that for a simple evasion. Later, however, I learned it was true, paradoxical as it may seem. I didn't learn this until two months later, in my last meeting with Leibbrandt, when he explained why they had called me to Berlin.

It seems that in mid-June Rosenberg and Leibbrandt thought that after war had begun, it might be a good idea to form an anticommunist Russian government. They couldn't think of a Russian who was fit to do it. Whether it was a result of my action in Finland or Mannerheim's opinion of me, they came to envisage my candidature, so they called me to assess me (if Leibbrandt can be believed, they judged me favorably). War, however, began a few days later, and Rosenberg became minister for the Eastern occupied regions (a long-expected appointment) with Leibbrandt as his first assistant. The first time Rosenberg reported to Hitler to get his orders, he said: "My Führer, there are two ways to administer the Eastern occupied regions—first, under German administration, with gauleiters, or second, by creating a Russian anti-communist government, which will also be a center to attract anti-Bolshevik Russian forces." Hitler interrupted him, "There is no question of any Russian government. Russia is to be a German colony and will be administered by Germans."[15]

After that, Rosenberg manifested no further interest and didn't call me again.

After my meeting with Rosenberg and Leibbrandt I was in a peculiar position. I was in possession of a secret of capital importance, and I lived in total isolation. The morning of 22 June when I went out and saw the serious faces of people reading newspapers, I understood. The papers contained Hitler's manifesto on the war. The manifesto said nothing about a Russian state or the liberation of the Russian people. On the contrary, the only question was one of acquiring living space in the East for the German people. It was clear: Hitler had started the war to make Russia his colony. To me, it was an absolutely idiotic scheme. As far as I was concerned, Germany had already lost the war; it was merely a question of time, and communism would win. What to do?

I told Deringer I wanted to see Rosenberg. He replied politely that he would pass along my request to Dr. Rosenberg. Several days later he sent word that Rosenberg was very busy forming up his new ministry and couldn't receive me. I stayed in Berlin, twiddling my thumbs. I wanted to return to Paris, but according to Deringer only Rosenberg or Leibbrandt could authorize it. So, I waited.

A month later, Leibbrandt suddenly called for me. He already ran the new ministry, and the waiting room was full of gauleiters in generals' uniforms. He asked me if I still obstinately stuck to my prognostics, in light of recent events (the German army advanced victoriously, taking prisoners in the millions). I replied that I was absolutely certain that Germany would be defeated: her war policy was senseless. It was all clear, the press called Russians subhumans, and prisoners of war were allowed to starve to death.[16] The conversation came to no result, and Leibbrandt responded evasively to my wish to return to Paris: wait a bit longer. What could I do?

I spent another month as a prisoner, on my honor. Suddenly, Leibbrandt called for me, and asked me again: the German army was going from victory to victory, there were already several million prisoners, and the populace greeted the Germans by ringing church bells. Do I still predict the same? I replied, "More than ever. The people greet the Germans with bells, the soldiers surrender, but in two or three months all Russia will know that you starve your prisoners and treat the people like cattle. Then they'll cease surrendering, they'll begin to fight, and the populace will shoot your men in the back. The war will start to turn against you." Leibbrandt told me he had called for me to propose that I direct political work among the POWs. "You did it with such success in Finland!" I refused, point blank. What kind of political work would it be? What could the prisoners be told? That the Germans wanted to make Russia into a colony, the Russians into slaves, and that they should contribute to it? The prisoners would, rightly, tell such a messenger to go to the devil. Leibbrandt eventually lost his patience. "You're just a poor émigré, yet you speak as if you were the ambassador of a great power." I replied, "I am, in effect, the representative of a great power, the Russian people. As such, I am the only Russian with whom your government is speaking, and it is my duty to tell you what I think." Leibbrandt replied, "We can shoot you, or send you to break stones on the roads, or force you to apply our policies." "Dr. Leibbrandt, you are wrong. You can certainly shoot me or send me to break rocks in a camp, but you can't force me to apply your policies." Leibbrandt's reaction was unexpected. He got up and shook my hand. "It is because we believe you are an honorable man that we chose you as interlocutor. A great number of Russians line up at the ministry to offer to work for us. But they want to be our servants, and they don't interest us."

Again we discussed German policy, and I didn't pull any punches, telling him that at our level of political discussions we had to be blunt. Leibbrandt protested, but more and more feebly. Finally, forcing himself, he said, "I have full confidence in you, and I'll tell you something very dangerous for me: I believe you are quite right." I jumped: "And Rosenberg?" Rosenberg thought as I did. "Then why doesn't Rosenberg try to convince Hitler that his policy is completely disastrous?" "You don't understand," said Leibbrandt. "Hitler can't be convinced of anything. He is the only one to speak, and he lets no one else talk and listens to nobody.

If Rosenberg tries to convince him, the only result will be that Rosenberg will immediately be relieved of his job for being incapable of understanding and applying the ideas and decisions of the Führer, and he will be sent to the Eastern front as a simple soldier. That's all." "But if you're convinced that Hitler's policy is absurd, how can you apply it?" "It's much more complicated than you think," said Leibbrandt. "It's not only our problem, it extends to all the leaders of our movement. Once Hitler began to make decisions we thought were foolish—occupation of the Ruhr, violating the Treaty of Versailles, the arming of Germany, the occupation of Austria, then of Czechoslovakia—we waited each time for failure and disaster. But each time he won. Little by little, we came to believe that perhaps this man saw and comprehended things we neither saw nor comprehended, and that there was nothing for it but to follow him. It was thus with Poland, France, and Norway, and now in Russia we are winning and we'll soon be in Moscow. Maybe once again he's right, and we're wrong?"

"Dr. Leibbrandt, I've no place here, and I want to go back to Paris." "But as you're against our policies, perhaps you will work against us?" "I can give you my word of honor that I will neither work for nor against anyone. I can't work with the Bolsheviks, as I am an enemy of communism. I can't work with you; I don't agree with either your ideology or your policies. I can't work with the Allies either, for they have betrayed Western civilization by concluding a criminal alliance with communism. I can only conclude that Western civilization has decided to commit suicide, and there's no place for me in all of that. I will occupy myself with science and technology."

Leibbrandt agreed. Before leaving I told Larionov and the leaders of the solidarist organizations (Poremsky, Rozhdestvensky, etc.) about my meetings with Rosenberg and Leibbrandt. The solidarists had come to Berlin and wanted to enter Russia behind the German army. I told them it was absolutely hopeless: all the population would soon be against the Germans. To be with the population would be to fight with the partisans against the Germans. For what? To help the Bolsheviks resume power over the people? But the solidarists wanted to try anyway. They were soon to see that the situation was hopeless.

Back in Paris, I also reported to representatives of the Russian émigré organizations. My conclusions were very pessimistic. Among the audience were Gestapo informants. One of them asked me a provocative question: "According to you, should one collaborate with the Germans, or not?" I replied negatively: such collaboration made no sense.

Of course, the Gestapo learned of it. I have to credit the Germans that I was able to live peacefully in Paris until the end of the war, busy with physics and technology, and the Germans never touched me.

At the end of the war, before the occupation of Paris, I had to go to Belgium for a while. It was thus that communist bandits sent to kill me didn't find me.

Conclusion

During World War II, I distanced myself from politics, and during the next thirty years I was busy in science and technology.[1] However, my experience at the center of the communist regime and my knowledge of communism that came from it have enabled me to study communism and its evolution during all those years. That study, which has confirmed the observations of my active communist experience, permits me to conclude my book with comments that I want to share with the reader.

I've already spoken of the futility of Marxist economic theory. Marxist predictions of events have been shown to be false and have been contradicted in practice. Let's recall the analysis and prognostication of Marx: rapid industrialization brings about a proletariat and with it poverty of the masses, as well as concentration of capital in the hands of a few. That is why the proletarian social revolution will happen in the most industrialized countries.

In reality it was quite the contrary. The developed industrial countries didn't suffer proletarization and poverty of the masses but a substantial betterment of living conditions. The process of evolution of capital is also known. In the United States, the stage of millionaires has long gone, as has the stage of immense business companies whose directors had decisive influence. Now they are in a stage of wide democratization: the immense majority of shares of the large corporations are in hands of labor and of employees, who are coproprietors of the enterprises. The United States is ahead by ten or twenty years, and what happens there takes place later in the other developed industrial nations.[2]

As for the social revolution, it didn't occur in any of the developed industrial countries. On the contrary, it had mostly invaded poor, backward, and uncultured countries.

Let's leave Marxist theory and look at the real world. The experience of the communist revolution is the experience of Lenin and Leninism. It starts from the assumption that the poorer a country, the more it is savage, backward, ignorant, and uncultured, the better chance the communist revolution has to succeed. On reflection, it is not surprising: the essence of communism consists of inciting hatred by the poor against the rich. The poorer people are, the more simple and ignorant they are, the more they are susceptible to communist propaganda and the better the chances of the communist revolution succeeding. It is ensured in the countries of Africa and the miserable human anthills of Asia. In the developed countries of Europe, it could only be implanted by force, with the help of Soviet tanks. It is evident that envy and hate are used only to raise one portion of the population against another, to produce social hostility, repression, extermination, and to acquire power. Then, the entire country becomes a well-organized prison run by a small group of communist chiefs.

The object of the operation is universal pillage by force of arms and the creation of a universal slave society, robotization of the entire world, cruelly directed by dull and soulless "Party" bureaucrats who benefit from their absolute power.

It signifies the ruin of our western civilization. Civilizations are mortal: the barbarism which wishes to succeed ours carries a name—communism.

(I can just imagine the indignation those lines will cause in a fervent communist. When I joined the Communist Party in 1919, I would have rejected them just as indignantly. But now we've had sixty years' experience of communism. Have they convinced anyone? Alas, only those who suffer under communism. For the young, indignant communist to understand that what is written in this book is true, it will need communism to take over his country and last ten years. But then, again alas, it's too late: communism exists to take power and benefit from it, and once it has that power it keeps it. There is no going back. If, by chance, there is a Dubcek[3] at the top of the hierarchy who wants to establish a humane socialism, even if the entire party or the entire population is for him, Soviet tanks will come and quickly put things back in their place.)

Does our civilization intend to defend itself, to defend all that is its essence: liberty, freedom to live and create, humanism, peaceful and amicable coexistence?

Our civilization is, historically, Christian. In past centuries, the Christian religion has been its cement and its basis. But these times are gone, and we are in a period of fast and difficult mutation in which the structure of our life is changing at a constantly growing speed. Science, technology, and economics have altered life more in twenty or thirty years than in all the century before. In contrast, the psychology of the masses is changing much more slowly and is falling more and more behind these altering conditions of life. Political thought and the public's aspirations remain way behind the radical shifts in our existence. This causes real, profound catastrophes. One might think that it's the duty of a country's political leaders to understand these changes, draw conclusions from them, to lead, with their ideas, the slower thinking masses, and propose solutions that are needed to respond to the new situation. But democratic systems don't allow that. Politicians are elected by the masses. Those unfortunate politicians who try to lead the masses with their thinking, aren't understood, supported, or elected. They are obliged to follow the masses rather than guide them.

Mass political movements are divided into two large concepts. One, looking to the future, is socialism. The other, the voice of the past, is nationalism.

Let's stipulate up front that the ideas of nationality, and nationalism, are two different things. The idea of a nation is normal, acceptable. Man has known for a long time that people handle their problems differently in Beijing or in Paris, that ways of loving or hating differ greatly from the banks of the Yangtse to the banks of the Seine. Culture can develop only in a national context, which gives an original, unique, and necessary way of life. Nationalism is something quite different. It is, "My country above all others, and I support its interests above those of other nations." Nationalism is the doctrine of a fierce national egoism. It was, perhaps, valid 150 or 200 years ago, when nations were isolated and had almost no relations among each other. But the nineteenth century brought rapid changes with the development of the economy, technology, rail and ocean transport, world commerce and interdependence of the world economy, and colossal possibilities in military technology. Then, at the beginning of the twentieth century the fact that this nationalistic doctrine was the guiding doctrine of the great powers made it the prime world danger. This was confirmed by World War I, which was a great catastrophe, a serious blow to our civilization. It brought erosion of world order and loss of the white race's world leadership. It permitted the communist revolution in Russia, and the start of world civil war. And what did this teach national leaders? Apparently nothing. For Germany and Italy, wishing to create a bulwark against communism, found no better weapon than this same catastrophic nationalism already condemned by bitter experience: they went further, to the ultimate of ultranationalism. The only salvation for civilization is the union of civilized peoples against communism. There is nothing worse than ultranationalism which, rather than uniting peoples, divides them against each other and not only separates their strength but provokes senseless wars between them. Nothing is more beneficial, more welcome, to communism than this nationalism. The communists fan its flames, develop it by all their means, for it is the essential condition for their victory.[4]

The experience of World War I taught the leaders of the great powers nothing, and they heedlessly threw the entire world into a second colossal catastrophe. The masses and their leaders were guided by this same nationalistic doctrine, and the communists knew that for them there was nothing better: revolution would inevitably follow the war. Had the political cretins leading the great powers foreseen that after World War II half the world would be in communist hands? They had foreseen nothing at all. They only demonstrated how dangerous it is when the political thoughts of leaders are worthless, and how important it is, if our civilization wants to defend itself and survive, that its leader be guided by other political ideas. How different things would have been if it had been accepted as the basis of relations between peoples that *properly understood national interests were always to mesh with the interests of all other nations* [Bazhanov's emphasis]. National egoism today can only cost the free world its defense. Its salvation rests solely on union.

The other way, which slowly gains favor with the masses, is socialism. It can be said that the fundamental process of recent change in our society has been transfer of the base of the Christian religion to the base of the socialist religion. But what is socialism? A marshal of France said, "To formulate well is to understand well." It's not easy to understand what is true socialism, above all because the communists, as usual, use false terms for their lying propaganda, thus introducing them into general usage by constant repetition. The communists have everyone today talking of "capitalism" instead of "free market societies." When the communists describe their ferocious slave regime as socialist, the world accepts the term (Union of Soviet *Socialist* Republics). It is evident that the communists cover their regime with the word *socialist,* to mislead the masses. True socialism "with a human face" has nothing in common with the barbarous socialism of the Marxists.

Let's say that in the best case, for the masses who believe in it, socialism represents a vague idea of a better life and more social justice. It is also the ideal of free, liberal societies whose adherents don't accept the term "socialist," first because it has been sullied by the communists and their disreputable allies, and second because it allows the dubious false Marxist "socialism."

We know that religions are based on faith and that reason is not applicable to them. We also know that despite this, the new victorious religions possess substantial power. It's a fact that religions quickly divide into sects and heresies which possess a remarkable degree of mutual intolerance. The great spread of the socialist religion in the world signifies not so much its victory as the appearance and development of new varieties of internecine struggles. Had socialism carried the world, there would have appeared as many socialisms as there are countries, if not more, with fierce hostility and fighting among them. For communist China, communist Russia is more of an enemy than any "capitalist" country.[5]

The weakness of the concept of free liberal societies is that they promise no paradise. The weakness of the concept of a socialist society, in contrast to Christianity (which promises paradise and eternal life hereafter, verifiable only by trying it), is that it promises a socialist paradise on earth, which is verifiable by experience. The communists get around it by making it impossible for the population to change its condition, no matter what they think of it after experiencing it. You can't even flee their paradise: it's surrounded by barbed wire and machine guns. Such a condition must be foreign to, and its perspectives difficult to comprehend by, true socialism.

However, as with nationalism, socialism is not the basis upon which our civilization can establish its defense. Even in its best (non-Marxist) varieties, socialism starts off with criticism and negation of our civilization, wishing to replace it with something else that it thinks is better.

The scene appears somber, and it's difficult to answer the question of whether the West intends to defend its civilization.[6] The masses are attracted by communist propaganda, by socialist propaganda, and [our] most rational and stable elements can see no other solution than the old, dangerous nationalism. As for the political leadership, the same that failed to see or understand at the beginning of the twentieth century that their nationalistic ideology would bring the world to catastrophe and revolution still play the little games of the great powers and of nationalistic egoism and don't understand that the world is on the road to being lost.

Nor do they notice that the world is at a crossroads. Our civilization can take another road, one that will save it.

If there were only a firm desire to take another road, it wouldn't be that difficult. Fortunately, there's reason for such a change, if only the political leadership would see it.

Look carefully at the history of the twentieth century. It began with a euphoric atmosphere: everything was developing rapidly; technology, economies, national wealth. Faith in infinite progress was widespread, as was the belief that life would never stop getting better, that extraordinary

social changes would bring better conditions for the poor and unfortunate. Came World War I, and world catastrophe. Empires crumbled, and
so too did the prestige of Europe and the white race, and world civil war
began. But man kept on thinking that everything would be all right, so the
old games continued with the old dice of national ego and racial rivalry.
Then came the second world catastrophe, and despite the triumphant
alliances of the grand victory (in fact the principal victors were subversion, communist revolution, and they trumpeted their glorious victories
louder than the whole world), doubt set in and swept the globe. The result
was total catastrophe, and society's dissolution became all too certain.

A reevaluation and reassessment of the situation got underway. Once
we were well along this road, there remained little of the optimism of the
century's start and man's faith in infinite progress. It seemed we were well
on the way to complete catastrophe. Galloping population increases make
the world unable to nourish itself. Man rapaciously destroys the thin
veneer of arable land, mineral reserves of primary materials and energy
are fast being used up, nature's ecological equilibrium is shattered, the
sea—our future food store—is dying, poisoned by man. All that science
and technology have developed for the good of man, he has turned against
himself. The apotheosis of all this is the atomic bomb, with its unprecedented potential for destruction including, for the first time in human
history, the possible annihilation of the entire human race itself. There is
also the menace, not at all theoretical, suspended over our heads, of world
war, with the arsenal of atomic destruction of humanity multiplying at a
mindless rate. Where, then, is the prospect of a better social life? The great
experience of the Russian social revolution, in which the world's workers
all believed so fervently? The truth of this experience has been trying to
surface for a long time, but in vain. Now its time has come, the bomb of
Solzhenitsyn's *Gulag Archipelago* has exploded taking this illusion with
it, in the wake of sixty million assassinated witnesses.[7]

If all that had taken place a hundred years ago it would have brought
about a long and painful awakening of conscience, and a reassessment of
values among a small circle of the elite. Nowadays radio, newspapers, and
above all television, deluge, daily and hourly, the population with the
most up-to-date and complete information on world events. Thus all the
process of rethinking, all understanding of threats, all fear of danger, are
quickly available to the masses. The peoples of the industrialized countries
live in fear, even terror.

It is this very understanding, this fear of looming catastrophe, which
constitutes today the greatest chance for a significant change: it is the basis
which can permit our civilization to journey on another road.

The choice of roads requires major participation and approval by the masses. But they are indifferent to intelligent solutions based strictly on reason and are motivated only by sentiment and emotion.[8] A [major] change of direction requires an emotional basis, and it exists. That change is now closely intertwined with the salvation of the human race, that it has immense, global, importance far above questions of war and defense. We must find solutions to all these questions, while at the same time escaping enslavement under the bureaucratic communist regimes, which by incompetence and lack of creative thinking are incapable of resolving mankind's very considerable and challenging problems.

This change of direction may be necessary, and it may be possible, but it is by no means inevitable. It can very easily not occur. There is a basis for it, a chance, that didn't exist twenty or thirty years ago. We must find the right way, the right methods, and men truly capable of effecting it. The impetus for it must come in a new way, a new style, a new dimension than ordinary political agitation. The future of the human race is at stake.[9]

Postscript to French Edition

When my book was translated into French, the first readers thought that it would raise some questions, to which my answers weren't clear, in the minds of the French public. This postscript attempts to answer those questions.

The first comment made to me: I don't speak enough about myself in this book, and I remain a mysterious personage to the reader.

That remark greatly astounded me. I had thought, on the contrary, that I spoke too much of myself. Voltaire, I believe, said that there's only one subject on which man never tires: talking about himself. But I think I cannot be accused of this flaw, because it is unavoidable to speak of oneself in one's memoirs. I have tried to do it only when it was indispensable. In particular, I had to speak at length about my Bolshevik career. That enabled the reader to be quite clearly aware of the fact that I was witness to these historic events, saw them with my own eyes, heard them with my own ears, and that my words are not hearsay.

Even when citing episodes in my life of little importance, it was always in the same vein—to confirm my role as a witness. For example, I devoted a page to the period when I directed the Financial Publishing House. In and of itself, that is of little interest, but it permitted me to cite characteristic traits of the bureaucratic machine of the Soviet institutions and enterprises.

I have emphasized this criticism by the first readers because I was no less surprised when my very first reader, Solzhenitsyn, made the same criticism.

That is why, to clarify, I must also reply to the following questions.

First question: How it is that I survived? How could it be that, having become anticommunist and fled to the West with a large number of very important secrets of communist power, I escaped the vengeance of Stalin with his seemingly limitless ability to annihilate his enemies, even outside the USSR (it is enough to remember Kutepov, Agabekov, Krivitsky, Trotsky, etc.)?

There is no question that Stalin wanted me exterminated, not only for general political reasons but also for personal reasons: he must have been very embittered by the fact that, maniacally suspicious and distrustful as he was, he had nevertheless let himself be fooled by a twenty-year-old adolescent, putting him in a ridiculous position vis-a-vis the other Party leaders.

The OGPU manhunt unleashed against me by his orders, went through various stages. The fiercest and most open was in Persia, where everything was tried to kill me or effect my extradition. Once in France, the next stage was less convenient for the OGPU. There were three possibilities: simply to kill me, to kidnap me like Kutepov, or to camouflage my assassination as an accident. The first and second methods presented some political inconveniences: I wrote for the press, and I was more or less known. French public opinion wouldn't have appreciated at all such settling of scores on French territory (as illustrated by the violent public opinion reaction over the kidnapping of General Kutepov).

There was another circumstance that made the first two methods very difficult: I was too well informed on OGPU customs and had no illusions on this subject. I was armed, always ready to face an attempt against me and shoot immediately, without hesitation. I had already foreseen, in Moscow before I fled, the possibility of such attempts. I had taken courses in rapid, precision shooting, and the OGPU knew very well that I was an expert, cold-blooded, shot. That was why it wasn't easy to find OGPU volunteers for the job: it was clear that unless I were killed right off, the attempted assassin would himself have very little chance to survive.

For all those reasons the OGPU preferred the third method, to simulate an accident. They tried various ways, but without result. Finally, the celebrated chekist Bliumkin came to Paris in 1929 to organize my assassination and hit upon the following plan: knowing that I often took the express to Nice, he decided to have me fall from the train at full speed, without witnesses, as if by accident. At that time, I was unaware of the plan. Even when, after one of my trips, I read in the papers that a passenger had fallen from the Paris-Nice express and been killed, I didn't think the Cheka had caused someone else to fall in my place.

In retrospect I believe that may have happened because of the following chain of events: Bliumkin announced at once in Moscow that his mission was accomplished, and Stalin, very satisfied, hastened to inform the Party leaders. From then on, Stalin and the Party would consider me dead.

This news was widely distributed, even coming to Solzhenitsyn to whom it was presented as an irrefutable fact. In the first volume of his *Gulag Archipelago* he mentions Bliumkin's voyage to Paris and his successful attempt.

But here, a question arises: why, into the 1960s, did the Party consider me dead when for the past thirty years I had furnished quite a lot of proof that I was alive? An example is the Russian volunteer army I formed in Finland in 1940.

The answer can only by hypothetical, but for me personally, knowing Soviet practice perfectly, there is a hypothesis that provides a very plausible explanation.

I think that the OGPU, having informed Stalin of the brilliant success of their mission and having discovered afterward that I was alive and that they had deceived Stalin, didn't dare, knowing Stalin's nature, admit the mistake. They preferred to wait. Obviously, in the years that followed, OGPU agents knew I was alive, but since Stalin received only news that came through, and was carefully filtered by, the OGPU, neither he nor the other Moscow leaders knew I was still alive.

I find confirmation of this hypothesis in three facts:

1. The French communist press was strictly forbidden not only to engage in polemics with me but even to mention my name.

2. During the purge trials of the 1930s, when quite absurd charges of espionage and counterrevolution for foreign interests were leveled against Zinoviev, Kamenev, Sokolnikov, and others, I could logically have been included among their ["foreign"] contacts: all the accused knew me personally and had been abroad (Sokolnikov was ambassador in London, Kamenev in Rome, etc.). However, there was not one mention of me, which is easy to explain if one accepts that the OGPU preferred that Stalin continue to believe me dead.[1]

3. The OGPU was, of course, very well aware of my activity in Finland, but they carefully hid it from the Party leaders, i.e., Stalin, and nobody in Russia heard about it. The reason could be that a long-dead Bazhanov couldn't raise an anti-Soviet army in Finland.

(Here I must interject an interesting detail. Bastamov, brother of two officers in my "army," who himself served in the general staff of the Finnish army and who knew all about my activity, was delivered to the Soviets after the second Finno-Soviet war and spent many years in Soviet prisons. During many interrogations OGPU [officials] questioned him on a wide variety of subjects, but they never said one word about my enterprise. Bastamov was astonished but preferred to keep silent. Liberated finally, he returned to Finland and told me this story.)

I imagine I lived in the shelter of this smoke screen until the death of Stalin. When Stalin died in 1953, everything changed for me. I had been Stalin's personal enemy. For his successors, Khrushchev and Brezhnev, I was one of many enemies of the Soviet regime, and I was of no particular interest. They had no personal reasons to hate me. Then, too, times had changed: not only were chekists no longer assassinating their enemies abroad, but they now preferred expelling sworn enemies of the regime.

It is thus that I explain to myself how I went through all those dangers without damage.

The second question posed by the readers of the French translation of my book also needs an answer: Why did I abandon politics in 1941, and why have I now come back to it with the publication of this book?

I wrote earlier that when I got to France at the end of the 1920s, I encountered great difficulties getting my account of Soviet Russia past the barriers erected against publication of my book and that it had to be mutilated before I could get it published. More, I was far from being able to write about all I wanted to. I couldn't say much about the people who'd remained in Russia, in Stalin's hands. Neither could I relate a number of facts, even secrets of the regime. I'll illustrate that with an example.

In this book I have mentioned that Stalin could listen in on all conversations between Party leaders. It was, for him, a weapon of the greatest importance. I knew this secret, but I kept it. Why? Because, as well as being a great weapon for Stalin, it could become a great weapon against him. Imagine a group, wishing to overthrow him, forming in the Politburo and the Central Committee. Stalin would know all their secret thoughts, as the members spoke freely on the [Kremlin] phone system. But if I had secretly advised the group that Stalin was listening, they could have agreed among each other only to have phone conversations which would have given Stalin misleading information about their plans and actions. It would then have been a great advantage for them.

I kept this secret because I hoped there would be an occasion to use it. When Trotsky and Zinoviev started their struggle against Stalin, I hadn't the slightest intention of telling them the secret. Their group was just as communist as Stalin. I was waiting for a group to form in the Politburo or the Central Committee which understood the absurdity and harmfulness of communism and which wanted at least to move to "socialism with a human face," as was the case in Dubcek's Czechoslovakia, for example.

I waited for that until 1930–31, but in vain. After that Stalin's power became so absolute that no Central Committee group could have been up to the task of overthrowing him. By then, for the same reason, Stalin had no further need to listen to the conversations of any adversaries.[2]

Returning to the 1920s, everywhere my story banged against a wall of incomprehension: for the left, communist Russia was an excellent socialist experiment; for the right, it was an operation by inept leftist extremists which would crumble on its own because of its absurdity and its utopian character. My thesis was completely different: Socialocommunism has an immense future despite its absurdity, because it is a religion which seeks to replace Christianity; it represents an enormous danger for our civilization, the number one danger. If Western civilization doesn't understand that in time, it is mortally menaced. Furthermore, the world civil war began in 1917. That is the most important fact, and all the problems of our civilization should have been posed and resolved differently from then on.

Nobody, above all not the political leadership, was ready to see things in this manner. Hence the unfolding of events that led to World War II, the collapse of Europe, and the gigantic development of communism.

By 1941 the catastrophe was already absolutely evident. At that moment I decided to abandon politics. For me, the world war was a stupid crime. I didn't want to take part in it. To fight against communism was impossible: it was considered to be a fascist activity against our valorous Soviet allies.

I turned to physics and technology. For a long time after the war, the situation remained the same. The left, which had won the war and crushed the right in all the Western countries, consolidated its successes. I busied myself with the theory of the structure of matter, my technical inventions, and the fabrication of precision instruments for laboratories (these last years, for the Pasteur Institute).

When things began to change in the 1960s, I knew that it would take the West a long time to appreciate the true value of the Soviet socialist experience, but my life was already approaching its end and I could no longer play an active role in the struggle that was beginning to be possible. Furthermore, I had never liked to occupy myself with minor matters, and my age didn't allow me to envision a struggle on a large scale.

One day I read in *Gulag Archipelago* that I had been killed by chekists. I wrote to Solzhenitsyn, starting the letter thus: "As Mark Twain said, rumors of my death are greatly exaggerated." I met Solzhenitsyn when he came to Paris. He persuaded me to write a book of memoirs. At first, I refused.

Solzhenitsyn believed it of capital importance to reestablish the real history of Russia in this century: we know it has been totally falsified and distorted by the communist powers.

I agreed with him but not without a certain scepticism: history is not the events that took place but what we today think of those events. Did my testimony have any importance?

In the end Solzhenitsyn persuaded me, and I wrote this book. Thus I returned to the political struggle.

Another reason played an important role in this return. The struggle against the communist regime that began in Soviet Russia created groups of heroic fighters inside the country, and a part of them had been expelled to the West. Unlike what happened in the past fifty years, the West now displays lively interest in their testimony. Their critique and their description of the Soviet regime is now accepted. But there is another aspect to the supportive attention the West now gives them. The West has begun to understand that it has followed a wrong road, one that leads to communist barbarism. Understanding this, the West seeks to know what path it should follow? It seeks the reply first of all among those who have lived and endured the Soviet socialist experience.

Meanwhile all these heroic combatants find themselves in a very difficult situation for the creation of an ideology. They've been cut off from the world, from books and ideas, by years of prison, exile, or concentration camp. Even if one is at liberty in the USSR there is no possibility of meeting Western thinkers, of learning about human experience, of having contacts with friends and trying to understand with them the entire world and its evolution. Each one has to search alone, surmounting the greatest difficulties.

Those who reach the West must overcome the obstacle of language, of the harsh nomad life, of progressive assimilation of the experience of the world and the study of problems to be solved.

As soon as I had met these men, I understood that I was in a privileged situation: having peacefully lived all these years in the West, having studied all the problems which we must answer today, and starting with my own Soviet experience, I had much reflected, studied, and understood, and I could now be very useful to my [new] friends, the "dissidents." They had brought out on the soles of their shoes not only the future of Russia but perhaps also a beacon for the West's pathway.

After this book, which is a testimony, I shall prepare another on the change of direction Western civilization must take if it wishes to survive. That path is indicated by the hard road Russia has followed and the dangerous experience of the West.[3]

Party Congresses

Congress	Date	Remarks
1	March 1898	Minsk (RSDLP)
2	July/August 1903	Brussels and London (RSDLP)
3	April/May 1905	London
4	April/May 1906	Stockholm
5	May 1907	London
6	August 1917	Petrograd
7	March 1918	Moscow (all thereafter were in Moscow)
8	March 1919	
9	March/April 1920	
10	March 1921	
11	March 1922	
12	April 1923	(Lenin's last Congress)
13	May 1924	
14	December 1925	
15	December 1927	
16	June/July 1930	
17	January/February 1934	
18	March 1939	
19	October 1952	
20	February 1956	(Khrushchev denounced Stalin)
21	February 1959	
22	October 1961	
23	March/April 1966	
24	March/April 1971	
25	February 1976	
26	February/March 1981	
27	February/March 1986	(Gorbachev's *glasnost*, socioeconomic reforms)

Notes

Introduction

1. Bazhanov's "trade" documents included the original of the spoof Politburo decision on the Lena-Goldfields/Ramsay MacDonald situation (chapter 16), and the Politburo minute on Politburo session records (chapter 3, p. 25). These "trade" documents and other information Bazhanov carried in his head established his credentials and saved his life and that of his OGPU fellow-defector Maksimov.

2. According to Gordon Brook-Shepherd in *The Storm Petrels* (chapter 4), the initial interrogation alone, which was conducted under the supervision of Lieutenant Colonel Josse (first name unknown), went over two hundred typewritten pages. It is interesting to note that the impression Bazhanov made on Brook-Shepherd closely parallels the impression I got of Bazhanov from his text: that he was an excellent observer and reporter; his nature was calm, honest, straightforward, courageous, and very determined; and his habits were modest.

3. General A. P. Kutepov (1882–1930?) was a career tsarist army officer who fought with Vrangel's White Army during the Civil War. In 1929 he was head of the Union des Combattants Russes in Paris, in effect the leader of the Russian military émigrés in France. His abduction by OGPU agents in January 1930 caused a scandal in France and almost brought about a rupture in French diplomatic relations with the USSR. Bazhanov's book, coauthored by one N. Alekseev, described the OGPU coup and subsequent successful OGPU efforts to throw French authorities off the trail. Bazhanov named as one of his principal sources on the OGPU abduction, the former Soviet chargé d'affaires in Paris, Grigory Zinovievich Bessedovsky, who had defected a few months earlier and who apparently was knowledgeable of the OGPU plan.

4. Bazhanov briefly describes the attempt on his life by Yakob Bliumkin (chapter 17) and alludes to other such attempts. He told Gordon Brook-Shepherd that at least six such attempts were made in the first ten years of his stay in Paris. Bliumkin was a chekist whose most famous coup was the 1918 murder (actually performed by (fnu) Borizov, a sailor) of German Ambassador Count Wilhelm von Mirbach in Moscow. Aleksandr Solzhenitsyn (*The Gulag Archipelago*, vols. 1–2) mentions Bliumkin's effort to kill "Bazhenov" (which was indeed touted by Stalin

as having been successful, as a warning to other potential defectors). Bliumkin, former friend and military secretary to Trotsky (Trotsky, *Writings, 1929–39*), was Trotsky's first visitor to Prinkipo (Princes' Islands), the latter's Turkish exile. He took a letter from Trotsky to the Trotskyist opposition in Moscow, was betrayed to the OGPU and shot in December 1929, at age 30.

5. Georgy Agabekov (aka Georgy Sergevich, Aruntov, Nerses Ovsepian) defected in June 1930 from his post as OGPU *Rezident* in Constantinople. Prior to taking over the Constantinople post from Yacob Bliumkin, Agabekov (as OGPU *Rezident* in Tehran) had directed the manhunt for Bazhanov in Persia. Bazhanov's 1930 book describes how they met in Paris after Agabekov defected and Bazhanov then learned the details of the OGPU manhunt for him to eastern Persia.

Aleksandr Barmine defected late in 1937 in order to evade certain retribution from Stalin.

Grigory Z. Bessedovsky defected in Paris on 2 October 1929 from his post as chargé d'affaires at the Soviet embassy. Bazhanov is very critical of him.

Walter Krivitsky (aka Samuel Ginsberg, Martin Lessner, Edward Miller, Walter Poref) defected in Paris on 6 October 1937 from his post as illegal NKVD *Rezident* in Holland, where his cover had been as an Austrian art dealer named Dr. Martin Lessner. He died in Washington, D.C., in 1941, while there to testify to the U.S. Congress, under circumstances suggesting an NKVD execution.

General Aleksandr Orlov (aka Aleksandr Berg, Leon Berg, Blackstone, Aleksandr Feld, Leon Feldbin, Leon Koornik, Leon Nikolaev, Schwed) defected on 12 July 1938 to France from his post as NKVD chief in Spain. Prior to his defection, he organized and supervised the famous Soviet heist of the Spanish state gold reserves, a crime still uncompensated by the USSR.

Boris Souvarine, historian and founding member of the French Communist Party, defected in 1939 from the party and from his position as a leader of the Comintern.

6. Much of their testimony had already been mentioned by Khrushchev in his Twentieth Party Congress speech and later publicly disseminated.

Preface

1. The book, of course, was *Avec Staline dans le Kremlin*, op. cit. In it, he not only obscured the date he became anticommunist but stated without equivocation that he had, from the beginning, deliberately penetrated the Kremlin.

2. Grigory Z. Bessedovsky must have been Bazhanov's principal source for this information.

3. It isn't clear if Bazhanov is referring to Lidia Aleksandrovna Fotieva, or Maria Ignatievna Glyasser, both of whose roles he describes in chapter 3.

Chapter One

1. Mogilev-Podolsky (48°.27′N, 27°.48′E) is about two hundred miles southwest of Kiev.

2. P. P. Skoropadsky (1873–1945) was a Russian general. His tenure as hetman (Cossack chief or headman) of the Ukraine was based entirely on the

German military occupation, and he was their puppet dictator. A man with no military following, he was a monarchist, not a Ukrainian nationalist, and his regime was highly unpopular. He escaped on the last German train to leave Kiev in March 1918, disguised as a wounded German officer.

3. S. V. Petliura (1879–1926) was a Ukrainian schoolmaster who served as war minister in the Ukrainian Rada until 1918 when he became leader of the Ukrainian Peoples' Republic, a semi-Bolshevik armed nationalist movement. He was one of five Directory members in this short-lived government (during a period when fifteen governments came and went in four years). His forces battled for supremacy against the Red Army, the *ghaidamaks* (Ukrainian Cossacks), peasant rebels under Makhno, the Germans, and assorted guerrilla bands. His forces steadily lost personnel to the Red Army and finally in 1919 were driven from most of the Ukraine, where the peasants preferred the better disciplined Bolsheviks who were promising them their land (and had yet to steal their grain, promote communes, and inflict on them a "foreign" government and its dreaded Cheka). In April 1920 he signed an agreement with Polish General Pilsudski, exchanging eastern Galicia for Pilsudski's armed assistance in driving the Red Army out of the Ukraine—an agreement that made him a virtual puppet of the Poles. The Soviet-Polish war ended in October and with it Petliura lost the last of his influence on key events.

4. Zimmerwald and Kienthal were the 1915 and 1916 conferences of European Socialist internationalists held in Switzerland to try to find common ground for stopping the war and pursuing the goal of an international association of socialists. Lenin tried, without success, to persuade the conferences to seek to turn the war into a common (socialist and communist) front to bring the movement to power, on the basis of a rigidly controlled Third (Socialist) International.

5. The Soviet State Security Committee (now the KGB) is referred to by Bazhanov as Cheka or GPU. It was founded in 1917 as Cheka, and in the years until he defected in January 1928 it was called consecutively Cheka, vCheka, GPU, and OGPU.

6. Vinnitsa (49°.14'N, 28°.29'E) is about one hundred miles northeast of Mogilev-Podolsky.

7. Zhmerinka (49°.02'N, 28°.06'E) is about seventy-five miles north-north-east of Mogilev-Podolsky.

8. The Yampol he refers to is probably the one about forty miles southeast of Mogilev (48°.16'N, 28°.17'E).

9. Andreev and Trofimov are not otherwise identified by Bazhanov. Henceforth in the text, in such cases and where I have felt that further identification has been unnecessary, last names will appear without first names or patronymics, and there will be no footnote.

10. A. G. Shliapnikov (1884–1937) was a well-known Bolshevik self-educated workman, labor leader, and labor minister in the first Soviet government. Shliapnikov headed the Workers' Opposition, suggesting a trade union role in running the economy as a counterweight to the Politburo and the government. Stalin had him shot in 1937. His memory was rehabilitated in 1956 but never reinstated in the party because of his role in the Workers' Opposition. See Solzhenitsyn, *Lenin in Zurich* (n. 293).

11. Georgy Vladimirovich Akimov (1901–53) roomed with Bazhanov in Moscow. He became a well-known professor of metallurgy.

12. Lemberg appears again in Bazhanov's chapter 15, as a "traitor . . . on Yagoda's side."

13. Moisei Markovich Volodarsky (1891–1918, né Gol'shtein) was leader of the Petrograd Committee and was assassinated by the Left Socialist Revolutionary Sergeev in June 1918. Volodarsky had returned earlier in 1918 from Philadelphia, where he had lived in exile until the tsar's abdication. After his return, he was one of the most active figures in the Petrograd Committee and was its press commissar. His brother, Aleksandr (Sasha) Markovich Volodarsky was presumably married to Lida Volodarskaya mentioned in chapter 2.

14. Ksenofontov (1884–1926) joined the party in 1903 and became a "Party Figure" (Soviet terminology). He attended the Second Congress (1903), which made him a member of the All-Russian Central Executive Committee. From 1914–17, he was a Party activist while in the tsar's army. He took part in the October Revolution and then helped Dzerzhinsky organize the Cheka. He was a Cheka collegium member from 1917–21 and vice chairman of Cheka, 1919–20. He participated in crushing the Kronstadt Insurrection in 1921, and from 1922–25 he was in the Central Committee administration (and concurrently chief of the Cheka Executive Action Department, also known as the Operations Department). In 1926, before he died, he was deputy peoples' commissar for social security.

Chapter Two

1. Bazhanov is probably referring to Nikolai Petrovich Rastopchin (1884–1969), a well-known revolutionary and Party figure who worked in the Central Control Commission in the 1920s and was a Red Army political commissar in World War II. He retired in 1952.

2. Lazar Kaganovich (1893–?, né Kogan), prominent Party figure, was a strong, authoritarian administrator who staunchly supported Stalin. After Stalin's death he was one of four deputy premiers under Malenkov (the others were Beria, Molotov, and Bulganin). Kaganovich was one of the men "of almost impersonal" character (along with Molotov, Mikoyan, Zhdanov, and Andreyev) who seem to have best fitted Stalin's portrait of a new leader: "not a man of letters, feared as well as respected." (Stalin, *Sochinenya*, vol. 7, pp. 42–47). Kaganovich faithfully helped Stalin throughout his career, and Stalin had complete confidence in him despite the fact that he was jewish. When, in 1937, the "Yezhovshchina" purge was at its height, Kaganovich saved himself by sacrificing his subordinates in the Transport Commissariat. According to one source, after World War II when his brother Mikhail (see n. 16, below) was being examined on charges of treason by Mikoyan, Lazar palmed him a revolver in Mikoyan's office. Mikhail went to the nearby restroom and shot himself. Lazar Kaganovich lost his positions and influence in 1955, when Malenkov was pushed aside by Khrushchev.

3. Petr Adolfovich Otsup (1883–1963) was the famous, quasi-official Soviet photographer. Thirty-five of his pictures of Lenin taken between 1918–22 have survived. From 1925–35 Otsup operated the All-Russian Central Executive Commission's photographic studio.

4. M. Tomsky (1880–1938), an ex-worker, was a prominent early Bolshevik and supporter of Lenin. For years he was head of the Trade Unions Council. In 1922 he was elected to the Politburo at the same time as Zinoviev. He earned a

reputation for integrity, realism, and great caution but strength as an administrator. He was close to the very top by 1927, but eventually the shifting sands of the Politburo brought him Stalin's enmity and Tomsky was replaced as Trade Union head by Shvernik and Kaganovich, in December 1928. Tomsky had objected to the scale of the sacrifices demanded of the workers and of the forced collectivization of potentially prosperous farmers. In February 1929 he was expelled from Trade Unions Council membership. During the next few years his situation deteriorated as he recanted and then recanted his recantations, in and out of exile. In early 1938 he committed suicide rather than have to declare himself a Trotskyite traitor in the Yezhovshchina trials.

5. Balashov is probably Semyon Ivanovich Balashov (1874–1925), a weaver from a peasant family who joined the Party in 1898. He became a Party figure and worked in Moscow from 1919 until his death.

6. V. M. Molotov (1890–1986, né Skriabin), well-known Party figure, joined the Russian Social-Democratic Labor Party (RSDLP) in 1906. He became a candidate member of the Politburo in 1921, and a full member in 1925. He was a consistent acolyte and supporter of Stalin throughout his career. He was rewarded with the chairmanship of the Council of Peoples' Commissars in the mid-1930s and the Foreign Ministry in 1939. His rather tedious, pedestrian mind, his great patience, and his capacity for hard work are well reported. Bazhanov's characterization of Molotov is, however, a useful addition to the chorus, since it adds detail from a source who worked with Molotov daily for several years. Molotov was dropped from the Central Committee in 1957 for his continued posthumous loyalty to Stalin. He held a number of relatively minor jobs, including the ambassadorship to the Mongolian Peoples' Republic, and died in November 1986 shortly after being rehabilitated.

7. Several times in his book, Bazhanov's choice of words makes it clear that he understood early the nature of Stalin's interest in the acquisition of total power by any means, including liquidation of almost all his friends and supporters. There seems to be little doubt that Bazhanov aided Stalin's implacable accumulation of bureaucratic power at this early stage. He certainly did nothing to stop it. Bazhanov does not credit Stalin with any but the most selfish motives, whereas current historians believe he was a far more complex person than has been attributed to him either by his detractors or by his defenders.

8. Anastas I. Mikoyan (1895–1978), well-known Party figure, was elected to the Politburo in 1927, where he was a consistent supporter of Stalin. Like Kaganovich, he was one of Stalin's chosen "new leaders," one of his "impersonal men" of substantial bureaucratic talents. He held a number of important posts in the trade arena, including pre–World War II minister of foreign trade, and minister of domestic trade (as well as a vice-chairman of the Council of Ministers) under Malenkov. Curiously Bazhanov only mentions him this once in his book, although Mikoyan played a substantial role in Stalin's rise to power. He was the first Politburo member to retire and write his memoirs.

9. Boris Pilniak (1894–1942?, né Vogau), well-known author, almost paid with his life for his 1926 book, *Tale of an Unextinguished Moon*, alluding to Frunze's murder. In 1929, he was expelled from the All-Russian Writers' Association on trumped-up charges of deliberately publishing his critical book *Mahogany* (in Germany) abroad when it was not published in the USSR. In fact a decision to publish it in the USSR had been rescinded without his prior knowledge, at the last

moment. The regime also chastized him for his book *The Volga Flows into the Caspian Sea,* and he was arrested in 1938 and died in prison, supposedly in 1942. Pilniak is sometimes referred to as the "father of Soviet letters."

10. Rozalia S. Zemliachka (1876–1947, née Zalkind), a Party figure, was a notorious and fanatical Bolshevik. She joined the Communist Party in 1896, was elected to the RSDLP Central Committee in 1903. In 1918 she became chief of the political commissariats of the Eighth and Thirteenth Red Armies. During the 1918 aftermath of General Wrangel's evacuation of the Crimea, she and Bela Kun (the former Soviet dictator of Hungary) reportedly arranged the execution of thousands of persons believed to have supported Wrangel, whether or not they did. In 1920 she became secretary of the Russian Communist Party (Bolshevik) (RCP(B)) Crimean Oblast. From 1939–43 she was vice-chairman of the USSR council of peoples' commissars, then the All-Union Communist Party (Bolshevik) (ACP(B)) Party Control Commission. She was buried in Red Square at the Kremlin wall.

11. Georgy Malenkov (1902–1988), a very well known Party figure, joined the Party in 1920. In 1928 he became Stalin's secretary. In 1930 he was secretary of the Party's Moscow section. In 1934 Stalin moved him to the Orgburo as head of the personnel department. In 1939 the Eighteenth Party Congress elected him to the Central Committee, which made him one of its five secretaries. In 1941 he became a candidate Politburo member and joined Molotov, Beria, and Voroshilov on the State Defense Committee, which Stalin headed. Stalin sent him to the battle of Stalingrad to urge Russian troops and workers to hold out. In 1943 he was decorated for organizing aircraft production. In 1946 he was made a full member of the Politburo. With Zhdanov, he was Soviet delegate to the forming of the Cominform in 1947. In 1952 he gave the main report at the Nineteenth Party Congress and was elected to the Presidium, thus being viewed as Stalin's successor. In March 1953 he succeeded Stalin but resigned in February 1955. Whether or not Bazhanov's characterization of him is fair is difficult to determine, since Malenkov and his wife revealed little of themselves outside their inner circle.

12. German Tikhomirnov (1899–1955) joined the RSDLP as a student in 1917 and served with the Kazan Red Guards, then the Red Army in the Civil War. He worked on the Central Committee staff from 1920–25 and in the Marx-Lenin-Engels Institute from 1925–37. From 1937–38 he chaired the Council of Peoples' Commissars, then from 1947–55 served in the Institute of Marxism–Leninism.

13. Viktor Tikhomirnov (1889–1919) joined the Party as a student in 1905, helped organize (and finance) *Pravda* in 1912, and was exiled quite often for revolutionary activity. He was active in the February 1917 Revolution in Petrograd and in 1918 helped form the militia.

14. Helena Stasova (1873–1966), a Party figure, joined in 1898 and was an early RSDLP propagandist with Krupskaya. She was exiled from 1913–16, became secretary of the Central Committee from 1917–20, and from 1921 she held executive jobs in nascent Soviet international organizations including the Comintern and the Profintern. She became increasingly arrogant toward her peers and was eased aside in the 1920s. She is buried in Red Square, at the Kremlin wall.

15. Bazhanov intermixes vCheka, Cheka, OGPU, GPU, and NKVD throughout the book. In fact it was Cheka and vCheka from its founding in 1917 until 1919, when it became GPU and then OGPU until 1933. The NKVD existed from 1934 to 1946, headed by Lavrenty Pavlovich Beria. After some years as NKGB, MVD, and MGB, the modern KGB was born in 1954, when Malenkov appointed

Beria to be its first chairman and then had him shot after Beria tried to pull off a coup d'état.

16. Mikhail Kaganovich (1889–1941), a metalworker, joined the RSDLP in 1905 and thereafter was often arrested for radical behavior. From 1917–20, he was engaged in Party organization in the military. From 1921–27 he held a series of local Party positions and then attended the Fifteenth and Sixteenth Party Congresses (1927–28), which elected him to the Central Control Commission. In 1931 he was deputy chairman, Sovnarkhoz (National Economic Councils), in 1932 deputy commissar for heavy industry, and 1935 head of the main administration of the aircraft industry. He was elected a member of the Central Committee in 1934 and became a candidate member of Orgburo. He was arrested in 1941 on charges of being a German spy and shot himself.

17. V. M. Mikhailov (1894–1937) joined the Party in 1915, and in 1917 was a member of the Moscow Party Committee and chairman of the Gorodskoy Raion Cheka. During the Civil War he was a Red Army political commissar and became a Central Committee secretary in 1921. From 1922–24 he was secretary of the Moscow Party Committee, then chaired the Moscow Trade Unions Council from 1925–29. In 1930–37, already in eclipse, he held various executive jobs in construction.

Chapter Three

1. Y. M. Sverdlov (1885–1919), first president of the Soviet Republic and "unofficial secretary general" of the October insurrection, was one of the leading non émigré Party organizers. A strong, capable administrator with vast knowledge of the cadres, he played a key role in both the revolution and the Civil War. From 1912 to 1917 he was in exile in Siberia, the first year with Stalin, whom he thought "inconsiderate and rude." Like Stalin, he was an early editor of *Pravda* and a strong supporter of Lenin. In October 1917 he was one of Trotsky's "military centers" at Petrograd, sometimes called "master organizer of the dictatorship." In the two years before his death he was a member and secretary of the Central Committee, and a member of the Second Politburo (with Lenin, Trotsky, and Stalin). At times during the Civil War he mediated for Lenin between Trotsky and Stalin. He died of typhus.

2. Serebriakov is almost certainly Leonid Petrovich Serebriakov (1879–1937), although it is not clear why Bazhanov uses the wrong first name and patronymic. L. P. Serebriakov was a prominent communist, member of the Central Committee, and until replaced by Molotov, one of the three Central Committee secretaries— the others being Preobrazhensky and Krestinsky. All three were supporters of Trotsky and were expelled from the Party in 1927 along with most of Lenin's former closest collaborators. Serebriakov was exiled to Siberia in 1928, capitulated and returned in 1929. He was tried in January 1937 and disappeared, probably shot.

3. N. N. Krestinsky (1883–1938) was an early, prominent communist and supporter of Lenin and Trotsky. An able, energetic militant, he was one of the three secretaries (with Serebriakov and Preobrazhensky) in 1919 when the primitive Party bureaucracy had a joint secretariat for the Politburo and Orgburo. The three were expelled from the Central Committee in 1921 for their support of

Trotsky. In the early 1920s the Troika sent him to Berlin as ambassador. In 1927 he was expelled from the Party, but in 1928 was one of the important Party leaders who recanted, his defection being one of the first signs that Trotsky had finally lost to Stalin. He was tried in 1938 and shot.

4. V. V. Kuibyshev (1883–1935) was a prominent communist, an able bureaucrat, and very much Stalin's man. In 1923 Stalin made him president of the Party Control Commission. In 1926 he replaced Dzerzhinsky on the Economic Council and became a member of the Politburo. When he died in 1935 he was vice president of the Council of Peoples' Commissars. His death has been attributed to alcohol by some, and by others to a drug overdose (organized by Yagoda).

5. J. E. Rudzutak (1887–1938) was a Bolshevik trade unionist, close colleague of Tomsky and an early supporter of Lenin. In the 1920s he became a loyal Stalin collaborator and was promoted to the Politburo in 1926, replacing Zinoviev. He was tried in 1938 as one of the "21," disappeared and was probably shot. (The "trial of the 21" was the last of the great Moscow purge trials. The three principal trials of nonmilitary officials are often referred to by the number of accused on trial.)

6. S. Syrtsov (1893–1937) was an obscure senior bureaucrat, head of the Central Committee's propaganda section, until Stalin promoted him to replace Rykov, in 1929, as premier of the Russian SSR (Soviet Socialist Republic) and president of the USSR Council of Commissars. Formerly very much Stalin's man, he joined the 1932 opposition to Stalin. He was imprisoned and eventually disappeared in the 1937 purges.

7. S. N. Smidovich (1872–1934), a noble's daughter, joined the Party in 1898 and became a Party figure. After work in Moscow Party organizations from 1917 on, she was head of the Womens' Section [*Zhenotdel*] of the Central Committee from 1922–24. She served on the ACP(B) collegium, Central Control Commission, and Central Executive Committee until 1930.

8. G. Y. Zinoviev (1883–1936, né Apfelbaum) joined the RSDLP in 1901. He was Lenin's closest companion in World War I and was the first president of the Comintern. He played key roles in the Revolution and the Civil War, becoming a member of the first Central Committee and the first Politburo. He was nominal head of the Troika in 1924. In 1925, he joined with Trotsky's Left Opposition and was expelled from the CPSU by the Fifteenth Party Congress in December 1927. Sent to Siberia, he recanted, was reinstated in 1928; he was again exiled and repeated the recantment and was again reinstated in 1932. In 1935, after the Kirov murder, he was sentenced to nineteen years for "complicity." In the first Moscow trial of August 1936 he was, in Trotsky's absence, the leading target and was executed after he "confessed."

9. L. B. Kamenev (1883–1936, né Rosenfeld) joined the RSDLP in 1901, headed the Bolshevik faction in the Duma prior to 1914, and was exiled to Siberia from 1914 to 1917. In 1917 in Petrograd he and Stalin headed the Bolshevik movement until Lenin returned from Switzerland. He was a member of the Troika with Zinoviev and Stalin but was expelled from the CPSU in 1927. He recanted, was readmitted, and like Zinoviev, he again was expelled, recanted, and was readmitted in 1932. He was executed in 1936 for "moral complicity" in the Kirov murder. Kamenev was Trotsky's brother-in-law.

10. A. G. Bieloborodov (1891–1938) was a leading communist militant who, during the Civil War, was in charge of the Ural communists when they executed

the tsar and his family. He was a supporter of Trotsky, for which, like so many, he paid with his life. He disappeared in the 1938 purges.

11. O. A. Piatnitsky (1882–1939, né Tarshis), prominent revolutionary and Comintern leader, joined the RSDLP in 1898. For many years from 1901, he smuggled copies of Lenin's *Iskra* into Russia and was imprisoned and exiled. He returned from Germany for the 1905 Revolution but again went into exile from 1908–17. He was on the All-Russian Central Executive Committee from 1918 until 1921, when he joined the Comintern. He served there as a senior executive the rest of his life. He was a Central Committee member from 1927–34, was expelled, recanted, and was finally executed in the purges. He has since been rehabilitated.

12. A. A. Solts (1872–1945), joined the RSDLP in 1898 and became a Party and government figure. He was arrested, exiled and escaped several times, and in 1917 was a member of the Moscow Party Committee. He was active in the Moscow Bolshevik revolution. In 1920 he became a leader of the Party Central Control Commission and was a Presidium and Supreme Court member from 1921–34. He was a member of the Comintern's International Control Commission. Solts was a regular contributor to *Pravda* (he was on the editorial board), urging stricter discipline within the Party.

13. Y. K. Peters (1886–1942?), a Latvian and famous Cheka executive, was a man of ferocious cruelty. He was briefly vCheka chairman in July and August 1917, one of its deputy chairmen (and concurrently chief of its secret political department) from then to 1919, and chief of the eastern department from 1922–28. He was reportedly put to death in the 1938 purges, although other reports claim he died in prison in 1942.

14. M. I. Latsis (1888–1938, né Ian Fridrichovich Sudrabs) was a Bolshevik leader during World War I in Friborg. In 1918 he was made a deputy chairman of the Cheka (and concurrently chief of the counterintelligence department) and spent his career in the security services. Like Peters he had a reputation for ferocious cruelty and was also a victim of the 1938 purges.

15. V. N. Mantsev (1889–1939) was a prominent Cheka and OGPU official. His death at age 50 would seem to indicate that he was also purged in 1938 or 1939.

16. G. Kanner (1900?–1937) was a bright, talented man who was with Stalin for over ten years. Stalin treated him almost as a son. When Stalin eventually gave him permission to leave, he graduated from the Industrial Academy and was rewarded with top jobs in the Heavy Industry Commissariat. He tried to protect senior industry officials from the purges, and Stalin had him executed.

17. I. P. Tovstukha (1889–1935) joined the Party in 1913 after nine years of arrests and exiles for revolutionary activities. He was in exile in France from 1912–17 and returned and held Red Guard and Party jobs until he went to the Central Committee staff in 1921. He served there until 1930, with two years (1924–26) absent while assistant director of the Lenin Institute. In 1931 he was named assistant director of the Marx-Engels-Lenin Institute of the Central Committee. The Seventeenth Party Congress in 1934 elected him a candidate member of the Central Committee. Bazhanov reports him as dying of tuberculosis, but others have found his death in 1935 mysterious. He is buried at the Kremlin wall.

18. E. M. Yaroslavsky (1878–1943, né Mini Israelevich Gubelman) was secretary of the Central Control Commission but was perhaps best known for his

"authorship" of the famous "short course" history of the Bolshevik Party, written under his direction and for Stalin's benefit. His hatred of Trotsky and servility toward Stalin weren't enough to shield him from being charged in 1931 with "Trotskyism" (Stalin did have a certain sense of humor). He confessed, saving his Party position, but was disavowed as a historian when Stalin needed history rewritten—the history Stalin had so depended upon when it served him. Yaroslavsky was the Party's wartime head of propaganda in 1942 and leader of the Society of the Godless.

19. N. N. Yudenich (1862–1933) was a famous White Army general who commanded the northern armies and led the march on Leningrad in 1919. Only Trotsky's almost superhuman efforts to stiffen the Red Army's front stopped Yudenich's advance, which got to the gates of the city. Yudenich's "victory" was announced all over Europe, making Trotsky's action all the more impressive (and Zinoviev's panicky failure all the more obvious).

20. The "military experts or specialists" were former tsarist officers drafted into the Red Army by Trotsky.

Stalin's anti-semitism seems to be generally accepted, although he was at pains to hide it during much of his career.

21. Fanny Kaplan (1890–1918, née Feiga Efimova Roidman) used other names: Fania (Fanny) Royd and/or Dora Kaplan. She was arrested as early as 1906 for a bombing in Kiev and spent some years in prison. She was freed in the amnesty following the February 1917 Revolution. She thought Lenin a traitor to the revolution because of his dispersal of the Constituent Assembly and his support of the treaty of Brest-Litovsk. On 30 August 1918 she fired two bullets at point-blank range into Lenin, who almost died and never fully recovered. Kaplan, a jewish fanatic member of the Socialist Revolutionaries, was caught and her summary execution by Kremlin Commandant Pavel Malkov was announced publicly. There are, however, doubts that she was actually executed, and she is reported to have been seen as late as World War II. It has not been determined if her attempt on Lenin was at the behest of the Central Committee of the Socialist Revolutionaries.

22. "Sergo" Ordzhonikidze (1886–1937) joined the RSDLP in 1903 and in 1910 graduated from Lenin's school in Italy. A former Georgian worker, he became a very close friend and supporter of Stalin. He was on the Central Committee's executive bureau (in the USSR) in 1912. He was an early Bolshevik leader in the Caucasus. In 1923, Lenin chastised Stalin and Ordzhonikidze for their violent and repressive policies against the Georgian nationalists. In 1924, he and Stalin provoked, then brutally suppressed, the Georgian insurrectionists. He was brought into the Politburo as an alternate in 1925 by Stalin, then chaired the Rabkrin in 1926 and the Central Control Commission. Although an acolyte of Stalin, in 1927 he opposed expulsion of Trotsky. From 1928 to 1936 he was given various senior jobs in the endless oligarchic musical chairs that Stalin composed, including head of the Supreme Economic Council for some years and Commissar for Heavy Industry. He was purged by Stalin in 1937 and died under mysterious circumstances.

23. Feliks Dzerzhinsky (1877–1926) was a founder of the Social Democratic parties of Lithuania and Poland. In 1906, he was elected to the Central Committee. He was also the founder of the Cheka (Extraordinary Commission to Combat Counter-Revolution, Speculation, and Sabotage) and its first chairman. Born in

Lithuania to a Polish Catholic upper middle-class family (known as the minor nobility in Russia), his radical revolutionary bent appeared early—possibly as a result of his younger brother's death at the hands of the Okhranka (the Russian pre-revolutionary secret police, often transliterated as Okhrana) for writing seditious poetry. Lenin took him as an intellectual equal, and when the time came to protect the Revolution, this brutal disciplinarian was the logical choice. The new regime was on very shaky ground and if Trotsky gave Lenin the revolution with his military victories, Dzerzhinsky ensured it for Lenin with the police and prisoner skills he had learned during his fourteen years in tsarist jails between 1897 and 1917. His role as commandant at Smolny (and wire-tapper for Lenin and Trotsky) provided intelligence that was a key to victory in Leningrad. In 1919 Lenin vastly expanded the scope of the Cheka's already wide powers by putting the Cheka's Special Department (Osobyi Otdel, OO) in charge of security in the armed forces, down to platoon level. In 1919 Dzerzhinsky was put in charge of the GPU and then OGPU. His support of Stalin was not always consistent, and his strength was such that he was talked of as a replacement for Stalin as Party general secretary after Lenin's death. In 1926, a few hours after he made an emotional and threatening speech to a joint plenum of the Central Committee and the Central Control Commission, he had a heart attack, which many believe was somehow contrived by Stalin. His death removed a serious impediment to the rise of Stalin to absolute power, and it may rank with the mysterious death of Frunze, or the murder of Kirov, both of which also removed obstacles in Stalin's path.

24. Bazhanov's assertion that Lenin had syphilis has not been documented.

25. N. K. Krupskaya (1869–1939) was the daughter of a tsarist official. She formally married Lenin in 1897 in order to accompany him into exile in Siberia. She spent her entire life with him, as his wife, confidante, secretary, and coworker. She was not a success as a writer in her own right on educational matters, but she wrote extensively for the Party and was widely respected as Lenin's accurate representative. After his death she missed several opportunities to help block Stalin (whose faults she knew very well) in his rise to power; the first such opportunity being when she had a chance to make Lenin's testament widely known and heard. Instead, with an honesty misplaced among the Kremlin hierarchy at that time, she respected Lenin's precise instructions and the chance was lost. In 1924–25 she sided with Zinoviev and Kamenev against Trotsky, although she must have known it would greatly strengthen Stalin, and again sided with them against Stalin but only when it was too late. She was silent during the purges, and in their wake she was one of the Party seniors who falsified their memoirs to suit Stalin. That, and her silence, probably permitted her to remain almost sacrosanct and die naturally at age seventy.

26. L. A. Fotieva (1881–1975) joined the Communist Party in 1904. She was arrested and exiled several times and helped Krupskaya with *Iskra* in Geneva and Paris. In 1917 she was on the *Pravda* editorial board and a member of the RSDLP(B). In addition to being Lenin's private secretary from 1918–24, she was secretary to the Council of Peoples' Commissars and the Council of Labor and Defense. She survived the purges and in 1938 went from the Central Energy Administration to the staff of the Central Lenin Museum. From 1941–45 she was a member of the Central Commission of International Organizations for Aid to Fighters for Revolution. She was pensioned and awarded the Order of Lenin in 1956.

27. Zinoviev and Kamenev were so blinded by their fear of Trotsky that they ignored Lenin's Testament, although they knew very well what it said. It is a mystery that they could be so far off in their assessment of Stalin as a lesser threat than Trotsky to Russia and to themselves.

28. M. I. Glyasser (1890–1951), like Fotieva, worked for Lenin daily and was privy to his most secret thoughts. In addition to being Lenin's private secretary 1918–24, she worked in the Secretariat of Peoples' Commissars. Later, she worked in the Lenin Institute.

29. Voloditcheva (first name unknown) is relatively unknown, although many sources confirm her role as one of the three secretaries closest to Lenin (although not nearly as close as Fotieva and Glyasser).

30. A. M. Nazaretian (1889–1937) joined the Party in 1905 while a law student in Petrograd. From 1911–13 he was imprisoned, escaped, and lived in Switzerland. He went back in 1913 to Petrograd, where he was a Party activist until he returned to his native Tiflis in 1916. There, he held several top Party regional jobs, including the Caucasus Central Committee and Presidium. He went to Moscow in 1922 and was concurrently on the *Pravda* editorial board and head of the Central Committee's secretariat for two years. In 1924 he returned to Tiflis and held regional Party jobs. From 1931–37 he was back in Moscow, on the Central Control Commission and the Council of Peoples' Commissars. He was arrested in 1937 and died in prison in 1937 or 1938. See Souvarine (p. 344) for a different account of Nazaretian being discovered to have forged the results from a Kiev Party resolution favorable to the minority. Souvarine has it that Trotsky, Piatakov, and Radek appealed the case to the Central Control Commission only to have the plaintiffs censured, not the forger.

31. Maxim Maximovich Litvinov (1876–1951, né Meer Genokh Moissevich Vallak) born in Russian Poland, met Lenin during the Second RSDLP Congress in London in the summer of 1903 and was thereafter a disciple of Lenin. In 1903 he was a frontier agent, smuggling and running cross-border operations for the Party. In 1908 he was arrested in Paris for passing ruble notes stolen by the Party in Tiflis. He escaped to London, where he lived for many years as "Mr. Harrison." In 1917 he married Ivy Low, an English woman. In 1918 he was the chief Soviet diplomat in the United Kingdom and later that year was exchanged for British SIS (Secret Intelligence Service) officer Bruce Lockhart. Back in Moscow, Litvinov was assigned to the Foreign Ministry (Narkomindel) and in 1921 became its deputy chief under Chicherin. When Chicherin was forced to retire in 1930, Litvinov replaced him and, in 1933, negotiated US recognition of the USSR directly with President Roosevelt. In 1934 Litvinov was elected to the Central Committee but never carried much weight there. He was forced into retirement in 1939, replaced by Molotov, and was in official limbo (due to his foreign policy "failures") until he was rehabilitated in 1941 to be the wartime Soviet ambassador to Washington. In 1943 he was again shelved, as deputy to Molotov in the Foreign Ministry, was retired in 1946, and died of natural causes in 1951.

32. G. V. Chicherin (1872–1936), a leading Menshevik intellectual, rallied to the Bolsheviks in 1917. In 1918, he replaced Trotsky as Foreign Commissar. He organized and trained the Soviet diplomatic corps, and during the period 1921–24 he obtained recognition of the USSR by all the major world powers except the United States. He was elected to the Central Committee in 1925 but soon after took a cure at Wiesbaden and almost stayed there. He was enticed back to the

USSR to avoid the appearance of a defection. Litvinov replaced him in 1927 when he retired but was not actually promoted to foreign minister until 1930. Chicherin lived quietly in retirement in Moscow until his death from diabetes and poly-neuritis in 1936. He was almost ignored by Stalin and the hierarchy in his last decade of life, largely because he had failed to obtain foreign monetary credits that Stalin required, and because he had stayed out of politics (which probably saved him from the purges). Since Stalin's death Chicherin has been somewhat rehabili-tated, and he is now officially credited with having formed up the Soviet Narko-mindel.

Chapter Four

1. Bazhanov's description of his twin roles, running the Politburo secretariat and being assistant to Stalin, is detailed and unique even today. There seems to be grudging admiration, as the book unfolds, for Stalin's techniques of acquiring power and his persistence in seeking it.

2. Except for Bazhanov, his Politburo secretariat staff were evidently all fe-male.

3. These notes make no attempt to provide routine biographical information on such well known figures as Lenin, Trotsky, or Stalin.

In exile, Trotsky and Bazhanov took each other to task in their writings. What they say about each other should be viewed with caution.

4. Nadezhda Alliluyeva (1901–32) was Stalin's second wife. They met when Lenin and Stalin were hiding in 1917, in the Petrograd apartment of her father (Sergei Yakovlevich Alliluev). She joined the Party in 1918, and they were married in 1919. She differed with Stalin on the brutality of forced collectivization and frequently asked him to be lenient with her friends. She is reported to have committed suicide in 1932, after a bitter argument about collectivization, but many believe she was murdered by Stalin. There is no firm evidence either way. She left a son (Vassily) and daughter (Svetlana).

5. "Pearl" in English.

6. Bazhanov is broadly hinting that Stalin was sexually involved with Tamara during this period.

7. A. A. Andreev (1885–?) has been characterized by others as a docile sup-porter of Stalin. He joined the Party in 1914 and was in the RSDLP(B) in Petrograd until 1917. He participated in the October Revolution and then did Party organi-zation work in the Urals and Ukraine until 1920. From 1920–22 he was secretary of the All-Union Central Trade Unions Council. From 1922–25, and again from 1935–46, he was secretary of the Central Committee of the All-Union CP. He joined the Politburo in 1926 as an alternate member and was promoted to full member in 1932. He chaired the Central Control Commission from 1930–31 and 1939–52 and chaired the Supreme Soviet from 1938–45. From 1943–46 he was peoples' commissar for agriculture, and from 1946–53 deputy chairman of the Council of Ministers. In 1953 he was elected to the Presidium and was an advisor to that body from 1962 on.

8. Marshal K. Y. Voroshilov (1881–1969) became a communist in 1903 and in 1917 helped Dzerzhinsky organize the Cheka. During the Civil War he com-manded large Red Army units on the southern fronts, including the Tsaritsyn

group of forces, the Tenth Army, and he was deputy commander of the southern front. He helped put down the Kronstadt Insurrection and from 1925–34 was commissar for the military and navy and chaired the Revolutionary Military Council. From 1946–53 he was deputy chairman of the Council of Ministers and from 1953–60 chaired the Presidium. He served in the Central Committee from 1921–61, the Politburo from 1926–52, and the Presidium from 1952 until he was pensioned.

9. Stalin (né Iosip Vissarionovich Djugashvili) used the pseudonym Koba until 1912, when he began to use the pseudonym Stalin. The name Koba was coined, in Kazbegi's *Patricide,* for a heroic Caucasus outlaw. All told, Stalin used eighteen pseudonyms during his revolutionary career.

10. L. Z. Mekhlis (1889–1953) joined the Party and the Red Army in 1918. He was an army political commissar until, in 1919, he joined the Workers and Peasants Inspection Commissariat. He joined Stalin's secretariat in 1922. In 1930 he became editor-in-chief of *Pravda* and concurrently chief of the press section of the Central Committee. From 1937–40 he was chief of the main political directorate of the Red Army and was derisively referred to by Trotsky as "Stalin's agent in the Red Army." In 1940 Mekhlis became peoples' commissar for state control. In 1941 he was deputy peoples' commissar for defense. In 1942 he was dismissed from the Crimean Front for undue political interference in military affairs, but by 1946 he had recovered and was commissar (then minister) for state control. He worked with Yezhov in the purges, rose to be a colonel general in the Red Army, and was in the Central Committee from 1939–53. He is reported to have died of natural causes and is buried at the Kremlin wall.

11. Bazhanov also refers to Fomenko as courier for Stalin.

12. G. G. Yagoda (1891–1937) joined the CP(B) in 1907. In 1919 he worked in the Commissariat for Foreign Trade. In 1920 he became a member of the Cheka presidium. He was deputy chairman of the OGPU from 1926–34, and chairman of the NKVD from 1934–36. He was executed in 1938 as a traitor in the same purge group as Bukharin and Rykov.

13. I have not seen any account elsewhere of this telephone tap or execution of the Czech who installed it. The Czech remains unidentified. In his 1930 book, Bazhanov only hinted at this phone tap: "Comrade Stalin speaks little, but he knows how to listen."

14. Trotsky affirmed his own view of the military importance of horses and their shortage. See "Writings," 1933–34, p. 254.

15. N. I. Bukharin (1888–1938) joined the Party in 1906. In 1912 he was working with Lenin in Krakow, on early *Pravda* editions. In 1917 he was appointed editor of *Pravda,* a job he held over twelve years. In 1926 he replaced Zinoviev as chairman of the Comintern Executive Committee. During the period 1928–30 he headed the "right-wing deviation" in the Politburo, along with Tomsky and Rykov. In 1937 he was expelled from the CPSU as "Trotskyist," and he was executed in 1938 in the "group of 21," after which only Stalin (and Trotsky in exile) remained alive from Lenin's Politburo.

16. A. I. Rykov (1881–1938) joined the RSDLP in 1899. In 1924 he succeeded Lenin as head of state. In 1925 he was president of the Council of Peoples' Commissars. On the NEP question he joined right-wing forces with Bukharin. In March 1938, at the third trial, he "confessed" and was shot.

17. A. D. Tsiurupa (1870–1928) joined the RSDLP in 1898 and was one of

those frequently arrested and exiled during the next twenty years. In 1922–23, he replaced Stalin as peoples' commissar of Rabkrin (Workers and Peasants Inspection Commission). From 1923–25 he chaired Gosplan, after being elected to the Central Committee in 1923. From 1925–26 he was peoples' commissar for Domestic and Foreign Trade. He was a personal friend of Lenin.

18. M. I. Kalinin (1875–1946) joined the RSDLP in 1898 and in 1912 was a candidate member of the Central Committee of the Bolshevik wing. He was one of Lenin's first adherents. He was elected to the Central Committee of the CPSU in 1919 and became chairman of the All Russian Central Executive Committee. He was elected to the Politburo in 1926. A popular man who avoided intrigues, he survived the purges, and from 1938–46 headed the Presidium of the Supreme Soviet. He is written off by Bazhanov as being, like Rykov, more decorative than substantive. Deutscher classes him as one of the "liberals" in the Politburo, along with Rudzutak, Kirov, and Voroshilov.

19. K. B. Radek (1885–1939, né Soibelsohn in Poland) was active from 1914 in the Polish and German Social Democratic parties. In April 1917 he returned with Lenin from exile and joined the Bolshevik Party (he was an early disciple of Lenin). In 1921 he was made secretary of the Comintern. In December 1927, at the Fifteenth Party Congress, he was expelled from the CPSU for "Left Oppositionism" and was banished to the Urals but soon recanted and was reinstated. In 1932 he was the Comintern representative in Germany. In the late 1930s he was the senior foreign correspondent for many Moscow publications. In January 1937 he was sentenced in the second purge trial, to ten years in prison, where he is reported to have been murdered by a fellow prisoner.

Chapter Five

1. "Ivry" Piatakov (1890–1937), already a militant revolutionary as a fourteen-year-old student, joined the RSDRP in 1910. He was arrested several times, and banished to Siberia in 1913. He made his way to Switzerland and in 1915 (with Bukharin) formed the nucleus of the Left Communists. He returned to Kiev to chair the city Bolshevik Committee in 1917. The next year he headed the Orgburo of the Ukrainian Communist Party (Bolshevik wing—KP[b]U), then was secretary of its Central Committee. In 1921 he was elected candidate member of the Central Committee, and (with Bukharin) was cited by Lenin's December 1922 testament as one of the two outstanding younger Communist Party leaders. He coauthored the Trotsky opposition from 1923–27, was expelled from the Party by the Fifteenth Congress, then readmitted in 1929 as director of the State Bank. From 1930–36 he was Ordzonikidzhe's deputy commissar of Heavy Industry. In 1936 he was arrested, with Radek and others, and was a central figure of the 1937 trials. He was tortured, then shot right after the trials.

2. I. S. Unshchlikht (1879–1938), a Lithuanian electrical engineer, joined the Polish-Lithuanian Social Democrats in 1900 and the RSDLP(B) in 1906. Between 1902 and 1916 he was arrested and imprisoned or exiled several times. In 1917 he was a member of the Petrograd soviet. During the Civil War he held several Party posts in the Red Army. From 1921–23 he was deputy chairman of the GPU. In 1925 he was elected to the Central Committee. From 1923–25 he was a member of the Revolutionary Military Commission and chief of logistics for the Red Army,

and from 1925–30 deputy head of the same commission. He was deputy head of Gosplan from 1930–35. He was a victim of the 1938 purges.

3. V. V. Shmidt (1886–1940), a St. Petersburg lathe operator, joined the RSDLP(B) in 1905 as a Bolshevik labor activist. From 1907–11 he was a militant laborer in Germany, where he had fled to escape arrest. From 1911 to 1917 he was again in St. Petersburg as a labor (metalworkers) leader and a member of the city Bolshevik commune. An energetic, fearless disciple of Lenin, he was arrested several times in that period. From 1918–28 he was a member of the Presidium and the All-Russian Council of Trade Unions, and a candidate member of Orgburo from 1921–30. In 1928 he became deputy chief of the Council of Peoples' Commissars. In 1930 Stalin began to strip him of his titles, on the grounds that he had "vacillated" in his posture toward the right opposition. He was declared a member of the "anti-Party group" by the 1933 plenum of the Central Committee and sent to Siberia to head the Far East Coal Trust. In 1937 he was arrested and reportedly died in prison in 1940.

4. The Maslov–Ruth Fischer group was a minority faction of the German Communist Party in 1923. This group was given leadership of the Party by Moscow after the Brandler group was expelled from the Comintern, but by 1927 the Maslov–Ruth Fischer group had joined the Trotsky opposition and formed the nucleus of the German supporters of Trotsky's Fourth International.

5. Heinrich Brandler (1881–1967) headed the majority faction of the German Communist Party in 1923 and was held largely responsible by the Politburo and the Comintern for the failure of the German revolution.

6. E. M. Skliansky (1892–1925) was Trotsky's military deputy and a member of all the supreme war councils from 1918 to 1923. Trotsky called him "the Carnot of the Red Army."

7. M. V. Frunze (1885–1925), an old revolutionary with years at hard labor in Siberian exile, was one of Trotsky's most capable field commanders during the Civil War. Trotsky was very suspicious that Stalin had Frunze murdered by the doctors who tended him during the 1925 operation that caused his death (*Stalin: An Appraisal of the Man and his Influence*, p. 418). Whether or not Trotsky's suspicions were well founded, it is remarkable that Stalin was able to arrange, as early as 1925, that the Politburo could order Frunze to undergo an operation he quite rightly feared.

8. N. P. Komarov (1896–1937) was listed as a Presidium member of the Eleventh Party Conference of December 1921, a list that did not, incidentally, include Stalin.

9. S. Dmitrievsky is the former Soviet diplomat cited several times, usually with disdain, by Trotsky, who described him more caustically than did Bazhanov: "a chauvinist and anti-Semite, who temporarily joined Stalin's faction during its struggle against Trotskyism and later, while abroad, deserted to the Right Wing of the White emigration . . . [but even so] continues to regard Stalin highly, to detest all of his opponents, and to repeat all the legends of the Kremlin." (*Stalin: the Man and his Influence*, p. 71).

10. N. Osinsky (1887–1938, né V. V. Obolensky), a Party and government figure, joined the Party in 1907. In 1917 he was appointed director of the Russian Soviet Federated Socialist Republic (RSFSR) state bank and first chairman of the Supreme Council on National Economy. From 1921–23 he was deputy commissar of agriculture. He supported Trotsky in 1923. He was made Gosplan

president in 1925. From 1926–28 he directed the Central Statistical Administration, and in 1929 he was deputy chairman of the Supreme Council on National Economy. The Tenth, and Fourteenth through Seventeenth congresses made him a candidate Central Committee member. Osinsky objected violently, at the Eighth Party Congress of March 1919, to the Politburo's decision making powers, pointing out that it made the other members of the Central Committee "second rate." His objection was prophetic; as Bazhanov pointed out, the Politburo slowly moved from handling only urgent matters, to handling all matters (urgent or routine) in lieu of the Central Committee. Osinsky was tried and purged in 1938, but has since been rehabilitated.

11. V. M. Smirnov (1887–1937), an old Bolshevik and former World War I artillery officer, was one of the leaders of the Left Communists who vigorously opposed the treaty of Brest-Litovsk. He participated actively in the Civil War and was purged by Stalin in 1937.

12. Y. N. Drobnis (1890–1937), a state and Party figure, joined the RSDLP in 1906, and from 1908–17 was arrested and exiled several times. In 1918 he was in the Ukranian Central Committee. From 1919–20, he fought Petliura and the Whites. From 1922–27 he chaired the RSFSR Small Council for Peoples' Commissars but was expelled from the CP for Trotskyism by the Fifteenth Party Congress. He recanted and was reinstated in 1929, but was accused of Trotskyist sabotage and executed in the 1937 purge.

13. T. V. Sapronov (1887–1939), government and Party figure, joined the Communist Party in 1911. He was active in the Moscow revolutions of 1917. He was in the Ukranian Central Committee from 1919–21 and in 1923 became a full Central Committee member. He and Preobrazhensky were the leaders of the Democratic Centralist (Decemist) opposition to Party centralism. Sapronov was sent into internal exile in 1929, recanted, was exiled again in 1932 and finally arrested and jailed in 1935. He died in prison.

14. Y. A. Preobrazhensky (1886–1938), an old Bolshevik, was elected an alternate member of the Central Committee in 1917. In 1920 he was elected to both the Politburo and Orgburo. A respected, ethical opposition leader, he was too humane for Party police work, and the following year he was removed from the Politburo, the Orgburo, and the Central Committee, leaving room for Molotov and other Stalin supporters.

15. Y. V. Kossior (1893–1937) was one of three militant brothers. He joined the Bolshevik party in 1907 and was arrested several times and exiled to Siberia. He escaped in 1917 and joined the Red Army, where he was a political commissar and a senior field commander at the front, from 1918–22. From 1923–27 he headed some key heavy industry trusts, and by 1927 he was deputy head of the Supreme Council for the National Economy (Vesenkha). He was elected a candidate member of the Central Committee in 1925 and a full member in 1927. In 1932 he was appointed deputy commissar for Heavy Industry. He died in 1937, officially of illness, but since his brother Vladislav had been executed, it was rumored that he also was put to death or at least enticed to commit suicide.

16. The Thermidor ideology refers to the conservative reaction in revolutionary France, which came to a climax when the conservatives took over after Robespierre was overthrown on the ninth of Thermidor. Trotsky believed that Stalin, "the outstanding mediocrity in the party" was the epitome of the Thermidorean reaction in Russia to the Revolution, and that it was inevitable that

Stalin, "this colorless mediocrity" would rise to be Russia's dictator, needed and supported "by all the worms that are crawling out of the upturned soil of the manured revolution" (Trotsky, *Stalin,* p. 393).

17. I. A. Zelensky (1890–1938), statesman and Party figure, joined the Communist Party in 1906, was arrested and exiled several times, and in 1917 was active in the Moscow revolutions. He had Moscow Party jobs from 1918–29, and in 1921 became secretary of the Moscow RCP(B) Committee. From 1924–31 he was a Central Committee member, secretary, member of Orgburo, and head of the Central Asian bureau. From 1931 he chaired the USSR Central Union Consumers Societies but was purged in 1938.

18. I have not been able to identify Bombin, Makhover, or Youzhak.

19. A. N. Poskrebyshev (1891–1966?) joined the Party in 1917. He held a series of local Party jobs until 1922, when he was employed in the Central Committee staff. He has been called "one of the most mysterious and perhaps also most powerful figures in the CP apparatus during Stalin's years in power." (*Modern Encyclopedia of Russian and Soviet History*); this source claims that Poskrebyshev was listed as head of the Special Section of the Central Committee from 1928 until 1953. The job included gathering information on prominent members of the Party and government, being head of Party headquarters and Kremlin security, and overseeing Stalin's personal security force. He was elected a candidate member of the Central Committee at the Seventeenth Party Congress in 1934, and a full member in 1939. He seems to have played a key role in the purges, helping Yezhov and Malenkov draw up lists of victims. At some point in the 1930s Stalin's secretariat and the Special Section merged, and Preobrazhensky headed the new unit, which reportedly had some kind of supervisory powers over the OGPU and then the NKVD. During and after World War II he was the gateway to Stalin and was made a lieutenant general after the war. He was a principal speaker at the Nineteenth Congress in 1952. Khrushchev claimed that Stalin fired Poskrebyshev shortly before his death because he suspected his assistant of having leaked secret documents.

20. S. V. Kossior (1889–1939?), brother of Yosif Kossior, joined the RSDRP in 1907 and was arrested several times during the next few years. He was exiled in Siberia but in 1917 was in the Petrograd Military Committee. In 1919 he was a member of the KP(b)U central committee and in 1922 was in Moscow as head of the Central Committee's Siberian section. He was made a full member of the Central Committee in 1924 and joined the Politburo (as a supporter of Stalin) in 1927 as a candidate member and in 1930 as a full member. In 1938, partly due to his success in forming a political base in the Ukraine, Stalin "promoted" him away from his power base. He was arrested in the 1939 purges and either executed that year or died in prison the next year.

21. "Leon" Sedov (1906–1938), Trotsky's only son, was murdered in Paris in 1938, on Stalin's orders, by the infamous NKVD agent Mark Zborovsky, who later entered the United States and managed to acquire U.S. citizenship, possibly as a prelude to an attempted murder of the KGB defector Aleksandr Orlov.

Chapter Six

1. D. B. Ryazanov (1870–1938, né Goldendach) was a labor leader, friend of Trotsky, and a prominent Marxologist. He adhered to the Bolsheviks in 1917 and

in 1922 founded and directed the Marx-Engels Institute (the official repository of documents by or about Marx and Engels). An individualist, he insulted Stalin's intelligence on several occasions and was dismissed from his directorship and expelled from the Party in 1931 on trumped-up charges. By 1934 he was under house arrest in Leningrad, and in 1938 he died in prison.

2. S. I. Gusev (1874–1933, né Yakob Davidovich Drabkin) had a good Civil War record as a commander of Red Army units at the front. In 1919 he was elected to the Revolutionary War Council and in 1920 to candidate membership in the Central Committee.

3. N. M. Shvernik (1888–1970), a Party, government, and trade union official, joined the Communist Party in 1905. He was arrested and exiled several times. In 1917 he chaired the All-Russian Artillery Workers union. In 1923–25 he was on the Presidium of the Central Control Commission. He attached his star to Stalin and was moved up to CC membership in 1925. From 1927–38 he was on the All-Russian Central Executive Committee. In 1941 he chaired the State Defense Committee, and in 1944 became deputy chairman of the Presidium. In 1946 he moved up to chair the Presidium, thus becoming head of state. A dull plodder, he was removed in 1953 and replaced by Voroshilov. He was reinstated as a member of the Presidium, in 1957.

4. Trotsky's own account of the incident lays the blame squarely on Stalin, whose telegram said, "The funeral will take place on Saturday. You will not be able to return on time. The Politburo thinks that because of the state of your health you must proceed to Sukhum. Stalin." No one informed Trotsky, who stayed in Sukhum, that the funeral had been changed to Sunday. Trotsky, relating the foregoing, added, "Stalin . . . might have feared that I would connect Lenin's death with last year's conversation about poison . . . and demand a special autopsy. It was, therefore, safer to keep me away until after the body had been embalmed, the viscera cremated and a post mortem inspired by such suspicions no longer feasible." But if Trotsky thought that at the time, he could have called for a post mortem from Sukhum. Once more he mysteriously failed to act on his suspicions. Perhaps he only firmed up his suspicions in retrospect, when later he wanted to revenge himself on Stalin, for no other *competent* source thought Stalin might have poisoned Lenin.

5. Trotsky describes (*Stalin,* p. 392) how Menzhinsky (1874–1934), "who was carried away by the machine of police repression . . . was not interested in anything except the GPU," supported the *Troika* when it was in power, then Stalin when the *Troika* fell apart, but Yagoda (hence Stalin) knew that Menzhinsky had warned Trotsky about Stalin's anti-Trotsky intrigues during the Civil War.

6. According to several sources, including Trotsky, by then Yagoda was already Stalin's inspector in the OGPU and had a very close rapport with Stalin. It is clear from Bazhanov's text that Yagoda and Bazhanov engaged in a personal vendetta that played a significant part in (and after) Bazhanov's defection.

7. A. S. Bubnov (1883–1940), a state, Party, and army figure, was a historian. He joined the RSDLP in 1903. He was an early supporter of Trotsky but by 1918 was pro-Lenin. From 1907–17 he did Party work in Moscow and various provinces, with several arrests and exile periods. In the October Revolution he was in the Bolshevik Central Committee and a member of Trotsky's Revolutionary Military Committee (RMC). He joined the Ukraine left-wing dissidents in 1918 and was a partisan leader and member of the Ukraine central committee during the Civil War. From 1922–23 he chaired the Agitprop bureau of the Central Commit-

tee. In 1925 he was made a full member of the Central Committee and an Orgburo secretary and was chief of Political Administration of the Red Army. He was a Democratic Centralist, and his descent began in 1927. From 1929–37 he was commissar of education, RSFSR. From 1934 he lived in the shadow of the purges and was finally executed in 1940.

8. Marshal S. M. Budenny (1883–1973), a farmer who became a cavalry sergeant-major in the tsarist army in 1908, was founder of the Soviet cavalry. He fought with great bravery in World War I, joined the CPSU in 1919, and fought and commanded Red Army troops in the Civil War. He became a very close friend of Stalin and Voroshilov. By 1923 he was on the Revolutionary Military Council, inspector of cavalry, and director of cavalry maintenance. In 1935 he was promoted to be one of the first five Soviet marshals. He joined the Presidium in 1938, and in 1941 was appointed first deputy commissar of defense. In 1941, commanding the southwest front (with Nikita Khrushchev as his political commissar), he was responsible for the Kiev fiasco, which cost the Red Army 600,000 men. He was removed, had no further battle commands, but remained a highly popular public hero.

9. S. S. Kamenev (1881–1936), born into a tsarist military family, was a colonel in command of the Thirtieth Poltava Regiment in October 1917. Trotsky drafted him into the Red Army and put him in command of the eastern front in 1918. In 1919 he was promoted to commander in chief of the Soviet armed forces, replacing Joachim Joachimovich Vatzetis, and served in that capacity until in 1924 the post was abolished as Bazhanov describes. Both Bazhanov and Trotsky have called the post decorative, but in fact Kamenev (unrelated to Lev B. Kamenev) played a very active operational role during and after the Civil War. He joined the Communist Party after the Civil War, and died a natural death, prior to the purges.

10. A mission with diplomatic immunity was a vital requirement for the Soviet plan to use "safehaven" bases (the embassy and its ancillary missions such as consulates and trade missions with diplomatic status) for a variety of legitimate and clandestine purposes. It still is. All Soviet diplomatic, media, trade and commercial (Amtorg included), and consular missions overseas are routinely used today for cover purposes by the KGB and the Glavnoye Razvedyvatelnoye Upravleniye—Soviet military intelligence (GRU).

11. Maxim Gorky (1868–1936, né Aleksei Maksimovich Peshkov) was the only major Russian writer actively involved in the Social Democratic movement. He joined the RSDLP(B) in 1905 and gave the movement prestige as well as his influence and his ability to raise money. He exiled himself from Russia from 1910?–13 and 1921–31, but meanwhile wrote extensively and pursued his goal of reviving Russian cultural life. Gorky, who was opposed to the concept of a proletarian-ruled state (on the grounds that the masses need expert help), split with his former close friend Lenin because of this difference.

12. Yakob Sverdlov was the first Soviet official to attempt to set forth the relationship between the Party and the Soviet government and its administrative organs.

13. Nikolai Vasilievich Krylenko (1885–1938), officially a state and Party figure, joined the Party in 1904, was a St. Petersburg militant until 1913, when he served in the Russian Communist Party (Bolshevik wing) (RCP(B)) Duma and afterward exiled himself to Switzerland. He returned in 1917 and was a member of the Petrograd Military Revolutionary Committee (MRC). In November 1917

he was made supreme commander in chief and political commissar for military affairs. In March 1918 he was removed, but surprisingly he had a good career from 1918–1931. He organized the Soviet courts and was principal prosecutor in major political trials. In 1931 his descent began, and he was a second-level figure in tourism and chess until he was purged in 1938. I have not been able to trace Emshanov.

14. One wonders if Bazhanov is saying this to protect his friend German Sverdlov.

15. Bazhanov's account of this episode has the ring of truth. It was apparently quite a significant factor in the upward motion of his career.

16. Dr. N. A. Semashko (1874–1949), a state and Party figure, was a founder of the Soviet public health service. He was a Marxist in 1893, and joined the RSDLP in 1904. He was arrested and exiled and emigrated to Switzerland, then France, 1906–17. In 1918 he was peoples' commissar of public health, RSFSR, and from 1921 until his death he taught medicine at Moscow University.

17. K. A. Mekhonoshin (1889–1938), a military figure, joined the Party in 1913. He was arrested and exiled several times, 1909–14. In 1917 he was in the Petrograd RMC, and was deputy peoples' commissar for military affairs. He held various jobs in RMCs for the next two years and from 1921–34 was deputy, then chairman, of universal military training, member of the peoples' commissariat for communications, military attaché in Poland, and director of the all-union oceanographic and naval management scientific research institute. He was purged and died in 1938.

18. G. Y. Sokolnikov (1888–1939, also known as Briliant), a Party and government figure, joined the Party in 1905. He received both law and economics degrees in Paris and was one of the few really well educated Bolsheviks. He was in exile in Switzerland from 1914–17, at first helping Trotsky, then Lenin. He was in Lenin's first Politburo in 1917 with Lenin, Zinoviev, Kamenev, Trotsky, Stalin, and Bubnov (although all the real work was done by Trotsky's RMC). He was a leader in various RMCs in the Civil War and at one point commanded the Turkestan front. From 1921–26 he was deputy, then chairman, of Narkomfin, but his descent began in 1925 when he joined with Zinoviev, Kamenev, and Krupskaya in opposition to Stalin. He was sent to the United Kingdom as ambassador in 1929, lost his Central Committee seat in 1933, was reinstated as a candidate in 1934, but was demoted to deputy peoples' commissar for forestry in 1935. He was purged in the 1937 "trial of the seventeen," and was sentenced to ten years in jail, where he died. He has not been rehabilitated, although he was a truly talented man.

19. Galina Iosifovna Serebriakova (1905–?), a well-known Soviet author, joined the Communist Party in 1919. She graduated in medicine from Moscow State University in 1925 and has written many books and articles.

Chapter Seven

1. See Trotsky's *Stalin: An Appraisal of the Man and His Influence,* ed. Charles Malamuth (London: MacGibbon & Kee, 1968), p. 376 of the English edition.

2. Bazhanov makes quite a lot of this error on Trotsky's part, and it would seem possible that he elevated it to this level in order to draw particular attention to the fact that Trotsky cited his eyewitness account. In fact, reading Trotsky's

account, one can draw an alternate conclusion, that Trotsky was merely using his words loosely and didn't mean to imply that Lenin was still alive. He could have meant to underline that Stalin was already aware of the testament and its threat to him, before the 1924 CC plenum, and so realized very clearly what was at stake.

3. Whether or not he had become anticommunist by this time, Bazhanov was apparently still pursuing his own scramble for position and power.

4. Lazar Chatskin (?–1937) was founder and director of the Komsomol. Bazhanov's selection as one of two future leaders of the USSR must have been the determining factor in his claim that, had he stayed in the Kremlin, he might well have been Stalin's successor. Curiously, Chatskin doesn't appear either in the Great Soviet Encyclopedia or in the Modern Encyclopedia of Russian and Soviet History.

5. Muzyka and (first name unknown) Babakhan are not further identified. They do not appear again, and I have not been able to trace them. Muzyka is also the name of the Soviet Music Publishing House.

6. Tarkhanov is almost certainly Oskar Sergeevich Tarkhanov (1901–38), youth leader, Komsomol founder, and orientologist. He was active in the Odessa communist youth underground movement in the Civil War and became secretary of the Komsomol central committee and the Communist Youth International in the 1920s. He was expelled from the Communist Party for Trotskyism but reinstated in 1928. From 1932–34 he was in the Far East, serving in the army and as an embassy counsellor in Mongolia. He was purged and has since been rehabilitated.

7. Since Bazhanov wrote his book Trotsky has been partially rehabilitated in a number of communist societies.

8. Most serious scholars would agree that Lenin did not seek power for its own sake but because he had a novel agenda that he wished to put into effect at no matter what cost.

9. The Kronstadt Insurrection took place during the Tenth Party Congress, in March 1921, and was an uprising of workers and sailors at the Kronstadt naval base on an island near Petrograd. The uprising, rooted in anger against the Party's brutality, repressions, censorship, and forcible grain requisitions, was put down by the Red Army, but it was a major element in Lenin's abrupt switch to NEP. The 1918 Antonov Rebellion (also known as the Tambov Rebellion) was the largest and most nearly successful peasant uprising against the Soviet regime. The leader, Antonov, organized the bitter peasantry against forcible grain seizures and at one time controlled an area the size of France. The rebellion was put down by Trotsky's Red Army, at substantial cost in lives and effort.

10. Bazhanov's interpretation of Adam Smith and David Ricardo is at best a crude summary of some rather complicated thinking that basically pertained to an agricultural economy and farm labor. Curiously, Bazhanov on Karl Marx is also lacking in depth of understanding.

11. There was no congress in 1926, but he probably means the Fourteenth Party Congress, which ended on 31 December 1925.

12. The question of Soviet recognition of tsarist bonds and other paper debts was of significant interest in Western Europe throughout the period from 1917 to the late 1940s, when some optimists still thought the USSR might in fact pay at least a percentage of the face amounts. I recall European friends discussing the

subject as if it had the possibility of a favorable solution, as late as the end of the 1940s.

Chapter Eight

1. Bazhanov's French and Russian texts both read "half a lung," but the implication is that he was untrustworthy, which in Russian slang would be "only one lung."

2. Mekhlis replaced Bukharin as chief editor of *Pravda*. Bukharin resigned.

3. The single most important impetus for the cult of Stalinism was the occasion in 1929 of Stalin's fiftieth birthday anniversary. Not only *Pravda* but all Soviet media and hundreds of celebrities eulogized him as the second Lenin, the best revolutionary, Leninist, Marxist theoretician, military genius, Civil War leader (and so Trotsky was eclipsed), and builder of socialism.

4. V. P. Kolarov (1877–1950) joined the Bulgarian socialist party in 1897 and in 1905 adhered to the Bulgarian Workers Socialist Democratic Party (Narrow Socialists) (BWSDP[NS]). He was a delegate to the Second International conferences of 1907 and 1910 and sat in the national assembly 1913–23, when he led (with Dmitrov) an anti-Fascist uprising. He fled to the USSR, where he headed the Central Committee's foreign bureau until 1944 (in addition to his Comintern executive position). He returned to Bulgaria in 1945, presenting himself as a leader of wartime resistance, and chaired the national assembly until his death, also serving as provisional president, deputy chairman, then chairman of the Council of Ministers.

5. A sovkhoz is a state farm owned and totally supervised by the state, whereas a kolkhoz (officially called "autonomous producer cooperative") is a collective farm on land leased from the state but operated by local farm management. Net profits from a sovkhoz go to the state, and its personnel are paid by the state. Net profits from a kolkhoz are used by the kolkhoz or divided among its workers. Under Gorbachev, the agricultural reform efforts started by Khrushchev are being pushed forward quite vigorously. These reforms have included upgrading farm labor to the same rank as industrial workers and official permission for farmers to use their spare time for private ventures. The latest Gorbachev experiment in decontrol is in his home district, Krasnodar, where on the oblast level six-person brigades (interestingly, a unit of six closely relates to the 1987 farm family) are given great autonomy in crop selection, production, sales, and disposal of net profits.

6. For the Lena-Goldfields tale, see chapter 16, page 197–98.

7. 18 Brumaire refers to the French revolutionary calendar. It was the time of the 9–10 November 1799 coup by Napoleon Bonaparte, which overthrew the Directory and established a military dictatorship, thus "completing the Thermidor (1794) process of counterrevolution" so often referred to by Russian communists in and before Bazhanov's era.

8. Pogosiants is almost certainly Dr. Ovsep Ambartsumovich Pogosian (1887–1938), a prominent Caucasus communist. He attended Tiflis Seminary, Moscow Commercial Institute, and organized Red Army units in the Caucasus during the wars. In 1921 he did Party work in Armenia and chaired the Armenian Gosplan

from 1925–28. He is listed in GSE as having been a member of the Armenian Central Committee, not the RCP Central Committee.

9. In fact, Trotsky had reason to infer that Bazhanov suggested a Frunze plot. The wording of Bazhanov's 1930 book (*Avec Staline dans le Kremlin*, p. 108) was: "Then, relentlessly pursuing his project of a Bonapartist coup d'état, Frunze chose . . . authentic military men upon whose support he could count. He . . . waited for a favorable occasion." Bazhanov evidently meant that Frunze had coup ambitions but had not recruited any coconspirators. There is no evidence that Bazhanov ever tried to discuss the matter with Trotsky, who by this time had written Bazhanov off as a turncoat against communism.

10. Voroshilov was kept on until he was pensioned in 1961.

Chapter Nine

1. The mystery of Stalin's arm remains. He himself told his sister-in-law, A. S. Alliluyeva (*Vospominania*, Moscow, 1946), that he was rejected by the tsarist army in 1916 partly because of a chronic stiffness of his left arm, and partly because of his political unreliability. B. Z. Shumiatsky (1886–1938) joined the Communist Party in 1903, and in 1905–07 he led the Siberian revolts. From 1910–20 he headed the Siberian bureau of the Central Committee and from 1923–25 was Soviet ambassador to Iran. In 1926 he became rector of the Communist University of the Workers of the East and headed the mid-Asian bureau of the Central Committee. He was a prominent and loyal Stalinist and in 1933 was appointed chief of the Central Board of the Motion Picture Industry, a position that enabled him to control the arts for Stalin.

2. This penchant for going with, and using, the majority may help explain how Stalin achieved power and survived at the top.

3. In fact, there is no evidence that Lenin lacked physical courage.

4. *Burevestnik*, one of Maxim Gorky's better-known works, was also the pseudonym used by Gorky in later life.

5. Semyon Arshakovich "Kamo" Petrosian (1882–1922 aka Ter-Petrosyan), a Caucasian bandit and close friend of Stalin, joined the Party in 1903. He organized, under Stalin's supervision, 1907 bank robberies in Tiflis and Kutaisi that earned him several death sentences and the epithet "the expropriator." Kamo worked in the Cheka from 1917 until his death in a 1922 auto accident.

6. Whether or not Stalin displayed physical courage is a matter of which author you believe, since—as Bazhanov points out—no specific instances of heroic behavior have been either cited or proven other than by Stalin or his partisan biographers such as Tovstukha. However, the point is somewhat academic since Stalin frequently displayed the kind of perseverance, cool calculation, and cold ruthlessness in critical situations that must overlie a rare kind of psychological courage. Physical coward or not, he duped his colleagues, terrorized his enemies, and killed almost everyone in Russia who stood in his way.

7. As explained in greater detail by Trotsky (see *Stalin*, pp. 385–95, for example).

8. Ekaterina Svanidze married Djugashvili (who was then using the pseudonym Nizheradze) in 1902. She bore him Yakob in 1908 and died about a year

later of illness. Her death reportedly caused Stalin considerable unhappiness and he didn't marry again for ten years.

9. Precise reasons for Nadezhda Sergeevna Alliluyeva's suicide have been the subject of considerable speculation and differences of opinion, but they have never been convincingly detailed. Bazhanov's account may well be based on reliable sources. *Khrushchev Remembers* (pp. 43–44) explicitly credits Nadezhda with extolling Khrushchev as a loyal Party-liner to Stalin when they were both at the Industrial Academy, thus materially helping Khrushchev's career along. Khrushchev claimed that Nadezhda liked him, which is quite the opposite of Bazhanov's account. The specific incident of the Industrial Academy students being shot has not, as far as I know, been confirmed.

10. Bazhanov's account of Yakob's relations with his father, his capture, and Stalin's refusal to negotiate for him is essentially the same as Svetlana's account (*Twenty Letters to a Friend*, pp. 157–63). It is also interesting to note that Svetlana said of her father, "He was a bad and neglectful son, as he was a father and husband. He devoted his whole being to something else, to politics and struggle. And so people who weren't personally close were always more important to him than those who were." (*Twenty Letters*, p. 154.)

Chapter Ten

1. Trotsky's famous Clemenceau speech at the November 1927 plenum was also included in Bazhanov's 1930 book (*Avec Staline dans le Kremlin*, pp. 99–102), in much the same words as he uses here. Bazhanov's speculation in 1930 that Stalin hadn't arranged Trotsky's death inside the USSR in some subtle way because he might see an advantage to have Trotsky die outside the USSR (see note 7, below) was amazingly prophetic and is a clear indication of just how well Bazhanov understood the dictator. Trotsky was condemned to death in absentia in the purges of 1936–38, and Stalin doubtless hastened to execute the sentence when it was clear that World War II was coming and that it might give Trotsky the chance to put his Clemenceau thesis into some form of action against Stalin. Trotsky's small but dedicated and violent Fourth International activists were (and still are) of substantial security concern to Soviet leaders and to the KGB/GRU complex.

2. L. B. Krasin (1870–1926), an engineer and diplomat, was an early Bolshevik from the Caucasus who put his business and technical experience to use installing and managing revolutionary printing presses and publications. He was a delegate to the Brest-Litovsk treaty negotiations and attended numerous international conferences as peoples' commissar for foreign trade. He was appointed ambassador to France in 1924, and to London in 1925 (where he died).

3. Which is, of course, what happened during the post-Revolution intervention on the side of the White forces by France, Britain, Japan, and the United States. The noncommunist countries, however, used insufficient force and skill and thus ensured that, when they lost, communist Russia would survive as a mortal enemy. To this day the intervention is clear in Russian memories and has helped make it extremely difficult for Western leaders to convince Soviet leaders that the West basically has peaceful intentions toward them.

4. The USSR now claims that it has abandoned its objective of seeking world

communism by any means including subversion and violence and truly seeks "peaceful coexistence." Most leaders of the Western nations have difficulty believing this "renunciation," which has yet to be clearly demonstrated. Western distrust of Soviet intentions is, ironically, almost a warped reflection of Soviet distrust of Western intentions. Both are rooted in hard experiences and veneered with opinions, many of which long since ceased to be as clear as they initially were. Both sides have changed substantially in both intentions and capabilities, but the nature of the confrontation has not kept pace with those changes.

5. The Interdistrict group was strong in the Petrograd neighborhood Party communes, arguing for uniting the two Socialist Democratic factions.

6. Trotsky's *Stalin: An Appraisal of the Man and his Influence*, contains twelve chapters and two supplements. The work was interrupted when Trotsky was murdered in August 1940 by Ramon Mercader (also known as [aka] Jacson, aka Jacques Mornard) at Stalin's behest. Trotsky's translator and editor, Charles Malamuth, left the first seven chapters much as Trotsky had written them and as Malamuth had translated and edited them while Trotsky lived. Malamuth constructed the remaining five chapters from Trotsky's notes, worksheets, and other fragments in a remarkable work of painstaking care. The result was a book that is a curious mixture of truth, insight, and polemics. Despite Bazhanov's critique, however, Trotsky presented a picture of Stalin that makes Trotsky appear to have understood (too late, in the event) Stalin's capacity for evil. For example, Trotsky's description of the Central Committee session at which Kamenev first made Lenin's Testament known is followed by this passage (p. 376): "Lenin's return to activity could only mean the political death of the General Secretary. And conversely only Lenin's death could clear the way for Stalin." Then Trotsky went on to describe the strange manner in which Stalin kept insisting that Lenin was asking for poison and hinting that it might be best to give him some. Of Stalin's demeanor Trotsky said, "This episode is one of those that leave an indelible imprint on one's consciousness for all time. . . . Stalin's behavior, his whole manner, was baffling and sinister."

Discussing Stalin's role in Frunze's death, Trotsky said (p. 418), "The very nature of the suspicion is significant. It shows that by the end of 1925 Stalin's power was already so great that he could rely on a submissive concilium of physicians armed with chloroform and the surgeon's knife."

The question is not so much how naïve was Trotsky, as when did he begin to understand that Stalin was capable of anything *and* that therefore Stalin would stay in power? Bazhanov seems to have had significant influence on the erosion of Trotsky's innocence.

7. It is worth repeating in translation what Bazhanov said in his 1930 book (*Avec Staline*, p. 101–4):

I don't recognize my Stalin. If he had remained loyal to his methods, he would have acted with more finesse in this matter. He would, for example, making a grand gesture, have reconciled himself with Trotsky by offering him a portfolio . . . Moscow's most insignificant one. We have, at least, made some progress since Caesar Borgia. Then, a dose of lethal powder in a cup of Falerne, or perhaps the enemy would perish by biting into the golden skin of an apple. Now, the procedure is based on the latest conquests of science. A culture of Koch bacilli systematically and slowly mixed into the food will produce a galloping consumption and rapid death, without anyone having the slightest right to accuse the restaurant waiter of having sent an enemy to his maker. General Vrangel died of galloping consumption. I heard several times in the Politburo that the Bolsheviks considered him their most dangerous adversary. He died at a time when the Soviets were in dread of a war in which he could have played a role fatal to them. Vrangel's illness revealed typical intestinal phenomena. But who would have dared affirm that the Bolsheviks had poisoned Vrangel?

Had Trotsky, in his turn, died of tuberculosis, Stalin would have found himself in an advantageous situation. The doctors would have found typical intestinal phenomena, but attributed them to stomach lesions. Furthermore, everyone would recall Stalin's cordiality in regard to Trotsky. A guard of honor would have been sent around his bier, his name given to some small city, and there would have been long discussions in the public press about how, underneath, Trotskyism didn't differ at all with Leninism and, to the contrary, complemented it, and that it was only on lesser tactical points that the head of the opposition strayed a bit from orthodox doctrine, and that, in the view of History, had no importance and merely illustrated Trotsky's scope. It's difficult to see why Stalin didn't use that method, so much in line with his habits and his character . . . but it is, after all, very possible that Stalin finds an advantage to seeing Trotsky die, not in the USSR, but abroad.

Chapter Eleven

1. Grigory Aleksandrovich Potemkin (1739–91), famous statesman and army marshal, was a favorite of Catherine the Great. In 1787 she toured the south to inspect his zealous construction activities and was very pleased with the result. She didn't realize that he had managed to conceal the many defects in his program. The deception included temporary false fronts of unbuilt houses in whole villages that she took to be completed. Hence the saying, "Potemkin village."

2. Olga Davydovna, Trotsky's sister, was Kamenev's wife.

3. Sten was a Marxist philosopher.

4. G. Dmitrov (1882–1949) joined the Bulgarian Workers Social Democratic Party in 1902, served in the Bulgarian parliament from 1913–23, and then emigrated first to Germany then to the USSR. He became a Soviet citizen, lived in the USSR from 1934–45 and as general secretary of the Comintern from 1935–43 was a reliable Stalin mouthpiece. He returned to Bulgaria in 1945 and became general secretary of the Bulgarian Communist Party and chairman of the Council of Ministers.

5. Now, in Gorbachev's glasnost and reform of the late 1980s, for the first time in the USSR, the Party is publicly accused of making mistakes. The theme, however, is still soft-pedaled.

6. Marshal Blucher (1889–1938, also spelled Bliukher) joined the CP(B) in 1916. In 1919 he commanded the Fifty-first Soviet division fighting Kolchak, was commander in chief Far East from 1921–22, and for three years from 1924 was chief military advisor to Kuo Min Tang (KMT) leaders Sun Yatsen and Chiang Kai-shek. He was made candidate member of the Central Committee in 1934, promoted to marshal in 1935, and in 1938 purged, tortured, and killed in prison. Marshal Egorov (1883–1939) joined the CP(B) in 1918, organized and commanded Red Army staffs and in the Civil War commanded two fronts and later three Soviet military districts. He was chief of the general staff from 1931–

37, promoted to marshal in 1935, and purged in 1937. He died in prison, either in 1939 or 1941. Blucher and Egorov, professional soldiers, have been rehabilitated.

7. Beginning in the 1980s the Soviet regime began to take an interest in revising the official view of Bukharin, as ancillary to the revision of NEP, which is of such interest in the light of Gorbachev's reform drive. It is unlikely, however, that Bukharin (or indeed many former leaders) will be completely rehabilitated in the near term, partly for the reasons Bazhanov gives. It is also unlikely that Trotsky and Zinoviev, still completely ostracized from Party history, will be even partly exhumed by either the USSR, its close Eastern European allies, or the Peoples Republic of China in the near term. *Always* is, however, a very strong word, as Bazhanov eventually said.

8. Stalin made them full members in 1925.

9. It is more or less generally accepted now that this was the position of Molotov, Malenkov, and Kaganovich—and very likely many thousands of other hard-line bureaucrats whose security was then and is still threatened by *glasnost* and economic reform.

10. Molotov died in 1986.

Chapter Twelve

1. M. G. Bronsky (1882–1941, né Varchavsky), a revolutionary government official, joined the Polish Socialist Party in 1903. He took refuge twice in Switzerland between 1907 and 1917, worked for *Pravda* in 1917, and joined the Narkomfin management in 1924. In 1927 he was an economics professor at Moscow University and edited *Socialist Economy*. He was purged in 1938 and died in prison in 1941.

2. Professor Aleksandr Vasilievich Chaianov (1888–?) joined Gosplan and the Peoples' Commissariat for Agriculture in 1918. A prolific author, he wrote extensively about the peasantry.

3. M. M. Lashevich (1884–1928) joined the Communist Party in 1901. In February 1917 he headed the Bolshevik faction of the Petrograd Soviet and in October was a member of the Petrograd military revolutionary committee. He commanded the Third Red Army in 1918–19. From 1920–25 he commanded the Siberian military district. In 1925 he was made deputy commissar of military and naval affairs, and deputy chief of the military revolutionary council of the USSR. He ran the Chinese Eastern railroad from 1926–28. He was expelled from the party in 1927, recanted, then killed himself. G. E. Evdokimov (1884–1936), one of the more prominent purge victims, joined the RSDLP in 1901. He was an active Party organizer in Petrograd and the provinces in 1918–22, was chief political commissar for the Seventh Army in 1922, and in 1925 headed the Petrograd trades council. In 1925 he joined the Central Committee and was a strong supporter of Trotsky in 1927. He was expelled from the Party in 1935, recanted, then was purged with Zinoviev and Kamenev and executed in 1936.

4. The "Doctors' Plot" was a supposed Jewish conspiracy to poison Kremlin leaders. The plot was invented by Stalin. See also Alliluyeva, *Twenty Letters to a Friend*, p. 196.

5. Bazhanov probably meant not only internal passports, still required for all

citizens in the USSR but also the external (international) passports carried by those Soviet Jews who are allowed such documents.

6. The policy has since been somewhat modified, with new passports issued and selective emigration allowed.

Chapter Thirteen

1. G. Belenky (1885–1938) joined the RSDLP in 1901 as a propagandist. He was arrested, imprisoned, and exiled several times. In 1910 he worked for the CP(B) in the provinces and St. Petersburg. He was a Party organizer in Moscow in 1917 and from then until 1925 was a Comintern agitprop agent. He was allied with Trotsky, Zinoviev, and Kamenev in 1926, was expelled from the Party in 1927, recanted in 1928, was purged in 1938, and died in prison.

2. G. G. Yagoda (1891–1938) was credited by Trotsky in his book *Stalin* as having been the organizer, if not the inventor, of the entire system of forced confessions to crimes that weren't committed.

3. In the light of what is known about Stalin's modus operandi at the time, this use of members of his secretariat to watch the OGPU rings true.

4. A. Y. Vyshinsky (1883–1954) joined the RSDLP (Menshevik) in 1903. In 1905 he was secretary of the Baku Party committee. He joined the Public Prosecutor's office in 1918, the Red Army in 1919, and the Communist Party in 1920. He read law at Moscow State University, 1921–22, and from 1923 held junior- and second-level jobs in the Public Prosecutor's office. His infamous, frenzied performance in the first of the 1936–38 purge trials won him the post of Prosecutor General (1935–39) and brought him to the top circles of Stalin's regime (Central Committee, 1939–54). He became deputy foreign minister in 1940 and Soviet ambassador to the United Nations in 1947.

5. Once again Bazhanov is repetitive here, but the full translation has been rendered in order accurately to give the flavor the author wished to convey.

6. Bazhanov often sees things in pure black or white, and in this case he lumps Lenin and Stalin together in the same mold, which is very much an over simplification.

7. Bazhanov has just used, in the preceding paragraphs, a significant portion of the CPSU's lexicon of the approximate period 1920–1980 for describing perceived threats to the regime.

8. Svetlana Alliluyeva said of her father, "It was as though my father were at the center of a black circle and anyone who ventured inside vanished or perished or was destroyed in one way or another." (*Twenty Letters to a Friend*, p. 222.)

Chapter Fourteen

1. A. V. Lunacharsky (1875–1933), an early Bolshevik propagandist and leading element of the faction's ultra left wing, broke with Lenin (whom he criticized as not being sufficiently radical) but rejoined the Bolsheviks in 1917. He was a leader of the July 1917 Congress and was appointed commissar of education in Lenin's first government, on 26 October 1917.

I. M. Vareikis (1894–1939), a prominent early Bolshevik political writer and organizer, headed the Central Committee's press bureau from 1920 until he broke with Stalin in the mid-1930s over the question of forced collectivization. He was tried in 1938 and executed in 1939.

2. A. A. Blok (1880–1921), one of the most popular and influential Russian symbolist poets, a gifted man dedicated to change, strongly welcomed the Revolution. By early 1921 he was complaining that freedom of the arts was being taken away and life had lost its meaning. He died, disillusioned, later the same year.

3. A. A. Akhmatova (1888–1966, née Gorenko) was a well-known Russian poet. She was rehabilitated between the 1954 Second Congress of Soviet Writers and the Twentieth Party Congress of 1956. But the Twentieth Congress gave Soviet literati mixed signals, mainly due to the unpredictable Nikita Khrushchev's secret speech, which seemed at least in part to close the doors that speakers at the congress had vociferously opened in support of Soviet writers. Solzhenitsyn, who learned her famous "Poem without a Hero" by heart, called her "the soul of Russia."

4. M. A. Bulgakov (1891–1940) was a well-known Russian author. Like Akhmatova, his works were banned during the Stalin dictatorship but crept into covert circulation during the early Samizdat period of the mid-1950s. He and Akhmatova are now Russian folk heroes.

5. Vladimir Vladimirovich Mayakovsky (1893–1930) joined the CP(B) in 1908 and actively supported the Revolution with his poetry, eventually turning his art into a public spectacle.

6. Blinis are Russian buckwheat pancakes, eaten either as hors d'oeuvres (spread, for example, with caviar or fish paste) or as dessert (spread with sweets).

7. A. B. Kusikov (1896–, also known as Kusikian), revolutionary futurist (then imaginist) poet, was published in Russia from 1917 until he emigrated abroad in 1922.

8. A play on the Russian word for taste, *vKus*, the diminutive plural form being *vKusikov*.

9. I. P. Utkin (1903–1944), revolutionary poet, took a lyric view of the fervor of the Bolsheviks. He was killed in an air crash returning from the front.

10. Another play on words, centered on the fact that *ytka* means a "duck," and *gus'* is a "goose."

11. A. N. Ostrovsky (1823–1886) was a famous Russian dramatic author. He wrote both comedy and, later in life, more serious dramatic works. He established a modern theater and a school of dramatic art in Moscow and founded the Society of Russian Dramatic Art and Opera Composers. Bazhanov's view of Eisenstein seems extreme and pays no attention to the possibility that Eisenstein had his own subliminal sarcastic agenda that Stalin didn't have the wit to detect.

12. N. I. Podvoisky (1880–1948) joined the Communist Party in 1901. He was arrested several times for fomenting labor unrest, and emigrated to Switzerland in 1907. He was active in Pravda and Svezda while abroad. He returned and played a leading role in 1917 in the Petrograd soviet and revolutionary military committee but remained basically second rank among revolutionary leaders. He chaired the all-Russian collegium on organization and formation of the Red Army in 1918. He was president of Sportintern from 1921–27 and was pensioned in 1935.

13. A. M. Kollontai (1872–1952) was simultaneously ambassador to Sweden

(as well as Norway). She was a leading Menshevik who came over to the Bolsheviks in August 1917, largely due to her friendship with Lenin. She was immediately elected to the Central Committee, where she stood out as a forceful, brilliant, colorful debater and pamphleteer. A vehement advocate of the monopoly of power by the Communist Party, she remained a prominent Bolshevik leader until at the Tenth Congress Lenin won over the Democratic Centralists. Kollontai was thereafter best known for her key role in the Workers' Opposition and her post–Civil War negotiations with the Finnish, Norwegian, and Swedish governments.

14. *Carmen* was written with four acts, hence has a total of three intermissions. Bazhanov probably saw a version of the opera translated into Norwegian not long before by opera star Kirsten Flagstad's father. Flagstad herself sang the role of Micaela in *Carmen*, in Oslo, in 1926, and that may be the performance that Bazhanov heard (Kirsten Flagstad, *The Flagstad Manuscript*, pp. 5–6, 30). This kind of detail is worth recording since it adds to Bazhanov's credibility (the general reader might, at first glance, doubt that *Carmen* was performed in Norwegian in the 1920s).

Chapter Fifteen

1. Sindeyev, Budavey, and Prokofiev are not further identified. Budavey was a staff captain, equivalent in rank to somewhere between lieutenant and captain in the U.S. Army.

2. Bazhanov's index lists Chalkushyan as "Counselor, State Bank."

3. V. A. Larionov (1897–), a fervent anticommunist militant, was one of the last of the 1920s militants to penetrate communist Russia so deeply and get out again safely.

4. A. P. Kutepov (1882–1930 also transliterated Koutiepov or Kutiepov, depending on the languages involved), a famous White general, was kidnapped by the OGPU in Paris in 1930. See Bazhanov's 1930 account of the kidnapping (*l'Enlèvement du Géneràl Kutepov*, op cit).

5. The association was indeed penetrated and controlled, through Tretiakov (first name unknown) by the OGPU.

6. Skoblin was an OGPU agent. The abduction of General Miller was a well-known scandal at the time.

7. The foregoing paragraph does not appear in the Russian text.

8. Askhabad is at 37°.57′N, 58°.23′E.

9. Yakob Bliumkin (1899–1929) was Trotsky's military secretary during the Civil War. Trotsky's *Writings, 1929–39*, mentions Bliumkin as his friend and first visitor in Constantinople. In 1929 Bliumkin took a letter from Trotsky to the Opposition in Moscow, probably to Radek. Bliumkin was betrayed and shot by the OGPU without trial in December 1929. His attempt to kill Bazhanov in France was mistakenly reported as successful by Solzhenitsyn in *Gulag* (vols. 1–2, p. 370n).

10. In his 1930 book Bazhanov mentioned but did not identify Maksimov as his companion in the escape to Persia "who shared my desire to leave the communist paradise." The 1978 version is a more likely one.

11. Ambassador A. Griboyedov (1795–1829), the great Russian dramatist, was perhaps best known for his famous masterpiece *Woe from Wit*.

12. Lotfabad is at 37°.32′N, 59°.20′E.

Chapter Sixteen

1. Pasban (first name unknown) is not further identified and does not appear again.

2. Quchan is at 37°.06′N, 58°.30′E.

3. It is interesting that Bazhanov doesn't comment on why he stopped Maksimov, clearly a potential redefector to the OGPU (which in fact happened in Paris) from drinking the poisoned coffee. Bazhanov's index identifies Koltukhtchev (first name unknown) as an OGPU agent.

4. Pachayev (first name unknown) is not further identified and does not appear again.

5. Georgy Sergeevich Agabekov (also known as Aruntov, aka Nerses Ovsepian) an Armenian by origin, wrote *The Russian Secret Terror*, a book which contains many errors of fact. He was a mysterious, devious figure who may in fact have survived the OGPU attempt against him in the Pyrenees. He is the subject of chapters 6 and 7 of Gordon Brook-Shepherd's *The Storm Petrels*. It is interesting to note, incidentally, that Bazhanov's own account of his voyage through Persia and into India differs in many details from the account in *The Storm Petrels*, although both were apparently based on direct translation of Bazhanov's words the same year (1976–77).

6. Duzdab, near what is now the Pakistan border with Iran, is now more often called Zahedan. It is at 29°.30′N, 60°.52′E.

7. In his 1930 book Bazhanov discreetly avoided all mention of his lengthy discussions with British intelligence in India.

8. Urquart was president of Lena-Goldfields. The reference to collars was a sarcastic prod at British officialdom of the time, who usually wore high, starched collars and were sometimes themselves referred to pejoratively as "starched collars."

9. Bazhanov's 1930 book made no mention either of the Lena-Goldfields or the MacDonald episodes.

Chapter Seventeen

1. P. N. Miliukov (1859–1943) was a historian and well-known author (*The Russian State under Peter the Great, Essays on the Russian Culture*, etc.). He played an active role in the February 1917 Revolution and became minister for foreign affairs in the first provisional government but resigned in May 1917 in disagreement with the majority over foreign policy matters and passed into the opposition. Bazhanov's index describes Miliukov as a "Russian publicist."

(I recall clearly as a small boy in Brussels, living in an American household constantly visited by Russian émigrés of all political persuasions, the heated and persistent arguments that Bazhanov has just touched upon. The amount and variety of wishful thinking about Russia's coming "liberation from Bolshevism" was apparent even to my young ears, as the partisans growled at and insulted each other's views. Ed.)

2. This translated excerpt from Bazhanov's 1930 book *Avec Staline dans le Kremlin*, pp. 2–3, typifies what he refers to here:

Soldier of the anti-Bolshevik army, I had taken on myself the difficult and perilous task of penetrating to the heart of the enemy headquarters. I reached my objective [appointment as Stalin's assistant and Politburo secretary]. It was highly risky, but I didn't let myself be stopped by thoughts of risk. After all, I was only risking my skin, the least one should risk in a civil war.

One wonders whether the crudity of this pretense, which evidently seriously embarrassed Bazhanov in later years, came from his own imagination or that of his publisher. It goes beyond what he could have said and still have honored his promise to his friends in Russia. It appears to be one of the few areas where Bazhanov departed unnecessarily far from the truth.

3. Based on OGPU (and successor) Soviet security practice, it seems likely that the OGPU, not aware of how many Politburo documents Bazhanov had brought out with him, manufactured the fakes to discredit Bazhanov as well as to generate foreign exchange.

4. G. Z. Bessedovsky (1896–?, aka Cyril Kalinov, Ivan Krylov) defected on 3 October 1929. He was only the second senior Soviet official (and the first diplomat) to defect. Bessedovsky's jump over the embassy wall just ahead of the OGPU has been well documented. An interesting account of it appears in Brook-Shepherd's *The Storm Petrels*, chapter 5. Bessedovsky is often referred to as "the ambassador to France," whereas in fact he was the chargé d'affaires. Like some Soviet defectors then and since, he wrote what he knew would sell to the general public, regardless of the validity or the source of his words. He later resumed his Soviet connections as business partner of Bogovut-Kolomiets (see n. 6 below).

5. V. S. Dovgalevsky (1885–1934) joined the Communist Party in 1908, was arrested, exiled, and escaped several times and emigrated later that year. He was a party activist in France (left wing, French Socialist party), Belgium, and Switzerland until his return to Russia in 1917. From 1919–23 he held various postal and communications jobs, and from 1924 until his death he headed Soviet diplomatic missions to Sweden, Japan, the United Kingdom, and France. He is buried near the Kremlin wall.

6. V. Bogovut-Kolomiets (or Kolomitzev) was a Russian émigré who lived, as the British put it, "by his wits." He was motivated by greed and worked secretly for the OGPU while professing anticommunism.

7. I. A. Roizenman (1878–1938) joined the Communist Party in 1902. As a Ukrainian Party activist he was arrested and exiled several times between 1905–17. He held minor Party posts until he was appointed a member of the presidium of the Central Control Commission in 1924 and concurrently a member of the Workers and Peasants Inspection Committee. He was made deputy chairman of the Central Control Committee in 1934.

8. Veteran Bolshevik M. A. Trilisser (1883–1940) was deputy chairman of OGPU from 1926–30, and S. A. Messing (1890–1946) was deputy chairman from 1930–31. There were as many as three deputy chairmen at once, some simultaneously heading OGPU departments. Trilisser, a prominent revolutionary delegate to the Tammerfors conference in 1906, headed the Foreign Department

(now the First Chief Directorate of the KGB) from 1920–30 and was replaced by Messing.

9. Bazhanov evidently wants the reader to understand clearly that he was not in Paris when Maksimov died and learned of it by chance.

10. There are many versions of what happened to Bliumkin and to whom he was to deliver the documents. Most versions agree that he was trying to deliver the documents from Trotsky to Radek and was trapped and shot immediately to discourage other Trotsky allies.

11. For another view of why Bazhanov stayed out of the émigré group before World War II, here is an excerpt from personal correspondence with a more recent émigré in Paris: "in general, the old wave of emigrants related to him in a prejudiced manner. The closest contacts he seemed to have were among the new arrivals." Doubtless Bazhanov reacted in an antagonistic manner to a wall erected against him by the majority of the early émigrés, to whom he was suspect.

12. Alfred Rosenberg (1893–1946), longtime head of the Nazi party office of foreign policy and ideology, was Hitler's minister for the Occupied Eastern Territories from 1941 to 1944. He was as convinced as Hitler that Bolshevism was the final step in an international Jewish plot to conquer the world, but he didn't overtly believe in physical extermination of the Jews. Rosenberg favored exploiting rather than liberating Russia. By mid-1942 he and Goebbels openly admitted their realization that Hitler's Ostpolitik had failed, for the same reasons Bazhanov had given, but by then it was too late; the Russian population was irrevocably opposed to Hitler.

13. Deringer was then head of administration for the Nazi party's Berlin organization.

14. Georg Leibbrandt (1899–?), a Ukrainian of German origin, was in fact not Rosenberg's first assistant. Meyer was between them. Leibbrandt, as liberal as Rosenberg in respect to occupation policy, was fired by Rosenberg (for political reasons) in mid-dispute on the question of German policy toward the Russian population. The dispute lineup was: Bormann, Himmler, and Koch in favor of simple enslavement of the Soviet people (whom Hitler despised), versus Rosenberg, Meyer, and Leibbrandt who favored winning over the Russians to fight against Stalin's regime.

15. See Adolf (Schikelgruber) Hitler's *Mein Kampf,* for a clear prediction of what he had in mind for the USSR, repeated many times. Hitler saw Russia as the soil upon which Germany was to expand eastward, "using the sword only to acquire the land for her farmers" so that there would be living room for the 142 million Germans Hitler estimated for the year 1950. The Russian people would be their colonial servants. It seems likely that Rosenberg asked the question of Hitler in an attempt to change his mind.

16. I was in England in 1941–42 and can clearly recall the surprise with which the people realized that Hitler was, in fact, rejecting the Russian population's initial effort to greet his troops as saviors. It was one of the few signs, in 1941 and as 1942 began, that perhaps Germany might be in trouble. There were very few other signs of it. I can also recall, with even more clarity and remembrance of shock, the condition in which we found Russian prisoners of war in Germany. My unit parachuted into Germany in early 1945 and immediately we found Red Army POWs living in pigpens, crawling under barbed wire stretched two feet above their "runs," where they could "exercise" after their work in the fields. The pens where

they spent the night had no heat, no running water, no furniture; just a concrete floor and a bench and one wooden peg for each soldier to hang his clothes. They ate from common bowls. Ordinary German farmers, "Ma-and-Pa" types if you will, were an integral part of this bestial treatment and seemed then to feel little remorse. It was suddenly clear to us, relatively inexperienced U.S. soldiers who certainly had no sympathy for the Kremlin, why Hitler had lost the Russian war and with it his chance to win against the West.

Conclusion

1. During the period 1928–40, Bazhanov earned his living mostly by writing. In 1941 he turned to the design and fabrication of scientific instruments, some for the Pasteur Institute in Paris and was so engaged at least until the late 1970s.

2. Bazhanov's understanding of the facts of U.S. corporate ownership is, at best, very limited and quite dated.

3. Aleksandr Dubcek was first secretary of the Communist Party of Czechoslovakia and leader of the "Prague Spring" which was crushed by Soviet and other Warsaw Pact troops in the summer of 1968. The Soviet reaction to Czechoslovakia's "Prague Spring" was as brutal, offensive an act of naked power without ideology, as the Kremlin and its KGB has displayed anywhere.

4. Bazhanov's political monologues are a curious mixture of useful reminders and somewhat strident, harshly stated, and often simplistic, polemics.

5. Bazhanov's argument doesn't include the fact that they share the world's longest border, an important traditional source of mutual suspicion and disagreement.

6. Bazhanov (while perhaps unwittingly reflecting a bit of international communist propaganda) is paying no attention to the profound problems generated within free, liberal societies in the second half of the twentieth century, problems derived from the very liberties those societies defend. My nose tells me that our external competitors may eventually prove to be less dangerous to us than our internal problems. From that thought it would be logical to seek mutually acceptable accommodation and joint approaches to mutual problems with the *reformist* communist powers, not to maintain the starkly drawn battle lines that Bazhanov carried with him from Russia of the 1920–53 period. One wonders if Bazhanov's bitterness of exile would have been translated into a cynical scoffing at Gorbachev's reform program, or would he perhaps have applauded today's extraordinary changes in the heartland of communism?

7. We in the West sometimes forget that the Russian people suffered these dreadful killings and have far more reason to throttle the next Stalin in his political crib than we give them credit for.

8. Bazhanov has identified one of the free world's major dilemmas: how do you maintain an educated electorate, and sustain its upward evolution, when each person has a vote regardless of his or her knowledge and competence? How can you entice the majority to acquire learning when there are so many other, apparently more appealing things to do? He suggests the impetus must come from the top. On balance he would seem to be right, but his manner of saying it will offend many. His presentation is typical of the Russian intelligentsia.

9. When all the shouting is done, as it now is, it's worth remembering that

Bazhanov wasn't just another man expressing his views. Right or wrong, he spent many years actively supporting communism at its very center, then many more actively fighting it from exile. What he has to say, whether or not you agree with it, is of interest. It's one more glimpse into the agony that has tormented Russia for over sixty years, and we can all learn from it.

Postscript

1. It would seem to me just as believable that the prosecutors would have used a dead Bazhanov's (manufactured) words to help their cases. This bit of "proof" isn't convincing, although the hypothesis itself is very plausible.

2. In fact, Bazhanov came very close to spilling the beans in his 1930 book, where (p. 120) he wrote, "Stalin, king of three [telephone lines], had one at home and two in his office. The reason for the third is cloaked in mystery; the secret known to very few initiates. Comrade Stalin is a man of few words, but he knows how to listen . . ."

It seems probable, despite Bazhanov's view, that Stalin continued to use any means, including his Kremlin phone tap, to maintain his power, which, seen from the pinnacle, may not have seemed so absolute to him.

3. Bazhanov died in Paris in 1983, without having published the book he refers to.

Select Bibliography

Aleksandrov, Viktor. *The Kremlin: Nerve Center of Russian History.* St. Martin, New York, 1963.

Alliluyeva, Svetlana. *Twenty Letters to a Friend.* Harper & Row, New York, 1967.

Barmine, Aleksandr. *One Who Survived.* Putnam, New York, 1945. *Memoirs of a Soviet Diplomat.* Hyperion, Westport, 1973 (reprint).

Barron, John. *KGB Today: The Hidden Hand.* Reader's Digest Press, New York, 1983.

Bazhanov, Boris (Bajanov). *Avec Staline dans le Kremlin.* Editions de France, Paris, 1930.

———. *Stalin: Der rote Diktator, von seinen ehemaligen Privatsekretär.* Berlin, P. Aretz, 1931.

———. *l'Enlèvement du Général Koutepov.* Editions Spes, Paris, 1930.

———. *Vospominaniia byvshego sekretaria Stalina.* Third Wave, Paris, 1980.

Binyon, Michael. *Life in Russia.* Pantheon, New York, 1983.

Block, Russell (editor). *Lenin's Fight against Stalinism.* Pathfinder, New York, 1975.

Bortoli, Georges. *The Death of Stalin.* Praeger, New York, 1975.

Brook-Sheperd, G. *The Storm Petrels: The Flight of the First Soviet Defectors.* Harcourt Brace, New York, 1978.

Bulgakov, Mikhail. *The Master and Margarita.* Harper & Row, New York, 1967.

Chamberlin, William H. *The Russian Revolution, 1917–21.* MacMillan, New York, 1952.

———. *The Russian Enigma.* Scribner, New York, 1944.

Cohen, Stephen F. *Rethinking the Soviet Experience,* Oxford University Press, 1985.

Corson, William, and Crowley, Robert. *The New KGB: Engine of Soviet Power.* William Morrow, New York, 1985.

Costello, John. *Mask of Treachery.* William Morrow, New York, 1988.

Craig, William. *Enemy at the Gates.* Reader's Digest Press, New York, 1973.

Daniels, Robert. *Conscience of Revolution.* Harvard University Press, Cambridge, 1960.

Deriabin, Peter, and Gibney, Frank. *The Secret World.* Ballantine, New York, 1982 (reprint).

Deutscher, Isaac. *Stalin: A Political Biography.* Oxford, New York, 1949.

Duranty, Walter. *USSR: The Story of Soviet Russia.* Lippincott, New York, 1944.

Fischer, George. *Soviet Opposition to Stalin.* Harvard University Press, Cambridge, 1952.

Flagstad, Kirsten, and Bancolli, Louis. *The Flagstad Manuscript.* Putnam, New York, 1952.

Getty, J. A. *Origins of the Great Purges.* Cambridge University Press, 1985.

Gorbachev, Mikhail S. *A Time for Peace.* Richardson & Steirman, New York, 1985.

Gorodetsky, G. *The Precarious Truce, 1924–27.* Cambridge University Press, 1977.

Hitler, Adolf. *Mein Kampf.* Houghton-Mifflin, New York, 1943.

Katkov, George. *Russia 1917: The February Revolution.* Harper & Row, New York, 1967.

Kennan, George F. *Memoirs, 1925–1950.* Little, Brown, Boston, 1967.

Kerensky, Aleksandr. *The Prelude to Bolshevism.* Dodd, Mead, New York, 1919.

Koestler, Arthur. *Darkness at Noon.* MacMillan, New York, 1948.

Kulski, W. W. *The Soviet Regime.* Syracuse University Press, 1954.

Levine, Isaac Don. *The Mind of an Assassin.* Weidenfeld & Nicholson, London, 1959.

———. *Stalin.* Blue Ribbon Books, New York, 1931.

Lewin, Moshe. *Lenin's Last Struggle.* Pantheon, New York, 1968.

Lockhart, Robin B. *Ace of Spies.* Stein & Day, New York, 1968.

Lyons, Eugene. *Workers' Paradise Lost.* Paperback Library, New York, 1967.

McCagg, William. *Stalin Embattled, 1943–48.* Wayne State University Press, Detroit, 1978.

Medvedev, Roy. *All Stalin's Men.* Doubleday, New York, 1984.

Medvedev, Zhores and Medvedev, Roy. *A Question of Madness.* Random House, Vintage Books, New York, 1971.

Pirogov, Peter. *Why I Escaped.* Duell, Sloan, Pierce, New York, 1950.

Radkey, Oliver H. *The Unknown Civil War in Soviet Russia: A Study of the Green Movement in the Tambov Region, 1920–21.* Hoover Institution, Stanford, 1976.

Romanov, A. I. (pseudonym, true name unknown). *Nights are Longest There: A Memoir of the Soviet Security Services.* Little Brown, Boston, 1972.

Scammell, Michael. *Solzhenitsyn; A Biography.* Norton, New York, 1984.

Schapiro, Leonard. *The CPSU.* Random House, New York, 1960.

———. *The Origin of the Communist Autocracy.* Praeger, New York, 1965.

Seton-Watson, Hugh. *From Lenin to Malenkov.* Praeger, New York, 1953.

Shevchenko, Arkady N. *Breaking with Moscow.* Knopf, New York, 1985.

Shub, Anatole. *The New Russian Tragedy.* Norton, New York, 1969.

Solzhenitsyn, Aleksandr. *Lenin in Zurich.* Farrar Straus & Giroux, New York, 1975.

———. *The Gulag Archipelago, 1918–1956.* Harper & Row, New York, 1973.

Souvarine, Boris. *Stalin: A Critical Survey of Bolshevism.* Longmans, Green, New York, 1939.

Treadgold, D. W. *Twentieth Century Russia.* Rand McNally, Chicago, 1959.

Trotsky, Leon D. *The Russian Revolution*. Doubleday, New York, 1959 (reprint).
———. *Writings of Leon Trotsky (1929–1939)*. Pathfinder, New York, 1972 (reprint).
———. *The Challenge of the Left Opposition (1923–25)*. Pathfinder, New York, 1975 (reprint).
———. *Stalin: An Appraisal of the Man and his Influence*. Stein & Day, New York, 1967 (reprint).
Tucker, Robert C. *Stalin as Revolutionary, 1879–1929*. W. W. Norton, New York, 1974.
Tuominen, Arvo. *The Bells of the Kremlin*. University of New England, Hanover, N.H., 1983.
Urban, G. R. *Stalinism: Its Impact on Russia and the World*. Harvard University Press, Cambridge, 1982.
Vasiliev, A. T. *The Okhrana: The Russian Secret Police*. Lippincott, Philadelphia, 1930.
Wolfe, Bertram D. *Three Who Made a Revolution*. Dial, New York, 1948.
Young, George G. *Stalin's Heirs*. D. Verschoyle, London, 1953.

Reviews, Journals, Catalogs

National Union Catalog
Russian Review
Slavic Review
Digest of the Soviet Press

Problems of Communism
Radio Liberty Bulletin
Soviet Analyst

Bibliography

Bibliography of Russian émigré Literature. Ludmila A. Foster, G. K. Hall, Boston, 1970.

Encyclopedias

Great Soviet Encyclopedia. Macmillan, New York, 1973. (A. M. Prokhorov, Editor in chief.)
Modern Encyclopedia of Russian & Soviet History. Academic International Press, Gulf Breeze, Florida, 1978. (J. L. Wieczhinski, Editor.)
Encyclopedia of Russia and the Soviet Union. McGraw-Hill, New York, 1961. (Michael T. Florinsky, Editor.)

Index